The Justice and Development Party in Turkey

Turkish politics was dramatically reshaped in the early 2000s following the decline of the Islamist National View and the electoral breakthrough of the new Justice and Development Party (JDP), headed by Recep Tayyip Erdoğan. Alongside its Islamist credentials, Erdoğan's JDP consistently and convincingly presented itself as the 'populist' defender of the downtrodden sectors of Turkish society. However, with Erdoğan's rise as the popularly elected president in 2014, Turkey's already fragile democratic system was pushed in a more authoritarian direction.

Shifting the focus away from structural factors, this book analyses the political appeal and organization of the JDP that granted the party such unprecedented electoral resilience. With critical but accessible theoretical discussions, Toygar Sinan Baykan locates the JDP within the wider literature of populism, Islamist party politics, party organizations and authoritarianism. More than fifty in-depth interviews also help to relate the intimate story of Turkey's socio-cultural divides and the JDP's intra-party organizational dynamics, thereby offering a fresh account of Turkish politics.

Toygar Sinan Baykan is Assistant Professor of Political Science and Public Administration at Kirklareli University. He attended the Middle East Technical University and Leiden University for his post-graduate studies and has a master's degree in comparative politics from the London School of Economics and Political Science. He received his PhD in politics from the University of Sussex, with his dissertation focusing on the populism and organization of the JDP in Turkey. His reviews have appeared in *Party Politics* and *Political Studies Review.* His research interests include party politics, comparative politics and populism.

The Justice and Development Party in Turkey

Populism, Personalism, Organization

Toygar Sinan Baykan

Kirklareli University

CAMBRIDGE
UNIVERSITY PRESS

CAMBRIDGE
UNIVERSITY PRESS

University Printing House, Cambridge CB2 8BS, United Kingdom

One Liberty Plaza, 20th Floor, New York, NY 10006, USA

477 Williamstown Road, Port Melbourne, VIC 3207, Australia

314–321, 3rd Floor, Plot 3, Splendor Forum, Jasola District Centre, New Delhi – 110025, India

79 Anson Road, #06–04/06, Singapore 079906

Cambridge University Press is part of the University of Cambridge.

It furthers the University's mission by disseminating knowledge in the pursuit of education, learning, and research at the highest international levels of excellence.

www.cambridge.org
Information on this title: www.cambridge.org/9781108480871
DOI: 10.1017/9781108570725

First published 2018

Printed and bound in Great Britain by Clays Ltd, Elcograf S.p.A.

A catalogue record for this publication is available from the British Library.

Library of Congress Cataloging-in-Publication Data
Names: Baykan, Toygar Sinan, author.
Title: The Justice and Development Party in Turkey : populism, personalism, organization / Toygar Sinan Baykan.
Description: Cambridge ; New York, NY : Cambridge University Press, 2018.
  | Includes bibliographical references and index.
Identifiers: LCCN 2018030099 | ISBN 9781108480871 (hardback) |
  ISBN 9781108461658 (paperback)
Subjects: LCSH: AK Parti (Turkey) | Turkey–Politics and government–1980-
  | Turkey–Foreign relations.
Classification: LCC JQ1809.A8 A4339 2018 | DDC 324.2561/04–dc23
LC record available at https://lccn.loc.gov/2018030099

ISBN 978-1-108-48087-1 Hardback

Contents

Figures

Tables

Acknowledgements

If this work contributes even slightly to our understanding and knowledge of the relationship between electoral success, party organizations and Islamist party normalization, there is no doubt that my good fortune played a huge role in this. Now it is a huge pleasure for me to thank those people who, together, created these privileged circumstances for me. I have always been very lucky to come from one of those millions of families in Turkey – from all walks of life and with different social, ethnic and religious backgrounds – who have a firm belief in the collective and individual benefits of a proper education. My father and mother always stood behind me and supported me by any means at their disposal against the psychological and financial hardships of postgraduate studies. My gratitude to them is unending. I was also very lucky to be taught by very hard-working and inspiring teachers and educators from the time my formal education started. I consider myself extremely privileged to have attended these public schools and universities in Turkey. My postgraduate studies in UK, and my PhD research at the University of Sussex, have been supported by a scholarship from the Ministry of Education of Turkey. I have done my best to properly use this resource provided by the taxpayers of a country that is not very rich.

My good fortune regarding teachers and mentors was still with me when I began my PhD at the University of Sussex. As my PhD process continued I understood much better how privileged I was to have Paul Taggart and Aleks Szczerbiak as my supervisors. Without their guidance and suggestions I would probably have ended up with a text suffocated by extraneous empirical details and theoretical discussions. Alongside their invaluable contribution to my understanding of some of the essential conceptual and theoretical tools, and to the research in general, I learned many things from their intellectual and professional integrity. These are surely lessons with life-long consequences. When I started my PhD research, there was another lucky coincidence. Cristobal Rovira Kaltwasser was at the University of Sussex and, for a year, we conducted unusually crowded supervision meetings with him which were extremely intellectually stimulating. He made a very significant contribution to the formation of this research project in its initial stages.

I was also fortunate to receive comments and criticism from other people and friends in the department. It was very kind of Marko Stojic to take the time to comment on one of the chapters. I also had the chance to speak to Monika Bil on the various central arguments in the text and benefited immensely from her suggestions. Nikoleta Kiapidou, Stella Georgiadou, Gregor Zons, Roxana Mihaila, Daniel Keith, Rebecca Partos and Pedro Echeverria were among the people who made the politics department an extremely supportive and friendly environment. It was a privilege to have them around and have the opportunity to hear them speak on various dimensions of my research project as well as on other practicalities of the PhD process. At a very early stage of my research two anonymous reviewers read my research outline and recommended some very useful changes. Two other anonymous reviewers read a working paper I published in the second year of my PhD studies, and their comments later helped me to define the most appropriate approach to one of the central concepts of my work: populism. In fact, I received even more help and support from the department than I have already listed. In two presentations to the department and in other individual contacts, I received some extremely helpful comments and thought-provoking questions from the academics and other PhD students in the department.

I also attended some important events during my PhD research. I presented various parts of my research at the ECPR PhD Summer School on Political Parties in Luneburg, the BRISMES Annual Conference in London, the ECPR Annual Conference in Montreal, the Inaugural Symposium on Turkey of the Centre for Southeast European Studies and the Consortium for European Symposia on Turkey in Graz, and the Düsseldorf Graduate Conference. At these events I received some very important questions and comments from the participants.

In Graz I had a chance to meet in person Elise Massicard, whose studies on Turkey were one of those few that deeply shaped my approach to the case of the JDP organization. She was extremely generous in agreeing to read the first full draft of my dissertation and gave me some crucial feedback in a Skype meeting. Meanwhile, I also had a failed attempt to publish one of the chapters of my research. Despite this failure, I received extremely important feedback from two anonymous reviewers, which led me to write a (hopefully) much more robust theoretical background to the central chapter on the JDP's organization. It was very kind of Tanel Demirel, too, to agree to read and comment on a couple of key chapters of the first draft of this work. I benefited

x   Acknowledgements

significantly from his comments and recommendations. Since my undergraduate studies began, Fethi Açıkel has always been very kind to take the time to have long discussions with a group of his students and to encourage them to pursue careers in social sciences. I was lucky to have been one of those students. He was very encouraging during my postgraduate studies, too, and on a couple of occasions I had a chance to discuss various aspects of my PhD research with him.

Excepting only the role of my supervisors', Pierre Ostiguy's contribution to my research was second to none. He was very generous in spending long amounts of time replying to my many questions on his approach to populism via email. He read many parts of my dissertation and, on many occasions, took time to meet with me in person in Brighton and Santiago. Thanks to a Santander Mobility Grant, I was able to visit Pierre Ostiguy in Chile, and he and Umut Aydın helped to organize a seminar presentation for me at Catholic University there. I received some very crucial, thoughtful questions and comments there from the academic staff and PhD students, which helped me to think through various problematic aspects of my research.

There is no doubt that without the contribution of my participants this work would not have found a voice of its own. The overwhelming majority of my interviewees were very kind to me, and they taught me crucial lessons on party politics in Turkey. I would never have been able to acquire this insight through second-hand resources and without their generosity. Participants of my research from various hierarchical levels and localities of the JDP organization were in fact taking part in an unprecedented political experience which, I think, will have long-term political consequences for a much wider Muslim majority geography: the rise of an electorally successful post-Islamist party (or an electorally successful and politically resilient Islamist party normalization). I hope I properly grasped the important discursive/stylistic and organizational reasons for this process, which unfolded itself to me in the narratives of the actors of this historic transformation. My copy-editor Jenny Prince-Chrisley made a substantial contribution to this work by mediating my uneasy relationship with English language. I would like to thank my wife for her compassion and solidarity which made the whole process a much smoother and less lonely one.

After I submitted my dissertation at the beginning of July 2016, I continued to receive new comments, critiques and recommendations from many other established academics that I admire. At the 2016 APSA annual meeting in Philadelphia, I was lucky enough to present my paper as part of a panel on populism and get some encouraging feedback from Pierre Ostiguy and Francisco Panizza. The examiners of my dissertation,

Paul Webb and George Christou, provided me with some very important feedback in my viva in November 2016. In a second attempt, I got much closer to publishing a central chapter of my work. This time, too, I received highly detailed and helpful comments and suggestions from three reviewers as well as from the editors of the journal *South European Society and Politics*. Yaprak Gürsoy, very generously, read the entire text and provided me with extremely useful feedback. Murat Somer also read key chapters of my dissertation and recommended some key changes for the book in a very long meeting. It was very kind of him. I am indebted to all.

When this book started its life as PhD dissertation, the subject matter and the related problematics that occupied the minds of researchers and scholars in the social sciences were remarkably different. The JDP was still considered the 'democratic model' for the Middle East, and the Arab Spring could still be viewed in a positive light; there was hope for a more democratic, much more tolerant and prosperous region. Since 2012, Turkey and the wider region surrounding it have undergone profound, and mostly negative changes. There is no doubt that these changes have deeply shaped the manner and perspective in which I examined the JDP, as well as the final conclusions I have reached regarding the party. But I hope the desire to keep pace with these changes helped me to achieve a more up-to-date, theoretically and empirically richer account of the phenomenon of Erdoğan's JDP.

Two anonymous reviewers of this typescript provided me with invaluable comments and criticisms. They helped me to properly define the relevant gaps within it and achieve a better study of the JDP in Turkey, taking into account the country's authoritarian turn as well as the important political and social developments underlying this transformation. My repeated contact with Pierre Ostiguy, Yaprak Gürsoy and Murat Somer through recent academic activities and collaborative work that continued after I submitted the typescript to the Cambridge University Press for the peer review process made substantial contributions to its current form. I also attended some extremely stimulating academic events, including the PSA annual meeting in Glasgow, the ECPR annual meeting in Oslo and a symposium titled 'I am a people' in Eugene, Oregon, USA. In these events, I had a chance to hear very relevant comments and questions from extremely curious and interested audiences as well as prominent scholars of politics and populism. The editorial help I got from Maria Marsh and Abigail Walkington at Cambridge University Press was always timely and encouraging. Of course, errors and gaps in the text are entirely mine.

In memory of my sister Diyar Baykan

1   Introduction: Agency Matters

The Research Question and an Initial Glance at the JDP

Turkish politics was reshaped by a remarkable transformation at the beginning of the 2000s. The decreasing vote for the parties of the Islamist National View tradition (Milli Görüş Hareketi)[1] and of the total votes for the traditional centre-right[2] corresponded to the electoral breakthrough and success of a new party. The Justice and Development Party (JDP, Adalet ve Kalkınma Partisi), which was founded only a year before the general election in 2002 by politicians coming from different right-wing political backgrounds under the control of a formerly Islamist elite, won a landslide victory. Besides its Islamist (or, as discussed below, post-Islamist)[3] credentials, Recep Tayyip Erdoğan's JDP both consistently and convincingly presented itself as the 'populist'[4] defender of the downtrodden, excluded and despised sectors of Turkish society against the domestic and international elites who sought to oppress them.

After its first electoral victory, the JDP continued to receive 35–50 per cent of all votes until the presidential elections in 2014, when the JDP leader Erdoğan received more than 50 per cent of votes and became the

---

[1] These Islamist parties are the National Order Party (Milli Nizam Partisi) and the National Salvation Party (Milli Selamet Partisi) in the 1970s, and the Welfare Party (Refah Partisi), the Virtue Party (Fazilet Partisi) and the Felicity Party (Saadet Partisi) in the post-1980 period. For brief information on these parties as well as other significant political parties in Turkey, see Appendix 1.

[2] These are the True Path Party (Doğru Yol Partisi) and the Motherland Party (Anavatan Partisi).

[3] I borrow my definitions of Islamism and post-Islamism from Bayat (1996; 2007). Very roughly, while the former term refers to a strictly Islamist politics which follows a top-down strategy to Islamicize society, particularly through the seizure of the state, a post-Islamist movement refrains from such top-down strategies, adopts a perspective prone to reconciling religiosity with rights and liberties and embraces a pluralist stance where Islam is not considered the single truth and remedy for all social, political and cultural problems (Bayat, 1996: 44–46).

[4] In this book I am using the approach proposed by Pierre Ostiguy (particularly 2009c and 2017) which evaluates populism as a response to 'high' political appeals/styles. I elaborate on the concept in Chapter 3.

first president of the Turkish Republic to be elected by popular vote. Afterwards, in 2015, the JDP became the first party in a general election and regained the parliamentary majority in a snap election in the same year. In 2017, the party won a referendum on a constitutional amendment that transformed the Turkish political system from parliamentarism to presidentialism. This last development was emblematic of the changes Turkish politics has undergone under the rule of Erdoğan's JDP. The JDP not only won a series of local and general elections and referenda but, at least since the Gezi protests in 2013 and Erdoğan's rise as the popularly elected president of the Republic in 2014, it has also driven Turkey's already fragile democratic system in a more authoritarian direction.

Throughout this period, apart from intra-party organizational difficulties entailed by the initial formation of the JDP by politicians with different backgrounds, the party also encountered many problems stemming from the corrosive effects of incumbency[5] as well as social, political and economic crises. For example, in 2008 a legal case was initiated by the Constitutional Court (Anayasa Mahkemesi) attempting to ban the JDP, and the global financial crisis hit the country in the same year. In 2011 an earthquake left 600 people dead in provincial Turkey. Two years later, nine young people were killed under the circumstances of disproportionate police violence during the weeks-long wave of mass protests against the government. Episodic eruptions of armed struggle with the Kurdish separatists caused the death of many more people. Corruption probes against four ministers in 2013 imposed enormous damage on the image of the JDP government. A mine blast killed more than 300 workers in 2014, and many other 'work accidents' killed hundreds of workers throughout the JDP years. On top of all these, a huge humanitarian crisis emerged after the outbreak of Syrian Civil War, which brought more than 3 million refugees to the country. In the biggest terror attack Turkey has ever experienced, more than a hundred citizens who were attending an opposition mass meeting were killed. Finally, in July 2016, a foolhardy and bloody coup attempt by a faction of the Turkish Armed Forces tried to topple Erdoğan and the JDP government.

The extremely surprising fact was that these enormous problems neither influenced popular support for the party negatively nor caused any massive discontent within the JDP organization. In fact, Erdoğan's party tightened its grip over Turkish society and politics by gradually building a 'new authoritarian' (Somer, 2016) or 'competitive authoritarian' regime (Esen and Gümüşçü, 2016). Eventually the JDP emerged as a

---

[5] See Rose and Mackie (1983) for a consideration of incumbency in government as a liability for parties, negatively influencing their electoral fortunes.

'hegemonic/dominant party'[6] (Ayan Musil, 2015) that has remained in power for more than three terms through meaningful, free and competitive but increasingly unfair elections.

Thus, the rise of the JDP in Turkey was a very curious and interesting story of 'political success' in its own right when the term is understood in its Machiavellian sense as the party maintaining its grip on power. What kind of political circumstances paved the way for the rise of the JDP? More importantly: what strategic choices and actions of the JDP politicians substantially contributed to the party's unprecedented electoral achievements and political resilience[7] and, eventually, to its transformation into a hegemonic/dominant party in Turkey? What distinguishes Erdoğan's JDP from other cases of populism that were less electorally successful and more politically vulnerable and, ultimately, incapable of transforming their political system according to their populist outlook? This book is a systematic explanation of the rise, the electoral achievements and the political resilience of the JDP in Turkey that particularly focuses on the political agency of the party, in other words, its political appeal and organization.

An Initial Glance at the Ideology, Organization and Policies of the JDP

One of the most illustrative documents defining the JDP's position *vis-à-vis* the party's Islamist legacy (the Islamist National View tradition), its electoral and elite competitors in the Turkish political system, and its position within the Turkish political history in general is a booklet written by one of its ideologues and prominent figures, Yalçın Akdoğan (2004), entitled *The Justice and Development Party and Conservative Democracy* (*AK Parti ve Muhafazakar Demokrasi*). The suspicion of the powerful secularist circles regarding the Islamist past of this new party pushed JDP leaders to define their ideology in a very careful manner, and Akdoğan's work was an outcome of this concern.

It is interesting to see that, in line with Bayat's (1996) observations regarding Islamist politics and its transformations in the middle of the 1990s, the party's most prominent ideologue defines political Islam as a

---

[6] I borrow the terms 'hegemonic' and 'dominant' parties from the excellent studies of the phenomenon by B. Magaloni (2006) and K. F. Greene (2007).

[7] I use the term 'resilience' to refer to the durability as well as the cohesion of the JDP that enabled it to withstand consecutive social, economic, political and geo-political crises as well as interventions by powerful non-party elites, in contrast to its predecessors in Turkish politics.

strategy which pursues a top-down method to Islamicize society through the seizure of the state and political power (Akdoğan, 2004: 92). Akdoğan defines the political stance of the JDP quite differently from this understanding, calling it 'conservative democracy' (2004: 12–21). In order to avoid calling the party Islamist, he defines the JDP as the party of those with religious sensibilities (Akdoğan, 2004: 111).

Akdoğan also discusses the importance of democracy, human rights and secularism to the identity of the party, and their position within it. Akdoğan underlines the compatibility of these concepts with the demands of Islam (2004: 62–87). Hence, in line with Bayat's definition of post-Islamism, the JDP and its conservative democratic identity were, initially, a decisive enterprise in reconciling 'religiosity with rights and liberties' and incorporating 'Islam, freedom and pluralism' (Bayat, 2013a: 8). This is why I define the JDP as a pioneering, electorally succesful 'post-Islamist' party in the Muslim world. In contrast to its predecessor, the Islamist Welfare Party (Refah Partisi), the JDP was much keener to develop relationships with the West and with the European Union in particular, especially during its initial years, and was much more careful about protecting the democratic and secular qualities of the regime (Akdoğan, 2004: 106).

In the economic sphere, Akdoğan emphasizes that the JDP was in favour of a free market economy and a competitive economic under-standing, which were compatible with the global system (2004: 13). Indeed, in the economic field, the JDP followed the structural adjust-ment programme of the International Monetary Fund (Ekzen, 2009: 475), which imposed widespread privatization and a drastic reduction in the size of the state. Nevertheless, the JDP also sought to improve income distribution through the use of public sources (Bakırezer and Demirer, 2009: 166). The JDP also deployed the networks of religious charities in order to reduce poverty (Buğra and Keyder, 2006: 224). Buğra and Keyder (2006) also argue that the JDP had an inclination to transform the very hierarchical and uneven corporatist welfare regime which ignored the majority who worked in the informal sector.

Following this post-Islamist phase, however, the JDP's populist cre-dentials have become more and more obvious, and ultimately it emerged as a hegemonic party that propelled Turkey into a competitive authoritarian regime. Over the years, the JDP has undergone profound changes. The publication of a recent book by Akdoğan (2017) entitled *The Leader: Political Leadership and Erdoğan (Lider: siyasal liderlik ve Erdo-ğan)* was emblematic of these changes. During the party's initial years, as documented above, Akdoğan was trying to define a party identity based on a political-ideological stance. In this recent hagiographic account, however, he has given Erdoğan centre stage.[8] This particular change in Akdoğan's themes was a strong indicator of the transformation of the JDP from a post-Islamist conservative democratic vanguard into a populist and personalistic hegemonic party. Thus, this study also represents an answer to the question, 'What kind of sources, instruments, and strategic choices and actions have made this transformation possible?'

Identifying the Theoretical Puzzle of the JDP: From Post-Islamism to Populism to a Hegemonic Party Autocracy

The case of Erdoğan's JDP has always been a multi-faceted phenomenon, and since its rise to prominence, as the literature review below documents, students of Turkish politics have examined it from a variety of angles. So far, Erdoğan's JDP has been evaluated as a case of the 'normalization'[9] of a religious party (or a case of post-Islamism or Islamic liberalism), a case of populism and, more recently, a case of authoritarian predominance. In this book, I will touch upon all these problematics regarding the case of the JDP to varying extents, but the main focus here is to explain the political success of the party, that is, its extraordinary capacity to stay in power for such a long time. Therefore, the main problematic here appears to be the electoral success of the party and its capacity to transform the already fragile democratic system of Turkey (or its electoral democracy) into competitive authoritarianism. This was a very puzzling case of political success in three interrelated theoretical respects: firstly, regarding the 'transformation of Islamist politics'; secondly, regarding 'populism in power'; and, thirdly, regarding 'the rise of a hegemonic party autocracy'.[10]

---

[8] For a detailed review of Akdoğan's book in English, see Baykan (2017a).

[9] For the term 'normalization', see the volume by Mecham and Hwang (2014b), and particularly their introduction in which the authors propose the term 'normalization' instead of 'moderation' since the latter term also assumes an ideological liberalization of Islamist movements. According to Mecham and Hwang, 'normalization is a process by which Islamist parties increasingly accommodate themselves to the rules of the political regimes in which they operate; in other words, they become less unique and more normal political actors when compared with other parties in the competitive system' (2014a: 6–7). Hence, 'normalization' has less-normative implications than terms such as 'liberalization' and 'moderation'. It should however be noted that the concept of 'normalization' does not help researchers to grasp how the 'normalizing' political actor transforms the 'normal'.

[10] I do not claim that this new regime has already been established. As I discuss in Chapter 8, the rise of competitive authoritarianism and the hegemonic party autocracy in Turkey is still an ongoing, transitory process, although it has already passed a legally constitutive moment with the referendum on 16 April 2017.

How and Why Did an Islamist (and Later, Post-Islamist) Party Embrace Populism? The rise and subsequent electoral and political predominance of the JDP were, first of all, a solid example illustrating one of the potential trajectories of the transformation of Islamist politics. In its struggles with strictly secularist forces of the country (as delineated in Chapter 2) which did not shy away from certain repressive measures, Islamist political actors (most notably the National View movement) in Turkey gradually embraced a more conciliatory posture. It was from this tradition that the JDP finally emerged as a conservative democratic (or a post-Islamist) force. Nevertheless, since it came from a strictly Islamist political background, there has always been a very deep suspicion of – and even hostility towards – the JDP on the part of the secularist elites and secular social segments of Turkey. The JDP's political success was achieved despite these widespread unfavourable attitudes and feelings towards both the party and Erdoğan among broad segments of Turkish society and elites. Hence, the JDP's long-lasting hold on power was a very puzzling story of success given its political background and the highly intolerant secularist traditions of Turkey. While liberal Islamism or post-Islamism represented a certain phase and strategy of the normalization of Islamist politics in Turkey, it was a temporary and, more importantly, insufficient strategy for the survival of this particular political tradition. This is why populism, sometimes latently and sometimes more manifestly, has always accompanied the normalization of Islamist political actors in Turkey and gained a critical prominence as the threats and risks for the JDP and Erdoğan increased. Hence, the case of JDP very puzzlingly illustrates that the transformation of Islamic inclinations within politics and society may lead to results other than liberal democracy and violent Islamic fundamentalism. In the case of the JDP, this route led to populism (and then competitive authoritarianism). Given the fate of other Islamist and post-Islamist actors across the Muslim world, this was an exceptional outcome. How and why did an Islamist (and later, a post-Islamist) party embrace populism? What set of circumstances and, more importantly, strategic choices and actions paved the way to this particular outcome?

How Did a Populist Party Defy the Expectation That Populists Are Destined to Fail in Government? Populism is a problematic strategy for any party in office, and the JDP has always been required to counterbalance its populist responsiveness. This responsiveness has usually been in contradistinction to the responsibility required by a long-term tenure in office. Given the fact that the JDP has remained in office for such a long time, it is plausible that the party and Erdoğan relied on different sources and invented new methods and instruments that other populist parties and actors across the world could not. In other words, in contrast to the common expectation, the case of Erdoğan and the JDP illustrated that populist forces are not destined to fail in government and that they are on the political stage to stay. So how did a populist party defy the expectation and common wisdom that they are destined to fail in government? What sources and methods granted such a long political life to Erdoğan and the JDP? How were the JDP and Erdoğan able to combine populist responsiveness with the precise amount of governmental responsibility to prevent any crises?

How, in the Absence of Required Symbolic and Economic Resources, Did a New Political Actor Build a Hegemonic Party Autocracy? Another puzzling aspect of the JDP phenomenon is in regard to the regime change that it achieved. How did this new populist party with an Islamist background rise to a hegemonic/dominant party status under unfavourable conditions that included the lack of historical legitimacy granted by being the founding party, such as that enjoyed by the Party of Institutional Revolution (Partido Revolucionar Institucionel) of Mexico; the lack of extensive natural resources that could be used to improve the repressive capacity of the state, such as those relied upon by Putin's United Russia; and the lack of control over a massive public economic sector, such as that exerted by Chavismo in Venezuela. In the absence of these usually necessary symbolic and economic resources, how could a new political actor like the JDP rise to obtain hegemonic party status and transform the entirety of Turkish politics? What kind of sources, strategic actions and choices allowed Erdoğan's JDP to build a competitive authoritarian regime under these unfavourable circumstances?[11]

Throughout this book, I draw attention to how agency-based factors (such as populism and party organization) to a great extent explain the theoretical puzzles posed by the case of Erdoğan's JDP. First of all, this case shows that a particular political strategy – namely, 'low-populism' – is the best way to cope with the obstacles raised against Islamist party normalization and ensure the survival of the post-Islamist party in a setting that includes hostile and powerful secularist actors. More importantly, the theoretical argument of this study is as follows: the case of Erdoğan's JDP demonstrates that, if a particular organizational model (which I refer to as the 'personalistic mass party' in this book) is

---

[11] I owe this formulation of the puzzle of the JDP, as well as some of the arguments examining the party's hegemonic position from an agency-based perspective, to a joint work with Murat Somer. See the draft paper by Somer and Baykan (2018).

embraced by populists in power in a political environment where the liberal democratic architecture is weak and where the symbolic and economic resources that other authoritarian political actors enjoy are missing, the rise of a 'hegemonic party', and therefore the growth of competitive authoritarianism, as a consequence of populist predominance is much more likely than other national contexts where populist parties and leaders do not have such organizational and economic resources, and where the political systems have strong liberal and constitutional institutions.

In this book, therefore, I propose an overwhelmingly agency-based explanation for the normalization and electoral achievements of the JDP and its authoritarian turn that focuses on the organizational and strategic reasons behind the party's political success. This approach also complements the current literature on the party, which frequently focuses on the external-structural reasons for the rise and electoral success of the party. I argue that the JDP's upward trajectory and political resilience, as well as its success at establishing a competitive authoritarian regime under the unfavourable circumstances in Turkey at the time, relied on the 'low-populist' appeal of the party and its tightly controlled, massive membership organization which was active year-round and which penetrated the remotest corners of the country. This massive and pervasive organization was built by and around a personalistic leadership and was supported by political marketing techniques. Therefore, in this book, the JDP is called a 'personalistic mass party'. In short, I define the political appeal and organization of the JDP – the 'low-populist appeal' and the 'personalistic mass party' – as the essential agency-based factors behind the unprecedented political predominance of this new party in Turkey for more than fifteen years.

The Literature on the JDP

The rise and enduring electoral success of the JDP in Turkey have drawn remarkable attention from students of political Islam, Middle East politics and party politics in general.[12] The JDP's exceptionally successful 'normalization', as a party with an Islamist background, was one of the underlying reasons for this enormous interest. The JDP was strikingly successful, too, in protecting and increasing its vote steadily during previous elections, despite its position in power, or the negative

---

[12] See Atacan (2005), Atasoy (2009), İnsel (2003), Jang (2005), Mecham and Hwang (2014b), Mecham (2004), Somer (2007), M. Şen (2010), Tanıyıcı (2003), Taşkın (2008), Tezcür (2010), Tuğal (2009) and Yavuz (2009).

incumbency effect – a situation that has also increased scholarly interest in the party. More recently, following the authoritarian turn of the JDP, a series of academic studies have appeared that seek to describe and explain how Erdoğan's JDP established its current authoritarian predominance (Ayan Musil, 2015; Esen and Gümüşçü, 2016 and 2017; Özbudun, 2014 and 2015; Somer, 2016). The wide-ranging literature focusing on the rise and electoral achievements of the JDP and its authoritarian turn, as I will illustrate, predominantly embraces the following perspectives: economy-based explanations; ideology/ discourse-based perspectives; leadership-based approaches; and constituency-based perspectives (the rise of the so-called Islamic bourgeoisie).

In this part of the Introduction, I will show that the majority of the literature on the JDP focuses on factors other than the role of the party's strategic and organizational agency in its electoral and political resilience. As I will illustrate in the following sections, even the most agency-based explanations do not fully focus on the role of the JDP's organizational dynamics in the success of the party; they see the JDP (and therefore its political agency) simply as a reflection of wider external social, economic and political circumstances. This book, then, aims to contribute to the broad literature on the rise and electoral and political success of the JDP by highlighting the role of organization and strategy, in short, the agency of the party.

Research Focusing on the Economy

One of the oft-cited factors behind the electoral success of the JDP in the literature has been the growth of the Turkish economy, notably the decrease in consumer price inflation throughout the JDP's rule and the dramatic rise of *per capita* income. Studies by Kalaycıoğlu (2010: 39), Dağı (2008: 29), Çarkoğlu (2007: 515–516) and Öniş (2012: 137) underline the role of the economy in the electoral success of the party. One of the most prominent economists in Turkey, Korkut Boratav, also explains the political success of the JDP as an outcome of global economic cycles. According to his analysis, while the failure of previous coalition governments preceding the JDP corresponded to the downturn in the global economic cycles, the electoral breakthrough and the rise of the JDP are explained as resulting from the global economic recovery and rising foreign investments in Turkey (Boratav, 2009). There are also other economy-based explanations of the success of the JDP as resulting from its redistributive policies. In this sense, the studies of Bakırezer and Demirer (2009), Öniş (2012: 137), D. Yıldırım (2009: 102) and

Yücesan-Özdemir (2012: 143–144) highlight the role of redistributive strategies in the party's success.[13] More recently, students of Turkish politics have pointed to new patronage-based relationships as the basis of the competitive authoritarian regime established by the JDP (Esen and Gümüşçü, 2017). In short, there is a remarkable literature highlighting the economic reasons for the JDP's success that focuses on the role of macro-economic trends and redistributive mechanisms.

Research Focusing on Social Structural Dynamics and Constituency

Second, many studies of the rise and electoral success of the party highlight the role of the 'Islamic bourgeoisie' in Turkey. Until the 1980s, the state supported the businesspeople close to the secularist world-view of the establishment elite of the country (the Kemalist military and bureaucratic elite).[14] Nevertheless, since the 1980s, and through the introduction of a more liberalized economic regime by the centre-right Motherland Party (Anavatan Partisi) governments that replaced the import substitution regime of the previous era, small and medium-sized businesses that were conservative and religious in orientation gained momentum and started to grow. These business networks, or the 'Islamic bourgeoisie', tended to support, firstly, the Islamist parties of the National View tradition such as the Welfare Party, and then the JDP.

The historical and ideological transformations leading to the formation of a pious bourgeoisie are well documented in the literature. In an ESI (2005) report, prominent examples can be seen of the development of the pious small and middle-range enterprises and the role of religious factors in their achievements. Studies by M. Şen (2010) and Atasoy (2009) reveal the ideological and economic transformations that gave rise to the formation of the pious bourgeoisie. In a comparative study, Buğra (1998) analyses the development of the business association of the pious bourgeoisie. Jang (2005) illustrates the close relationship between the JDP and the pious bourgeoisie. Tuğal (2009: 8), İnsel (2003: 299–300), Gümüşçü and Sert (2009: 957–958), Yavuz (2006: 1) and

---

[13] The studies about the JDP that focus on the role of patronage, clientelism and vote-buying should be seen within the framework of economic explanations and the redistributive agency of the party. Although I agree that these mechanisms and instruments contributed to the party's success to a certain extent, I also propose a more nuanced understanding of the redistributive agency of the JDP, particularly in Chapter 5. I highlight the discursive, stylistic and organizational factors that differentiated the JDP's engagement with patronage and clientelism from its centre-right predecessors.

[14] See Keyder (2003) for these economic developments.

Hoşgör (2011: 355) also point out the role of the Islamic bourgeoisie and highlight the relationship between this social group and the party. There are also various accounts illustrating the socio-economic accord between the JDP cadres and JDP voters. One of these studies is the research of Aydın and Dalmış (2008). According to Aydın and Dalmış's interpretation of polling data and public opinion surveys, JDP supporters had a lower educational level as well as a lower profile in terms of professional training than had voters of other parties (2008: 218). Aydın and Dalmış also argue that 'when the socio-political identities favoured by the deputies were examined, it was seen that they shared similar identities as their supporters' (2008: 217). This social resonance between party members, in particular party deputies in the parliament and the electorate of the party, in combination with the support of the Islamic bourgeoisie, to a certain extent facilitated the rise and electoral and political success of the party.

Studies Focusing on Discourse/Ideology and Hegemony

Some studies in the literature have a stronger emphasis on the JDP's agency. For instance, Hale and Özbudun (2010: 24), Yıldız (2008: 46) and Cizre (2008a: 5) argue that the JDP had a more pragmatic and less essentialist and dogmatic strategy than its Islamist predecessor. These studies do not directly address the contributions of these ideological and strategic stances to the party's electoral achievements although they imply the role of moderation in the rise of the JDP.

The Populism of the JDP: A Controversial Issue The more challenging and promising aspect of the literature on the JDP is the emphasis on the concept of populism. Economic and political-ideological explanations of the party's rise and electoral achievements frequently deploy this concept. While some of these analyses underline the 'non-populist' character of the JDP, some studies emphasize the 'populism' of the party as a factor in its rise and electoral achievements. This contradiction in the literature on the populist qualities of the JDP specifically highlights the conceptual ambiguities within the literature, particularly that on the concept of populism. For instance, in his study, Yıldız argues that the JDP could be characterized by 'less populism and more economic rationality' (2008: 43). Similarly, Duran argues that the JDP's leaders tried to construct a political stance that was free from 'populism' (2008: 82). According to Öniş, the JDP implemented in the redistributive field a 'controlled populism' quite unlike the 'old-style populism' of the former centre-right parties in Turkey (2012: 137). Deniz Yıldırım describes the redistributive social policy approach of the JDP as 'neo-liberal populism' (2009). In contrast, according to White, 'Erdoğan's populism' articulated the diverging desires of rising pious middle classes and the politically alienated young conservatives (2008: 373). Along the same lines as White, Dağı defined the JDP as a 'populist political party' (2008: 30). Taşkın, too, argues that the outsider character of the founders of the JDP made their 'populist claim' much more persuasive (2008: 59).

More recently, a few studies more vocally (and more accurately, from a theoretical standpoint) described the JDP as a populist actor. Aytaç and Öniş (2014) stress the redistributive aspect of the JDP's brand of populism in Turkey, while Yabancı (2016) points out its ideological content and Dinçşahin focuses on the discourse of the JDP (2012) in order to identify the party's populism. Selçuk (2016) also focuses on the discursive-strategic dimension of the party's populism. The common gap in these recent, theoretically more nuanced analyses of the JDP's populism is that they do not put enough thought into the question of why we need to look at either redistributive tactics, ideology, discourse or strategy (or all of them) in order to define populism. These are questions that I will address in the theoretical section of Chapter 3 with reference to the methodological and theoretical diversity that characterizes the currently available broader literature on the concept.

Thus, it is fair to argue that there is a marked disagreement in the literature on the populist qualities of the JDP. This 'disagreement' signifies a gap in the literature which is closely related to the overestimation of the role of Erdoğan and redistributive strategies and, therefore, to an underestimation of the role of party organization and strategy (namely the discursive and behavioural responses to the electoral-political environment as well as the emotionally and stylistically broad and intense linkages built between the party and the electorate that surpass the discourse) in general. In other words, while some of these studies see populism as a redistributive strategy, some evaluate it only as the particular discourse and popular appeal of the party leader. Populism is understood, by many scholars working on Turkey, either as an economy-based electoral strategy or as a popular-telegenic leadership and his/her discursive interventions. These understandings lead most of these studies to overlook the broader role that party organization and strategy have played in the JDP's political success.

The JDP's Hegemony There is also a remarkable literature on the party in which the JDP's electoral and political success is evaluated as a part of a wider hegemony based on a cross-class coalition including 'popular sectors' (low-income, peripheral and provincial segments of society). Roughly, these works in the literature see the JDP as an outcome of the Islamic-leaning dominant classes articulating low-income, subordinate segments of society via a cultural bond. This stream of studies implies that this articulation depended mainly on the overplaying of cultural cleavages, controlled redistributive policies and, hence, the absorption of the dissent of popular sectors by the dominant classes which had vested interests in the running of neo-liberal processes (Atasoy, 2009; Tuğal, 2009; Yalman, 2012; D. Yıldırım, 2009). Nevertheless, these analyses of the JDP have mostly focused on the cultural-ideological dimension of the JDP hegemony and demonstrated little about the political-organizational dynamics of the process.

Research Focusing on the Organization and the Leader

Apart from the work of Kumbaracıbaşı (2009), most of the research on the JDP treat the issue of the organization as part of a wider framework and deal with this dimension in passing. Given the fact that one of the widespread truisms in Turkish political science literature is that all the Turkish political parties were very centralized and dominated by their leadership (Massicard and Watts, 2013) due to the framework defined by the Law on Political Parties (Law No. 2820), it is hardly surprising that in the literature we do not see party organization examined as an explanatory variable of party success. There are, however, some studies on the role of leadership and party organization, and these studies can be evaluated as evidence of the contribution of a certain political and organizational strategy to the electoral success of the JDP. This encourages further examination of organizational factors beyond the analysis of formal evidence such as laws, statutes and other written party material.

One of the most comprehensive analyses of the JDP is the oft-cited study of Hale and Özbudun (2010), although their examination devotes only a single chapter to party organization. Hale and Özbudun underline the fact that local JDP organizations were the most active, motivated and elaborately organized among Turkish parties (2010: 49).[15] In a work on the Islamist social movement in Turkey, Eligür (2010) also devotes a chapter to the organizational dynamics of the Islamist National View parties (2010: 182–213) as well as a section on the JDP's organization (2010: 243–275). Eligür especially underlines the role of 'strong

---

[15] Hale and Özbudun provide very accurate details about these kind of sub-provincial organizations of the JDP through the example of Gaziosmanpaşa sub-province in İstanbul (2010: 49–50).

organizational networks of the JDP' (2010: 258) in distributing selective resources to the urban poor.

Many accounts of the rise and success of the JDP also highlight the role of its leader, Erdoğan (Çağaptay, 2017; Cizre, 2008a: 5; Hale and Özbudun, 2010: 154–155; Heper and Toktaş, 2003: 160; Tezcür, 2012: 122; Tuğal, 2009: 176; Yavuz, 2009: 79–117). In a crucial chapter in his book Yavuz strongly underlines the personalistic organizational structure of the JDP and the party's lack of a well-defined ideology and identity. Indeed, previous works on the JDP affirmed the importance of Erdoğan within the organization as the glue holding together what would otherwise be 'too many diverse groups within the party' (Yavuz, 2009: 85) and 'a set of informal networks' (Yavuz, 2009: 99).

That the above-mentioned studies emphasize the importance of the JDP's leader, on the one hand, and the role of organization, on the other hand, in the party's electoral success does indicate a certain political and organizational strategy. Nevertheless, as I have illustrated so far, the literature on the JDP focuses either exclusively on the image of Erdoğan or on the role of redistributive mechanisms and, therefore, has overlooked party organization and strategy in general. In fact, the centrality of the leader of the JDP was complemented by its very centralized and hierarchical party structure. According to the analysis of the JDP's organization by Kumbaracıbaşı, the party was mainly characterized by a 'lack of internal democracy and leadership accountability' (2009: 124). These characteristics, according to him, also caused members and activists to be excluded from decision-making processes (Kumbaracıbaşı, 2009: 124–153). According to Kumbaracıbaşı, alongside the 'charisma' of the JDP leader, a highly autonomous leadership and strong centralization were decisive in protecting the party from fragmentation by different ideological elements (2009: 146).

In short, as Özbudun maintains, what has been observed in the case of the JDP is 'a highly centralized and hierarchical' organization (2006: 552). Özbudun also notes that, although local organizations were tightly controlled by the centre, they could not be seen as absolutely submissive extensions of the central organizations (2006: 552). Hence, it seems that the party had a very fragile balance between absolute leadership control and widespread grass-roots participation in intraparty politics.

In this context, it is also necessary to note that many studies pointed out the role of 'normalization' or 'moderation' in the electoral success of the party (Mecham, 2004: 350; Somer, 2007). Nevertheless, further normalization of Islamist parties in Turkey and the rise of the JDP contributed to the enlargement of the party base (as a result of the move beyond core Islamist constituency) and, therefore, also to ideological and socio-economic pluralization within the party and its electoral base. It seems that the organizational structure of the JDP was, to a large extent, shaped by the problems imposed by normalization. In other words, the party itself started its political life as a coalition of former Islamic cadres, centre-right politicians, far-right politicians and members with divergent ethnic and class backgrounds. This fragmented party leadership also corresponded to a fragmented electoral base as a coalition of the 'Islamist core constituency', 'part of [the] far right constituency', 'centre-right votes' and the 'Kurdish Vote' (Aydın and Dalmış, 2008; Erder, 2002). Thus, the normalization of Islamism and subsequent electoral victories of the JDP imposed a dual problem on the party: a fragmented party organization consisting of people coming from diverging political backgrounds and a fragmented electoral base consisting of diverse voter groups. For the JDP elite, keeping the party together and protecting and enlarging its fragmented electoral base have required a very specific political, organizational and discursive strategy.[16]

In his study, Kumbaracıbaşı (2009) outlines a very similar problem for the party. He argues that the JDP gradually found itself in a situation where it was wedged between the restrictions of a secular system, and the expectations of a non-Islamist centrist electorate and its own grass-roots' radical ideological leanings (Kumbaracıbaşı, 2009: 19). According to Kumbaracıbaşı, in order to overcome this problem and protect and enlarge its electoral base, the JDP leadership deployed 'tight [. . .] control over the party base and factions that [might] be more partisan in nature' (2009: 78).

This is to say that the JDP elite was not able to accept further grass-roots participation, and at the same time the JDP leadership was not able to increase its control over the external environment by strongly appealing to median voters. Increased participation by the radical-leaning grass roots of the JDP would cost it the median voter, and further moves towards policies designed to target median voters and consolidate the party vote and image in such a way that allows the party to exert control over its systemic environment – such as the establishment elite of the country – would cost it the core grass-roots support.

Thus Kumbaracıbaşı defines the main dilemma of the JDP as that between its allegedly more radical-leaning grass roots and its leadership's inclination towards targeting the median voter (2009: 19). According to Kumbaracıbaşı, this dilemma was solved 'through tight leadership

---

[16] In Somer and Baykan (2018), we frame this empirical puzzle from a theoretical perspective which considers the party's organizational development.

control over the party base and factions' (2009: 78). Relying on one of his senior interviewees from the JDP, he underlines that the JDP elite 'believed an equilibrium needed to be found among religious, conservative nationalist, liberal, and traditionalist ideas within the party. The leadership of Erdoğan is the primary factor that keeps these groups under control and prevents break-aways' (2009: 146).

Nevertheless, Kumbaracıbaşı's work demonstrates little about how the JDP leadership exerted this tight control over the party base and over the diverse groups within the organization and the party's electoral base in general. One of the main undertakings in this book is to illustrate empirically how the JDP leadership exerted this tight control over the party base without alienating its massive membership organization. In other words, this study illustrates the organizational mechanisms that helped Erdoğan to tighten his grip over the party organization and helped the JDP to encapsulate a very heterogeneous constituency.

Apart from the works analysed so far, more recently, a couple of empirically very rich studies have appeared that fully focus on the organizational agency of the party in different localities of Turkey (Doğan, 2016; Ocaklı, 2015). Doğan (2016) provides a very vivid account of the organizational activity and activist profiles of the JDP in a peripheral local context in İstanbul. Ocaklı (2015) comparatively underlines the role of a cohesive organization that selectively incorporates local elites and presents itself as a united front to local constituencies, which were key factors in the electoral success of the JDP in different localities. Nevertheless, just like Doğan's study (2016), Ocaklı's work, apart from passing references in his dissertation (2012: 68–9, 77, 168), says little about the links between the local-provincial organizations and the central JDP leadership which, from my point of view, played a crucial role in the cohesiveness and the proper strategic articulation of local elites in the majority of Turkish localities and enabled the party's electoral predominance. This book also aims to complement these recent works on various local organizations of the JDP in Turkey by focusing on crucial vertical intra-party relationships and by highlighting the national-scale organizational agency of the party.

The Approach and Purpose of the Research: Shifting the Focus from Structures to Party Agency

The main issue addressed by all relevant major works on the JDP examined above is the articulation of diverse tendencies, segments, social classes and political actors by the JDP. Most of the works reviewed above try to explain the coexistence of the dominant and the subordinate segments of society under the banner of the JDP. Which mechanisms and processes provided the consent of the subordinate sectors and convinced them to remain loyal to the (formerly Islamist, then post-Islamist) dominant social segments? The works I have evaluated above point out discursive-ideological change/interventions (such as emphases on cultural differences and the language of democracy, rights and liberties), redistributive policies of the dominant sectors, or social transformations of the Islamist elite and Islamist sectors of society as the basis of this coalition. Hence, on the one hand, they treat the JDP either as the generator of ideological-discursive interventions or as a redistributive mechanism. On the other hand, most of the studies analysed above tend to see the JDP as a simple reflection and political expression of the Islamic business community. In a sense, these accounts evaluate the JDP simply as an outcome of a wider social process and tend to underline the external-structural conditions of the current predominance of the JDP.

All of these external-structural processes highlighted by the major scholars, in fact, had an impact on the rise and electoral and political predominance of the JDP. However, while these accounts highlight the structural processes, and to a certain extent the discursive agency of the party, they fail to notice the role of the party's broader organizational and strategic agency. This is why, in most of these accounts, the JDP was everything but a party organization. These works, which focus predominantly on the wider structural reasons for the rise, electoral achievements and political resilience of the JDP, are characterized by a lack of interest in the JDP's organizational mechanisms because most of them consider the party a homogeneous given, a reflection of the social hegemony of conservative dominant classes. In fact, my argument in this book is that the party organization played a crucial role in the success of the JDP, and was at the heart of the current conservative hegemonic party autocracy in Turkey. In other words, consent was first and foremost produced within the party and extracted from the party base, and then extended beyond other spheres of the public life. As an intense and intricate relationship[17] between diverging segments, tendencies and desires, party organization was the kernel of the JDP's hegemony where dominant and subordinate social elements met each other on the basis of a particular organizational dynamic. This is the broader rationale that led me to focus primarily on the party's organizational agency.

---

[17] In line with Massicard and Watts, I take parties to mean 'relational entities' (2013: 1–6).

This review also points out a couple of interrelated theoretical and methodological lacunae in the literature on the rise and electoral success of the JDP. First of all, studies focusing on external-structural economic and social reasons for the JDP's rise and electoral achievements have a predominant position in the relevant literature. In addition, when it comes to the analysis of the party's agency, past studies have either showed a conceptual inaccuracy – as in the case of the concept of populism – or they exclusively focus on the role, and more precisely the image, of Erdoğan and the ideological-discursive aspects of JDP politics from a narrow perspective. Furthermore, analyses of the JDP's organization have not properly demonstrated its crucial, national-scale intra-party dynamics, which played a central role in the cross-class coalition of the party and the conservative hegemony in Turkey in general, either. In other words, exclusively focusing on the leader, or on patronage/pork-barrel politics, or on ideology/discourse (as 'words' [Ostiguy, 2017: 77]), has overshadowed a much broader organizational-strategic dynamic behind the rise and electoral achievements of the JDP. One of the theoretical and methodological aims of this research is to fill this gap in the current literature on the JDP by analysing the case through more rigorous conceptual tools borrowed mainly from literature on party politics (and, to a certain extent, from the literature on populism).

Given the state of current literature analysed above, the lack of a systematic focus on the role of party agency – the immediate discursive/ stylistic and organizational mechanisms connecting the JDP with its electorate and protecting the party from fragmentation – becomes rather puzzling. After all, the JDP as a party has capitalized upon convenient economic circumstances and social transformations within Turkey, and the party's agency was not restricted to redistributive tactics, its leader's image, official messages indicating moderation and normalization, and, more recently, repressive measures restricting fair competition among political actors in favour of the JDP. The party's agency was also about emotionally engaging with its voters and supporters and creating and sustaining a unique organizational culture conducive to winning elections. As popular commentators in Turkey have argued, there existed indeed an 'economy' (careful economic management according to pro-JDP columnists and 'pasta and coal' according to the opponents of the party), a specific 'sociology' (conservative wealth and bourgeoisie and/or devout and humble Anatolian people) and a 'leader' (Erdoğan's image) behind the JDP's success.

But there was also 'politics', things done by the party as an organization, the actions and choices made by its elite, their engagements with the organization, and their emotional and stylistic appeal to the electorate beyond discursive and programmatic links. In my view, the political agency of the party in this sense was key to transforming these external-structural economic and social circumstances, as well as the redistributive mechanisms and the leader's image, into concrete electoral gains for the JDP. Thus, in this research I wanted to focus on this 'politics' with a highly empirical and, to a large extent, inductive approach. I wanted to explore and demonstrate discursive/stylistic and organizational mechanisms behind the JDP's electoral success and political resilience through a dense narrative built upon empirical evidence.

Ultimately, therefore, this study has implications regarding a fundamental discussion in social sciences around the role of structure and agency in social and political processes. Following Hay (2002: 91–92), I contend that the separation between structure and agency is not an empirical but a theoretical and analytical one that helps us to understand this social and political phenomenon. Hence, no empirical investigation can provide a definitive answer as to whether structure or agency is more decisive in the formation of outcomes in social and political processes (Hay, 2002: 93). In other words, whether we assert the role of structure or agency in the political analysis is strongly related to the ontology we embrace regarding the social and the political. It is therefore legitimate to have a certain ontological – and thus epistemological – position regarding the role of structural or agency-based factors. In this analysis, I am inclined to assert the role of individual and collective agency and contingency in social and political processes. This perspective also corresponds to a particular understanding of social and political reality: as Almond and Genco (1977) highlighted in a classic study, social and political realities cannot be seen as clockwork processes in which outcomes are determined by mechanical configurations of various variables. Social and political realities are, as Popper's metaphor goes, cloud-like processes that are always open to contingency and, therefore, to the effects of human agency.

Structure is certainly a very elusive concept, but embracing the idea of structure is, at the same time, inevitable if we are going to understand the constitutive context of political phenomena (Sewell, 1992: 1–3) and, more practically, if we are going to have a guide before our empirical investigation of politics begins. I use the term 'structure', following the classical discussion by Sewell (1992), to mean both material and immaterial constraints and opportunities, including rules, resources, mental schemas, sedimented human interactions, cultural values and predispositions. I also embrace a dynamic understanding of the interaction of structure and agency. In other words, I see structures as subject to continuous transformation as a result of the actions of the actors created by these very structures – an interaction that changes agents as well.

As discussed above, with reference to the theoretical significance of the puzzles posed by the case of the JDP, Erdoğan's party was a collective actor[18] that was a product of the economic, political and cultural structures of Turkey, and was successful under highly unfavourable structural circumstances; it was both the outcome of these structural conditions and, at the same time, the agent that struggled with and reshaped these economic, political, institutional and cultural structures. As agents, the Islamist political actors and Erdoğan's JDP underwent profound changes throughout this struggle that led them from Islamism to post-Islamism to populism and, finally, to an authoritarian predominance only very loosely related to an Islamic agenda.

During the mid 1990s, the heyday of the strictly Islamist Welfare Party of Necmettin Erbakan, 'The army won't let them bring in sharia law!' was a common cry among secular upper and middle classes. In today's Turkey, however, the Turkish Armed Forces are no longer an invincible component of the political structure, nor does there remain a major political party with a strictly Islamist agenda. The rise of the JDP as a populist and personalistic mass party that catapulted Turkey into competitive authoritarianism was the contingent – and quite unexpected – outcome of the continual structure–agency interaction in Turkish politics. In fact, the whole story of Erdoğan's JDP – in other words the transformation of the structural aspects of Turkish politics and, more precisely, the establishment of a hegemonic party autocracy by this particular actor, who was himself created by the social, economic and political structures of Turkey – is strongly related to the plasticity of the structure–agency interaction in social and political reality. Both the political structure of Turkey and the agency of Erdoğan's JDP have changed remarkably since the foundation of the JDP. This book is an attempt to grasp the role of the latter in these extraordinary transformations.

---

[18] One might assume that the party, as an organization, should be considered part of the structures in analytical terms. This may or may not be the case depending on the history and circumstances surrounding the party. In the case of Erdoğan's JDP, I see the organization as a vehicle for agency given the low degree of the party's institutionalization and the high degree of external-environmental resistance that the party as a whole has had to face since its foundation (I discuss these points later in the book). More recently, the party could be considered as becoming an element of a new structure. For analytical purposes, however, I will keep taking the party as a vehicle for the agency of the JDP elite containing complicated intra-organizational relations that produce co-ordinated, meaningful and effective collective action.

Method, Fieldwork and Sources

In the literature review, I pointed out that specific organizational mechanisms and strategic choices, which protected the balance between diverse desires and interests of different groups within the party and the party's electoral base, were central to the JDP's electoral and political success. In this sense, as illustrated above, the study of Kumbaracıbaşı (2009) underlines a very similar point in the organizational and strategic problems and choices of the party and diverges from the rest of the literature. Nevertheless, his study mainly depends on a top-down perspective and focuses on the central organizations of the party. In order to see the effect of the specific organizational dynamics and strategic choices of the party elite that helped the party to protect its unity and electoral predominance, I embraced a broader – and, to a greater extent, a bottom-up – approach[19] which takes into account the different levels of party organization ranging in size and influence. This is in line with the perspective of Levitsky (2003), who places a special emphasis on the intra-party relationships of various hierarchical units within parties.

Neither the examination of the central organization nor the examination of the local or provincial organizations of the party alone could accurately depict the political and organizational strategy of the JDP. This is why I conducted in-depth interviews with JDP deputies and central elites as well as provincial (*il*) and sub-provincial (*ilçe*) chairs, and neighbourhood representatives across Turkey. I asked my interviewees open-ended questions about the organizational characteristics of the party[20] and these characteristics' contributions to the JDP's electoral success. The length of my interviews varied between half an hour and two hours. I spoke to more than fifty people[21] during my interviews.

---

[19] The overwhelming majority of my interviewees came from the provincial and sub-provincial levels. See Table 1.1 for information on the distribution of my interviewees.

[20] A typical interview usually revolved around (but was not limited to) the following questions and any follow-up questions, depending on the answers: 'What do you think about the role of political circumstances (institutions and competing political parties) in the rise and electoral success of the party?', 'In terms of organization, what characterizes the party compared to its Islamist predecessors and its competitors in the Turkish party system?', 'How has the organization of the party transformed since its foundation?', 'Have the profiles of the members and activists changed since the foundation of the party?', 'Have the candidate selection processes changed?', 'Have the research strategies of the party changed?', 'Has the reliance on opinion polling activity increased over time?' and 'Have the party's electoral strategies changed?'

[21] In fact, I spoke to more than fifty people for my research – the exact number is fifty-five. Nevertheless, a few of my interviewees told me in advance that they would speak but that they did not want to be cited in the research. I also had a chance to speak with a few people coincidentally while conducting interviews with others. I indicate them in the

I conducted interviews with participants from the JDP as well as people who were neutral observers or indirectly related to the party. Of my interviewees, forty were JDP members; twenty-six were active members and fourteen were former members at the time of interview. The rest were experts from bureaucracy, journalism and academia and politicians from other relevant parties. I started my fieldwork in September 2013 with several initial interviews, and I conducted the overwhelming majority of my interviews with the JDP members and relevant participants between January 2014 and May 2014.[22] Before discussing issues of validity and reliability of the research regarding the locations and sample of interviewees, in the following sub-section I would like to give some details about the constraints and opportunities that stemmed from the particular timing and conjuncture of the research, and then I will provide a brief reflection on my own position as the researcher.

The Impact of the Timing and Conjuncture of the Research and a Brief Self-Reflection

I encountered many unexpected yet quite illustrative obstacles stemming from the timing and conjuncture of my research which, to a certain extent, reshaped the methods and research design that I had initially had in mind. The first thing that bears mentioning is that I started my interviews just after the Gezi protests that took place in the early summer of 2013. This event had a deep, traumatizing impact on the JDP. Until then the JDP was much more convincing at presenting itself to large sectors of Turkish society as a pro-democratic force, the political bifurcation between the pro- and anti-JDP/Erdoğan sectors in Turkey was tolerable, and it is plausible that, before this particular event, it would also have been much easier to conduct field research on the party.

Further, just before I moved back from the UK to Turkey for the main bulk of my fieldwork, the corruption probes by allegedly

total numbers but I do not cite them in the Bibliography of this research. However, they also contributed to my overall understanding, which is why I wanted to acknowledge their participation. At their request, I use numbers for identifying my interviewees and omit their real names and any other information that could lead to the identification of the individual participants in the research. I only indicate the place and the position of my interviewees if it was not possible to determine individual interviewees from this information. Hence, in the Bibliography, I do not indicate the provinces of party chairs or any sub-province name that might lead to the identification of individual participants among a limited number of names.

[22] The exact date of each interview can be seen in the Bibliography.

Gülenist[23] prosecutors against JDP ministers were initiated in the middle of December 2013. These began just before the local elections on 30 March 2014. Hence, I started my research at a critical moment when the insecurities of the party had increased, its capacity to generate consent in a genuinely competitive environment had started to fade away, and its authoritarian tendencies had become visible. This was certainly an extremely difficult context that entailed decisive constraints for the research on the party.

All of these circumstances were components of a remarkable political crisis, even for such a strong political organization as the JDP, in terms of its electoral performance and leadership. These circumstances naturally caused considerable difficulties in getting in touch with even junior and local party members, let alone senior party members from headquarters. Yet this difficulty provided some first-hand insight into the organizational characteristics of the JDP.[24] It seems that, in times of political crisis, highly hierarchical and centralized parties like the JDP show a natural tendency to be much more vigilant and conservative about external demands such as interview requests. One should also note that other researchers investigating party politics and organizations in Turkey frequently had similar difficulties, and even in quite stable periods party elites and members have held a deep suspicion towards these kinds of requests.[25]

As the organizational heir of the Islamist National View tradition, which had long dealt with the pressure of systemic actors such as the army and high judiciary, the JDP revealed a remarkable resistance to extra-political influence thanks both to the skilful interventions of its leadership in the public debate regarding graft probes and to its disciplined organization (I focus on the impact of this Islamist past on the current organizational discipline of the party in Chapters 2 and 5). After the initial waves of corruption probes, the party leadership reinterpreted these investigations as a conspiracy planned by Western powers and staged by the Gülenist 'parallel state' embedded in the bureaucracy. The results of the local elections on 30 March 2014 proved the success of this strategy. The JDP received 45 per cent of the popular vote.

---

[23] Under JDP rule, the Gülen Community, an influential religious group, has become one of the main components of elite-level power structures in Turkey. I elaborate on the relationship between the Gülenists and the JDP in some length in Chapter 8.

[24] As Dexter stated, 'frequently the circumstances of the refusal, the way in which it is done, the excuses given, the reaction to the interviewer, may provide valuable data or, at least, hypotheses about the situation' (Dexter, 1970: 31).

[25] See research conducted nearly twenty years ago by Çarkoğlu et al. (2000: 22).

The failure of my initial attempts at getting in touch with active JDP members implied a very particular quality of the party: the intensity of their internal communications and the hierarchical connectedness of the different regional branches and layers of the party.[26] Even after these March 2014 local elections, I had difficulties in getting in touch with some of the active members of the party. In a provincial city, I arranged an interview with the chair of the youth branch of the JDP. Later on he called my contact and told him that he was not allowed by the party to do the interview. This could be considered to be an indication of a tightly interconnected, highly disciplined party organization and the difficulties this situation posed for the research. This was only a single instance among many that I encountered in attempting to reach research participants from the JDP. This particular combination of the nature of the JDP as an organization and the timing and the conjuncture of the research were making it remarkably difficult to conduct field research.

The above-mentioned difficulties of the fieldwork process, and particularly its timing, led me to find some new ways of locating participants. I started to look for and identify former members of the party, contacting former candidate deputies of the party, former provincial and subprovincial chairs, and former candidates for the local elections. In this sense, the period before the local elections provided some unexpected opportunities. Once the party published the names of their candidates for local government on the party website, I had an extensive list of names, and after the party made its final decisions regarding its candidates in the middle of February 2014, failed candidates within the party became available. It was at this point that I started to find some interviewees. This also provided some vivid information about candidate selection processes within the party. These narratives contained some very useful information about the distribution of power within the organization as well as the negotiation of power among members from different levels of the party.

[26] One could also form an idea about the degree of the party's systemness through a consideration of the stability of its corporate identity. In this sense the JDP had clear standards for the shape and colour of its party emblem and provided specific directions to the provincial and local branches and individual candidates on the visual representation of the party. See the webpage of the party, where detailed directions for the visual appearance of the party identity on personal cards, office papers, billboard posters, advertisements on the sides of buses, etc. can be found: www.akparti.org.tr/site/akparti/kurumsal-kimlik (accessed: 17 June 2017). During my fieldwork, I also observed that the use of the party emblem and its corporate identity in general was quite similar across distinct corners of the country. One can also observe that the webpages of the different provincial branches of the party reveal a remarkable degree of similarity.

In addition, I also carried out some interviews with senior members of the former centre-right Motherland Party, as well as sympathizers and senior members of the Islamist National View party (at the time of my research it was called the Felicity Party [Saadet Partisi]) in Turkey before the JDP's victory in the March 2014 local elections. These people had no official connection with the JDP but had close, informal ties with the party. These interviews, particularly those with the Motherland Party members, provided a crucial comparative point of view for the research. Further, after the local elections on 30 March 2014, I found many opportunities to interview both senior and junior JDP members in particular settings, and even this fact revealed a considerable degree of transparency in JDP activities, as well as a high degree of responsiveness among the JDP elite, despite the widespread interest in the party and the political crisis and transformation (namely the increasing authoritarian inclination) that have been highlighted in the previous sections.

Nevertheless, my initial interviews with former party members and failed candidates, and their more critical voices, provided me with a 'control narrative' against which I could test the more reserved and 'diplomatic' narratives of active party members that depicted an idealized picture of party life and remained within the limits of the 'official story' of the party as defined by Katz and Mair (1994). This is also to say that, by talking to the active members of the party after the elections, I obtained yet another 'control narrative' with which I could test critical but potentially biased interpretations of some of the former members and failed candidates of the party. The composition of the group of my interviewees with regard to their regions, hierarchical positions and timing of interviews can be seen in Table 1.1.

It is also important here to reflect on the potential opportunities and constraints, and the advantages and disadvantages, that stemmed from my position as a researcher. There is no doubt that, as someone brought up in Turkey, I was deeply embedded in the research context in social, political and cultural respects. Although as a Turkish citizen and student of Turkish politics, I had some sort of orientation regarding the political field of Turkey, from a much wider perspective the difficulties I had in getting in touch with the interviewees largely stemmed from the fact that most of the JDP members came from a particular social and political milieu to which I had little access. In this regard it is crucial to highlight the role of common informal networks, similar social environments, educational backgrounds and common business circles as well as common political socialization processes for most of the senior and junior members, sympathizers and supporters of the JDP. My social,

Table 1.1 *Details of interviewees*

High-ranking	Provincial level	Sub-provincial level	Non-JDP Experts	Non-JDP politicians
4 from the JDP headquarters, 2 active deputies, 2 former deputies, 1 vice-minister.	1 active chair, 5 active vice-chairs, 5 former chairs, 2 failed candidates, 2 active administration board members.	5 active chair, 4 active vice-chairs, 1 active mayor, 2 neighbourhood representatives, 4 failed candidates.	1 journalist, 3 academics, 2 bureaucrats, 1 researcher, 2 professional campaigners.	1 former minister from the Welfare Party, 2 former minister and 1 former deputy from the Motherland Party, 2 active executive committee members from the Felicity Party.
Total: 9	**Total: 15**	**Total: 16**	**Total: 9**	**Total: 6**

Total number of participants from the JDP: 40 (12 from Ankara, 8 from İstanbul, 6 from Trabzon, 6 from Konya, 5 from Mardin, 1 from Urfa, 1 from Diyarbakır, and 1 from Batman)

Total number of non-JDP participants: 15 (14 from Ankara and 1 from İstanbul)

Total number of participants: 55

	HQ	Provincial executives (chairs and vice-chairs)	Sub-provincial executives (mayors, chairs and vice-chairs)	Neighbourhood representatives	Non-JDP participants	Total
İstanbul		3	4	1	1	9
Ankara	9	2	1		14	26
Konya			5	1		6
Trabzon		3	3			6
Mardin		4	1			5
Diyarbakır		1				1
Batman		1				1
Urfa		1				1
Total	9	15	14	2	15	55

	Interviews conducted before the corruption probes of 17–25 December 2013	Interviews conducted after the corruption probes and before the local elections	Interviews conducted after the local elections of 30 March 2014	Total
Former JDP members	2	10	2	14
Active JDP members		7	19	26
Non-JDP participants	3	8	4	15
Total	5	25	25	55

political and educational background, to say the least, did not provide me with strong points of access to the conservative, centre-right political circles in Turkey. This should be considered a particularly challenging starting point for the research since informal personal relations are a key aspect of social and political life in Turkey, as researchers of Turkish politics point out (Meeker, 2001; Wuthrich, 2015). Nevertheless, this same unfamiliarity and my position as an outsider equipped me, I hope, with a fresh perspective (compared to a conservative insider) during the fieldwork since – other than second-hand sources – I had little informed insight and observation into the practical politics of the JDP. The interview process as a whole, apart from providing practical empirical insight on the internal operations of the JDP as an organization, substantially influenced my view of Turkish politics and society. As I will show in the rest of this book, this led me to interrogate some of the truisms in the Turkish political science literature regarding the factors that define electoral and political success.

The Effect of Interview Locations on the Research

I conducted my interviews in various cities and regions across Turkey such as Ankara, İstanbul, Konya and Trabzon, along with predominantly Kurdish – and economically underdeveloped – cities such as Diyarbakır, Batman, Şanlıurfa and Mardin, which can be seen in Figure 1.1. I conducted twenty-six interviews in Ankara, nine in İstanbul, six in Trabzon, six in Konya and five in Mardin. I also conducted three interviews each in Diyarbakır, Urfa and Batman. Each of these cities represents various degrees of electoral success of the party as well as diverging regional, economic and socio-demographic features, which can be seen in Table 1.2. While İstanbul and Ankara, more or less, represent the national average for the party in terms of electoral success, Diyarbakır, for example, represents the least successful and Trabzon and Konya the most successful locations for the party in my sample. Looking at these different regional settings also provided an idea about the degree of centralization of the party. By visiting these different settings I had a chance to see how the party could more or less successfully establish a nationwide common image and identity.

One might think that it was also necessary to observe the party in a local setting where the main opposition, the Republican People's Party (Cumhuriyet Halk Partisi), was dominant such as the Thracian, Aegean or Mediterranean coasts of the country. However, the interviews conducted in predominantly Kurdish local settings, as well as the interviews

Table 1.2 *Some basic statistics regarding the cities included in the research and JDP vote share*

Cities	GDP per capita in US dollars in 2011*	Car ownership per 1000 people in 2013	Electricity consumption per capita in 2012 (KWh)	Newborn deaths per 1000 births in 2013	JDP voter percentages in November 2015
İstanbul	13,865	152	2,388	8	48.4
Ankara	12,259	217	2,140	7.9	48.8
Konya	7,118	130	2,586	11.8	74.4
Trabzon	6,652	92	1,622	9.5	66.8
Batman	4,689	26	936	17.2	28.4
Mardin	4,689	26	1,397	14.4	28.5
Diyarbakır	4,282	31	829	14.2	21.4
Urfa	4,282	49	1,428	15.5	64.6

* Economic data for this and the following three columns received from Turkish Statistical Institute (2013). The precise figures for GDP per capita for Batman, Diyarbakır, Mardin and Urfa were not provided by the Turkish Statistical Institute.

Figure 1.1: Cities visited for the research
Source: Redrawn from www.mapsopensource.com/turkey-outline-map-black-and-white.html (accessed: 27 May 2016).

conducted in secularist strongholds in İstanbul and Ankara, to a great extent compensated for the lack of this kind of setting within the sample. In addition to the above, I also had difficulties in getting in touch with local party branches in peripheral, low-income and developing sub-provinces and the neighbourhoods of big cities such as İstanbul and Ankara. My attempts at getting in touch with any member of these JDP strongholds failed even in cases where I had the help of 'gatekeepers' such as relatives and friends. This situation represented a pattern, and it is plausible that the nature of the party's activity in these kinds of settings might be remarkably different than in party branches, where I mainly conducted my interviews. There were certain reasons to think that the nature of party activity in these settings might also be different in terms of the prevalence of selective incentives – providing goods and aid in particular to members and supporters – for the party branches.[27] Perhaps this was why, in these regions, it was unusually difficult to get in touch with the chairs or members of governing bodies of the party.

The lack of full access to these kinds of settings – low-income, peripheral sub-provinces in metropolitan cities such as İstanbul and Ankara – during my fieldwork could be considered the major limitation of my sample. However, I should also note that, although I could not speak to party activists from branches of the JDP in poor sub-provinces in İstanbul and Ankara, I was able to conduct interviews with party activists from relatively poor provincial and sub-provincial settings in other Anatolian cities. This gave me some solid impressions about JDP politics in localities where the overwhelming majority of inhabitants come from socio-economically lower-status groups.

In addition, some recent research has demonstrated the prevalence of clientelistic practices in Turkey already under the rule of the JDP (Çarkoğlu and Aytaç, 2015; Çeviker-Gürakar, 2016; Marschall et al., 2016). It should also be mentioned that after I completed my fieldwork some up-to-date and empirically robust accounts of the JDP in these sorts of contexts were published (for example, Doğan, 2016). Overall, however, during fieldwork I was able to observe vertical ties among various JDP branches and the leadership. Despite its limitations, the fieldwork process provided rich empirical material for my book, and its contribution to my understanding of the JDP's political appeal and organization was invaluable.

---

[27] A few classic and empirically robust studies on Islamist party politics in low-income, peripheral local settings in İstanbul and Ankara contain vivid accounts of these kinds of practices by the JDP's predecessors, namely the Welfare and Virtue Parties of the 1990s. See Delibaş, 2015; Tuğal, 2009 and White, 2002.

The Effect of Interviewee Sample on the Research

I have already underlined the variety of my interviewees with regard to their links with the party at the time of fieldwork. To summarize, I conducted interviews with former as well as active JDP members, which provided me with remarkably different insider perspectives. I also conducted interviews with members of the JDP who represented different hierarchical positions, as can be seen in Table 1.1. On the one hand, I carried out interviews with JDP deputies and vice-ministers, members of the JDP Central Executive Committee (Merkez Yürütme Kurulu) and Central Decision and Administration Board (Merkez Karar ve Yönetim Kurulu) and advisers to the chairman as well as provincial, sub-provincial party chairs and vice-chairs.[28] On the other hand, I also conducted interviews with chairs of the youth and women's branches of the party and neighbourhood representatives.[29] There were nine high-ranking interviewees among the sample, including deputies, ministers and members of the Central Executive Committee of the party. There were fifteen members from provincial organizations and sixteen members from sub-provincial organizations of the party in various cities. This variety of interviewees provided me, as I expected, with a chance to see the vertical relationships between the party echelons as well as a better understanding of the implementation of JDP centralism. The rest of my interviewees were more or less neutral, non-JDP participants coming from academia, bureaucracy and journalism and from other relevant parties.

As can be seen in Table 1.1, I was able to interview JDP members from provincial and sub-provincial levels in almost every city I visited for the research, with the exception of Diyarbakır, Batman and Urfa. I was also able to speak to someone from the same rank (except headquarters) before and after the party's victory in the March 2014 local elections. But, as expected, I was able to speak with a larger number of active members after the electoral victory of the party. Nevertheless, former party members – as well as non-JDP participants – tended to be more

---

[28] The Central Decision and Administration Board of the party is a large central decision-making body in the JDP headquarters consisting of around fifty people. But, in practice, the highest ruling segment of the party is the Central Executive Committee which consists of only around twenty people.

[29] An important detail illustrating the hierarchical and socio-economic variety of the sample emerged in my attempts to get in touch with my participants. As could be expected, while it was very easy to get in touch with senior and central JDP members and receive answers via email, it was extremely difficult to get in touch with more junior, provincial members of the party in this way. Some of them did not check email accounts properly, or they simply did not have an email address or any computer literacy at all.

vocal in their criticism of the party. It can therefore be argued that almost one-third of my sample adopted a somewhat critical attitude. As mentioned above, I conducted interviews where the JDP was electorally weak. For example, eight of my interviews took place in predominantly Kurdish regions, and I also had interviews with several people from central sub-provinces of İstanbul and Ankara that were dominated by the secularist Republican People's Party. Hence, almost one-fifth of my interviewees came from settings where the JDP was electorally weak.

Other Sources

In-depth interviews and the personal observations that accompanied these were the main components of my research. As illustrated in the literature review section, I also relied on empirically robust studies on Islamist politics and the JDP in particular, as well as other accounts of Turkish politics in general, which were based on fieldwork in order to ameliorate the limitations of my own fieldwork. But apart from interviews and these empirically robust second-hand sources, there was already a vast amount of information on the organizational dynamics of the party on the internet. Thanks to the ease of internet publishing, it was possible to access local newspapers and the personal blogs and websites of politicians, as well as videos on local JDP activities such as consultation meetings (*istişare toplantıları*), non-binding elections among selected members (*teşkilat temayül yoklamaları*) and provincial conventions. I was aware that the use of personal blogs on local politics and media might entail specific problems for neutrality since I had a strong impression that these sources were often controlled by the local power holders and politicians. Thus, I tried to double-check the information from these types of sources with other websites and, if possible, with reports from national media. Apart from second-hand accounts and some newspapers close to the JDP such as *Yenişafak* and *Sabah*, I also examined the official publication of the party, *Turkey Bulletin* (*Türkiye Bülteni*), which, to a certain extent, helped me to understand the main emphases of the organizational activity in the JDP.

Another source that I drew upon extensively, as the reader will notice, was the work of Hulusi Şentürk. Şentürk, formerly a high-ranking member of the İstanbul branch of the Islamist National View parties and the JDP, has written several books regarding practical aspects of party politics and organizations in Turkey as guides for aspiring politicians. Apart from his book on Islamism (Şentürk, 2011), in which he briefly discusses the formal structures of the National View parties and the JDP, he has written some empirically rich works on intra-party politics which contain crucial information and clues about the formation of governing bodies of the party and candidate selection processes as well as about the world-view of the JDP elite (Şentürk, 2006; 2007; 2008a; 2008b; 2008c). It is plausible that all of these publications depend mostly on Şentürk's experience in the Islamist National View parties and the JDP.[30] These works should be considered some of the most important publicly accessible observations by an insider of the Islamist National View parties' and the JDP's organizational and strategic features. As this provided relatively neutral and, from time to time, humorous accounts of intra-party politics of the National View parties and the JDP, I have extensively used the empirical evidence provided by Şentürk's works throughout this book.

Structure of the Book

As I have illustrated in the literature review section, a considerable majority of the works on the JDP focused on the external-structural social and economic reasons behind the extraordinary electoral and political achievements of the party. In this book, by diverging from these over-whelmingly structural explanations, I put a strong emphasis on the role of party agency – the 'low-populist' appeal and the robust organizational leverage firmly controlled by the leadership – in the rise, electoral success and political resilience of the JDP. Hence, the majority of chapters following this Introduction focus on the organizational characteristics of the JDP as well as the strategic discursive and stylistic manoeuvres and preferences of the party elite. Although I highlight the role of party agency, all the chapters of the book, in one way or another, take into account the inevitable interaction and interpenetration of external-structural and agency-based factors in the rise and electoral and political resilience of the party. After all, from the party elites' discursive, strategic and stylistic preferences to the organizational characteristics and leader-ship modes within the party, agency-based factors in the electoral and political resilience of the JDP cannot be understood unless they are evaluated as responses to certain socio-political and historical develop-ments in Turkey. Yet, as I make clear throughout the book, the party agency of the JDP was the crucial dynamic that capitalized upon the opportunities – and ruled out obstacles – for electoral and political success created by these socio-political and historical developments.

---

[30] See also Çarkçı's (2006) interview with Şentürk.

Each chapter in this book gradually constructs an empirical and theoretical argument regarding the lasting electoral success of this formerly Islamist new political actor and, ultimately, its rise to authoritarian predominance in a political environment that included powerful elite and party competitors. *To put it more theoretically, this book is about the rise to authoritarian predominance of a new party in a multi-party setting within a short period of time and under highly unfavourable political, economic and social circumstances (that is, the rise of a hegemonic party autocracy).* I argue that, if a particular strategic and organizational agency (populism and the personalistic mass party) is embraced by a new party, it is possible, firstly, to overcome the reactions of secularist elite competitors embedded in the establishment, then, to achieve lasting electoral predominance and, finally, to gradually transform this electoral predominance into competitive authoritarianism. Hence, the JDP represents an example of a very successful case of populism in power (successful enough that it was able to fundamentally alter the political system of Turkey, moving the regime from an electoral parliamentary democracy to a 'competitive authoritarian presidentialism', as termed in Chapter 8) that emerged under specific political and historical circumstances (a weak liberal institutional heritage, which I call 'selective pluralism' in Chapter 2, as well as a specific, established way of representing sociocultural divisions of society in politics, namely the 'high–low divide' in Chapter 3) with a specific mode of agency (populism and the personalistic mass party, which are analysed in Chapters 3–8).

The book gradually constructs the argument regarding the agency-based factors behind the rise of the JDP into authoritarian predominance by embracing a logic of presentation that follows a line stretching from the analysis of structural contexts (Chapter 2 and, partially, Chapter 3) to various agency-based dynamics (Chapters 3–8) that could be summarized under the label 'populism-cum-personalistic mass party'. In Chapter 3, I introduce the political appeal of the party and Erdoğan: low-populism. In Chapter 4, I examine the role of Erdoğan, who was both a product of historical and structural context of Turkish politics (delineated in Chapters 2 and 3) and the strategic mastermind centrally located within the group of elites that shaped responses for political success against this background of historical and structural constraints and opportunities. In other words, Erdoğan represents the nexus between the structural aspects of Turkish politics and the agency-based features of the JDP. Therefore I placed Chapter 4 just after the analyses on the structural aspects of Turkish politics (Chapter 2 and, partially, Chapter 3) and before the examination of strategic (Chapter 5) and organizational and elite responses (Chapters 6–8) to these structural circumstances. The final chapter of the book focuses on the theoretical lessons that could be drawn from the case of Erdoğan's JDP regarding the relationship between (post-)Islamism, populism and authoritarianism.

In Chapter 2, I focus on the broad political structural factors that facilitated the rise of Islamism and eventually the post-Islamist JDP. Even here, in this most structural part of the book, I put special emphasis on the interaction of the political actors who created the political institutional settings that facilitated the JDP's rise and electoral and political resilience. I illustrate how the establishment elite of the country after the 1980 coup prepared the ground for the rise of Islamism, and eventually post-Islamism, through the inhibition and destruction of leftist organizational networks, through a virtual consensus with the conservative-Islamist elite, through the introduction of a new conservative and nationalist indoctrination of the masses, and through selective limitations on the political space with restrictive constitutional and legal regulations. This strategy, which I call 'selective pluralism', later became a political and institutional opportunity space for the Islamist and post-Islamist elite that facilitated the electoral and political resilience of the JDP.

After this rather structural chapter, I focus in Chapter 3 on the political appeal/style of the JDP. Here, I again highlight a relatively structural aspect of Turkish politics: its 'populist emphasis'. In this chapter, I adopt the perspective of Ostiguy (2017) on populism, taking the concept as a political appeal/style and using his high–low divide in order to locate the JDP's political appeal. This chapter makes it clear that, more than the party's position along a left–right or secular–religious divide, the JDP's success at reaching economically and culturally underprivileged segments of society was strongly connected to a 'low-populist' political appeal/style that created a strong sense of similarity between the party elite and the ordinary people. I demonstrate evidence from both the party's discursive interventions in the public debate and its communication and propaganda style.

In Chapter 4, I focus on the JDP leader, Erdoğan, since he was key to the political appeal and organizational formation of the JDP. After a theoretical discussion on closely related concepts such as charisma, personalism and personalization, I evaluate the role of Erdoğan within the party by relying on my interviews and some secondary sources such as biographies written about him. I highlight the central role of organization building and 'robust action' (Ansell and Fish, 1999) in his leadership style. In contrast to existing descriptions of him as a charismatic leader, I define him as an inventive and diligent organization man (teşkilatçı) who exclusively focused on achieving and maintaining power. Hence, I call the relationship between Erdoğan and the JDP 'non-charismatic personalism' (Ansell and Fish, 1999).

In Chapter 5, I elaborate on the JDP's strategic approach to redistributive tactics, organization and communication. In this chapter, I again focus on the historical background, and demonstrate the contribution of the organizational and strategic experience of the JDP elite, who came from different backgrounds such as centre-right parties and the Islamist National View parties. I demonstrate that these previous experiences provided the JDP elite with a highly effective strategic inclination, which led them to certain organizational and electoral-tactical preferences. In order to maintain electoral and political predominance, the JDP elite embraced an organizational and electoral strategy that struck a balance between the short-term requirements of elections (responsiveness) and the long-term requirements of government processes (responsibility), between collective and selective incentives, and between idealism and pragmatism. The combination of robust organizational leverage – a tightly controlled massive membership party, active year-round and present in neighbourhoods – with a strong and decisively pro-JDP media was key to this balance and, therefore, to the JDP's electoral predominance.

In Chapter 6, I exclusively focus on the JDP's organization by following the classics of the party organization studies as well as new perspectives highlighting the importance of the interaction between various hierarchies within parties (Levitsky, 2003; Massicard and Watts, 2013). In this chapter, I illustrate the formal territorial and membership structure of the party and put a special emphasis on how this massive membership organization was kept under the control of the central JDP elite. Here, I demonstrate the details of the central control mechanisms in the JDP, such as public opinion surveys (*anketler*), technological communications instruments and party co-ordinators. I also underline the role of 'controlled participation' channels in the JDP, such as regular consultations (*istişareler*), non-binding elections among selected members (*teşkilat temayül yoklamaları*) and women's branches, which together made a vital contribution to the absorption of the potential dissent against firm leadership control through the creation of a very strong sense of participation among the party base. In this chapter, relying on a discussion of party typologies, I also argue that these organizational traits of the JDP made it difficult to identify the party's organization simply as either a mass-based (mass party) or an elite-based one (such as a cadre, catch-all or cartel party). Instead, I propose to diverge from Eurocentric conceptualizations regarding party organizational typologies and define the JDP organization as a hybrid electoral machine, or more precisely 'a personalistic mass party', combining a firmly controlled massive membership organization with political marketing techniques.

In Chapter 7, I take a closer look at the elite recruitment processes of the JDP. I demonstrate the rise of the leadership domination within the party just after its foundation. I also focus on how the provincial and local governing bodies of the party were accurately designed by the central party elite and how candidate selection processes were kept under the firm control of the party leadership. Here, I also focus on the different narratives deployed by, on the one hand, high-ranking party elites and, on the other hand, junior party members, failed candidates and 'true democrats' in struggles over elite recruitment within the JDP. In this chapter, I also focus on the characteristics of the relationship between local and provincial elites and the JDP leadership, which represents one of the novel elements in JDP politics compared to its right-wing predecessors in Turkish politics.

In the final chapter before the conclusion, I place the rise of the JDP as a hegemonic party, and the rise of a competitive authoritarian regime in Turkey in general, into the historical context of elite-level power struggles in Turkey. In this chapter, I illustrate that the skilful, pragmatic and opportunistic manoeuvres of the JDP leadership at this level – in other words a series of fluid political coalitions the party established with powerful, elite groups – paved the way to the irreversible demise of the elite power contenders of Erdoğan's JDP in Turkey. Although these manoeuvres (which were components of a slow and turbulent *reforma* in Turkey that started with the rise of the JDP) increased tensions and paved the way to a bloody military intervention, the instruments and methods (populism-cum-personalistic mass party) embraced by the JDP during this process gave the upper hand to the JDP elite in the critical conjuncture that occurred after the coup. The JDP took advantage of this moment of unexpected *ruptura* by declaring a state of emergency and transforming the electoral democracy of Turkey into a *de jure* competitive authoritarianism (or to a peculiar, all-powerful presidentialism designed by the JDP to accumulate power in Erdoğan's hands).

In the conclusion, I summarize the crucial empirical findings and broader theoretical implications of the research regarding the literature on the JDP and Turkish politics in general. Erdoğan's JDP in Turkey was a case of extremely successful populism in power, winning consecutive elections by shaping the political environment by overwhelming its elite enemies and political rivals, and by dismantling the institutional structure of the previous establishment to a degree that transformed the political system in Turkey from an electoral democracy to competitive authoritarianism. In this final chapter, I take a closer look at the JDP as a case of electorally successful normalization of an Islamist party (or the rise of a post-Islamist one) that gradually and vocally became a populist force which has driven the political regime surrounding it into competitive authoritarianism. I then highlight some of the theoretical implications of the analysis of the case of the JDP in the book in general through a discussion on the relationships between Islamism, populism, organizations and the rise of competitive authoritarianism.

2 The Transformation of the Turkish Party System: Selective Pluralism and the Rise of the JDP

Introduction

The literature on the transformation of Islamism and the rise of the JDP in Turkey usually highlights the role of pressure from external actors such as the army and judiciary.[1] In this chapter, I argue that a much more complicated relationship between external actors and Islam and the Islamist elite caused the transformation of Islamism in Turkey and the rise of the JDP.[2] Without the permissive attitude of the powerful external actors and a degree of consensus between them and the Islamist elite, prospects for Islamism in Turkey would have been remarkably different. Thus, this chapter is mainly concerned with the political-institutional and historical-structural background that shaped the strategic inclinations and organizational approach of the formerly Islamist, then populist JDP leadership throughout the 1980s and 1990s. These strategic and organizational lessons of the decades preceding the 2000s were, as will be illustrated in Chapters 4–8, constitutive of the agency-based factors of the future hegemonic party system the JDP would establish over the years.

I employ two central concepts in this analysis: 'establishment elite' and 'selective pluralism'. I use the concept of 'establishment elite' to refer to the high-ranking ruling cadres of the military and judiciary as well as the president of the Republic, who always had a decisive effect on the formation of Turkey's legal political space and the 'official doctrines': a restrictive official ideology and a restrictive narrative on national identity. The establishment elite in Turkey – like its counterparts in other Muslim

---

[1] For this kind of approach to the transformation of Islamism and the rise of the JDP, see Atacan (2005: 196), Çarkoğlu (2007: 504–505), M. Çınar (2006a: 473–474), Dağı (2008: 27), Hale and Özbudun (2010: 10), Jenkins (2003: 51), Öniş (2001: 286–287), Özbudun (2006: 547) and Taşkın (2008: 58–59). All translations of excerpts from interviews and Turkish sources in the text are mine.

[2] My perspective in this chapter has remarkably benefited from the approaches of Cizre (2008b) and Turam (2012) which put an emphasis on the interaction between Islamists and the external environment.

countries where the concept might refer to royal monarchies, high-ranking religious clerics, high-ranking military officers, established ruling families, or personalized dictatorships[3] – tried to protect its power position, and frequently the wider status quo, through defining the boundaries of the legal political space and the official doctrines.

The strategy of 'selective pluralism' mainly refers to the exclusion of the particular elite groups and their organizations from political competition and representation through legal and coercive means while including others who are seen as compatible with the status quo.[4] Most of the establishment elites across the Muslim world chose the strategy of authoritarianism and monopolized the legal political space by inhibiting the existence of opposition through legal as well as coercive means. However, in Turkey, the establishment elite chose to engineer a peculiar pluralism which excluded the meaningful political representation of the left and the Kurdish opposition through high national electoral thresholds and a restrictive party and election law as well as coercion. The very same strategy was relatively permissive towards the Islamist elite and their organizations. In addition, the establishment elite also initiated the semi-official indoctrination of nationalist and religious values from the beginning of the 1980s, like its counterparts in the Muslim world; this created the wider social context for the rise of Islamism and post-Islamism in Turkey. Gradually, selective pluralism started to work against the establishment elites themselves due to the fragmentation of the party system and the decline of the legitimacy of the political system in general throughout the 1990s. Thanks to selective pluralism, the JDP enjoyed a disproportionate majority in the parliament (particularly after its first electoral victory in 2002) and relied on this majority as well as a discourse of reform and democratization in their struggle with the establishment elite.[5]

---

[3] For the diversity of the political power holding elite in the Middle Eastern context, see Owen (2002).

[4] From a historical institutionalist point of view, 'selective pluralism' can be considered a strategic decision taken by the establishment elite in Turkey at a critical juncture, namely during the 1980 coup which created a certain 'developmental pathway' for every political actor of the country. Gradually, this strategic decision, compatible with the restrictive political cultural legacy of the country, became a formal as well as an informal institutional context which defined the rules and boundaries of the political game in Turkey. For historical institutionalism, path dependency and critical junctures, see Thelen (1999).

[5] One cannot miss the similarity between the political context characterized by the tutelary position of the establishment elite and the strategy of selective pluralism described here, and regimes called 'electoral democracy' by students of authoritarian politics (Özbudun, 2011: 41). Thus, for a long time after the transition to multi-party politics, excepting intermissions caused by coups, Turkey remained an electoral democracy. I will analyse

One of the widespread convictions in the literature on Islamism and the JDP is that the Islamist elite, and later the JDP elite, had to overcome secularist[6] systemic pressure. There is no doubt that there was always a certain tension between the establishment elite and first the Islamist, and then the JDP, elite. However, focusing on this tension usually over-shadowed the ultimately consensual nature of this relationship. Hence, apart from Eligür's work (2010), few studies underlined the contributions of the strategic choices of the allegedly secularist elite of the country in the rise of Islamism and the JDP. Similar to the 'inadvertent elite ally' argument of Eligür, which underlines the contribution of the introduction of Turkish-Islamic Synthesis and repression of organized leftist networks by the military elite in the rise of Islamist movement (2010: 277), I argue that, without the strategic choices of the establishment elite of initiating a gradual Islamization of society and of constructing a selectively pluralist political space, the JDP's spectacular electoral achievements and its resilience in the face of the establishment elite would have been impossible. Although my argument is in line with Eligür's work, I put a special emphasis on the selectively pluralist political space and the electoral system of Turkey since the foremost beneficiary of the exclusion of small, organizationally weak and more ideological parties through the 10 per cent national electoral threshold, and the restrictive electoral and party laws in general, was the JDP.

In the following section, I firstly describe the introduction of selective pluralism by the establishment elite in the 1980s through legal and coercive interventions as well as the gradual Islamization process, which created unexpected opportunities for the Islamist political elite. In the third section, I briefly describe the fragmentation in the Turkish party system and the decline of the legitimacy of the regime in the 1990s, which caused the rise of Islamism and the backlash of the establishment elite near the end of the decade. Following this, in the fourth section, I demonstrate how the JDP benefited from the fragmentation of the party system and the political environment that was created by the strategy of selective pluralism in the previous period after it came to power. In the following section, I illustrate the impact of this environment on the

---

the long-lasting influence of this aspect of the political regime in Turkey (and its change) since the transition to multi-party politics more thoroughly in Chapter 8.

[6] I use the term 'secularist' to refer to a particular world-view consciously embraced by the establishment elite in Turkey which relies upon a highly exclusionary modernizing attitude towards religious symbols in public and political life and devout segments of society. 'Secular', in this context, unlike 'secularist', refers to the spontaneous predominance of non-religious attitudes and mentalities in the public and political space as is the case in the Anglo-Saxon world.

organizational and strategic formation of the JDP. In conclusion, I argue that, to a certain extent, the JDP owed its electoral success and political resilience against the assaults of the establishment elite of Turkey to the political environment created by the strategy of selective pluralism.

The 1980s: Restoration through Selective Pluralism

The Coup and Selective Pluralism

The politics of Turkey after the military coup on 27 May 1960 was characterized by a rapid pluralization of the political space on the basis of a liberal constitutional framework (Çavdar, 2008: 110). This liberal legal framework, alongside the accelerating urbanization and industrialization of the country throughout the 1960s, gave rise to leftist movements as well as Islamist parties and ultra-nationalist political actors. In other words, the pluralization of the political space unintentionally created fertile ground for the radical political forces. During the 1970s, the country also witnessed the leftwards turn of the Republican People's Party[7] as a response to these political and socio-demographic changes. The overall result of these changes was the rising salience of the left–right cleavage in the country (Özbudun, 2013: 43). This pluralization and simultaneous radicalization of the political scene throughout the 1960s and 1970s resulted in unstable and weak coalition governments and rising street violence among militant leftist and rightist groups, particularly during the last seven years of the 1970s (Zürcher, 2004: 261–264). A crisis of the import substitution economy completed this bleak political picture towards the end of the decade (Boratav, 2005: 139–145).

On 12 September 1980, the military elite decided to intervene on the grounds of the rising economic problems and the lack of public security (Ahmad, 2003a: 181). In the eyes of the military elite, the conditions triggering the intervention were mainly the excessive plurality of the political system and its radicalization. In the military junta's view, the political instability was mainly due to the weak coalition governments that were in power throughout the 1970s. The rising violence between ultra-nationalist forces and the leftist movements in particular was seen as a major destabilizing factor by the military elite. Thus, the military

---

[7] For brief information on the Republican People's Party and other parties mentioned throughout this chapter and their positions in the Turkish political system, see Appendices 1 and 2.

coup grimly crushed these movements (Ahmad, 2003a: 184–185; Zürcher, 2004: 279–280).

The military elite's strategy ruthlessly crushed some movements and drove some of them towards a decisive and prolonged armed struggle with the armed forces. As Belge underlined, the coup created a 'political exodus' for leftists due to torture and brutal interrogations in prisons and caused thousands of them to flee to European countries (2008: 43). Most notably, facing the heavy repression of the military regime was the main body of the Kurdish left, namely the PKK (Partiya Karkeren Kurdistan, Kurdistan Workers' Party). Unlike the Turkish left, thanks to their underground organizations and timely flight to Syria just before the military coup, the PKK could protect its organizational strength and, to a great extent, avoid the heavy repression (Romano, 2006: 49–50).[8] The PKK later followed a much more nationalistic direction (Bozarslan, 2008: 860–868). Apart from state repression towards the left, the armed struggle between Kurdish separatists and the state drove the more centrist left-wing actors of the country, namely the Republican People's Party and the Democratic Left Party (Demokratik Sol Parti), towards a more nationalistic direction, particularly throughout the 1990s. Hence, unlike the previous period, the political space of the post-coup period in Turkey was deeply shaped by the absence or the weakness of the organizational networks of genuinely leftist movements.

At this point, it should be noted that the mainstream Islamist movement among the radical political forces – in other words the Islamist National View Movement – avoided street violence throughout the 1970s (Eligür, 2010: 24). These strategic choices of the Islamist actors and the military elite, to a great extent, protected the Islamist movement and its organizational networks from heavy repression after the military coup in 1980. The organization of the National View tradition was characterized by a tight leadership grip over the grass roots, and this, to a large extent, prevented the movement from using violence.[9]

In electoral politics, the military junta was also aiming for the elimination both of potential tendencies towards radicalization and of the possibility of coalition governments through sustaining a two- or a two-and-a-half-party system (Özbudun, 2013: 73). The main devices introduced for this purpose, and hence the main components of the

---

[8] For further information on the PKK, see also Marcus (2007).

[9] A similar point was also underlined by a high-ranking Felicity Party member in a personal interview. In a response to a question regarding the reaction of the National View supporters after the soft military intervention on 28 February 1997, he underlined the role of the tight leadership control over the organization in avoiding violent political reactions (Interviewee 1, 2013).

establishment elite's strategy of selective pluralism, were the Law on Political Parties and the Law on Election of Deputies (Milletvekili Seçimi Kanunu), which were both accepted in 1983. The main measure introduced to inhibit the excessive fragmentation of the party system, and hence radicalization, was the 10 per cent national electoral threshold. Another measure introduced against the pluralization of the system was the inhibition of participation for parties without a certain number of branches across the country in elections. Hence, the Law on Election of Deputies and the Law on Political Parties effectively inhibited the representation of small, organizationally weak and somewhat more ideological parties in the parliament.

The Gradual Islamization of Society

In the eyes of the military elite, the remedy for the rising polarization between left and right and for the violent outcomes of this polarization was a more religious and conservative society. In order to construct such a society, the military elite embraced the Turkish-Islamic Synthesis, which was proposed by the conservative nationalist intellectual circle known as the 'Hearts of the Enlightened' (Aydınlar Ocağı), as the semi-official doctrine of the recently restored regime (M. Şen, 2010: 65–66).

A heavily religious curriculum became a part of the education policies of the new regime (S. Kaplan, 2006: 73–124; Copeaux, 2006). The military elite also opened state institutions and civil society associations to the influence of the religious brotherhoods and groups (Cizre, 1998: 107–108). The main outcome of the implementation of this new semi-official doctrine of the Turkish-Islamic Synthesis, alongside the harsh repression of the left, was a narrower political space and the predominance of more conservative and nationalist views on politics in society (Çarkoğlu and Kalaycıoğlu, 2009: 10).

The Reintroduction of Party Politics and the Rise of the Motherland Party

After three years of junta rule, the military elite decided to reintroduce party politics. In the first general elections in 1983 after the coup there were only three parties: the Nationalist Democracy Party (Milliyetçi Demokrasi Partisi), the Populist Party (Halkçı Parti) and the Motherland Party. The military elite was in favour of rule by the Nationalist Democracy Party, and the party was explicitly supported by Kenan Evren, the leader of the junta. The Populist Party was expected to be the loyal,

Table 2.1 *Results and significant actors in eight general elections between 1983 and 2011*

	Elections	1983	1987	1991	1995	1999	2002	2007	2011
Nationalist Democracy Party	Vote share	23.3							
	Seats	71							
Populist Party	Vote share	30.5							
	Seats	117							
Motherland Party	Vote share	45.1	36.3	24.0	19.6	13.2	5.1		
	Seats	211	292	115	132	86	-		
True Path Party	Vote share		19.1	27.0	19.2	12.0	9.5		
	Seats		59	178	135	85	-		
Welfare, Virtue, Felicity *	Vote share		7.2	16.9	21.4	15.4	2.5		
	Seats		-	62	158	111	-		
Democratic Left Party	Vote share		8.5	10.8	14.6	22.2	1.2		
	Seats		-	7	76	136	-		
Republican People's Party *	Vote share		24.8	20.8	10.7	8.7	19.4	20.8	20.8
	Seats		99	88	49	-	178	112	135
Nationalist Action Party	Vote share				8.2	18.0	8.4	14,3	13.0
	Seats				-	129	-	71	53
Young Party	Vote share						7.2	3,0	
	Seats						-	-	
JDP	Vote share						34.3	46,6	49.8
	Seats						363	341	327

Source: Election results from the Turkish Statistical Institute (2012).
* Due to the political bans the Republican People's Party was represented in the parliament as the Social Democratic Populist Party (Sosyal Demokrat Halkçı Parti) until 1995. The Islamist Welfare Party also reappeared under different names due to party closures during the 1990s and the beginning of the 2000s.

slightly left-wing opposition (Zürcher, 2004: 282). The Motherland Party was not expected to take part in the parliament at all. The result of the first election after the coup was perhaps the least desired outcome by the junta since the Motherland Party, which was seen more democratic and independent alternative compared to other two, won a landslide victory, receiving the 45 per cent of the vote (2004: 282).

In the following general elections, the Motherland Party was still predominant despite the significant decrease in its total number of votes. However, thanks to new electoral regulations prior to the 1987 general election, the Motherland Party gained more seats in the parliament than in the previous election, receiving 36 per cent of the votes, and maintained a single-party majority government from 1983 to 1991. Thus, throughout the 1980s, the military junta's idea of a stable two- or a two-and-a-half-party system seemed to be realized, albeit under the dominance of an unexpected political actor (see Table 2.1). Table 2.1 illustrates the fragmentation of the party system in Turkey starting with the 1991 general election. In 1987, the ban on the parties and leaders of the pre-coup period was lifted through a referendum (Kalaycıoğlu, 2002: 49). In the 1991 general election, the monopoly of the Motherland Party over the centre-right votes was broken by the re-emergence of Süleyman Demirel and his True Path Party (Doğru Yol Partisi) on the Turkish political scene. The centre-left also gave signals of fragmentation with the re-emergence of Bülent Ecevit and his new Democratic Left Party.

Although the establishment elite's strategy ran smoothly at the beginning, the military regime's top-down project of creating a slightly more religious and nationalist society in order to save the country from the 'perils of the left' gradually created some unexpected consequences from the point of view of the secularist segments of Turkish society by paving the way to the rise of Islamism at the beginning of the 1990s. As illustrated in the next section, rising conservatism, the Turkish-Islamic Synthesis and the repression of the leftist and ultra-nationalist forces created unexpected opportunities for the Islamist elite in Turkey.

The 1990s: Fragmentation in the Party System and the Legitimacy Crises

The Decline of the Motherland Party and Fragmentation in the Party System

The importance of favourable political and electoral circumstances – such as high levels of electoral volatility and fragmentation throughout the 1990s – in the rise and electoral success of the JDP has been already underlined (Tezcür, 2012: 119–122). Indeed, Turkish politics was characterized by the fragmentation of the centre-right and centre-left in the 1990s. Governments formed by these parties throughout the 1990s were not successful in terms of government stability, either. The strongest party of the post-coup period, the Motherland Party, started to lose momentum at the end of the 1980s after the election of its influential leader, Turgut Özal, as president of the Republic (Kalaycıoğlu, 2002: 58). This period also overlapped with the return of the experienced centre-right politician Demirel to the political game. As a result, during the 1990s the centre-right in Turkey was represented by two political parties: the Motherland Party and the True Path Party.

It is striking that between 1991 and 2002 Turkey had nine different governments (see Table 2.2 for government types between 1983 and 2013). From 1991 to 2002, Turkey was ruled by various weak minority and coalition governments. Political instability was a major visible and persisting feature of Turkish politics alongside other social and economic problems such as the armed struggle with the PKK, inflation, financial crises, corruption and natural disasters in the background. It would not be an exaggeration to argue that voters, to a great extent, saw the minority and coalition governments, and the fragmentation of the party system, as being responsible for the economic and social problems that they suffered.

In 1987, there were only three parties in the parliament, and the Motherland Party had a clear majority with 299 deputies. During the 1990s, the number of parties increased and the number of the deputies of different parties became almost equal. In this sense, the composition of the parliament (which can be seen in Table 2.1) after the general elections in 1999 is very striking. This almost even distribution of seats among five parties in the parliament created many opportunities for different configurations of coalition governments but, at the same time, the very same abundance of coalition possibilities in the parliament brought great instability.

The Legitimacy Crises of the Establishment and the Rise of the Islamist Elite

The fragmentation of centre-right politics and the instability of the minority and coalition governments in Turkey exacerbated the demise of the legitimacy of the political system in general. During the 1990s, some scandalous incidents of political corruption, including the notorious Susurluk incident and many other less sensational incidents, were

Table 2.2 *Government types since 1983*

No	Years	Party or Parties	Government type	Prime Ministers
45	1983–1987	Motherland Party	Single majority	Özal
46	1987–1989	Motherland Party	Single majority	Özal
47	1989–1991	Motherland Party	Single majority	Y. Akbulut
48	1991	Motherland Party	Single majority	Yılmaz
49	1991–1993	True Path Party and Social Democratic Populist Party	Majority coalition	Demirel and E. İnönü
50	1993–1995	True Path Party and Social Democratic Populist Party	Majority coalition	Çiller
51	1995	True Path Party	Single minority	Çiller
52	1995–1996	True Path Party and Republican People's Party	Majority coalition	Çiller
53	1996	Motherland Party and True Path Party	Majority coalition	Yılmaz
54	1996–1997	Welfare Party and True Path Party	Majority coalition	Erbakan
55	1997–1999	Motherland Party, Democratic Left Party and Democratic Turkey Party	Minority coalition	Yılmaz
56	1999	Democratic Left Party	Single minority	B. Ecevit
57	1999–2002	Democratic Left Party, Nationalist Action Party and Motherland Party	Majority coalition	Ecevit
58	2002–2003	JDP	Single majority	A. Gül
59	2003–2007	JDP	Single majority	Erdoğan
60	2007–2011	JDP	Single majority	Erdoğan
61	2011–2015	JDP	Single majority	Erdoğan

Source: Author's compilation.

publicized (Şener, 2001).[10] According to research published in 1997, although Turkish people had a commitment to democracy, there was a widespread distrust in the political institutions of the country such as governments, the parliament and the bureaucracy towards the end of the decade (Akgün, 2000: 18).

The 1990s were also characterized by the crimes committed by the forces of the Turkish 'deep state' against civilian Kurdish dissidents. The war waged against the PKK frequently crossed the borders of legitimate

---

[10] The investigation of the 'Susurluk' accident did not go too far and, therefore, the bonds between the state and organized crime, to a great extent, remained intact and unexplained (Baran, 2000: 137–139).

action with the involvement of criminal underground organizations in the process (Hamdan, 2009: 234). Paramilitary techniques deployed in coping with the PKK caused massive human rights violations during the 1990s and had a corrosive effect on the image of the Turkish state as a 'state of justice'.

In contrast with this picture, the clean image of the Islamist Welfare Party was consolidated by the performance of Islamist municipalities in two major cities of Turkey in the mid 1990s: İstanbul and Ankara. The relatively transparent and efficient management of these two cities under the rule of Welfare Party mayors increased the image of managerial competence of the Islamist elite in the eyes of the electorate (Öniş, 2001: 286). The electorate started to see the Islamist National View parties as a decent political alternative against the corrupt centrist politics of the country. In the absence of robust leftist organizational networks that could channel the grievances of the poor urban masses stemming from the declining legitimacy of the system and rising economic problems, Islamist politics started to be seen as the only reliable political choice for the disillusioned and unprivileged urban voters.

The outcome of these circumstances was a remarkable victory for the Islamist Welfare Party in the 1995 general election with 21 per cent of the votes. Afterwards, the formation of a coalition government of the centre-right True Path Party and the Welfare Party under the leadership of Erbakan from the Welfare Party in 1996 (Ahmad, 2003b: 168–169) triggered the resistance of the establishment elite, which was already alarmed by the rise of the Islamism in the middle of the 1990s.

The Establishment Elite Strikes Back: The Soft Intervention of 28 February 1997 and the Rise of Post-Islamism

The coalition government quickly became the target of high military circles after a number of controversial activities such as Prime Minister Necmettin Erbakan's visit to Libya and the political scandal caused by Muammar Gaddafi's public comments on Turkey (Ahmad, 2003b: 170). Some very controversial speeches by Welfare Party members addressing the issues around sharia rule and the secularism of the country were publicized on numerous occasions through mainstream media during the tenure of the Welfare–Path (Refah–Yol) coalition government.[11] A very debatable plan for the regulation of working hours according to the local

---

[11] Later these controversial speeches were used as proof of the anti-secular and anti-constitutional activities of the party in the investigation initiated by Vural Savaş, the chief prosecutor of the High Court of Appeals of the era, in order to ban the party. These

fast-breaking (*iftar*)[12] times by the government was also followed by the fast-breaking invitation made by Erbakan in the prime minister's residence (Sabah, 1997). This invitation was harshly criticized in the mainstream media due to the attendance of sheikhs and leaders of religious brotherhoods and communities in their religious attire (Ergin, 1997). The last highly controversial event was the 'Jerusalem Evening' (Kudüs Gecesi), where a theatre play on the Palestinian resistance against Israel was staged under the sponsorship of the Welfare Party municipality of Sincan, a sub-province of Ankara, in January 1997. This event was followed by 'practice manoeuvres' by military tanks on the streets of Sincan at the beginning of February 1997 (Ahmad, 2003b: 171–172).

One of the prominent researchers of the Islamist movement in Turkey, Hakan Yavuz, evaluated all these minor incidents as signs of frustration since the Welfare Party elite was not able to implement the redistributive economic programme called 'Just Order' (Adil Düzen) under the constraints of the coalition government and International Monetary Fund agreements (Yavuz, 2009: 64). One, however, should also note that this political picture was preceded by a wider process in which assassinations of some of the country's prominent secularist intellectuals had already started to represent a concrete threat. The most dreadful incident was when a mob set fire to a hotel full of secularist-leftist intellectuals and artists in 1993. The latter had come to the inner Anatolian province of Sivas for the celebration of an Alawite religious festival. The attack resulted in the death of thirty-six people.

The enmity of the military elite against the ruling Islamist Welfare Party ended with the declaration of a series of 'anti-reactionary [*irtica karşıtı*]' measures imposed on the coalition government in a notorious National Security Council (Milli Güvenlik Kurulu) meeting on 28 February 1997. These measures included taking control of non-registered Quran courses by the Ministry of National Education; the implementation of eight years of continuous education, which would undermine the educational strongholds of Islamist politics in Turkey, namely the Imam and Preacher Schools; and a ban on religious brotherhoods (Zürcher, 2004: 300). These measures were unacceptable for the Welfare Party elite in terms of the party's strictly Islamist ideology and the expectations of its core constituency. After a few days of hesitation, the prime minister and leader of the Welfare Party, Erbakan, had to sign

---

excerpts from the speeches of prominent party figures can be found in the indictment for the case (*Hürriyet*, 2008).

[12] According to the Islamic calendar, the month of Ramadan is considered holy, and observant Muslims do not eat or drink from sunrise to sunset throughout the month.

the document known as the 'February 28th Decisions', which was prepared by the military elite.

Later, the Welfare Party was banned by the Constitutional Court (Anayasa Mahkemesi) on the grounds of anti-secular activities (*T. C. Resmi Gazete*, 1998). The leaders of the party, most notably Erbakan, had their political rights suspended for five years (Zürcher, 2004: 301). After the closure of the party, prominent figures of the Welfare Party took the case to the European Court of Human Rights (ECtHR). The court's decision (ECtHR, 2003) confirmed the anti-secular and anti-constitutional activities of the Welfare Party and, to a large extent, was in accordance with the decision of the Turkish Constitutional Court. This was a decisive point in the history of the Islamist National View tradition (Yavuz, 2009: 69). After the decision of the ECtHR, the Islamist political elite must have recognized the importance of the support of domestic and foreign democratic circles in the survival of Islamist political movement.

The military elite's soft intervention, or its non-violent methods of dealing with the Islamist forces, should also be underlined. Despite the tensions between these two political forces in Turkey throughout the 1990s, the interaction between them had been sustained, particularly within a non-violent framework. In a sense, there was a kind of 'virtual consensus'[13] between the establishment elite and the mainstream Islamist elite. According to Cizre, there was a strong connection between the transformation of Islamism in Turkey and the fact that the members of the Islamist movement were not jailed and their sympathizers were not tortured or massacred by the establishment (1998: 116). This 'virtual consensus' between the Islamist elite and the secularist establishment elite should also be evaluated as a dimension of the strategy of selective pluralism elaborated above.

After the military intervention in 1997 and the collapse of the Welfare–Path coalition government, Islamist politics entered a period of decline and reformation. In fact, the Islamist National View movement had already started to gain a new direction with the rise of internal opposition to the decades-old dominance of the party leader Erbakan. Experiences in consequent elections and in office, particularly in local governments, had a crucial influence on the younger generation of the Islamist

---

[13] When defining this relationship as a 'virtual consensus', I have in mind a scholarly literature that focuses more on the 'politics of expediency' based on concessions, negotiations and arbitrations, rather than on coercion and indoctrination in power relationships. For theoretical works, see de Certeau (2002) and Scott (1990). For works emphasizing this dimension of Turkish politics, see Erdoğan (2000), Aymes et al. (2015) and Baykan (2015b).

National View tradition. This experience had a decisive impact on the would-be leader of the JDP, Erdoğan. According to Dağı, Erdoğan had become much more pragmatic and less ideological and had embraced a 'service'-oriented outlook during his years as the mayor of İstanbul from 1994 to 1998 (2008: 28). Indeed, some of the Islamist politicians, and particularly Erdoğan, noticed the opportunities that lay beyond a narrow Islamist appeal due to their municipal experience.

In the literature, as underlined in the introduction to this chapter, repression by the secularist elite has been frequently addressed as the main factor behind the moderation of the Islamist movement in Turkey. But it seems that the pressure from the secularist forces was only a catalyst for the internal transformation of the movement triggered by the opportunities of a permissive democratic system, or a selectively pluralist environment, which accommodated Islamist parties of the National View tradition within the system and which did not choose to criminalize them as it did the leftist and Kurdish nationalist forces.

As one member of the Islamist Welfare Party, who later became a JDP deputy, underlined in an interview, 'intensive state interventions or the closures by the oppressive coups provided merely an opportunity for the party to interrogate itself' (Interviewee 29, 2014). Another interviewee explained the transformation of the Islamist Welfare Party along similar lines: 'we went beyond this more Islamic discourse of the National View because we wanted to be a more inclusive party. You cannot make it with an Islamic discourse. This is why we remained at 18, 20, 22 per cent. [When the party was using an Islamic discourse] we got 24, 25 per cent in our best performance' (Interviewee 26, 2014). Another experienced former member of the Islamist National View parties and the JDP underlined the same inclination of the Islamist elite prior to the intervention of the establishment elite:

The National Salvation Party [Milli Selamet Partisi – the Islamist National View party of the 1970s] received 11 per cent in the general election in 1973 and 7 per cent in 1977. Hence, the number of deputies was reduced from forty-eight to twenty-four. So there was an electoral failure. If there had been no September 12th [the military coup in 1980], the party would have received many fewer votes. Because you can't reform yourself, and people start to move away. The Welfare Party received 22 per cent of the vote in the 1995 general elections but the Virtue Party [Fazilet Partis] received 15 per cent in the general elections in 1999. These were electoral failures. Why did the votes of the Virtue Party decrease? People started to discuss these things [...] The February 28th intervention was unfair but why was this unfair treatment of the party not corrected by the electorate? These discussions within the party gave rise to the change (Interviewee 21, 2014).

As argued above, the soft intervention of the military elite was only a catalyst for this transformation. As one of the experienced National View members of the era pointed out in an interview, the main dynamic behind the transformation of the Islamist elite and the rise of the post-Islamist JDP was the desire to be more successful in elections: '[In 1999,] for the first time in Turkey, local and general elections were held together [...] an 8–10 per cent gap, almost the vote of a single party, appeared between the votes received by the Virtue Party municipalities and the Virtue Party itself. The local level was much more successful and this was an indication of the fact that the headquarters could not bear the young cadres anymore and there would be an interrogation of this situation [within the party]' (Interviewee 29, 2014).

Thus, it would be fair to argue that the divide within the Islamist National View tradition and the rise of the so-called reformist wing within the party were results of internal interrogations of the party's electoral failures rather than a response to external pressures.[14] On the grounds of the developments and dynamics discussed so far, at the 2000 convention of the Virtue Party – which became the home to many members of the Islamist Welfare Party after the latter was banned by the Constitutional Court – Abdullah Gül challenged the authority of the old guard of the Islamist National View tradition. He lost the competition for the party leadership by a very slim margin. Nevertheless, in 2001, the JDP was founded by this same, younger, reformist generation of the National View movement led by Erdoğan and Gül, and which was influenced, to a lesser extent, by figures such as Bülent Arınç and Abdüllatif Şener, with the support of some centre-right and even left-wing politicians.[15]

When we focus on the wider political scene of the decade we see that the years following the 28 February 1997 intervention and the decline of the coalition government, including Islamists, did not change much in terms of the fragmentation and volatility of the Turkish party system and the instability of the governments. The first general elections in 1999 after the military intervention brought five parties into the parliament with roughly the same numbers of seats. The first party of the elections, the Democratic Left Party, and its old and experienced leader led the coalition government formed from his party, the Nationalist Action Party (Milliyetçi Hareket Partisi) and the Motherland Party, against the Islamist Virtue Party (Ahmad, 2003b: 173).

[14] For a very rich empirical source revealing the pragmatism and electoral concerns of the reformist wing of the Islamist National View, see Selim (2002).
[15] For a detailed description of this process, see Mecham (2004).

The already declining legitimacy of the system was made worse in 1999 by the biggest earthquake since the 1940s. The coalition government's inability to deal with this catastrophe, particularly in the immediate aftermath (Jalali, 2002: 124–126), was never erased from the public memory. The 2000 and 2001 financial crises followed this tragic event (Uygur, 2001). As Öniş made clear, there was a dramatic decline in GNP and per capita income, and the crises affected highly skilled and educated people, small and medium-sized businesspeople, and the very poor (2003: 14–15). Despite the technocratic steps taken with the appointment of Kemal Derviş, a former World Bank executive, as the minister of economic affairs (Öniş, 2003: 18), the image of the managerial incompetence of the coalition governments barely improved and was made even worse by the illness of Prime Minister Bülent Ecevit.

2002 Onwards: The Rise of the Post-Islamist Elite

The JDP Benefits from Fragmentation and Selective Pluralism

Under the above-mentioned political and electoral circumstances, the JDP achieved a spectacular electoral victory in the November 2002 general elections. The JDP won 34 per cent of the vote and gained 363 seats in the parliament, a clear majority. The Republican People's Party received 19 per cent of the vote, gained 178 seats and became the only force in the parliament other than the JDP. Although the True Path Party and the Nationalist Action Party won 9 per cent and 8 per cent of the vote respectively, they could not gain any seats in the parliament due to the 10 per cent threshold. The other coalition parties of the pre-election period, namely the Motherland Party and the Democratic Left Party, did much worse in the 2002 election. While the Motherland Party won 5 per cent of the vote, the Democratic Left Party could only manage 1 per cent (see Table 2.1). Apparently, the coalition partners were heavily penalized by the voters. The following years and elections brought a total dissolution of the centre-right parties of the period before 2002.

However, the relatively poor performance of the Republican People's Party remained unexplained. The Republican People's Party's absence from the parliament in the period between 1999 and 2002 to a great extent protected its image from the negative impacts of the deterioration of the political and economic circumstances after 1990 – a very similar situation to the clean image of the JDP. Electoral fragmentation, government instability, managerial incompetence on the part of the coalition governments, the economic crises of 2000 and 2001, and the decline of the legitimacy of the regime in general during the 1990s might have also worked in the Republican People's Party's favour. However, this was not the case, and the party could not reach beyond the traditional electoral limits of the centre-left in Turkey in the post-1980 period. As I will discuss in the following chapters on the political appeal, organization and leadership of the JDP, the relative failure of the Republican People's Party in this particular election illustrated the importance of effective political agency: the role of a robust organization as well as suitable political appeals. Hence, convenient political circumstances were not a sufficient condition for electoral success in its own right. In other words, agency matters.

After its electoral victory, the JDP formed a single-party majority government. The first years of the JDP corresponded to the recovery of the Turkish economy thanks to the upwards trend in global economic cycles (Boratav, 2009: 463) and to regulations introduced by Derviş in the period before the 2002 election. Within a couple of years, the consumer price index had dropped dramatically and the GDP per capita had begun to increase (Öniş, 2012: 140). This promising picture was also complemented by the determination of the early JDP government in the European Union accession process. The consecutive liberal and democratic reforms created optimism towards and trust in the democratic credentials of the party in the country and abroad (Hale and Özbudun, 2010: 55–67).

Resistance of the Establishment Elite

Despite the ideological change of Islamist politics and the initial liberal image of the JDP, the party had to deal with the resistance of the establishment elite. The clear majority the party gained in the 2002 general elections, which was an outcome of the strategy of selective pluralism (particularly the 10 per cent threshold) elaborated above, made a remarkable contribution to the resilience of the JDP before the attacks of the establishment elite. In the absence of other centre-right and right-wing parties in the parliament, the JDP found an opportunity to stand as the only representative of the right-leaning majority of the country *vis-à-vis* the establishment elite. As a result, the establishment elite lost its social support, which stemmed partly from its right-wing political allies such as the former centre-right parties.

The relationship between the establishment elite and the Republican People's Party was not that crucial in providing social legitimacy to the interventions of the former since the Republican People's Party was usually seen by the majority of the population as the political representative of the establishment elite. As Sayarı highlighted, 'in the absence of an effective political opposition in the parliament, the Constitutional Court and the Presidency have emerged as the two principal institutional sources of counter-majoritarianism in Turkish politics' (2007: 203). In the following parts of this section, I will give a brief descriptive account of this tension between the JDP elite and its elite opponents through some critical interventions of the establishment elite.

The Presidency of the Republic The presidency of the Republic, despite its lack of effective executive authority, always held significant veto power in Turkey. According to article 104 of the Constitution of 1982 prepared on the order of the military junta, the president of the Republic had the authority to return laws prepared and decisions made by the parliament and call for elections (TBMM, no date: 50–52). Hence, the ideological leanings of presidents made a great difference to the country's politics. One should also underline the fact that this position had been traditionally occupied by persons who were more or less in consensus with the establishment elite of Turkey until the selection of Gül by the parliament in 2007.

In its initial years, the JDP had to work with committed secularist and jurist Ahmet Necdet Sezer until 2007. After the JDP came to power, the relationship between Sezer and the JDP immediately started to grow more tense. Sezer frequently resisted the changes and regulations that favoured the JDP (Demirdöğen, 2007a, 2007b, 2007c). He also showed a ruthless and rough symbolic resistance to the JDP elite stemming from his firm secularist world-view. For instance, he did not accept or invite headscarf-wearing spouses of JDP deputies to presidential receptions (Demirdöğen, 2007b, 2007c). He was one of the most active presidents in the history of the Republic in terms of the laws that he vetoed and returned to the parliament (Demirdöğen, 2007d).

High Judiciary, Constitutional Court and the Military Towards the end of Sezer's term in office in 2007, the election process of the new president triggered a political crisis between the secularist establishment elite and the JDP. With a clear majority in the parliament, the JDP wanted to elect its own candidate to the presidency. Secularist circles, given the above-mentioned veto power of the president, advocated the idea of reaching a meaningful political and social consensus on the next presidential candidate. In other words, they were not willing to accept a candidate from the ranks of the JDP. At this point, secularist high judicial circles were involved in the discussion, and the election process was annulled by a decision of the Constitutional Court (Eroğul, 2007: 171). This crisis led the JDP elite to call for a snap general election.

The military were also involved in the discussions. On the evening of 27 April 2007, a declaration was published on the website of the Turkish armed forces. The declaration indicated that the military was determined to reassert its role in Turkish politics. The discussion about secularism, triggered by the crisis regarding the election of the new president, gave the Turkish armed forces the pretext that they were looking for.[16] This declaration was later called 'e-memorandum [e-muhtıra]'. Unlike the previous obedient attitude of the elected political cadres of the country towards military interventions, the JDP elite strongly criticized the declaration. Immediately after the e-memorandum, the government spokesman, Cemil Çiçek, underlined the fact that the chief of staff was bound to the prime minister but not the other way around (Yetkin, 2007).

In the 2007 election, the JDP increased its share of the vote dramatically mainly due to the notion that the JDP had been treated unfairly by the establishment elite. The party won 46 per cent of the popular vote and gained 341 seats in the parliament. This was slightly fewer than the number of seats the party gained in the previous election as a result of the reappearance of a third party in the parliament, the Nationalist Action Party, which passed the 10 per cent threshold in the 2007 election. Afterwards, the party was able to elect Gül as president without any legal discussion thanks to the presence of the Nationalist Action Party.

The most significant political event that followed the JDP's 2007 electoral victory and presidential election was the case opened by the Constitutional Court for banning the JDP. On 14 March 2008, the chief prosecutor of the High Court of Appeals of the era, Abdurrahman Yalçınkaya, initiated a case against the party in the Constitutional Court on the grounds that the JDP had become the 'focal point of anti-secular activities' (Bianet, 2008). The prosecutor demanded the closure of the party and a ban on seventy-one people from politics for five years, including Erdoğan and Gül. In the end, the Constitutional Court found the party guilty but decided not to close it, instead cutting its financial support from state sources (Milliyet, 2008). During this process, both conservative and liberal circles in Turkey criticized the case as a gross mistake and a massive violation of democratic politics.

As the course of events illustrated, the JDP elite were much more resilient than their Islamist predecessors. The disproportionate parliamentary majority enjoyed by the JDP since its early years was the main basis of this resilience. Hence, the 'selective pluralism' introduced in Turkey after the 1980 coup worked in the JDP's favour. As a

---

[16] For a longer version of the e-memorandum and the screenshot of the Turkish version, see http://en.wikipedia.org/wiki/E-memorandum (accessed: 27 May 2016).

consequence, the JDP could secure 66 per cent of the seats in the Grand National Assembly of Turkey after receiving 34 per cent of the vote in 2002. Hence, almost 50 per cent of the votes cast in the 2002 election could not be represented in the parliament. Relying on its parliamentary majority and a new language of reform and democratization, after 2002, the post-Islamist JDP elite gained the upper hand against the establishment elite in Turkey. After all, as noted by Toprak, 'the military finds it difficult to show open resistance to civilian decisions when these are taken through legitimate democratic procedures and rest on consensual politics' (2005: 179). As long as selective pluralism worked in favour of the JDP, despite the discourse of change, reform and democratization, the party elite did little to promote further pluralization of the political system. They neither reduced the national electoral threshold nor changed the Law on Political Parties. In short, the strategy of selective pluralism remained intact and started to work to the benefit of the post-Islamist elite.

Political Conflict under the Conditions of Selective Pluralism and the Political Agency of Erdoğan's JDP

The discussion in this chapter in general, and the demonstration of the confrontations between the establishment elite and the Islamist political entrepreneurs in the previous section in particular, has pointed out a couple of important features regarding the political context in which the JDP – or initially the post-Islamist party – emerged and came to prominence. One of the main features of this political context is the weakness of the liberal democratic architecture. In other words, in Turkey, at least since 1980, there have been decisive restrictions upon certain political actors in the legal political space, and powerful, highly politicized, non-party systemic actors including the military, high judiciary and bureaucracy were always central to the political game. Although for a certain period these circumstances worked in the Islamist elite's favour, particularly from the middle of the 1990s onwards, political actors behind these restrictions decisively turned against the rise of the (post-)Islamist elite. Under these restrictive conditions, and in their encounters with powerful, non-party elites, organizational capacity was seen as key to political survival by the (post-)Islamist elite.

The Islamist and anti-systemic ideology of the predecessors of the JDP also consolidated this need to rely on a robust organizational network (Interviewee 40, 2014). Although the relationship between the establishment elite and the JDP did not include violent confrontations, it was not an entirely peaceful one, either. Given the methods used by the establishment elite, ranging from military memorandums to legal intimidation, and given the extent of the change desired by the Islamists, and later by the JDP elite – such as more freedom for religious expression in public life – the political conflict in Turkey was remarkably deep. These characteristics and the degree of political conflict described in this chapter deeply shaped JDP politics in terms of its political appeal and organization.

The impact, as I will discuss in the rest of this book, was twofold. While the resistance of highly visible, powerful and politicized non-party elites led the JDP to easily embrace a 'low-populist' appeal, the party also carefully protected its hierarchical, centralized and robust organizational legacy that stemmed from the party's Islamist past in order to counterbalance institutional leverages available to the establishment elite. In this context, 'political organizations' should be considered 'a means of collective empowerment', 'a countervailing power to the concentrated economic or institutional resources of elite groups' (Roberts, 2006: 136). It is plausible that the nature of conflict with the establishment elite, and the insecurities that these conflicts inscribed in the perception of the JDP elite, led them to perceive party organizations as something beyond an electoral apparatus in a peaceful democratic game – as it is in liberal Western democracies – and a potential resource that they could deploy against systemic pressure. As briefly discussed in Chapter 6, the failed coup attempt in July 2016 confirmed the fact that this expectation of the JDP elite was highly realistic. Hence, the JDP elite constructed a robust organizational leverage on the one hand, and a very strong leadership relying on a decisively pro-JDP media and a 'low-populist appeal' on the other. This paved the way to deepen the already hostile divides among political actors of Turkey in the following years and decisively shaped JDP politics – its political appeal and organization – as delineated in the following chapters.

Conclusion

In this chapter, in contrast to the widespread emphases on the struggle between secularist actors and the Islamist and post-Islamist elite, I have argued that the permissive attitude of the establishment elite paved the way for the rise of Islamism and post-Islamism in Turkey. As illustrated in the second section of the chapter, the military junta's strategy of selective pluralism against the fragmentation and radicalization of the political space destroyed leftist organizational networks, deepened the Kurdish opposition's armed struggle and drove the centre-left forces of the country in a nationalist direction from the 1980s. As a part of its strategy of selective pluralism, the establishment elite introduced highly restrictive regulations on political parties and elections and a very high national electoral threshold, which inhibited the representation of small parties in the parliament. The military elite not only used restrictive coercive and legal measures to inhibit the emergence of a genuinely plural political space, but they also initiated a societal process of gradual Islamization like its counterparts across the Muslim world.

Nevertheless, the military elite's desire to inhibit the fragmentation of the party system and the radicalization of politics was not fully realized. After the reappearance of the traditional leaders of the centre-right and centre-left on the political stage of the country, the Motherland Party lost momentum and this caused the fragmentation of the centre-right and centre-left from the beginning of the 1990s. Representation of five parties with more or less equal numbers of seats in the parliament throughout the 1990s caused political instability due to weak coalition and minority governments. Social and economic problems accompanied these political developments and accelerated the decline of the legitimacy of the political system in general. In the middle of the 1990s, this background gave rise to Islamism in Turkey, and towards the end of the decade it triggered the intervention of the establishment elite against the rise of Islamism. After the 'soft intervention' of 28 February 1997, and mainly relying on their experience in elections and in office, some of the Islamist elite developed reformist ideas, and an elite spinoff from the main body of the Islamist National View tradition founded the JDP.

In the election held on 3 November 2002, the JDP achieved a spectacular victory over the protest vote of the electorate against the existing political actors of Turkey that had held power throughout the 1990s. Thanks to selective pluralism – in other words, a restrictive party and election law, an unusually high national electoral threshold, and the gradual Islamization of the society – the JDP acquired a disproportional majority in the parliament, particularly in its first term. The deployment of a language of reform/democratization and the parliamentary majority of the JDP helped the party elite to overcome the resistance of the establishment elite. Hence, selective pluralism started to work in favour of the post-Islamist elite and against the establishment elite. In the last section of this chapter, I also pointed out that these characteristics of the political conflict in Turkey deeply influenced JDP politics in terms of its political appeal and organization. I argued that, despite its mainly non-violent framework, the hostility between powerful non-party elites and Islamist political entrepreneurs have led the Islamist elite and, later, the

JDP elite to embrace a 'low-populist' appeal and to construct a robust organizational leverage for electoral success and political resilience. As I illustrate in the following chapters, the role of agency – in other words, the political appeal and the organization of the JDP – was essential in the exploitation of the opportunities created by selective pluralism in Turkey.

3 The High–Low Divide in Turkish Politics and the Populist Appeal of the JDP

[Two prominent characters of traditional Turkish shadow theatre are] Karagöz and Hacivat. Karagöz is an extrovert, a tactless and frank man of the people who does not pretend to be someone else. People connect to him emotionally and ignore some of his little vices, such as cheating his business partner. Karagöz is representative of the morale and common sense of the ordinary people [...] He always struggles to make a living since he has got neither a particular occupation and education nor charm [...] He wants to use nice words like Hacivat does but cannot pull it off [...] He does not understand elegance. He is realistic and cannot stand dreams, pretensions and illusions too long [...] With his full beard and big eyes he is a real man of the people. On the other hand, Hacivat is pretentious, somewhat hypocritical [...] [yet] prudent and earnest [...] He gives advice, guides and mediates. He speaks well [...] He observes the minute details of manners and gives advice to Karagöz accordingly. His knowledge is superficial but he knows everything   (And, 1977: 297–300).

Introduction

There is a widespread tendency in various evaluations of Turkish politics to underline the conservative–religious content of the Justice and Development Party's political appeal.[1] In this chapter, by shifting the focus from religion to a wider socio-cultural bond between the party and the electorate, I argue that the JDP owed its political success, to a certain extent, to its 'low-populist' political appeal as defined by Ostiguy (2009c, 2017). The JDP was the last actor playing the role of Karagöz, 'a rough-voiced man of the people', and skilfully pushed its political opponents to

---

[1] There are many studies focusing on the centrality of religion for the JDP and its supporters (Başlevent et al., 2005; M. Çınar, 2013). It is undeniable that religiosity is a central asset for the JDP leadership. But in this chapter I put a special emphasis on a wider context which made the JDP's appeal particularly attractive for the less-educated, provincial and low-income majority of the country.

play the role of Hacivat, 'a soft-voiced Istanbulite gentleman', in the political drama of Turkey.[2]

In the second section, starting with a discussion of the concepts of cleavage and divide and their relevance for Turkish politics, I briefly discuss the relevance of left–right, centre–periphery and high–low divides, and argue that the high–low divide, which consists of rival perceptions of the social and cultural inequalities in politics, provides the most appropriate lens to fully see the nature of the JDP's political appeal. This theoretical discussion, alongside the examination of the Turkish party system and the nature of elite conflicts in Turkey in Chapter 2, will provide a fresh perspective on the political and social structures of Turkey in order to better understand the role of agency that is elaborated in parts of this chapter and examined fully in the rest of the book.[3] In the third section, in order to complement this theoretical discussion of cleavages and divides I elaborate further on the concept of populism. In the fourth section, I give a brief political sociology of the JDP phenomenon by focusing on voter profiles of the JDP and the main opposition, namely the Republican People's Party,[4] and show the relevance of the high–low divide through several examples from Turkish political practice.

The second part of the chapter, starting with the fifth section, will focus overwhelmingly on the agency of the JDP and Erdoğan, which also represents a particular response to – and a particular positioning within – the socio-cultural and political divides of Turkey outlined in the second, third and fourth sections of this chapter. In the fifth section, I empirically support the argument for the importance of a wider socio-cultural divide over religious appeal for JDP voters through the speeches and writings of the JDP elite and the pro-JDP media, as well as through my interviews. In the analysis of these speeches, it becomes clear that the JDP elite and the pro-JDP media see the role of religion as part of a wider socio-cultural divide, which we can refer to as the high–low divide. In this section, I also focus on the presidential election in 2014 in order to consolidate my argument. The nomination of a highly conservative figure by the opposition parties for the 2014 presidential race against Erdoğan highlighted

---

[2] For these character traits of the Turkish shadow theatre figures, see And (2001: 402).

[3] I am indebted to one of the anonymous reviewers of the book manuscript for her/his recommendation to clearly spell out this aspect of the study.

[4] I also briefly discuss the ethnic and sectarian divisions of Turkey with reference to the theorectical framework embraced in this chapter in order to illustrate the limits and potentials of the JDP's populist appeal. For brief information on the Republican People's Party and parties other than the JDP cited in the chapter and for their relative position to each other, see also Appendices 1 and 2.

the salience of the high–low divide *vis-à-vis* a secular–religious divide for the JDP's political appeal. In the sixth section, I analyse the JDP's communication style. This also shows the highly conscious engagement of the JDP elite with 'low' political appeal and demonstrates the relatively unimportant place of religion in JDP propaganda.

Defining the Relevant Divide: How to Locate the JDP's Political Appeal

In this section, I briefly draw attention to an important theoretical discussion around the concepts of 'cleavage' and 'divide' and point out a few important characteristics of the social and political confrontations in Turkish history. I argue that the JDP's political appeal is understood best within the framework of the high–low divide proposed by Ostiguy in his various works.[5] In order to illustrate the importance of the high–low divide in the formation of the JDP's political appeal, I briefly discuss the relevance of the left–right and centre–periphery (or secular–religious) divides with regard to Turkish politics in the following sub-sections.

Cleavages or Divides? The Turkish Case and the High–Low Divide

A highly important concept for the analysis of political appeals in Turkey is 'cleavage'. In its original exposition in the seminal work of Lipset and Rokkan, the centre–periphery and state–church conflicts (which together represent the national revolution process), and land–industry and owner–worker (which together represent the industrial revolution process) conflicts prepared the formation of cleavage structures within Western party systems (1967). According to Kriesi (1998), Lipset and Rokkan's idea of 'cleavage structures' was an attempt to relate the social and cultural divisions of Europe to the European party systems. Kriesi also underlined two other features of the notion of cleavage: 'the groups involved must be conscious of their identity' and it 'must be expressed in organizational terms' (1998: 167).

Hence, the notion of 'cleavage structures' presumes relatively stable party systems where, at least for a certain period of time, political identities and organizations have more or less fixed relationships with certain

---

[5] Ostiguy developed the concept of the high–low divide based on his analyses of Argentinian politics (1997, 2009b). In this chapter, I rely heavily on his works, in which he proposed the high–low divide as a more or less universal, but not always present, political phenomenon that can travel across different contexts (2009a, 2009c, 2013, 2017).

social segments. However, in many party systems, it is rare to come across such institutionalized cleavage structures connecting parties and their identities relatively stably to clearly identifiable social segments. Hence, Deegan-Krause (2007: 539) has pointed out the necessity of using 'something less', in a sense, something softer and fuzzier than the concept of cleavage proposed by Lipset and Rokkan (1967), and later by Bartolini and Mair (1990). I therefore use the term 'divide' as suggested by Deegan-Krause (2007) in order to underline a fuzzier and less institutionalized relationship between political actors, political appeals and specific social segments of a society.

When analysed from this perspective, at first glance the main political confrontation in modern Turkey since the foundation of the secular Republic in 1923 appears to be a divide between secular urban nation builders (Kemalists) and conservative and traditional rural-provincial power holders (an amalgam consisting of social segments ranging from tribal leaders and local notables to respected religious authorities). Immediately after the foundation of the Republic, the Kemalist secular nation builders tried to politically incorporate popular sectors (low-income rural segments, either with or without land, and poor urban populations) through top-down ideological narratives of 'populism [halkçılık]' and 'peasantism [köycülük]' during the 1930s and 1940s.[6] The Kemalist elite ultimately failed to sustain lasting and widespread support from the popular sectors, particularly in rural-provincial Turkey.

One of the ideological hindrances for the early Republican elite that undermined their capacity to reach out to popular sectors was their strictly positivist-secularist world-view, which was deeply hostile to any religious symbol in politics (Hanioğlu, 1997, 2011). The outcome was the disappearance of a common language between secular nation builders and popular rural and urban sectors, which would provide a suitable ground to the regime in the initial stages of their attempt to mobilize and incorporate the popular masses. One of the strategic hindrances, on the other hand, was that the Kemalists were very reluctant to mobilize and eventually politically incorporate popular sectors to the Republican People's Party since they were extremely suspicious of the masses and mass mobilization (Karaömerlioğlu, 2006: 84; 1998: 70).

It was not surprising that one of the important attempts by Kemalists to incorporate rural popular sectors into the regime, namely 'Village Institutes' (boarding schools for poor peasant children across Anatolia), was prematurely cancelled before achieving any extensive outcome

---

[6] For populist and peasantist narratives during the early Republican period between 1923 and 1945, see studies by Karaömerlioğlu (1998, 2006).

because of criticism from opponents claiming that communist indoctrination was taking place in these institutions (Karaömerlioğlu, 1998: 65–67). And the 'people's houses [*Halkevleri*]', opened by the Republican People's Party to integrate the popular masses into the regime in urban Turkey through various social activities, lacked the proper language and organization to appeal to these social segments. These institutions ironically became centres of attraction for bureaucratic and intellectual upper and middle classes (Şimşek, 2005: 88). It also seems that another fundamental reason was the lack of sufficient financial and organizational capacity available to the Kemalist elite for a much fuller political incorporation of the rural and provincial masses.[7] Instead, the early Republican elite usually made deals with certain segments of traditional provincial and rural power holders of the country, giving them concessions in order to keep the popular sectors in provincial Turkey under the control of the regime.[8]

One should also add that Kemalist nation builders always had a very strong inclination towards economic liberalism (despite the hurdles of the 1930s, which led the regime to statist economic policies) and attached great importance to the growth of a national (Muslim and Turkish) bourgeoisie. Since the beginning of the Republic, the Kemalist elite supported a small business community that was submissive to the secularist world-view of the new regime (Ahmad, 2003a: 72–101; Buğra, 1997; Keyder, 2003). In addition, unlike their counterparts in Western Europe (Bartolini, 2000), secular nation builders in Turkey established a remarkably institutionalized organization,[9] the Republican People's Party – which was, to a large extent, articulated into state institutions – well before the formation of the party system and the transition to multiparty politics in the middle of the 1940s.

The transition to a multi-party system in Turkey was also made before the rise of the political salience of urban working classes in the 1960s and 1970s. Hence, a political divide between secular nation builders (the Republican People's Party) and their opponents (the Democrat Party [Demokrat Parti]) was already present and well established, suffrage for

---

[7] This, of course, does not mean that the early Republican regime was relying solely on repressive measures for survival. Recent research illustrates that the early Republican regime, to a considerable extent, was successful in generating consent, but that its hegemony was 'fragile' (Metinsoy, 2011).

[8] For evidence of the lack of financial and organizational capacity of the early Republican regime which prevented the Kemalist elite from directly reaching out to the provincial and rural popular sectors for a remarkably long time, see Meeker (2001).

[9] See Metinsoy (2011) for the remarkable degree of bureaucratization and institutionalization of the Republican People's Party even in the early decades of the new regime.

men and women had already been introduced and, therefore, the considerably weak working classes and poor rural segments were not able to establish their own political institutional expression in the form of an agrarian, mass socialist or social democratic party for the pursuit of political and social rights. Instead, the working classes, alongside poor rural segments, to a large extent, were incorporated by the elite opponents of the secular nation-building process (primarily conservative provincial-rural power holders such as segments of the large land-owners and local religious leaders), in other words, by the populist centre-right.

What followed the failure of the full incorporation of the popular sectors into the secular nation-building project during the 1930s, 1940s and 1950s was, from the 1960s onwards, accelerating industrialization, domestic immigration to urban centres and disorganized urbanization.[10] At this second critical juncture, the political institutions of Kemalist nation builders, and the Republican People's Party in particular, once again failed to incorporate popular sectors into the secular nation building process despite short-term success during the 1970s with Bülent Ecevit.[11]

These circumstances did more than simply contribute to the weakness of the 'left' on the one hand, and to a very well-organized, robust 'right' on the other, as usually argued by popular commentators in Turkey.[12] In fact, these circumstances were the main factors that inhibited the growth of a clear and predominant left–right cleavage in the country in general, since there was no clear and vigorous institutional expression of the working classes (either through an alliance with secular nation builders or through the construction of a mass socialist or social democratic party, as was the case in West European party systems).[13] Instead of a

[10] For these processes, see classic accounts of modern Turkish history by Ahmad (2003a) and Zürcher (2004).

[11] During the 1970s, the leftwards turn of the Republican People's Party under the leadership of Ecevit was accompanied by the latter's down-to-earth public image and highly populist discourse that located and defended the 'oppressed' and 'working' (*emekçi*) classes of the country against the 'dominant forces' (*egemen güçler*). In this period, with his peasant cap and blue shirt, Ecevit – who later retreated to the conventional 'high' politics of the left in Turkey in the 1980s and 1990s – started to be called the 'Black son' (*Karaoğlan*) and was embraced by the unprivileged segments of Turkish society. For an account of Ecevit's appeal to popular sectors during the 1970s, see Erdoğan (1998).

[12] Not surprisingly, during the 1960s, one of the prominent economists of the country, İdris Küçükömer, claimed that what was known as the 'left' (the Republican People's Party) in the country was actually 'right', and the 'right' (the Democrat Party and the Justice Party) was actually 'left' given the policies they defended and profiles of their supporters (1994).

[13] See Bartolini (2000) for a historical sociology of the development of the influential left-wing political organizations in Western Europe.

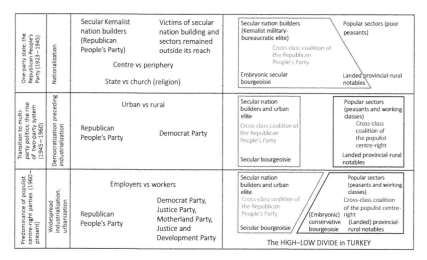

Figure 3.1 Cleavage structures and the formation of the high–low divide in Turkey

Source: Author's own compilation based on an interpretation of the classic account of Lipset and Rokkan (1967).

predominant left–right cleavage as a solid expression of the workers vs employers conflict, early political development of the Republican era created a predominant high–low (or anti-populism–populism) divide, as I will elaborate in the following sections. To put it succinctly, the critical historical dynamic behind the predominant high–low divide (and the lack of a neat left–right divide) in Turkish politics was the 'democratization – the introduction of universal suffrage and transition to multi-party politics – before rapid and widespread industrialization' or 'democratization before the rise of politically salient urban working classes'. A graphical summary of this discussion can be seen in Figure 3.1.[14]

As I will discuss at length in the rest of the chapter, what eludes observation when Turkish politics is evaluated around a secular–religious cleavage is that religion was only an element of a wider socio-cultural divide in the country, that of the high–low divide (elaborated below). Taking the centre–periphery (or secular–religious) divide as a cleavage is misleading because cleavages (in the fashion of Lipset and Rokkan's analysis) require relatively more stable party systems with highly institutionalized expressions of self-aware social forces (social classes or

---

[14] For the sake of simplicity I do not emphasize the exceptional populist turn of the Republican People's Party during the 1970s in the graph. See n. 11 for more information on this exceptional period.

denominational groups) such as socialist or social democratic working-class parties or denominational parties of liberal Western democracies (such as the Christian democratic parties of Europe). Instead, using divides rather than cleavages would help to better understand volatilities and fragmentations in the Turkish political system as well as the lack of predominance of highly institutionalized political actors associated with relatively homogeneous social segments such as the working classes, denominational groups or rural social groups. This kind of approach would help to grasp many hybrid forms, interpenetration and transitivity among political actors and their ability to articulate seemingly heterogeneous social groups and expectations, in other words the cross-class/cross-group nature of Turkish party politics since the transition to a multi-party regime.[15]

Left–Right Divide

As a consequence of the above-mentioned formation of Turkish party politics, strong social support for the centre-right political parties among most of the lower-income urban and rural masses has been one of the most enduring features of Turkish politics since the transition to multi-party politics. Since 1945, the continuing sequence of centre-right parties in Turkey, namely the Democrat Party, the Justice Party (Adalet Partisi), the Motherland Party and the JDP – except for a short period during the 1970s – have always been much more successful electorally than the so-called centre-left Republican People's Party due to the support of the most unprivileged social sectors of Turkey. Hence, it has always been very puzzling for Turkish leftists to see the workers and peasants supporting the centre-right parties in Turkey. For example, the first influential socialist political organization, the Labour Party of Turkey (Türkiye İşçi Partisi), was strikingly lacking in lower-class support compared to the centre-right Justice Party. Hikmet Kıvılcımlı, an important socialist political figure in Turkey and a prolific writer, notes at the end of the 1960s:

Two parties campaigning side by side were observed. Meetings of the Justice Party were full of shabby [külüstür] 'common rabble' [ayak takımı] with calloused hands [nasırlı eller], peasant caps [kasket], peasant moccasins [çarık] or black

[15] An alternative explanation of this situation can be found in Wuthrich's (2015) excellent account of the change in the Turkish party system over time. He mainly highlights the legal restrictions on ideologically oriented parties as the basis of the cross-class appeals and constituencies of Turkish political parties. Although the impact of legal constraints was effective, from my point of view, the cross-class appeal of Turkish political parties largely stemmed from the particular historical-sociological development of the Turkish party system outlined above.

rubber shoes [*kara lastik*]. Those who attended the meetings of the Labour Party of Turkey were more or less well and nicely dressed citizens with ties and leather shoes [*iskarpin*]. In Turkey, 'people', as everybody knows, refers to the congregation of the penniless [*züğürt*] poor. Despite the fact that the Labour Party of Turkey uses the language of the poor, the poor continue to support the Justice Party. Well-dressed gentlemen support the Labour Party of Turkey more than the Justice Party (Kıvılcımlı, 1974: 20).

Today, it is known that when competitive politics in Turkey began, with the foundation of the Democrat Party in 1945, there was a striking confusion among both the founders of the party and the public regarding the position of this new party along the left–right axis (Demirel, 2009: 417). Not surprisingly, the two dimensions of the left–right divide[16] in Turkish politics, the 'socio-economic policy' dimension and the dimension of 'political attitudes towards order and authority' (Ostiguy, 2009c: 13), usually could not help observers distinguish between 'left-wing' and 'right-wing' political forces in Turkey, particularly those close to the centre. On the one hand, with regard to economic policies, it is hard to distinguish the redistributive inclinations of the centre-right from the centre-left in Turkey, given that pro-market attitudes exist alongside redistributive political strategies in both political camps. On the other hand, with regard to the attitudes towards authority and order, in both the centre-right and the centre-left forces of the country there is an absence of 'liberal, non-hierarchical, anti-authority, and horizontalising attitudes' (Ostiguy, 2009c: 13–14).

When the Democrat Party started to gather momentum in the mid 1940s, there was, however, a remarkable conviction among the rural and urban poor people that, compared to the single-party rule of the Republican People's Party, this new party was 'taking them seriously [*adam yerine koymak*]' and 'treating people humanely [*insanca davranmak*]' (Demirel, 2011: 123). Not surprisingly, even from the perspective of the Turkish bourgeoisie, the successor to the Democrat Party, the Justice Party, was considered to be rural and far from civilized life, whereas the leader of the 'left-wing' Republican People's Party was considered to be more familiar, 'Westernized', 'refined [*kültürlü*]' and 'civilized [*uygar*]' (Demirel, 2004: 91). No surprise, then, that the historical tension between the centre-right parties of the country and the

---

[16] For elaborate analyses of the left–right divide, see Bobbio (2005) and Laponce (1981). I, to a great extent, embrace Ostiguy's interpretation of the left and right distinction and tend to see attitudes towards order and authority as the fundamental aspect of the divide (2009c: 13–14). As one accepts more hierarchical authority structures, s/he moves towards the right, and as one defends more horizontal authority structures and orders, s/he approaches the left.

Republican People's Party has been predominantly perceived as a clash between two lifestyles: an allegedly Westernized, modern, civilized (*çağdaş, uygar*) one vs an allegedly native, national (*yerli, milli*) one in line with custom and tradition (*göreneğe ve geleneğe uygun*).[17]

In each other's perceptions, rightist (those supporting centre-right parties such as the Democrat Party and the Justice Party as well as more radical right-wing parties such as the Nationalist Action Party and Islamist National View parties [Milli Görüş Partileri]) and leftist (those supporting the centre-left Republican People's Party, the socialist Labour Party of Turkey and other minor legal and illegal left-wing parties and factions) intellectuals attached great importance to socio-cultural differences. According to the leftist narrative in Turkey, rightists are, 'first of all, ignorant', and they are not 'individuals'; they are prone to violence; 'they do not read and interrogate'; they are peasants and/or provincial town dwellers; and therefore 'they lack horizon, and they are shallow and rude' (Demirel, 2009: 425). They are philistines, and they lack manners (Demirel, 2009: 426). They exploit the religious inclinations of the ignorant masses (Demirel, 2009: 427). On the other hand, according to the rightist narrative, leftists are anti-religious and anti-Islam. Left is the ideology of the anti-religious 'minority elite' (Demirel, 2009: 431). They are 'cosmopolitans' and they lack 'notions of country and nation' (Demirel, 2009: 435). They are 'rich', and as the 'heirs of the Westernized elite' they have been partaking of the 'cream of the system' (Demirel, 2009: 436).

Given the above-mentioned socio-cultural content of the left–right divide, it was no surprise that there was a strong quest for a new understanding of the main divide of Turkish politics. The centrality of attitudes towards religion in the perception of the left and right by the leftists and rightists illustrated above played a crucial role in the formation of a new understanding of the Turkish politics under the 'centre–periphery' divide.

---

[17] Wuthrich (2015) contends that the public political discourse that shapes the party competition and the system in Turkey has frequently changed since the transition to multi-party politics, and that there was no essential divide that structured Turkish party politics such as a secular–religious or left–right one. I agree, to a great extent, with this analysis regarding the change in the public discourse of the parties. However, I also think that solely examining written material consisting of party documents and speeches published in the media led Wuthrich to ignore a very resilient socio-cultural divide in Turkey that deeply shaped Turkish party politics. In the following sections of this chapter, I call this the 'high–low divide'. As I have cited throughout this chapter, accounts such as Demirel's works (2004, 2009, 2011) that rely on richer first-hand sources (including memoirs and popular narratives) include many details illustrating the resilience of socio-cultural divides in Turkish party politics.

'Centre–Periphery' Divide or 'Religious–Secular Polarization Perspective'

In the analysis of the multi-party politics in his highly influential study entitled 'Centre–Periphery Relations: A Key to Turkish Politics?', Şerif Mardin proposes to understand Turkish politics around the concepts of centre and periphery. He argues that in the 1950s 'the electoral platform of the opposition, especially as seen in Democrat Party political propaganda, in newspapers, and in the media, established the lines of a debate between "real populists" and "bureaucrats"' (1973: 185). Also, Mardin himself defined the contradiction between the Democrat Party and the Republican People's Party in a similar vein, whereby the latter 'represented the "bureaucratic" centre, whereas the Democrat Party represented the "democratic" periphery' (1973: 186). According to Mardin, especially after the foundation of the Republic, the secularist attitudes of the centre deepened the divide between the centre and the overwhelmingly religious periphery (1973: 182). The 'centre–periphery' approach has dominated the analyses of Turkish politics and society since the publication of Mardin's analysis in 1973 and has obtained, so to speak, a paradigmatic status (Hale and Özbudun, 2010: xviii).

The centre–periphery paradigm has recently received some very substantial criticism. First of all, it had some strong normative presumptions (Ahıska, 2006: 18). Centre–periphery analysts in Turkey, depending on their ideological stance, praised either the allegedly secularist high politics of the centre or the allegedly democratic and religious stance of the periphery. The centre–periphery paradigm depicted only two important conflicting actors in Turkish politics on the basis of secular–religious divide and a zero-sum political game: the secular state and the religious social forces, with nothing in between. This 'culturalist' and 'dualist' approach to politics (Açıkel, 2006) tended to identify the concept of centre with the state and ignored the plurality of the social forces, called the periphery (Gönenç, 2006: 131–132), while oversimplifying the complexities of the social and political struggles by reducing them to a simple struggle around the position of religion (M. Çınar, 2006b: 163). Apart from this, as many studies of Turkish political parties have illustrated, the centre–periphery approach led researchers to identify the centre-left and centre-right parties of Turkey with the concepts of centre and the periphery respectively.[18]

---

[18] Apart from the uses of the centre–periphery approach in various social science accounts on Turkey as an explanatory framework, to see the longevity of the effects of Mardin's approach on the analyses of political parties in Turkey, see Acar (1991), Karpat (1991), Levi (1991) and Sarıbay (1991).

Nevertheless, the centre–periphery paradigm implied a very resilient and fundamental dimension of Turkish politics. The resilience of the centre–periphery paradigm should be seen as connected to the resilience of the reflection of socio-cultural divides and the salience of different political appeals/styles in Turkish party politics. From this perspective, the main problem with the centre–periphery approach and its various interpretations appears to be the misleading identification of this divide with a full cleavage in the fashion defined by Lipset and Rokkan (1967) and Bartolini and Mair (1990), which corresponded to neat differences between two main identity-conscious social segments stably represented under highly institutionalized organizations and party systems.[19] Moreover, the centre–periphery divide usually led students of Turkish politics to associate the centre with the 'state', a highly contested and problematic concept in its own right. Besides, it also deprived researchers of a gradual understanding of the positions of political actors in Turkey along an ordinal axis, and therefore impeded a nuanced understanding of the Turkish political landscape.

In fact, the main divide in Turkish politics that gave scholarly predominance to the centre–periphery paradigm, as mentioned above, has always been 'something less' (Deegan-Krause, 2007: 539), something fuzzier and softer than a 'full cleavage'. This divide, which I will call the high–low divide in subsequent parts of the chapter in the fashion of Ostiguy (2017), stemmed from widespread reactions to a civilizing intervention, a 'proper' civilizational project which created an 'unpresentable Other'.[20]

Indeed, as illustrated above, attitudes toward religion played a crucial role in the formation of this divide. Nevertheless, I would argue that religion was an important yet subordinate dimension of a mainly socio-cultural divide. The puzzle of the lack of popular support for the Islamist National View parties of the old guard after the foundation of the JDP by a new reformist generation within the tradition indicated the true position of religious rhetoric and symbols in the formation of political appeals in Turkey. In other words, parties explicitly using religious

---

[19] For such an interpretation of the centre–periphery divide as a cleavage, see Özbudun (2013).

[20] 'Let us begin at the most *abstract* (and perhaps not most helpful) level, by conceptualizing populism, *independently of the continent*, as an antagonistic appropriation for political, mobilizational purposes of an *"unpresentable Other"*, itself historically created in the process of a specific "proper" civilizational project. The precise nature of that "proper", civilizational project can vary widely from liberalism, to multiculturalism, adapting to the ways and manners of the First World or the West, orthodox "textbook" economics, European integration, racial integration, colonial France's *"mission civilisatrice"*, or any other' (Ostiguy, 2017: 75) (italics Ostiguy's).

symbols and rhetoric in their political appeals were not able to be more successful than the centre-right forces, and particularly not more than the JDP.

The Concept of Populism

In order to understand the puzzle of the stronger popular appeal of the centre-right parties compared to that of the parties with predominantly religious or ideological appeals, it will help a lot to have a closer look at the concept of populism. In this section of the chapter, I will focus on four main conceptualizations of populism: those of Mudde (2004), Weyland (2001), Laclau (2005) and Ostiguy (2017).[21] The concept of populism, or the populism–anti-populism divide, might be seen as the proper approach to Turkish politics, given the highly socio-cultural nature of the competing political appeals in Turkey. This could be seen as the reason that the term 'populism' has been frequently deployed by students of Turkish politics, albeit with a surprising lack of attention to the definitional problems inherent to the concept.[22] Just like the centre–periphery approach, to see Turkish politics from the perspective of the concept of populism has usually reproduced dichotomous approaches. This could be explained by the fact that most of the general academic definitions of the concept were not ordinal and led researchers to only a nominal understanding of the political positions and actors. In other words, most of the definitions usually result in researchers labelling political actors as either populist or anti-populist, and generally inhibited a definition of the degrees of populism[23] since these definitions did not distinguish political actors from political appeals or styles.

---

[21] For a very similar approach to that of Ostiguy, see also Moffitt (2016). I embrace Ostiguy's (2017) approach since it also helps to understand the deep-rooted social, emotional and political factors that give rise to populism. Moffitt's approach puts a heavy emphasis on the transgressive, performative and grotesque dimension of this phenomenon. The 'transgressive' aspect is certainly an important feature, but I still contend that the 'social pain' and 'hidden injuries' caused by socio-cultural differences are also central to the phenomenon. Thus, in my point of view, Ostiguy's approach is much more potent at grasping the pathos of the phenomenon.

[22] For a discussion of the concept of populism with a special emphasis on the Turkish case, see Baykan (2014, 2017b).

[23] In this regard Sikk holds a special position. According to him, 'analysing degrees of populism in party rhetoric or programs is much more promising than the so far dominant dichotomous approach. To some extent, all parties are or appear to be populist' (2009: 12).

Populism as an Ideology, (Organizational) Strategy
and a Socio-Political Logic

Some highly influential current definitions of the term 'populism' are not particularly helpful here if we want to focus on the socio-cultural and political cultural stylistic aspects of a given party system. I share with Ostiguy (2013, 2017) his critique of two main, oft-cited conceptualizations of the term by Mudde (2004) and Weyland (2001). Mudde defines populism 'as an ideology that considers society to be ultimately separated into two homogeneous and antagonistic groups, "the pure people" versus "the corrupt elite", and which argues that politics should be an expression of the *volonté générale* (general will) of the people' (2004: 543).[24] Weyland's definition is as follows: 'populism is best defined as a political strategy through which a personalistic leader seeks or exercises government power based on direct, unmediated, uninstitutionalized support from large numbers of mostly unorganized followers' (2001: 14).

By focusing on 'discourses as words', as Ostiguy points out, the minimal populism definition as an ideology proposed by Mudde (2004) underestimates the centrality of the political styles/appeals in the populist phenomenon and might also cause 'misleading positives' (Ostiguy, 2017: 91) because many non-populist actors can use notions of 'people' and 'elites' and can depict these groups in confrontation in their discourse. The same problem, in other words the underestimation of style in the identification of the populist phenomenon, also weakens Weyland's definition (2001). This approach fundamentally ignores the centrality of style/appeal as the content of the 'direct and unmediated' link between the populist leader and the people (Ostiguy, 2017: 90). There is also the additional problem of focusing on organizations (or lack of organization) as one of the main criteria of populism in Weyland's approach.

Another influential approach to the study of populism is the discourse-theoretical understanding of the phenomenon by Laclau (2005). Laclau, very roughly, defines populism as a socio-political logic which articulates different demands against an enemy 'other' in an antagonistic fashion. Laclau claims that every political intervention that relies on this logic is populist. Laclau goes as far as to argue that only interventions and movements that embrace this logic deserve to be called 'politics'. For Laclau, populism is politics *par excellence* (2005: 155). Laclau certainly does not imply that the term 'discourse' encompasses only linguistic

---

[24] There is also the approach by Hawkins (2010), whose definition is very close to that of Mudde. However, he also emphasizes the moral dimension of the phenomenon and tends to understand it as a 'world-view'. Most of the criticisms in the following parts of the section regarding Mudde's approach are valid for Hawkins too.

elements. However, his approach to the phenomenon usually led his followers to analyse party discourse and ignore the extra-linguistic aspects of the phenomenon. When these aspects are ignored and the analyses start to focus on the antagonistic construction of political identities around the notions of people (or 'the poor' or 'working classes' or *'ezilenler'* ['the oppressed' in Turkish]) and elite (or 'dominant classes' or 'oligarchies'), many misleading positives – and particularly anti-liberal movements such as fascism or socialism that we know are not populist – may start to fall under the definition of populism.[25]

Hence, the understanding of populism as a Manichaean ideology separating the elite and the people as proposed by Mudde is problematic, since this kind of dichotomy can be seen in the discourse of many non-populist political actors as pointed out by Ostiguy. In addition, as the case of the JDP illustrates, the search for the systematic use of this kind of dichotomy can also lead researchers to underestimate the populist aspect of many political parties with a catch-all approach to the electoral processes. After all, as with the JDP, a party can most definitely be populist in style and appeal and avoid a systematic deployment of a Manichaean world-view and slightly underplay the moral dimension of populism in their well-thought-out written and spoken public material – the analysis of which is methodologically central to Mudde's (and Hawkins') definition and approach. These approaches, in short, do not consider the central role of social tastes and emotions in the formation of the political divides in a considerable number of political contexts.

Similarly, populism as an antagonistic logic that separates society into camps does not help to explain the populist dimension of Turkish politics in general and the JDP's political appeal in particular. While at certain moments this kind of conflict-driven language prevails in the political discourse of the JDP, it is hard to locate it systematically in public discourse that the party has produced. The party can sometimes adopt a very conciliatory form of language, and sometimes a very belligerent one. But, as I will demonstrate in the following sections, with regard to the JDP's appeal/style, to the particular way the party's leadership

---

[25] I do not claim that socialist or fascist movements and populism are mutually exclusive. There have been certainly some socialist (or fascist) movements that stylistically revealed populist characteristics. Nevertheless, if the researchers focus only on the discourse of these movements it becomes much more likely to put very different brands of socialism with remarkably different styles, appeals and constituencies into the same basket. For example, in Turkey, the style and constituency the Kurdish political movement represented were considerably different from the appeal/style and the constituencies represented by Mehmet Ali Aybar's Labour Party of Turkey. The former has always been much more populist than the latter.

connects with the popular sectors, and to its broader 'performance', it has certainly been systematically and persistently populist.

The case of the JDP also makes it clear that, as elaborated in the subsequent chapters of this book, populism can coexist with a highly routinized and remarkably bureaucratized organization. This is a substantial problem for Weyland's approach since it focuses on lack of a proper organization as the hallmark of populism. Hence, Weyland's approach helps little in grasping the populist component of the JDP politics since this party has a remarkably bureaucratized and routinized organization. However, Weyland's approach goes one step further than Mudde's and points out the extra-linguistic aspects of the phenomenon. Nevertheless, when the 'populist' strategy is understood simply as a specific way of establishing a power base that relies on the 'unorganized, unmediated' support of the masses, many 'misleading positives' – such as personalistic parties and other non-populist political movements – may also start to fall under Weyland's definition of populism.

In order to grasp the populist aspect of the JDP it is more productive to take populism as a political style/appeal,[26] as an 'emphasis' of politics.[27] In other words, populism should be seen as a relationship between performer, receiver and other political actors that are located together in a given political arena. Hence, 'reification of populism' as an intrinsic quality of parties and leaders should be avoided. In order to apply this approach, researchers should rely on other methods to understand populist phenomena such as the observation of the day-to-day activities of parties, listening to spontaneous speeches of leaders, and watching and observing numerous videos as well as meetings. Hence I, also consequently, rely to a large extent on methods proposed by Ostiguy.[28] Thus, this chapter embraces the definition of populism proposed by Ostiguy: 'the antagonistic, mobilizational flaunting in politics of the culturally popular and "native", and personalism as a mode of decision making' (Ostiguy, 2017: 84).

---

[26] Aside from Ostiguy (2017) and Moffitt (2016), it is de la Torre (1992, 2000) and Knight (1998) who previously put a special emphasis on style in their understanding of populism.

[27] Here, I see a certain proximity between the approaches of Ostiguy and Worsley. Worsley, decades ago, underlined the importance of seeing populism as something about style and political culture: 'Populism is better regarded as an emphasis, a dimension of political culture in general, not simply as a particular kind of overall ideological system or type of organization' (1969: 245).

[28] 'The political style of the low is clearly recognizable and delimited, empirically. It simply requires a different method of observation and a different acquired comparative expertise: the watching of innumerable videos of campaign rallies, political advertising, speeches, televised appearances, etc.' (Ostiguy, 2009c: 49).

Populism as a Socio-Cultural and Political Cultural Phenomenon:
The High–Low Divide

The high–low divide proposed by Ostiguy understands populism as a style/appeal.[29] But this approach also sees populism as something deeply related to the politicized socio-cultural divisions in a given party system. This can help researchers overcome the weaknesses of the centre–periphery (secular–religious) divide and problems with mainstream definitions of populism analysed above, and the insufficiencies of evaluating Turkish politics from the perspective of the left–right divide as well. Ostiguy's understanding of populism is not as much about labelling parties, leaders and movements as other common nominal understandings are (Ostiguy, 2013: 27), but about a space of symbolic, emotional, stylistic and discursive resources that parties and leaders can deploy. This helps the high–low divide travel extremely well across different settings (2009a: 2). According to Ostiguy, particularly in the contexts where the left–right and the liberal–conservative divides do not have strong salience, the high–low divide is a useful perspective in explaining the structure of political appeals (2009a: 2). Ostiguy emphasizes that the appeals that shape the high–low divide are about 'ways of relating to people, as such, they go beyond discourses as mere words, and they include issues of accents, level of language, body language, gestures, ways of dressing' (2009c: 5). He adds that this way of relating to people also covers different decision-making styles (Ostiguy, 2009c: 5) specified below, yet he also underlines the importance of a 'populist script' in which populist political entrepreneurs construct a narrative highlighting the struggle between 'the people [. . .] typically from here' and the hostile domestic and international minorities and elite power holders (Ostiguy, 2017: 76–77).

Ostiguy explains that the high–low divide consists of two components: a 'socio-cultural' and a 'political-cultural' one (2009a: 5).[30] The socio-cultural component of the high–low divide is about 'manners, demeanours, ways of speaking and dressing, and tastes displayed in public', while the political-cultural component is about 'forms of leadership and preferred decision making modes' (Ostiguy, 2009a: 6–8). He emphasizes

---

[29] Ostiguy, as explicitly stated in his various works, understands the term 'appeal' to mean something including discourse but at the same time something that goes beyond 'mere words': 'An appeal in politics is simply a way in which a politician or a political party attempts, usually voluntarily, to woo supporters' (2017: 11).

[30] In this chapter, I almost exclusively focus on the socio-cultural axis of 'low-populism' in Turkish politics. I analyse the political-cultural component of the 'low' in Turkey with regard to the leadership of the JDP in the next chapter.

that, while the high tend to be 'refined', the low tend to be 'crude', in socio-cultural terms. In political-cultural terms, the high tends to be 'formalistic and procedural', whereas the low tends to be highly 'personalistic' (2009b: 9). The key aspect regarding the political-cultural dimension of the phenomenon is the (virtual or real) 'immediacy'[31] which is in contradistinction to the mediated, non-personal, procedural and institutional logic of anti-populism. Finally, while the high tends to be 'cosmopolitan', the low is rather 'nativist' (Ostiguy, 1997: 5). As underlined by Ostiguy (2009c: 5–6), the high–low divide is also quite often connected to resentments deeply embedded in societies' history and existing group tensions.

By showing the attractiveness of each side of the high and low, this approach also helps researchers avoid certain normative biases (Ostiguy, 2009c: 4). This is why, when defining the assets of the high and low in socio-cultural and political-cultural terms, Ostiguy uses the mutual point of view of each side of the divide. According to him, in socio-cultural terms, the low tends to see the high as 'stiff, rigid, serious, colourless, somewhat distant and boring' (2009c: 6). On the other hand, the high tends to see the low as 'grotesque' (2009c: 6). According to Ostiguy, in political-cultural terms, while the high claims to be 'formal, impersonal, legalistic, institutionally mediated', the low tends to attach importance to 'personalism' and 'strong (generally male) leadership' (2009c: 9). It should be reasserted that, in this particular approach, populism is understood as a *relationship* between parties, leaders, supporters and other political actors in a given political space.

Methodologically, Ostiguy's approach requires the researcher to go beyond the analysis of the populist script – that is, the discourse in its linguistic sense – and to focus on a wider and more intense bond between populist performers and audiences. This approach also leads the analysis to take the anti-populist camp of the political system into account and present the phenomenon of populism in a belligerent dialogue – both linguistically and stylistically – with its constitutive other. It therefore requires more than illustrating and analysing a narrative consisting of catch-phrases and images. The approach necessitates the construction of a 'thick description' (Geertz, 1993) of the phenomenon that takes the historical-sociological context into account. However, one of the advantages of these arduous methodological requirements is that it gives researchers (and readers) a comprehensive, dynamic understanding of the context of the phenomenon as well as the phenomenon itself. It also

---

[31] Benjamin Arditi has underlined the importance of 'immediacy' in the phenomenon of populism (2005: 85).

helps researchers to locate the leader, party and movement under investigation gradually and historically along a political axis of populism and anti-populism which is 'orthogonal' (Ostiguy, 2017: 74) to the left–right axis. In the following parts of this chapter, I develop this thick description, which includes sociological, discursive and behavioural components.

The High–Low Divide in the Political Practice of Turkey and a Brief Political Sociology of the JDP Phenomenon

Before examining in detail the content of the the socio-cultural appeal of the JDP politically in the following sections by using the conceptual and theoretical tools introduced so far, in this section I will provide some examples of the relevance of the high–low divide in recent Turkish politics. A few significant political figures of the past couple of decades will provide a background for the later discussion on the 'low-populist' appeal of the JDP. In addition, I also underline in this section the similar socio-economic origins of the JDP elites and members. This similarity in the social profiles of JDP elites and voters supports the argument that the 'low-populist' appeal was central to the construction of a very resilient bond between the JDP leadership and its constituency. In the third part of the section, I give some brief information about the profiles of the JDP and the Republican People's Party voters which shows that the JDP supporters come overwhelmingly from underprivileged segments of Turkish society. In the fourth part, I relate the theoretical framework of high–low divide to the issue of ethnic and sectarian divisions in Turkey.

What Do High and Low as a Socio-Cultural Divide Mean in Turkey? A Glance at the Socio-Cultural Affinity between Voters and Leaders

Voters in Turkey have always been inclined to see political options through the prism of their socio-cultural experiences. Different political appeals ranging between extremely high-elitist and low-populist positions have articulated the voters' different socio-cultural experiences mostly stemming from their socio-economic and educational levels. Apart from the overall representation of parties in the media, one of the central channels that leads to association with a certain party is the party leader.[32] In this context, a closer look at a few recent leaders from

---

[32] See Akgün (2007: 197) for the importance JDP voters attach to the party's leadership.

prominent parties in Turkey will clarify the concrete meanings of high and low appeals in Turkish politics.

Compared to a series of leaders of the centre-right tradition in Turkey, leaders of the Republican People's Party have always had a relatively 'high' appeal. For example, Bülent Ecevit, one of the prominent leaders of the Republican People's Party in Turkey, despite the familiarity and popularity he acquired during the 1970s in the eyes of the lower classes, had a remarkably 'high' appeal. With his strictly urban background,[33] flawless manners, quite fluent English, perfect 'İstanbul Turkish' and intellectual and artistic occupations as a translator, poet and writer,[34] Ecevit's appeal could be predominantly located somewhere higher than that of Süleyman Demirel, the perennial leader of a series of centre-right parties in Turkey. On the other hand, Demirel – who was called 'father' or 'Shepherd Sülü [Çoban Sülü]' – with his upbringing in provincial-rural Turkey and slightly rural accent had always been a very familiar figure in the eyes of the electorate, who were socio-culturally more open to 'low-populist' appeals.

After the coup in 1980, the predominant figure on the centre-right, and with a 'low' appeal politically, was Turgut Özal. With his provincial upbringing in a Turkish–Kurdish family from Malatya, relaxed manners,[35] interest in popular culture and unpretentious religiosity, Özal was more familiar for voters socio-culturally open to 'low-populist' appeals in Turkey than the leader of the centre-left party of the era, Erdal İnönü. In contrast, İnönü, a physics professor with a doctorate from the United States, was the son of İsmet İnönü, a hero of Turkish National Independence War. Highly urban and intellectual, his appeal was more familiar for the voters prone to respond to 'high' appeals during the short period he was active in politics.

A similar pattern can be observed regarding the recent leaders of the Republican People's Party and Erdoğan, too. Deniz Baykal, the leader of the Republican People's Party for almost two decades, lectured as a professor of law in Ankara University until the mid 1970s. He is articulate when speaking, yet somewhat distant, serious and rigid. His successor, Kemal Kılıçdaroğlu, despite his origins in provincial Turkey in a very modest family and despite having 'lower', more populist appeal than his predecessor, would also be located somewhere 'higher' than Erdoğan in

---

[33] Ecevit was brought up in İstanbul as the son of a parliamentarian and went to the Robert Kolej, one of the most prestigious schools in the country.

[34] Besides writing several books on Turkish politics and a couple of poetry boks, Ecevit translated works of R. Tagore and T. S. Eliot into Turkish.

[35] On several occasions Özal was caught in inappropriate attire. He greeted soldiers in a military ceremony clad in sportswear and visited governors in shorts and a t-shirt.

terms of his appeal to the electorate. He had a successful career in state bureaucracy and worked in top positions in the Ministry of Finance and related state institutions. He was a latecomer to politics, with his political career starting only in the 1990s. With his proper and official appearance, his appeal was more 'high' than 'low'. One should also remember that, in a quite contemptuous way, Erdoğan used to call Kılıçdaroğlu 'general director [*genel müdür*]' in order to emphasize his bureaucratic origins and, perhaps, his alleged lack of political experience.

One should also add that for a very long time, and until recently, the primary position the Republican People's Party adopted in its political criticism of centre-right parties in power was to defend 'secularism [*laiklik*]'. Even their attempts at reaching out to the popular sectors of Turkish society were weakened by the terminological framing of their promises, such as arguing that the Republican People's Party was pro-welfare state (*sosyal devlet*). While criticizing the JDP, they usually under-lined the decline of institutions and of the state of justice (*hukuk devleti*) in the country. This style and discourse, which put a special emphasis on abstract notions such as 'secularism', 'welfare state' and 'the state of justice', usually failed to create an emotional bond between the Republican People's Party and the popular majorities of the country.

In contrast to the leaders of the Republican People's Party and the party's high appeal, the appeal of Erdoğan and the JDP was remarkably lower. The JDP leader Erdoğan was never bright academically[36] and, until he became the mayor of İstanbul in the mid 1990s, he had little idea about bureaucracy. However, he spent his youth and adult life in the midst of very intense party activity, and worked in every possible position in the Islamist predecessors of the JDP, which also helped him meet all kinds of people from every walk of life (Interviewee 28, 2014). As will be illustrated at length in the next chapter, he was the son of a low-income, immigrant family and he was brought up in one of the rough neighbour-hoods of İstanbul. He also had a very peculiar, slightly bulging posture, which resembled traditional Turkish roughnecks. There were many instances where he was quite rough and harsh. For example, he scolded citizens who complained to him and physically assaulted a man in one of the Turkish provinces after the tragic mine blast which killed more than 300 workers.[37]

Erdoğan loves football (soccer). It is well known that many popular media figures were very supportive of him, ranging from pop and *arabesk*

---

[36] There has even been some speculation regarding Erdoğan's university degree.
[37] See www.cumhuriyet.com.tr/video/video/72221/Basbakan_Erdogan_vatandasa_yumruk_atti.html# (accessed: 27 May 2016).

singers to former models and football players. Singers in *arabesk*[38] genres – mostly listened to by low-income, domestic-immigrant populations of urban centres in Turkey – such as Adnan Şenses and Niran Ünsal, were public admirers of Erdoğan. A fast-breaking (dinner) invitation by Erdoğan revealed this relationship between Erdoğan and popular culture. Unlike the one held by Erbakan (the founding figure of the Islamist National View tradition) almost two decades previously, which was full of sheikhs and religious personalites, the JDP's highly publicized fast-breaking dinner, this time, was full of popular media figures ranging from pop singers to soap opera actors, football players to TV personalities (*T24*, 2014). Not surprisingly, a pop singer wrote the following lyrics (which also highlighted the 'low-populist' appeal of the party) for the JDP in the 2014 local elections, and later became a JDP deputy:

> He is the strong voice of the oppressed,
> He is the free voice of the silent world,
> He is as he looks, he gets his strength from the nation,
> Recep Tayyip Erdoğan.
> The man of the people, the lover of the God,
> He is the light of hope to millions,
> He is confidant to the downtrodden,
> He is comrade of the excluded,
> Recep Tayyip Erdoğan.
> He has always been loyal to his word,
> He did not return from the way he started to walk,
> He is determined in his cause,
> He is in the prayer of mothers,
> Recep Tayyip Erdoğan.
> His word is true and he has no hypocrisy,
> He is the nightmare of the oppressors,
> He walks in the way he believed,
> He is the leader who has been awaited for years,
> Recep Tayyip Erdoğan.[39]

Erdoğan, however, has always been received with hostility by the cultural elite of the country – particularly by secularist artists and intellectuals, as will be illustrated at length below.[40]

---

[38] For accounts of *arabesk* demonstrating the genre's appeal to poor dwellers of Turkish metropolitan centres, see M. Stokes (1992) and Özbek (1991).

[39] For the song, see www.youtube.com/watch?v=j6jL95BaSeM (accessed: 27 May 2016).

[40] Fazıl Say, a world-renowned classical music pianist from Turkey, for example, was a fierce opponent of the JDP. He caused a heated debate when he stated that he was 'embarrassed by the *arabesk* indulgence of Turkish people [*Türk halkının arabesk yavşaklığından utanıyorum*]'.

A Glance at the Social Profiles of JDP Elites and Activists

There is a reason to believe that the majority of the JDP voters are highly open to a 'low-populist' appeal, since a study published in 2008 confirmed that supporters of the JDP came from lower and middling socio-economic status groups of Turkish society. According to Aydın and Dalmış, 'the JDP's support base lies in the peripheral elements of society' (2008: 215). The important point of Aydın and Dalmış's study, however, is the argument that the JDP deputies, despite their present high socio-economic and educational levels, overwhelmingly came from backgrounds similar to their voters. This is to say that the socio-economic status of families (including their wives and parents) of the JDP representatives in the parliament were by no means high (Aydın and Dalmış, 2009: 215). Another striking finding from Aydın and Dalmış's study was that more than half of JDP deputies spent a considerable amount of their childhood in rural Turkey, away from the cities (2008: 215).

This pattern regarding the backgrounds of JDP deputies was also clearly observable in my fieldwork.[41] For example, when one of my interviewees, a former JDP deputy, talked about his family, he mentioned that his father was an illiterate (ümmi) farmer (Interviewee 23, 2014). Another former JDP deputy highlighted that he came from a low-income, provincial family (Interviewee 21, 2014). One of the founders of the JDP in one province also argued that he had a blue-collar occupation when he started out in politics in the Islamist National View parties in the 1980s (Interviewee 18, 2014). Only relatively younger JDP members among my interviewees came from better-off families with roots in prominent urban centres of the country.

Voter Profiles of the JDP and the Republican People's Party

In this part I will underline a few important features about the profiles of the JDP and the Republican People's Party voters. Since the JDP's rapid rise, many studies have underlined the relatively strong support for the JDP among less-educated and low-income segments of the electorate. According to research conducted in 2002, voters with primary school education or below were the largest group of JDP voters (Erder, 2002: 74). Small shopkeepers and craftspeople comprised the largest segment

---

[41] See also N. Ergün's (2015) memoirs. A former JDP minister, he described living with his low-income family in a province near İstanbul. This book is an extremely valuable source for understanding the transformation of Islamist politics and the transformation of the majority of the Islamist elite from ideological, Islamist vanguards to pragmatic – and usually populist – politicians.

of JDP voters and, at the same time, voters with white-collar occupations comprised the smallest group (Erder, 2002: 74). In contrast, the largest group among the Republican People's Party in terms of education consisted of people with university degrees and those with white-collar occupations (Erder, 2002: 79). Akgün's research also confirms these findings. According to Akgün, as education levels increase, voters' tendency towards the Republican People's Party becomes stronger (2007: 209). In contrast, JDP supporters predominantly come from social segments with lower education levels, such as primary or secondary school graduates (Akgün, 2007: 209). It should also be noted that the JDP elites were also aware of the pattern to the extent that one of the former JDP ministers underlined the difficulties the party had in reaching out to well-educated voters.[42]

According to Şentürk, the Republican People's Party's votes also increase as the income level increases. Not surprisingly, support for the JDP is stronger among those segmets of voters with the lowest income levels (Şentürk, 2008b: 112). Another important point underlined by Şentürk is that support for the JDP among large families with many children and elders is stronger (2008b: 90). In Turkey, family size can be considered a proxy for the socio-economic and socio-cultural level of families. The larger the size of the family, the more likely they are to fall lower on the socio-economic and/or educational scale.[43] The following graph from Başlevent's study (2013) of the correlation between the JDP vote and lower levels of education in thirty-nine sub-provinces (ilçeler) of İstanbul overwhelmingly overlaps with previous evaluations of the voter profiles of the party.

To understand this graph I provide here some brief information about the two sub-provinces located at the extreme ends of the imaginary line stretching from the top left to the bottom right, between Sultanbeyli and Beşiktaş. According to data published by the Turkish Statistical Institute, in Beşiktaş almost one-third of the total population above fifteen years old – 150,000 people – are university graduates and almost 10 per cent of the population in the same sub-province have masters' degrees or doctorates (Turkish Statistical Institute, 2013: 107). In this sub-province,

---

[42] See www.youtube.com/watch?v=ZnsftqyDGLQ (accessed: 27 May 2016).

[43] Here one should also keep in mind that one of the widely debated political topics in Turkey was Erdoğan's repeated recommendations to newly married couples to have 'at least three children' (Haberler.com, 2014b). Fierce critics of Erdoğan usually did not understand that this was not simply intervening in people's lives, but was a way of enhancing bonds between the JDP and its supporters, most of whom came from large families with lower socio-economic status and education levels. Not surprisingly, Erdoğan has four children, and many JDP elite also have more than two children.

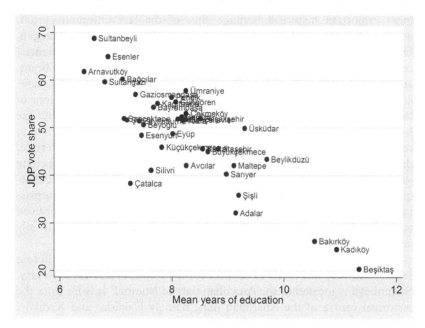

Figure 3.2 The JDP's vote share vs mean number of years of
education in thirty-nine sub-provinces of İstanbul
Source: Başlevent (2013).

the vote share of the JDP in the 2014 local elections was only 16 per cent.
In contrast, the Republican People's Party received 76 per cent of votes
in Beşiktaş. In Sultanbeyli the pattern is the exact opposite. In this sub-
province, the JDP received 61 per cent of votes and the Republican
People's Party received a mere 7 per cent. According to data from the
Turkish Statistical Institute yearbook, in Sultanbeyli, there are only
around 11,000 people with graduate degrees from universities in the
total population aged above fifteen (slightly more than 210,000 people)
(Turkish Statistical Institute, 2013: 111). Another data point from the
Turkish Statistical Institute mirroring this pattern is household size.
While the average household size in Beşiktaş is 2.49, it is 4.67 in Sultan-
beyli (Turkish Statistical Institute, 2013: 117).

It may be useful here to provide further context to the demonstration
of the difference between these two sub-provinces of İstanbul. Beşiktaş is
one of the central sub-provinces of İstanbul in the European part of the
city which stretches along the Bosphorus strait. The sub-province is
known for its tourist neighbourhoods (such as Ortaköy) as well as its
extremely wealthy ones (such as Bebek). Beşiktaş includes some of the

most important historical heritage sites of the late Ottoman period, which reflect the modernization efforts of the Empire, such as Çırağan, Dolmabahçe and Yıldız Palace. It also includes one of the financial centres of the city, Levent. Nightlife in Beşiktaş has always been vibrant, and the central parts of the sub-province are full of bookstores, cafés and live music venues. Some of the best higher education institutions of the country, such as Boğaziçi, Yıldız and Galatasaray University, are located in Beşiktaş. According to a socio-economic categorization report prepared by REIDIN, a real estate market information service, the highest socio-economic and socio-cultural records in Turkey belong to the Bebek neighborhood of Beşiktaş (*Trthaber*, 2014). As a consequence, real estate prices in Bebek are extremely high and, not surprisingly, in the 2014 local elections the Republican People's Party received around 3,000 votes in this neighborhood while the JDP received only around 500.[44]

When we look at Sultanbeyli, what we see is a remarkably different setting and very low levels of support for the Republican People's Party. Sultanbeyli is located in the Anatolian part of İstanbul. It is far from the historical centre of the Anatolian part, namely Üsküdar and Kadıköy, and therefore from the wealthy waterside. Sultanbeyli's population started to increase during the 1990s as a result of large numbers of domestic immigrants from provincial Turkey. Immigration to the region also brought rapid and unorganized urbanization.[45] Despite the remarkable development of Sultanbeyli under the JDP local government, and the further incorporation of the sub-province into the capitalist-consumerist urban development in İstanbul (including the recent construction of two big shopping malls), some of the longtime landmarks of the sub-province have been squatter buildings (*gecekondular*).[46] Within the sub-province, it is rare to come across pubs or shops selling alcohol. There are only a few bookstores in the centre of Sultanbeyli, and there are no higher education institutions within its boundaries. The sub-province is home to the poorly paid working classes of İstanbul. Unlike Beşiktaş, some of the cheapest real estate options in İstanbul can be found in Sultanbeyli.

[44] See the High Election Committee (Yüksek Seçim Kurulu) website for results: https://sonuc.ysk.gov.tr/module/sspsYerel.jsf (accessed: 22 March 2016).
[45] For the rapid urbanization of Sultanbeyli and the cycles of poverty it created for the new immigrants, see the works of Pınarcıoğlu and Işık (2001, 2008).
[46] These residences are built by new immigrants without the permission of state authorities. For a vivid literary account of this kind of urban development in Turkey, see the novel by Orhan Pamuk (2015) published in English as *A Strangeness in My Mind*.

Not surprisingly, one of my interviewees associated real estate prices with voting preferences in such a way that he was able to underline the proximity of the JDP to poor people:

I mean, if the real estate prices in an area are above 500,000 Turkish liras, the people living there most probably support the Republican People's Party [. . .] For example, in Ataşehir, when the sub-province was a slum [*varoş* was the term used by my interviewee] and prices were around 100,000 or 200,000 Turkish liras, the support for the JDP [was much stronger]. Now if you go and conduct research there you would notice that those people left their land and moved to Ümraniye [a relatively low-income sub-province of İstanbul] for the construction of new buildings worth a million dollars. Now, in Ataşehir, those people were replaced with people who can afford these prices and you have the fact that as people get richer they tend to support the Republican People's Party [. . .] It is very interesting that rich people lean towards the Republican People's Party [. . .] The JDP is still the hope for the poor people [*gariban insanlar*] (Interviewee 12, 2014).

The voting patterns in Turkey indeed confirm my interviewee's association of high real estate prices with the Republican People's Party vote. However, one can also find exceptions to this pattern in relatively wealthy strongholds of the JDP: a few relatively wealthier but conservative sub-provinces in metropolitan cities, such as Keçiören in Ankara and Başakşehir in İstanbul, and several cities in the conservative Anatolian heartland of the country, such as Konya and Kayseri. In the next part of this chapter, I will elaborate on the 'low-populist' appeal of the JDP and its central role in the party's connection with the constituency profile outlined above. However, before I begin, I would like to discuss briefly the position of ethnic and sectarian differences in Turkey with regard to the high–low divide.

The High–Low Divide and Ethnic and Secterian Divisions in Turkey

In this section I would like to provide a brief insight regarding the ethnic and sectarian limitations and opportunities facing the JDP's populism. For a very long time, apart from the pro-Kurdish political parties,[47] the JDP has been the only party that had a meaningful presence in the south-eastern regions of the country where, ethnically, Kurds were dominant. At the same time, the JDP was also an extremely successful party in the inner Anatolian Turkish nationalist heartland of the country. Thus, the JDP poses the puzzle of how a single party could contain ethnic Turks and Kurds under one roof. Apart from the conservative discourse and

---

[47] For these pro-Kurdish parties, see Appendix 1.

ideology of the party, which appealed to Turks as well as to Kurds (both of whom are majority Sunni), Erdoğan's populist appeal has been decisive in keeping these mutually exclusive segments of society together under the one roof of the JDP. The following examples are very typical in the sense that they illustrate the populist rapport between Erdoğan and the conservative Kurds and Turks from the lower classes of Turkey.

During a journey from Konya to Ankara, one of my travelling companions was a staunch JDP supporter from a provincial Kurdish city. His Turkish was not at all fluent and he was apparently an ethnic Kurd. During the time, we spent together he told me that he was visiting the capital because one of his relatives was ill and he was going to benefit from the social aid services in Ankara, which were largely under the control of JDP organizations. When the discussion turned to politics, his comments illustrated the importance attached to strong male leadership by the conservative lower classes of Turkey regardless of their ethnic differences. He told me, with a heavy accent, that '*Erdoğan aslandır!* [Erdoğan is the lion!]'. At the same time, many lower-class Turkish nationalists also had a deep sympathy for Erdoğan. It is common to see comments on social media from Turkish nationalists praising Erdoğan. For instance, one comment under a pro-Erdoğan YouTube video goes as follows: 'I wish you were leading the Nationalist Action Party Reis. We love you . . .'[48]

Hence, large swathes of ethnically Turkish and Kurdish populations that were expected to support the Nationalist Action Party and the pro-Kurdish political tradition have been extremely fond of Erdoğan. Populism has certainly played a key role in this situation alongside the impact of conservative Sunni beliefs. The fact that parts of the natural constituencies of these nationalist forces have supported the populist JDP was also related to the Janus-faced nature of these political traditions. Both Turkish and Kurdish nationalism in Turkey, alongside their impact on parts of the popular sectors of Kurdish and Turkish constituencies, have appealed to a sizeable population consisting of an urban upper- and middle-class intelligentsia. Therefore, Turkish and Kurdish political parties in Turkey could be located somewhere higher than the JDP along the populism–anti-populism axis, although they are located at the

---

[48] See www.youtube.com/watch?v=ddGnXDUWJOs&t=57s (accessed: 15 December 2017). Other comments under this same video (which shows Erdoğan scolding his opponents) celebrate Erdoğan's virility in vulgar terms, illustrating the importance populist audiences place on the masculine qualities of the leader. The point here is not just the celebration of these qualities *per se* but the interpretation of them as indicators of managerial competence (that 'he – or she – can get things done!') of the leader by the popular sectors.

opposite ends of the left–right divide (this is illustrated in Appendix 2). One of the reasons for this situation has been the fact that, despite lower-class support, these movements have mostly relied upon well-defined secular ideologies (Turkish nationalism and a hybrid of socialism and Kurdish nationalism) since their foundation. This certainly helped them to appeal to better-educated groups of society, which attach importance to bookish ideologies and neat political principles, alongside lower-class ethnic Turks and Kurds. However, the very ideological nature of these movements also made their lower-class constituencies vulnerable to populist appeals.

Here, the question of how Erdoğan compensated for the decrease in Kurdish support after the end of the 'Kurdish Opening [*Kürt Açılımı*]' due to the results of the 7 June 2015 general elections, and after the the urban battles between the PKK and the security forces in Kurdish regions, becomes relevant (these developments are examined further in Chapter 8). Erdoğan compensated for this decline in support by increasingly appealing to Turkish nationalists. Populism was the bridge that helped the JDP to move back and forth along the ethnicity axis since the constituencies of the seemingly mutually exclusive political positions of Kurdish and Turkish nationalism share a common populist sensibility.

However, it is misleading to think that populism was an almighty strategic instrument that helped the JDP to maneouvre back and forth without any restriction along the left–right, ethnic and secterian axes of Turkish politics. Most notably, the appeal of Erdoğan's JDP to the Alawite population of the country has always been ineffective, to say the least. The members of this heterodox Islamic sect (*mezhep*), who come from different socio-economic backgrounds in Turkey, overwhelmingly kept supporting their traditional political choice, the Republican People's Party. It could also be the case that Kurds from different walks of life may have remained ineffective in certain localities where ethnic Turks dominate the JDP branches, such as the specific peripheral sub-provinces of İstanbul. These sectarian and ethnic limitations of the JDP's populist appeal have been well illustrated by a recent work on Kağıthane, a peripheral sub-province of İstanbul (Doğan, 2016).

Political Appeals of the JDP: From 'High' to 'Low'

In this section I illustrate that, after a temporary engagement with a much more liberal and procedural (in a sense 'high') post-Islamist appeal, the JDP has adapted a full-scale 'low' appeal. In the first sub-section, I briefly illustrate this high appeal of the party, or 'conservative democracy'. Conservative democracy served the JDP in monopolizing the centre-right field of Turkish politics and in overcoming the oppression of secularist systemic forces through the implementation of pro-democracy and pro-EU reforms. In the following sub-section, I elaborate the subsequent 'low' appeal deployed by the JDP, which clearly emerged after the first term of the party between 2002 and 2007. I illustrate that the JDP elite and the pro-JDP media have constructed a 'peripheral identity' for the party that to a great extent overlapped with what is called 'low' by Ostiguy.

Conservative Democracy: A Relatively 'High' Prologue

During the foundation of the JDP, there was a vigorous debate around whether the founding cadres of the party had sincerely given up their Islamist convictions or not. Particularly in the critical secularist and Kemalist circles, there was a strong belief that the JDP had a hidden Islamist agenda, and that the party elite had engaged in religiously permitted dissimulation (takiyye). In response, the party leader Erdoğan and prominent party members repeatedly underlined that they had founded a new centrist party that had no connection whatsoever with the Islamist National View tradition. Party intellectuals (including Yalçın Akdoğan) made a remarkable effort at building a strong case in favour of this new identity. According to Akdoğan, then chief political adviser to Erdoğan, the JDP was not an Islamist party that saw the solution for change in the seizure of the state's apparatuses (2004: 92) but a 'conservative democratic' force. Thus, during the foundation of the JDP, the conservative democratic appeal, or post-Islamist appeal as described in Chapter 1, served two aims of the party: overcoming the boundaries of a classical Islamist party base by reaching the median voter, and overcoming the secularist sensitivities of systemic actors by downplaying religious symbols and language. By using this conservative democratic appeal, the JDP could easily engage with the pro-market and pro-European Union policies and overcome the systemic actors' resistance by supporting domestic and international pro-democratic forces.

Strategically, the period from 2002 to 2007 demonstrates what Duran, a close observer of the party, refers to as the 'politics of patience' (2013: 98). As underlined by Duran, after the crisis of the 2007 presidential elections and the case opened against the JDP in 2008 attempting to ban the party, the JDP entered a new phase in which the dominant strategy became 'controlled tension' instead of 'politics of patience'. It is plausible that these attacks by the establishment created the impression among the JDP elite that the post-Islamist high appeal was not sufficient to deter danger and ensure the party's survival. In addition, in the 2009 local elections, the JDP hit rock bottom electorally by receiving only 38 per cent of the vote. Apparently, a political appeal grounded mainly on democracy, the European Union process, and rights and liberties was neither emotional enough nor sufficiently flexible and simple to keep the party's core Islamist, nationalist, conservative and low-income constituency together.

These factors together paved the way for the adaptation of the overwhelmingly populist appeal and tension-increasing strategies by the JDP elite elaborated below. During this new phase, according to Duran, the JDP elite eroded the power of the Kemalist elite (2013: 98). This change of strategy and the decline of the systemic pressure on the party gradually entailed the total dissolution of the conciliatory, democracy- and rights-based post-Islamist appeal of the JDP, in other words the high appeal of conservative democracy. In its place, the JDP elite and the pro-JDP media substituted not an Islamist but a wider 'low-populist' appeal, which aimed to deploy the resentments of the majority of the electorate about the socio-cultural inequalities in the country. In the following subsection, I focus on this low appeal of the JDP through personal observations of the image and practice of the JDP politicians, my interviews with JDP members, examination of the JDP elite's speeches and writings, and the writings of the pro-JDP columnists.

Elitist Centre versus the JDP, the Defender of the Peripheral and Downtrodden Majority: The 'Low' in Turkish Politics

The strategic calculations of the JDP elite entailed the gradual downplaying of the conservative democratic framework or 'high' appeal of the party. This is why, in most of my interviews, conducted mainly in 2014, participants rarely identified themselves with the official narrative of the party, namely conservative democracy (Interviewee 10, 2014). Instead, in some of my interviews, party members tended to refer to a rather abstract notion of the party's 'cause [*dava*]' (Interviewee 11, 2014). In one of my interviews, I had a chance to listen to the content of the JDP's cause from a high-ranking party member in a provincial city (Interviewee 48, 2014). Surprisingly, the content of the party cause was very much in line with the centre–periphery analysis of Turkish politics provided by Mardin (1973), as outlined above. According to my interviewee, this narrative refers to the domination of minority elites over the peripheral majority of the country. Here, as illustrated through further examples in the following sections, a social science narrative, namely the centre–periphery approach, was transformed into a crucial element of the JDP's political appeal.

This 'populist script' (used by my interviewee in particular and the JDP elite in general), which also deploys some of the stereotypes of right-wing political discourses in Turkey such as 'the international Jewish conspiracy',[49] identified the authoritarian modernist and Westernist political traditions of the country since the late Ottoman period as a minority yoke over the segmented religious and traditional 'silent majority' of the country. This narrative also evaluated the Republican People's Party as a continuation of the central minority oppression over the silent majority until the centre-right Democrat Party's coming to power in 1950. Nevertheless, this same 'populist script', despite the centre-right and right-wing parties' long-lasting rule in Turkey since the 1950s, also suggests that Turkey could not shake off the central elite's oppression of the conservative majority until the rise of the JDP.

According to the same interviewee, with the help of American imperialism, 'White Turks, White Kurds, capitalists and elites' owned 90 per cent of the wealth of the country while the rest, the unprivileged majority, held only 10 per cent. Hence, he identified the cause of the party, 'Great Turkey [*Büyük Türkiye*]' (or 'New Turkey [*Yeni Türkiye*]' in its contemporary interpretation by the JDP elite), which has always been a centre-right motto, as the changing of this order by the JDP. As one of my interviewees, a close observer of the party and one of the experts on centre-right politics in Turkey, underlined, it seems that this 'populist script' also had a deep impact on the world-view of the central JDP elite (Interviewee 28, 2014). In the following sub-sections, I give other examples of this centre–periphery narrative from the speeches, interviews and writings of the prominent party figures as well as the writings of the JDP supporters in the media. I will also illustrate the highly exclusionary socio-cultural or, more precisely, 'high' attitudes of some of the JDP critics.

The JDP's 'Low' Appeal and Its 'High' Critiques

Particularly since 2008, Prime Minister Erdoğan's speeches have been dominated by elements recalling this centre–periphery narrative, and therefore a 'populist script' in general. Here one should also note that, in JDP discourse, the periphery was not simply a geographical entity, but a metaphor representing the excluded social segments in urban-metropolitan as well as provincial Turkey that the JDP elite was trying

---

[49] Hence, one should locate the conspiratorial speeches of the JDP elite and the conspiratorial style in the pro-JDP media in recent years within the context of the consolidation of the party's 'low-populist' political appeal.

to reach through its 'low' appeal. Erdoğan frequently complained about the bureaucratic oligarchy in the judiciary and the state (*Sabah*, 2012a). He frequently argued that the JDP represented the 'nation' against the 'happy minorities, privileged classes and shadow power holders' (*Zaman*, 2011). He defined the mission of the JDP as the 'liberation of the social segments despised and excluded by people who think that they are superior' (*Bugün*, 2012). He ridiculed old diplomats and academics who criticized his reaction to the Israeli prime minister for being inappropriate and undiplomatic[50] at the Davos Economic Forum in 2009[51] and called them '*monşer*'[52] (*Ensonhaber*, 2009), a term that apparently carried a pejorative meaning in Erdoğan's vocabulary and which implied the so-called Westernized elite's lack of courage and responsiveness.[53]

The following parts of Erdoğan's address to the crowd on the day he declared his candidacy for the presidency of the Republic were rather typical of the above-mentioned motives characterizing the discourse of Erdoğan and the JDP elite. Here we also find a symptomatic identification of religiosity with poverty and exclusion, which reproduced a certain distinction between secular, bourgeois, metropolitan segments and religious, poor, peripheral-provincial groups:[54]

We are in politics for our worker brothers who try to earn their life decently in the mines. We are in politics for the poor people in the suburbs of Sultangazi in İstanbul and of Diyarbakır [...] We are in politics for our girls who returned from the gates of the universities due to their headscarves [...] We are in politics for the man who is despised just because he is poor. We are in politics for those with pure hearts who were ill treated and despised in hospitals, schools and government offices [...] My brothers and sisters, from the years of our early youth those who did not understand us and did not want to understand us tried to keep us out of the equation by using disparaging adjectives. They tried to despise us when we

---

[50] 'The low generally does not worry overly much about appearing improper in the eyes of the international community and also at times apparently seems to enjoy it' (Ostiguy, 2009c: 10).

[51] For the details of the event, see CNN (2009).

[52] It seems that the term originally comes from the French expression *mon cher* ('my dear'). However, in Turkish it has gained a derivative meaning which refers to the elitist, somewhat feminine and out of touch attitudes of highly educated bureaucratic cadres and upper classes.

[53] See de la Torre, quoted in Ostiguy: '[Bucaram] ridicules his rivals' delicate manners and tastes, which he contrasts to his own and the common people's masculine ones. The representation of the oligarchy as imitators of foreign and effeminate lifestyles is well received by his audiences' (Ostiguy, 2009c: 38).

[54] Pamuk, son of a rich İstanbulite family, emphasized in his memoirs of childhood and early youth that when he was a child he used to think that religion was something belonging to poor people (2012: 167–176).

were studying in Imam and Preacher Schools. They called us cleaners of the dead.[55] They called us reactionaries just because we were using the salute to God, just because we were praying to God. They looked at people coming from among the nation from a different angle just because they were taking off their shoes in their homes,[56] crossing their legs when sitting for their meals.[57] They called these people reactionaries. They looked at us from a different angle just because we were defending the values of this land. They tormented our girls just because they were wearing headscarves for their faith. As our resistance became stronger they increased their insults and assaults. Sometimes they shut down our parties. They imprisoned us for reading a poem. They used headlines arguing that we cannot even become a village headman.[58] They argued that we cannot become prime minister or president and did not consider us human when it came to elections for high office [...] They excluded us but we increased our effort, we have become stronger with every blow. We confronted statutes, headlines against us. We did not look at who said what; we only looked at what justice said, what God said (Haberler.com, 2014a).

The motives and ideas outlined in Erdoğan's speech can hardly be seen as episodic and spontaneous reactions of the party elite; they are deeply embedded in the world-view of the JDP cadres. Hence, many examples of speeches referring to the centre–periphery narrative by high-ranking JDP members could be found. According to Şentürk, the former vice-chair of the JDP organization in İstanbul, for example, the JDP was the representative of the 'masses and values called the peripheral'. On the other hand, according to Şentürk, the Republican People's Party has

---

[55] Many JDP politicians received their secondary and high school education in Imam and Preacher Schools in Turkey, which are hardly the most elite educational institutions in the country and are usually ridiculed by their opponents as the 'home of reactionaries [irtica yuvası]' and schools of 'cleaners of the dead [ölü yıkayıcı]'. The latter term is used because one of the duties of the imams is washing the corpses before they are buried with a religious ceremony.

[56] After the appointment of Durmuş Yılmaz, a highly competent technocrat, as the director of the Central Bank of Turkey by the JDP, an interesting debate was triggered by the publication of a photo in a Turkish daily. In this photo, the new director's wife was seen with a headscarf, and there were shoes in front of the main entrance of his home. After the publication of this picture, an influential columnist, Ertuğrul Özkök, openly revealed in his column his distaste for the scene reflected in the photo (2006). Another columnist from the daily rather vulgarly criticized this scene and argued that leaving shoes outside the house was an uncivilized attitude belonging to peasants (Uluengin, 2006). The attitudes of these two columnists, who were also fierce political opponents of the JDP, illustrated the predominantly socio-cultural content of the political divisions in Turkey.

[57] A low-legged portable ground table is common in poor rural and urban houses where people have to sit on the ground to have their meals.

[58] After Erdoğan was found guilty by the High Court of Appeals and banned from politics for an indefinite time because of a poem which, it was argued, incited religious hatred among the people, a Turkish daily used the following heading for describing the political prospects of Erdoğan: 'He would not even be a village headman [Muhtar bile olamayacak]' (Radikal, 1998).

always been the representative of the 'centre', in other words, of 'elites' and their values (2008b: 53). For Şentürk, elite cadres reflected their vision of the periphery by calling the majority of the country's citizens 'fools' and 'ignorant' just because they voted for the JDP (2008b: 58). This perception of Turkish politics by the JDP elite was not unsubstantiated, and the JDP elite could usually find material to use to reproduce the 'low' political appeal which constantly marked the JDP as the representative of the downtrodden majority of the country. However, in contrast to the common belief, this material did not usually stem from the distinction between the secular state and religious society. As the following example will make clear, the material originated in sociocultural inequalities. It was not unusual to see that opponents of the JDP tended to belittle the JDP supporters, and the JDP elite skilfully exploited this tendency. In a widely debated blog post published after the local elections in 2014, for example, the blogger told of his experience in a huge JDP meeting in İstanbul, which he attended 'undercover' – in other words, he pretended to be a JDP supporter:

We have to talk about this mass of people. Who are these 1 million people? They are the ignored ones [. . .] yes, they are the people that we did not recognize, who we got bored of speaking to for a while, who we tended to ignore despite their existence in front of our eyes. They are these people [. . .] Our child's babysitter, Nermin [. . .] The security guard of our gated community, Kadir [. . .] Hatice, who is working in a textile factory without insurance. Her mother, Meliha [. . .] Her brother, Şanlı [. . .] Uncle Necati, who retired from the municipality. They are the police, [. . .] the firemen, [. . .] a bus driver, [. . .] workers in the subcontractor's building sites [. . .] They are the people who work without CVs [. . .] They are those people who did not bring a single newspaper with them [. . .] They are those people who do not look at their smartphones, look at the internet, who do not know about Twitter, who do not know how to take a 'selfie' [. . .] They are the people who raise their flags with an order, [. . .] who obey. They are the people who are shorter than I am because of malnutrition [. . .] They are the ones who have always been given orders throughout their lives [. . .] They are the people who obey lest they starve (Öztop, 2014).

One should also add that not only the supporters of the JDP but the JDP elite were usually despised by their opponents and, as is the case with Latin American populists, it is very common to hear such statements against the JDP politicians from urban upper classes: 'this kind of people should not be in the government' or 'this kind of people cannot rule over me'.[59]

---

[59] 'These characteristics are important not only or mainly as cultural markers of social differences, but as cultural modes, or ways of being, that play a large part in the "economy of affection and dislikes" in social relations – whether direct or imagined. This phenomenon comes to the fore in common utterances such as: "I don't want to

In addition to popular bloggers, some very well-known columnists and fierce opponents of the JDP also despised JDP supporters. Just after the JDP victory in the 2007 early general elections, a columnist and well-known opponent of the JDP in the Turkish daily *Hürriyet* blamed the JDP voters and argued that their votes were for sale at a very low price. He called anyone who voted for the JDP a 'barrel-head [*bidon kafalı*]' (Özdil, 2007). In the same daily, another columnist rather openly despised the JDP voters in his article entitled 'The Man Who Scratches His Belly [*Göbeğini kaşıyan adam*]':

He scratches his belly [. . .] He does not like news. He likes TV entertainment shows [. . .] He does not read [. . .] He does not know newspapers. The only newspaper that he knows is the newspaper from last year that he spread under the pickle jars. His most comprehensive view on leaders is that 'he is a Muslim guy' and on democracy, it is 'let him steal but get things done'. Then, he scratches his belly. This is the man that Tayyip Erdoğan trusted when he says 'ballot box for everything' (Coşkun, 2007).

As I have tried to illustrate, not only the self-identification of the JDP elite but also the opponents of the party have helped to create a very solid high–low divide in Turkish politics.

The Pro-JDP Media and Intellectuals against 'White Turks': 2014 Presidential Elections

Another stereotype that has become quite widespread in recent years, that of 'white Turks', is deeply embedded in the centre–periphery narrative outlined above, and therefore in the high–low divide of the country. One quite frequently comes across the use of this term by the members and supporters of the JDP to identify the opponents of the party.[60] According to a columnist who writes for the pro-JDP *Yenişafak*, for example, the white Turks were deeply disturbed by the fact that conservative people have become their flatmates instead of being their apartment staff (*kapıcı*). He also argued that white Turks could not take Erdoğan's rise, as he is an Imam and Preacher School graduate and has his background in provincial Turkey, in Rize (Esayan, 2014b).

This narrative and the images embedded in it were diligently reproduced by the pro-JDP media for the presidential elections in 2014.

associate with *ese tipo de gente* [that kind of people]" or "I don't want people *like that* in government", or even more simply: "Yes, I can relate to [name of politician]!'" (Ostiguy, 2009c: 10–11) (italics Ostiguy's).

[60] One of my interviewees also used the term to describe the critics and opponents of the JDP: Interviewee 37, 2014.

Although there was no doubt about his religious beliefs due to his previous position as the secretary general of the Organization of Islamic Co-operation, even the joint candidate of the opposition parties, Ekmeleddin İhsanoğlu, was delegitimized by the pro-JDP media on the grounds of his alleged elitism. According to a columnist in a pro-JDP daily, *Türkiye*, there was a crude elitism in every compliment to İhsanoğlu. According to this particular columnist, İhsanoğlu was a 'devout of the lounge [*salon dindarı*]' who was much closer to the 'white Turk circles' than to religious masses and who was always 'praised by the elite and the mainstream media due to his academic career' (Oğur, 2014a).

In contrast, pro-JDP journalists framed the story of Erdoğan as the son of a modest domestic immigrant family in İstanbul who received his education in an Imam and Preacher School. According to this narrative, Erdoğan knows the streets of İstanbul. He played football and came from within the political organizations of the Islamist National View by working within its every echelon. He suffered for his political ideals. In short, 'he has a story that appeals to the people [...] In his story we encounter someone who has come from the lower class and has climbed the ladder of life despite suffering due to various impediments' (Kaplan, 2014). According to Selvi, on the other hand, İhsanoğlu knew little about Turkey and the Turkish people, and he did not know the problems of the country: 'he has not smelled the sweat of this people and shared their bread. He has lived abroad three times longer than he lived in Turkey' (2014). Hence, while Erdoğan was described as a 'man of the people', his opponents were called a 'cosmopolitan elite'.

However, it would be misleading to evaluate the comments of the pro-JDP media on Erdoğan as a PR activity, a distorted public-image-making process. Some news reports indeed confirmed the 'low' political style of Erdoğan. According to a news article in *Radikal*, in a meeting with the JDP deputies Erdoğan harshly criticized some of them for not going to their electoral regions frequently and for spending too much time on Twitter. It was argued that he warned the deputies with the following words: 'Is it possible to be such a thing as a deputy who does not visit his electoral region? You either do not become the candidate for the parliament or, if you do, you have to do what this position requires. You cannot fulfil this requirement by using Twitter. You have to go in person and hug them, you have to smell the dung [*tezek*]' (*Radikal*, 2010). It was also argued by an opposition deputy that he slapped some of the deputies and ministers, and also insulted them quite frequently (*Radikal*, 2013). There were also some news reports on how Erdoğan scolded the deputies of the JDP (*Radikal*, 2004).[61] These incidents were indicators of the 'low' leadership style of Erdoğan. Erdoğan decisively, and to a great extent naturally, deployed the assets of 'low-populist' appeal/style.[62]

The Strategic Role of the Low-Populist Appeal for the JDP Politics

What exactly was the role of populist appeal in the overall scheme of JDP politics? The use of the term 'periphery' to identify the social segments represented by the JDP, and, therefore the use of the low-populist appeal in general, most notably, allowed the party elite to locate the party within a longer historical tradition of previous centre-right parties and thus in a wider social, cultural and political milieu.[63] The concepts of periphery and thus of the low appeal, which lacks rigid boundaries, have helped the JDP elite to reach more radical segments of the electorate, such as Islamists and Turkish nationalists, at the same time that they reached the median voter.

It seems that the concept of the periphery as the marker of a loose political identity, which flexibly included people from different political, social and ethnic backgrounds, was at the same time the framework of the elite alliance of the JDP. Since most of the members of the JDP high echelons, such as the Central Executive Committee and the Central Decision and Administration Board, came from different political backgrounds such as the True Path Party, the Motherland Party, the Islamist National View tradition and the Nationalist Action Party, overplaying a rigid party identity that explicitly referred to an Islamist, nationalist or liberal ideological framework would have been detrimental to the elite alliance of the party. It would also have limited the JDP's space for flexibility in terms of policies by decisively ruling out some of the options that might be seen as mutually exclusive with a less flexible political identity. Instead, the party leadership practically embraced the distinction between the centre and the periphery, which to a great extent overlapped with the high–low divide in politics. This also helped the party to contain seemingly contradictory social and economic policies at the same time.

---

[61]   Compare this with Ostiguy's arguments: '[the low] values and displays physical contact, use of slang. The body of the low is always at the forefront' (2013: 12–13).

[62]   I analyse Erdoğan's centrality to the party and his low appeal (more precisely the political cultural axis of the JDP's low appeal) in detail in the chapter on the JDP leadership.

[63]   Many discussions can be found on the role of the JDP with regard to the history of Turkish political parties. The party elite made a deliberate effort to place the party within the longer history of the centre-right tradition in Turkey. See Akdoğan (2004).

More importantly, and from the perspective of this work in particular, the 'low-populist' appeal of the JDP had another critical function: this kind of 'appeal/style' played a vital role in the construction by the JDP elite of the massive membership organization and its robust local presence in low-income, peripheral settings by successfully resonating with the vocabulary, language and imagination of the popular sectors of Turkey. The next section of this chapter reveals the fact that the central JDP elite had a sharp awareness of the importance of the low-populist appeal in electoral mobilization and prepares the ground for the following discussions regarding the party's organization in Chapters 5 and 6.

Form of the Message: A Conscious Engagement with the 'Low'

In the use of communication instruments, the JDP elite and cadres followed a strategy which was also consistent with the place of the 'low' in the party's political appeal. Simplicity, modesty and adherence to 'popular realism'[64] can be defined as the main stylistic characteristics of the JDP's communication activities. The JDP was always much more successful at interpreting its message into the receivers' language than any of its rivals in the party system.

Simplicity

One of the main pieces of advice given to JDP candidates by the party headquarters and the party elite was to use simple language for electoral campaigns. According to Şentürk, a former JDP vice-chair in İstanbul, messages sent by the parties or individual candidates should be aimed at the targeted constituency (2008a: 104). Şentürk's recommendations also reflect the wider relevance of the high–low divide in Turkish politics:

Socialist discourses in particular have no influence over large segments of society in our country. Why? There are of course many reasons, but the form of the message has a significant place among them [...] They not only use invented words instead of the words used by the people, but they also use very complicated

---

[64] I borrow the term 'popular realism' from Bourdieu's seminal work *Distinction* to identify the practical world-view of the working people, the majority of the electorate, who evaluate practices on the basis of their function, outside aesthetical and abstract frameworks (1984: 200). In politics, popular realism would also lead the majority of the electorate towards a much more cautious attitude regarding unrealistic economic promises of politicians, as well as towards political propaganda that depends on abstract concepts such as the welfare state, democracy and liberties.

words [...] In our country, the average education level of the electorate is the fourth year of primary school. Therefore, the message to the masses should be at the level of the fourth year of primary school (2008a: 105).

Şentürk contends that slogans like 'we are uncompromisingly going to protect the secular republic' or 'we will develop the welfare state' do not make any sense to the 'average citizen', the 'man on the street': 'How many people know the concept of the welfare state? In the coffee houses of the slums how many times is the concept of the welfare state used?' (Şentürk 2008a: 97). Hence, it is safe to argue that the JDP elite had a keen awareness of the importance of the use of the 'low' in Turkish politics.

The guide for candidate deputies published by JDP headquarters also repeatedly underlines the importance of modifying the message according to the circumstances and keeping it simple and straightforward. According to this guide, candidates and election office workers should have clear and straightforward answers to the questions of voters: 'We should [...] avoid polished narratives. We should not ramble and we must not forget that our main aim is not to feel good but to transmit our message to our addressee' (AK Parti, 2007: 14). According to the JDP elite, the party will not be successful in election periods if they are 'seen as intellectual', or use 'polished expressions' and 'heavy concepts' (Şentürk, 2008a: 84). Hence, the JDP embraces concrete language and defined concrete political targets in its electoral propaganda, for the JDP elite contends that the lower the education level of the electorate, the more they are prone to concrete as opposed to abstract thinking (Şentürk, 2008b: 41).

This was why the most widely known and enduring slogans of the JDP were those with a concrete and a simple message designed to appeal to large segments of society. Slogans such as 'We don't stop, we keep going [Durmak yok, yola devam]', 'It used to be a dream, it is now realized [Hayaldi, gerçek oldu]' and 'Always nation, always service [Daima millet, daima hizmet]' had simple and concrete messages that underlined the achievements of the 'hard-working' JDP cadres and their service-oriented outlook.[65] The JDP propaganda always pointed out the practical achievements of the party and always implied how 'resourceful' (or 'street smart') the JDP cadres could be.[66] Here one is also reminded of

---

[65] See Yavuz (2009) and M. Çınar (2013) for the importance of the emphasis on service delivery in JDP propaganda and politics.

[66] A sub-provincial mayor from the JDP defined himself with the following words: 'I do not have any extraordinary power. But I have the backing of this government as a mayor. I somewhat also have my own abilities: I have some lubricity, some gumption, some

the electoral slogan of the JDP: 'I do not look at words, I look at accomplishments! [*Lafa değil icraata bakarım!*]'. Hence, there has always been a classic statement about Turkish politics, particularly for ruling centre-right parties: 'They steal but they work hard! [*Çalıyorlar ama çalışıyorlar!*]'.[67]

Modesty

Not only the simplicity of the message but also the modesty of the candidate has been apparently seen as an important political asset by the JDP elite. For instance, according to Şentürk's recommendations, candidates should avoid expensive clothes lest the electorate feel a status gap (2008a: 123). Similarly, in her column, Ayşe Böhürler, one of the founders of the JDP, warns the individual candidates against 'branded, shiny or ostentatious accessories' (2013). Both the image and style of candidates and party members in general were taken seriously by the JDP elite. Hence, Böhürler also warned the candidates against transmiting an arrogant image (2013). The JDP guide for deputy candidates underlined the importance of being modest, too: 'you should not create the mood that you know the best, you should be moderate and you should avoid extravagance' (AK Parti, 2007: 12). According to the same guide, candidates should not use didactic language: 'The way to approach the people is by revealing that you are a part of the life they have' (AK Parti, 2007: 13).

Strikingly, the guide also emphasizes that the 'electoral process is not a didactic but an emotional one' (AK Parti, 2007: 15). In JDP propaganda, candidates are told to be 'friendly and sincere', and that they should avoid 'pretentious' attitudes (AK Parti, 2007: 11). This is why one of the founding figures of the JDP warns the candidates against excessively devout images: 'an excessively religious appearance makes people think that you are pretentious' (Böhürler, 2013). This recommendation is rather important since there is still a widespread belief that the JDP exploits the religious feelings of the masses. It seems that the JDP's appeal to the lower segments of the society had less to do with religious symbols than with a genuine engagement with the 'low' through simplicity, modesty and sincerity.

---

guile, and I use these for finding, for gouging money from the metropolitan municipality, from Ankara in order to deliver services in Beşikdüzü' (*Cumhuriyet*, 2017a).

[67] For a very similar situation in Latin America, see Ostiguy: 'These leaders often also claim that they "don't talk, but get things done", although most of them do talk more than their share. In a classic statement on Adhemar de Barros in Brazil, it was said without shame that: *"Rouba, mas faz!"*– that is, "He steals, but he gets things done!"' (2013: 8–9).

Another incident mentioned in the guide by Şentürk illustrated the importance of modesty as an asset in Turkish politics. It is hard to verify whether this anecdote conveyed by Şentürk is true or not. Yet even the fact that it was related by one of the JDP elites was emblematic of their stylistic approach to politics:

Let me tell you what is said about Recep Tayyip Erdoğan: 'They went to a poor household and inside it was dirty and smelled. While people around Erdoğan did not know what to do and their disturbance could be read from their faces, Erdoğan immediately crossed his legs and sat down in front of the [low-legged] table on the ground. He started to drink the soup in the common bowl with a spoon with such a great appetite that this established a warm connection between him and the owner of the house' (Şentürk, 2006: 155).

This example clearly illustrates the limits of understanding populism 'as words' and demonstrates the centrality of 'manners' and 'ways of doing things' (Ostiguy, 2017) in grasping the populist phenomenon. Party programmes and speeches of party elites only to a certain extent help to understand the populist phenomenon. This example also tells us a lot about the content of the direct and unmediated link between the leader and the supporters: it is the style as well as emotions (love, resentment, candour) that are central to the construction of populist rapport. Therefore, researchers should avoid reifying populism by simply focusing on the leader, the party and the 'text', and they should take into serious consideration the broader 'relationship' between performer and receiver/audience, as well as the wider political environment, including 'high' political opponents.

Taking 'Popular Realism' into Account: 'Cautious Promises' and 'Managerial Competence'

The necessity of simplicity, modesty and having concrete content as put forward in the political propaganda did not mean that the JDP used a simple strategy of abundant promises. The JDP elite contended that the electorate was not illogical and that they could easily distinguish realizable promises from unrealizable ones (Şentürk, 2008a: 46). As Çaha and Guida observed, this was indeed the practice in the JDP's campaigns. In contrast, the Republican People's Party, for instance, was not so careful with its promises in the 2009 local elections. According to the authors, the Republican People's Party's generous promises were not found to be convincing by the majority of the electorate (Çaha and Guida, 2011: 78–79). According to Çınar, the JDP, by comparison, always kept its promises limited, avoided binding redistributive strategies and gained a lot from fulfilling these 'downsized promises' in their time in office (M. Çınar, 2013: 38). Indeed, as one of my interviewees, a senior researcher for the JDP, emphasized, the party always avoided binding redistributive promises, and this contributed to the credibility of its leadership in the eyes of the electorate:

> You know, in the first JDP election campaign, the Prime Minister [Erdoğan] said this: 'do not expect anything from us for three or four years' [. . .] Citizens voted for such a party [. . .] What was our presumption? If you do not make promises to the citizens . . . I mean communication experts say such things like they should find the answer to 'what's in it for me?' [stated in English]. What is that? Unreserved promises. Citizens can find the answer of 'what's in it for me' in the other strategy, too. He says, 'Dude, I do not want anything from the state in a stable economy. [The only thing the state needs to do is] not steal the money in my pocket through inflation and interest rates, etc. I can already earn my living. [Let the government] not cast a shadow [over my life].' It was the concern of citizens. These were the results of our research (Interviewee 38, 2014).

Apart from the above-mentioned stylistic characteristics of the JDP propaganda, the party leader and his managerial achievements occupied a special place in the party's political appeal. This was why one of Erdoğan's frequent assaults (also in line with the 'low' appeal) against the opposition leaders of the Republican People's Party and the Nationalist Action Party highlighted their managerial incompetence: 'Never entrust three Karaman sheep to Baykal and Bahçeli. Believe me, they would lose them even in this Tayyare Square; they cannot herd them at all' (*Gazetevatan*, 2009). The JDP propaganda relied heavily on Erdoğan, his projects, his achievements and his so-called managerial competence.

Conclusion: The High–Low Divide and the Political Agency of Erdoğan's JDP

In the previous chapter, I illustrated the structure of the party system and the patterns in elite-level conflicts, and demonstrated how these structural aspects of Turkish party politics have deeply shaped the political appeal and organization of the party. The (formerly Islamist, and then populist) JDP elite responded to the structural constraints and opportunities that stemmed from the logic of party competition and elite-level power configurations by moderating its stance and appealing to the median voter (alongside a core Islamist constituency) as well as constructing a reliable, powerful party organization that can ensure its political survival *vis-à-vis* powerful secularist elite contenders.

In this chapter, I took a further step and focused on the details of the socio-cultural structures that lie beneath the political divides in Turkey and how the JDP has responded to these socio-cultural divides. I have shown that, after a temporary engagement with relatively 'high' conservative democratic appeal, the JDP elite quickly realized the ineffectiveness of this high appeal in indefinitely deterring any systemic pressure. The post-Islamist conservative democratic appeal was also insufficient to maintain a very heterogeneous electorate that included low-income segments, core Islamist voters and median voters. As a result, the low-populist appeal of the JDP came to the fore around 2007–2008. However, this decisive and irreversible inclination towards populism was more than a tactical manoeuvre for the JDP elite. Populism had in fact been waiting in the background to be deployed. Populism, in a sense, was the most compatible political appeal and provided a flexible identity for Erdoğan's JDP, given the socio-cultural basis of political divides in Turkey that have been illustrated so far in this chapter, and given the background of the JDP politicians and the composition of the party's electoral basis.

'Low-populism' as an appeal/style was also highly compatible with the resilient, warring organization that the JDP elite wanted to construct and sustain due to the hostile political environment that included powerful elite contenders. The resilience that the JDP elite were looking for certainly was not simply an ideological one (such as that sought by classical mass parties), but was instead related to the membership profiles that the JDP leadership sought. The populist appeal/style helped the JDP elite to create an organization that primarily relied on the most unprivileged segments of Turkish society. This was crucial, because the JDP elite had always waited for elite interventions and wanted to be prepared for these interventions when they came. They wanted to capitalize on the brinksmanship of the popular sectors. As I will illustrate in the following chapters, when this kind of intervention came in the form of a bloody coup on 15 July 2016, populism – and the robust organizational leverage built upon this appeal – proved itself extremely potent.

Thus, alongside Chapter 2, this chapter is an attempt to redefine the structural components of Turkish politics, but this time in socio-cultural terms, and to outline how the JDP elite has responded to them. In the next chapter, I will focus on the personalistic leadership of the JDP and the political cultural dimension of the party's populism. Through the discussions regarding the JDP's populism in this chapter and the personalistic leadership of the party in the next, I also aim to give the reader context for the following chapters, which focus on the JDP's strategy and organization. The JDP's populist appeal and its leader's personalistic political conduct, after all, not only provided the party with strong discursive and stylistic bonds with its low-income electorate, but also prepared the ground for the JDP elite to easily construct a massive membership organization, particularly in low-income localities across Turkey. I will remind readers of this particular role that populism and personalism played in JDP politics in Chapters 5 and 6.

4   The JDP and Erdoğan: Non-Charismatic Personalism

Introduction

Since its foundation in 2002, the Justice and Development Party in Turkey, under the leadership of Erdoğan, won several elections by receiving around 35–50 per cent of all votes. Many studies underlined the role of Erdoğan in this unprecedented electoral achievement by the JDP, and some of these studies explicitly argued that the achievements of the party could be understood primarily on the grounds of Erdoğan's 'charisma' and his direct appeal to the electorate.[1] In this chapter, I argue that, contrary to this widespread belief, Erdoğan was not a charismatic leader and that his authority over the JDP organization derived from another source: 'robust action' or 'diligence in organization building'.

Before analysing the relationship between Erdoğan and the JDP, I discuss the relationships between the concepts of personalization, personalism, charismatic personalism, non-charismatic personalism and personal party personalism in the second section. In the third section, I evaluate the case of Erdoğan and the JDP. I argue that, despite his very strong and popular public image (broadly his 'low-populist' appeal) and autonomy of leadership, Erdoğan's political ascent occurred within a stable political climate and he did not have any transformational impact on his followers, supporters and members of his organization in terms of their identities and world-views. Details of Erdoğan's biography demonstrated the fact that he is a diligent, innovative and pragmatic 'organization man [teşkilatçı]' exclusively focused on achieving and maintaining power. In order to do this, Erdoğan relied heavily on a large and pervasive organization personally constructed and firmly controlled by him. In the fourth and fifth sections, I incorporate the discussion in this chapter

---

[1] Many accounts of the rise and success of the JDP highlight the role of its leader. For instance, Hale and Özbudun (2010: 154–155), Tuğal (2009: 176), Cizre (2008a: 5), Tezcür (2012: 122) and Heper and Toktaş (2003: 160) stress the role of Erdoğan. Some other accounts, such as E. Yıldırım et al. (2007) and Sambur (2009), explicitly argue that Erdoğan's 'charisma' was vital in the party's electoral achievements.

on Erdoğan with the overall argument of the book on the role of agency (political appeal and organization) in the political success of Erdoğan's JDP. Defining the true nature of Erdoğan's leadership style is crucial, because as long as researchers evaluate him as a charismatic leader they will continue to ignore the remarkable contribution of a large and pervasive organization in the electoral achievements and the political resilience of the JDP.

Three Faces of Personalism

In this section, I discuss the relationships between the concepts of personalization, personalism, charismatic personalism, non-charismatic personalism and personal party personalism. I firstly demonstrate the difference between personalization and personalism. From the perspective of this distinction, I examine the concepts of charisma, non-charismatic personalism and personal party personalism as different reflections of personalism in politics.

Personalization and Personalism

The rising role of personalities in politics in the past several decades has been underlined by many political scientists. From the perspective of studies on political communication, the 'mediatization of politics' (Mazzoleni and Schulz, 1999) was strongly connected to the increasing importance of group leaders at the cost of collective identities. This was seen as one of the reasons behind personalized political leadership (Mazzoleni, 2000). From the perspective of studies on party politics, as the role of individual candidates within parties became more important, personalization in the media increased, and this in turn enhanced the personalization of the behaviours of politicians (Rahat and Sheafer, 2007). The rise of catch-all parties and new communications technologies, combined with the gradual retreat of squarely programmatic and ideological mass parties (and the social cleavages these parties relied upon), has provided a suitable ground for the increasing prominence of the candidates and, most notably, the party leaders (Blondel et al., 2010). This wider process of personalization of politics – in other words, the increasing role of personalities and the decreasing role of ideologies and programmes, together with the salience of political parties – has strong connections with the change of communications technologies (McAllister, 2007).[2]

[2] See also Balmas et al. (2014).

A very broad description of the 'personalization' of politics has been developed by Rahat and Sheafer, according to whom 'personalization should be seen as a process in which the political weight of the individual actor in the political process increases over time, while the centrality of the political group (i.e., political party) declines' (2007: 65). Ansell and Fish very similarly and broadly define 'personalism' as 'loyalty to persons rather than to impersonal ideologies, institutions, or rules' (1999: 286). However, personalization and personalism should be seen as different notions despite the common ground. As a broader phenomenon, personalization has implications for local and national leadership as well as the representation of politics in the media.

Thus, I tend to see personalism as a more specific concept, something particularly related to styles of top national leaders in political groups and organizations that are mostly working against collective-institutional arrangements and identities. Following this differentiation, the phenomena of charismatic personalism, non-charismatic personalism and personal party personalism can be considered to be different reflections of personalism in contemporary politics. However, these different reflections of personalism can be easily conflated due to their many common features, and this confusion could lead researchers to quick and misleading overestimations of the role of personalities in politics. In the following sub-sections of this theoretical section, I try to distinguish these different reflections for a better understanding of contemporary political leadership in context of its interaction with followers, supporters and organizations.

The Concept of Charisma

Like many other social science concepts, the concept of charisma has a much wider use beyond the academic sphere. This broad usage led to unsystematic and descriptive uses of the term 'charisma', which was frequently used simply as an adjective referring to a superior leadership performance or a popular image. In fact, the concept has a very specific meaning in its original use by Weber. In his wider discussion regarding the pure types of legitimate authority structures, Weber separately evaluates charismatic authority and distinguishes this form from the rational-legal and the traditional legitimate authority (1974: 46–47). In the case of rational-legal authority, obedience is owed to the 'legally established impersonal order', and in the case of traditional legitimacy structures, it is owed to the 'traditionally sanctioned position of authority' (Weber, 1974: 47). Unlike these pro-status quo legitimacy structures, in charismatic authority, obedience is mainly produced on the grounds of the personal qualities of the leader (Weber, 1974: 47).

Charisma was seen as an exceptional phenomenon by Weber. According to Weber, the phenomenon of charisma can be observed under the circumstances of 'distress', when the followers usually attribute 'supernatural gifts' to the charismatic leader (Weber, 1946: 245). Weber also defines charisma in contradistinction to any kind of bureaucratic, institutional and permanent structure (1946: 248). He underlines the role of personal strength and complete surrender of the followers to the charismatic leader as other indicators of the phenomenon (Weber, 1946: 249). According to Weber, charismatic personalities are, most of the time, outside family life and its routines (Weber, 1946: 248). In contrast to conservative and institutional routines, Weber states, one of the indicators of charisma is a revolutionary spirit:

Genuine charismatic domination therefore knows of no abstract legal codes and statutes and of no 'formal' way of adjudication. Its 'objective' law emanates concretely from the highly personal experience of heavenly grace and from the god-like strength of the hero. Charismatic domination means a rejection of all ties to any external order in favour of the exclusive glorification of the genuine mentality of the prophet and hero. Hence, its attitude is revolutionary and transvalues everything; it makes a sovereign break with all traditional or rational norms: 'It is written, but I say unto you' (1946: 250).

Given the indicators, circumstances and examples Weber has provided, such as 'national distress', 'prophets' and 'heroes', 'the attribution of supernatural powers to the leader' and a 'revolutionary spirit', it is clear that he considered charisma a genuinely rare and exceptional phenomenon. From the perspective of Weber's discussion, charisma can be seen as an original-mythical source for new, stable and legitimate authority structures. This is why Tucker underlines the fact that charismatic leaders were also defined by their radical proposal of a new way of life and existence (1968: 746).

In his later examination of Weber's notion of charisma, Tucker also underlines another important feature of charisma. According to Tucker, there will be a spontaneous formation of at least a small circle of followers identifiable at the early phases, before the leader has become politically powerful, if the concept of charisma is relevant for a given case (1968: 739–742). The concept of charisma should therefore be seen as something strongly affiliated with the circumstances of deep political crises as well as a revolutionary spirit which breaks ties with the current regime and existing institutional and traditional authority structures. Charismatic leaders usually introduce new ideological and intellectual narratives to their followers and expect them to follow this transformational narrative embodied by their personality. Charisma refers not only to superior leadership qualities or a popular image, but also to an intellectual and moral authority that reshapes its followers and provides them with a new identity.

A clear distinction between charismatic and other forms of leadership from the perspective of political organizations can be found in the seminal work of Panebianco on political parties. Panebianco differentiates more usual occurrences of prestige and authority from charisma. To a great extent Panebianco follows the distinction made by Weber and underlines the revolutionary character of charisma as well as its anti-institutional and anti-bureaucratic tendencies which observe no legal, permanent pattern except the charismatic leader's will (1988: 143–144). Panebianco also applies the Weberian concept to party organizations and underlines several indicators of a 'charismatic party'. For Panebianco, charismatic parties are defined by a 'cohesive dominant coalition held together by loyalty to the leader' that has no room for factional politics (1988: 145). Charismatic parties, according to Panebianco, do not reveal bureaucratic characteristics. He also asserts the 'revolutionary', 'anti-party' character of charismatic parties as well as the 'total symbiosis between the leader and the organizational identity' in these kinds of political organizations (Panebianco, 1988: 147). In a sense, Panebianco tends to see strong, highly routinized and remarkably bureaucratized organizations (like the one the JDP had, as I will illustrate in the following chapters) in contradistinction to the charismatic party, while underlining the importance of a revolutionary, 'transformational'[3] leadership with a high degree of autonomy *vis-à-vis* the leader's followers and supporters.

Non-Charismatic Personalism and 'Robust Action'

Non-charismatic personalism is a much more ordinary phenomenon than charismatic personalism. This is why Ansell and Fish strongly underline the exceptional features of charisma, stating that 'charismatic leadership is no ordinary occurrence. It transforms the audience [...] The charismatic leader is a prophet, not merely a personality' (Ansell and Fish, 1999: 284). In addition, Ansell and Fish contend that 'leaders of charismatic parties assume – or attempt to assume – transformational

---

[3] The distinction between transactional and transformational leadership is well established in the literature on leadership studies. It was introduced by MacGregor Burns during the 1970s (2010). For Burns, transactional leadership is based on exchange of goods or valued things between leaders and followers, whereas transformational leadership is based on strong emotional, ideological and moral bonds. In contrast to transactional leadership, transformational leadership seeks to provide a new identity and morality to its followers.

roles. They regard themselves as agents of massive social change tran-
scending the party or even any particular ideology or program. Their
main source of identity is themselves, and their personal style is
messianic. They maintain power by holding their followers in thrall'
(1999: 288). In contrast to the exceptional transformational roles of
charismatic leaders, non-charismatic types of personalistic leadership
have 'transactional roles' (Ansell and Fish, 1999: 288). Non-charismatic
personalist leaders are mainly brokers of power among different segments and groups within party organizations, and their authority derives
from this role. In other words, their identity is rooted in the party itself,
and they attach greater importance to the party's cohesion and effectiveness than to political principles (Ansell and Fish, 1999: 288). According
to Ansell and Fish, they maintain this role and make themselves indispensable through 'robust action', which refers to 'an aptitude for speaking effectively to multiple, often diverse, audiences within the party and
for convincing each audience that he or she represents its interests and
aspirations' (1999: 288–289).

For Ansell and Fish, in non-charismatic personalistic parties, leaders
have great personal authority and are symbols of their organizations.
However, they lack the exceptional features of charismatic leaders who
aim to transform their followers (1999: 283). In its place, non-
charismatic personalist leaders use 'robust action' – a multi-faceted,
proactive and energetic effort – to deal with multiple flows of requests
coming from diverging groups and local settings within the organization.
In the original exposition of the concept of 'robust action' by Ansell and
Fish (1999) and Padgett and Ansell (1993), the authors put a strong
emphasis on its transactional role in conciliating diverse interests. However, I see extremely tiring physical, bodily activity as equally essential to
robust action, which requires endless travelling, speeches and negotiations undertaken by the party leader. This is why, I tend to define
'robust action' as the transactional role undertaken by the party leader
via an extremely proactive political effort that consists of extensive travelling, numerous meetings and countless speeches with diverse audiences within the party for intra-party governance. Robust action
increases the party leader's control over the local and centrifugal tendencies within the party, and it also increases party cohesion. Hence, in line
with Ansell and Fish, it seems important to distinguish charismatic forms
of personalism from the more common form of non-charismatic
personalism. As underlined above, revolutionary and transformational
roles exceptionally claimed by charismatic personalist leaders are differentiated from non-charismatic personalism, which relies on a diligent
organization-building effort or 'robust action'.

The Personal Party

Another common reflection of personalism in contemporary politics which can help us better understand the case of the JDP and Erdoğan is the 'personal party'[4] and the overwhelming centrality of political leaders in rapidly rising and falling contemporary political parties. Alongside the ideal typical example of Berlusconi's various parties in Italy as analysed by McDonnell (2013), the rapid rise and fall of parties of many populist leaders in Latin America can be seen as examples of personal party personalism. According to McDonnell, personal parties are defined by the centrality of the leader's decisions and presence in the rise and fall of the party, the lack of any stable, permanent grass-roots organization, the absolute concentration of power in the hands of the leader and the centrality of the party leader in the campaign strategies of the party (2013: 222). Given the features underlined by McDonnell (2013), personal parties strongly resemble non-charismatic personalism. However, in line with Ansell and Fish (1999), one should strongly emphasize the fact that, unlike personal parties, in non-charismatic personalism leaders put enormous effort into organization building and attach importance to permanent organizational structures. Hence, while strategically the emphasis in non-charismatic personalism is on the organization, in the personal party the emphasis is on the leader.

Thus, it would be better to think of charismatic personalism, non-charismatic personalism and personal party personalism as related yet different – but not exhaustive – reflections of the broader notion of personalism in politics. I summarize the common and distinguishing features of these three faces of personalism in Table 4.1. A strong public image of the leader and the excessive concentration of power in the hands of leaders (leadership autonomy) represent the common ground of these different forms of personalism. This could also lead researchers to conflate these different forms of personalism since the prominence of a 'leader's persona' is essential to all. However, there are also decisive differences among these forms with regard to political and social circumstances and the linkages between leaders and their followers, supporters and organizations. While charismatic personalism is an outcome of extraordinary political and social circumstances, non-charismatic and personal party personalism are products of the status quo. In charismatic

---

[4] The first systematic use of the concept of 'personal party' is found in a book titled *The Personal Party*, written by Italian political scientist Mauro Calise, which was published in Italian in 2000 (McDonnell, 2013: 221). See also a short description of the concept by Calise (2005: 96–99) in English. In this part of the chapter, however, I rely extensively on McDonnell (2013) since I do not know Italian.

Table 4.1 *Three faces of personalism*

Types of personalism			
Features	Charismatic	Non-charismatic	Personal party
Public image of the leader	Strong	Strong or weak	Strong
Degree of leadership autonomy	High	High	High
Political and social context	Crisis/distress	Status quo	Status quo
Engagement with followers/ supporters	Transformational	Transactional	Transactional
Organization-building efforts	Low	High (robust action)	Low

Source: Author's compilation.

personalism, the leader enthrals the followers and supporters and transforms them in line with the leader's particular world-view – either a
narrow and specifically interpreted ideology, a new religion or a loose
yet peculiarly radical outlook.

In contrast, in non-charismatic and personal party personalism,
leaders have a transactional role. They are located either in the centre
of various politically salient social and individual actors through the use
of media and extensive patronage networks, and/or within a large and
pervasive organization through robust action. Instead of transforming
the audience, they connect various segments of their followers to
unified political action in return for material-selective-individual and/or
ideational-collective benefits. However, while the grass-roots organization in particular, and the party organization in general, can be seen as a
secondary instrument in this transactional political activity in the personal party, organization building has been the basis and the main aim of
the transactional role of leader in non-charismatic personalism, as the
case of the JDP reveals.

Charismatic Personalism and Contemporary Populism:
Examples from Turkey and Beyond

Before the detailed sections on Erdoğan, it would be useful to have a look
at a few genuinely charismatic leaders in order to highlight the true
nature of Erdoğan's leadership (and its non-charismatic quality).
I would like to discuss one from the context of Turkey and make an
overall comment on a few other charismatic leaders from other contexts

in order to illustrate their differences and commonalities. The only charismatic leadership at a national scale in recent Turkish history was Mustafa Kemal Atatürk (1881–1938), the founder of the modern Turkish Republic. From the perspective of the preceding discussion, there were at least three dimensions that made Atatürk a genuinely charismatic leader. First of all, from a very early age, Mustafa Kemal developed a unique, transformative vision of society based on Enlightenment ideas and their interpretation by the positivist/materialist intellectuals of the late Ottoman period (Hanioğlu, 2011).

In addition, not only did he experience the demise of the Ottoman Empire over a long and painful decade of dissolution from 1908 to 1918 personally, as a soldier, but he also occupied the leading position during the National Independence War of Turkey against the invading Greek Army backed by imperialist Western powers. The decades following the decisive victory in 1923 were characterized by a rapid and profound transformation of the political regime and social relations according to Mustafa Kemal's modernist/secularist world-view (Aydemir, 1981). Within a decade, Atatürk made considerable progress in forging a new national identity and a 'new man [yeni adam]' in line with the vision he had had in mind since his early youth. Hence, there was a 'revolutionary spirit' in the Kemalist project that unfolded under the circumstances of 'great distress'. More importantly, there was a solid intellectual basis for this transformative vision that attempted to surpass most of the rational-legal and traditional authority structures inherited from the country's imperial past. In short, Atatürk introduced a new way of life and exist-ence to the citizens of Turkey.

When other charismatic figures of the twentieth century are evaluated, a very similar combination of 'great distress', 'a revolutionary spirit' and 'a transformative intellectual narrative/project' appears at the heart of the phenomenon. A spectrum of leadership stretching from Lenin to Hitler, Mussolini to Gandhi, Mao to Gaddafi, and Castro to Khomeini repre-sents the tradition of transformative charismatic leadership of the past century. These figures were not simply political leaders: they emerged as 'prophets' in times of profound, existential crisis in their societies. They were not simply supported by the masses but, with greater or lesser success, they transformed the 'audience' according to their unique intel-lectual visions. These visions could be written down in many volumes (such as those left by Lenin) or in small 'red' or 'green' books (such as those left by Mao and Gaddafi); they could be systematically transcribed (such as those left by Khomeini) or could be non-systematic and ambigu-ous in terms of their doctrinal quality (such as those left by Gandhi); they could be more or less plausible (such as those written by Atatürk) or irrational (such as the anti-Semitic doctrines of Hitler). Here the content of the intellectual narrative in normative terms is not the point. The point is the presence of this new, original intellectual narrative – whether verbal or written, it was, regardless, systematically delivered – that is powerful enough to shape and 'enthral' the audience (this audience could be the broad masses or a narrower circle around the leader). In charismatic personalism, a leader personally represents a solution to his country's 'distress' through his leadership and his unique intellectual narrative.[5]

The other forms of personalism lack precisely these aspects: the circumstances of great distress, the revolutionary spirit and the unique, original intellectual narrative that is prone to transform the audience and forge new identities. Although it is common to see researchers and analysts labelling populist leaders as charismatic, from the perspective of the preceding discussion and the examples introduced in this particular section, the combination of populism and charisma is a highly unlikely one. It is, for example, difficult to think of figures such as Abdala Bucaram, Silvio Berlusconi or Donald Trump as charismatic figures with a new intellectual proposal powerful enough to enthral and transform the audience. Here, only Chavez could be seen as a (debatable) exception.

The overwhelming majority of populist leaders of our time neither appeared under the circumstances of great distress, nor did they have a unique, original intellectual narrative powerful enough to transform their society. Here, I might also go as far as to argue that there is a certain tension between charismatic leadership and populism. Populism is, by definition, non-charismatic unless the term 'charisma' is used to describe the popular appeal of the leader. This is because populism requires leaders to be in resonance with the values and expectations of the masses. It needs to appeal to the vocabulary and imagination of ordinary masses and it needs to be in congruence with the so-called true-authentic self of the nation or the people. Hence, it fundamentally lacks the intellectual-transformative capacity of the charismatic personalism of the twentieth century.

This quality of populism, however, could also be seen in a positive light. Charismatic leadership, after all, can be extremely destructive depending on the content of the transformative intellectual project. But the same thing – at least currently – cannot be said for the populist leaderships of our age. The impact of populism in governmental terms has been complicated, and the damage it caused has been, ultimately, incremental and largely contained, compared to the catastrophes caused

---

[5] Although all the examples I discuss in this section are male, this should not be considered an essential quality of charismatic leadership.

by twentieth-century charismatic leaderships.[6] In the following discussion of Erdoğan it will become clear that, in this case, we are talking about a phenomenon different from charisma.

The Case of Erdoğan and the JDP: Non-Charismatic Personalism

In this section of the chapter, I examine Erdoğan's personality and leadership style from the perspective of the discussion in the previous section. Following the features defined in Table 4.1, I firstly look at the public image of Erdoğan. Afterwards, I demonstrate some indicators showing Erdoğan's high degree of autonomy within the JDP. I also look at the context of his political ascent and his personal qualities. In the final, key sub-section of this section, I focus on the 'robust action' of Erdoğan, which mainly relied on massive organizational leverage constructed by him and kept under his firm personal control.

As early as 2004 the relationship between Erdoğan and the JDP was defined as 'charismatic' by one of the party ideologues (Akdoğan, 2004: 151). It is true that Erdoğan's personality had a dominant role within the JDP and it was one of the grounds of the elite coalition of the party as well as its broad and heterogeneous electoral base. Nevertheless, as I will illustrate, this dynamic was not charisma but non-charismatic personalism, which has always been a resilient aspect of Turkish politics. Through the personality of Erdoğan, like previous centre-right political forces, the JDP overcame the potential centrifugal impact of a lack of a well-defined ideological position, programme and institutional structure as well as a lack of a socially cohesive electoral base.[7]

It is not uncommon to see the term 'charisma' used in its adjectival form to describe the leaders of every major political party in Turkey by various scholars. This situation also represents one of the most common

---

[6] The contradistinction I depict here between charismatic and populist modes of leadership also leads me to question the emphasis Canovan (1999) places on the 'redemptive' aspect of populism. In contrast, I think, contemporary populism usually avoids redemptive, bookish, messianic appeals to its followers and tends to be more mundane, practical and short-term, at least in governmental terms.

[7] See Wikileaks document dated 27 March 2004: 'Just as at the national level, at the municipal level AKP [JDP] is trading on Erdogan as the party rather than on the identity and capabilities of its candidates' https://wikileaks.org/plusd/cables/04ANKARA1842_a.html (accessed: 27 May 2016). See also another Wikileaks document dated as 8 December 2005: '12. (C) AKP MPs are as divided by personality as by politics, but personality-based fault lines crosscut ideological ones. PM Erdogan is the glue that holds AKP together': https://wikileaks.org/plusd/cables/05ANKARA7215_a .html (accessed: 27 May 2016). Both documents were written by employees of US Embassy in Ankara.

yet rarely interrogated truisms of literature on Turkish politics. Prominent leaders of the centre-right and right in Turkey, such as Menderes, Demirel, Özal, Erbakan and Türkeş, as well as social democrat Ecevit, were called charismatic by students of Turkish politics.[8] Thus, mainstream political science literature on Turkey contains an unsubstantiated claim that Turkish politics has produced several charismatic political leaders in the past seven decades.[9] Erdoğan was a stronger case of charisma in the eyes of scholars since his direct appeal to the electorate and his authority over the JDP's organization was much stronger than that of the previous leaders in Turkey.[10] A closer look at the allegedly most charismatic leader ever in Turkish politics, the JDP leader Erdoğan,[11] also reveals the weakness of this sort of approach to political leadership in Turkey.

Erdoğan's Public Image

An outlier from Ansell and Fish's presupposition that non-charismatic personalist leaders are not usually telegenic characters (1999: 290), Erdoğan was a highly impressive public figure.[12] He was also a

---

[8] See Acar for 'Demirel's personality and charisma' (1991: 191). See Kalaycıoğlu's study on the 'charismatic leadership' of Özal (2002). For Ecevit's charisma, see Kınıklıoğlu (2000: 1 and 16). The perennial leader and founding father of the Islamist National View parties, Necmettin Erbakan, was also called charismatic (Şimşek, 2004: 124). See also Gümüşçü and Sert for 'Erbakan's charisma' (2009: 963). Cornell calls the founding leader of the Nationalist Action Party, Türkeş, as well as Erbakan, 'charismatic' (1999: 211). According to Gürgür, until the military coup on 27 May 1960, Adnan Menderes, the leader of the Democrat Party, 'was definitely the most charismatic and popular personality of the Turkish politics' (2009: 3).

[9] From the perspective of this chapter, all of these previous so-called charismatic leaders represented cases of personalism. In terms of personalistic leadership style, Erdoğan revealed very similar features to former centre-right leaders in Turkey. However, the importance attached by him to the construction of a large and pervasive organization as his power base differentiated him from most of his personalistic predecessors. While the previous generation of party leaders in Turkey constructed 'personalistic cadre parties' relying on a network of powerful local elites, and located themselves in the middle of this network, Erdoğan and the JDP elite preferred to construct a 'personalistic mass party' relying on a massive membership organization under the tight control of the central leadership. This distinction between the JDP and its predecessors in Turkish party politics is made clear in the subsequent chapters of this book.

[10] See E. Yıldırım et al. (2007). Throughout their study Yıldırım et al. repeatedly underlined the charismatic appeal and personality of Erdoğan but did not provide a satisfying conceptual discussion of the term. They also did not refer to the Weberian sources of the concept but explained charisma on the grounds of 'anthropology'.

[11] For instance, Sambur argued that 'the charismatic personality of Erdoğan is [the JDP's] real power' (2009: 121).

[12] One should also note that Erdoğan was much taller than the Turkish average, and his sympathizers in the (social) media sometimes called him the 'tall man [uzun adam]'. As

remarkable orator, which was partly a result of his education in Imam and Preacher School in İstanbul.[13] One of his advisers in his first significant electoral victory in the 1994 local government election for İstanbul implied that he was a very good actor who knew very well how to adapt to new conditions (Besli and Özbay, 2014: 121).[14]

Even before the foundation of the JDP, Erdoğan was a very popular political figure. One of my interviewees, a former provincial chair, related the following incidents which indicate the popularity of Erdoğan in the various corners of the country around the time of the official foundation of the party. This particular interviewee was a former chair of another right-wing party before the foundation of the JDP, and he joined Erdoğan during the foundation of the party, later becoming the first chair of the party in his province. The incidents he portrayed are especially important as he made some striking comparisons that indicated the role Erdoğan played during the foundation of the JDP and his attractiveness for masses:

For instance, for [my former] party to find people, establishing a party branch anywhere was extremely difficult. We could not establish party branches in most sub-provinces. We had had this experience just three months ago. For the Y sub-province that I mentioned previously, as I remember, three or four days after I became the provincial party chair [of the JDP], three or four different groups came to me. In addition, I was called by several people recommending various persons to me for the foundation of the party branch in Y [...] Later on, when we were founding party branches, chairman [Erdoğan] came to Z [a provincial city]. I think it was October. We went to Z. There is a huge square in Z called X Square. We had a meeting with Mr A [chairman of my previous party] there. That square is a huge one. I think it can hold up to fifty thousand people. In our

mentioned, he also had a very peculiar posture which bears the marks of his particular social background. Resembling the combatant lower classes in Turkey, his slightly forward-leaning posture looks both defensive and aggressive at the same time. Not unrelated to his posture, he frequently argued that his political attitude was neither challenging nor obedient with the following expression: 'we were not aggressive but we stand tall [dikleşmeden dik durduk!]'.

13 In Imam and Preacher Schools in Turkey students are taught rhetoric, and they are expected to become good public orators because one of the duties of imams is to give speeches to the congregation in Friday's sermons in mosques. Çakır and Çalmuk also mentioned in their oft-cited biography of Erdoğan that when he was a youth branch leader of the Islamist National View party in the 1970s he used to rehearse public speeches on his own (2001: 26).

14 In an interview with an experienced politician from the Motherland Party, he underlined the impact of the body image as an important political asset in Turkey: 'In politics, height, appearance, stature [boy, pos, endam] are extremely important' (Interviewee 17, 2014). It was not surprising that one of the members of the youth organization of the party told me during a lunch that it was even sufficient reason for casting people's vote for the JDP because of Erdoğan's height, appearance and posture (boy, pos, duruş) (Interviewee 42, 2014).

meeting with Mr A, there were a thousand, maximum two thousand people. Four months later in a meeting in the same square, you might not believe, but that space was not enough. Every corner was full; the avenues were full, too (Interviewee 25, 2014).

Hence, since the very beginning of his political activity as JDP leader there was a striking public sympathy towards Erdoğan and he was at the centre of party activity. His image has also been an extremely valuable asset for the JDP in the party's communications activities. A poster prepared by a non-governmental organization close to the JDP also strikingly illustrated Erdoğan's central role in the party (see Figure 4.1). In my fieldwork, I also examined catalogues of election posters in the library of the JDP headquarters. Not surprisingly, almost all posters officially published by the JDP and catalogued by the party library contained the image of Erdoğan and underplayed the party identity. One of my interviewees explained this situation to me as a communications strategy (Interviewee 49, 2014). Nevertheless, as I will try to illustrate, Erdoğan's role in the organization was always much more important than simply as a shortcut for the party's identity.

The striking thing about the above-mentioned poster seen on the billboards and newspapers is that the identity of the party cannot be seen and the poster refers to the personal 'will' of Erdoğan rather than that of the party. Since its foundation, as one of the JDP executives underlined in his book, the JDP has strategically and intentionally used the image of Erdoğan in its electoral campaigns (Şentürk, 2006: 185). Even in the local elections, the JDP mostly relied on the personal image of Erdoğan (Çaha and Guida, 2011: 64).

However, unlike the charismatic appeal in which followers are drawn in by the extraordinary personal qualities of the leader, and transformed by the new moral and/or ideological proposition by her/him, in the case of Erdoğan there was a strong affinity between the existing values and morale of the masses and the leader as delineated in the previous chapter. Erdoğan's popularity can be explained through an overwhelming sense among followers and supporters that they share many common values and characteristics with the leader – instead of admiration by the masses of the superior personal qualities of the leader and their consent to his new ideological and intellectual propositions.[15] The following narratives by two of my high-ranking interviewees indicated this situation.

[15] See also E. Yıldırım (2013): 'Today, conservative masses consider Erdoğan more than a party leader. They view the unjust treatment of Erdoğan not simply as against a prime minister or a party leader but as if it was against the conservative masses, values and existence. They see these as a violation of their identity and world-view.'

Figure 4.1 *'Sağlam irade'* ('Iron will')
Note: A billboard poster and a full-page newspaper advertisement prepared by a non-governmental organization that supported the government after the corruption investigation initiated on 17 December 2013.
Source: Photograph taken by author.

A Central Decision and Administration Board member related the following incident: 'A taxi driver told me this. He said, when this man talks, implying Erdoğan, the man inside me is talking' (Interviewee 36, 2014).

Not only Erdoğan's personality but also his family life were relatably familiar in the eyes of the average, low-income, conservative electorate. After emphasizing the electorate's sense of identity with Erdoğan and his rise from humble origins, one of my high-ranking interviewees from JDP headquarters underlined the people's affection towards Erdoğan's family too. According to her, in the eyes of the majority of the electorate, Erdoğan's family life and particularly his daughters – who wear head-scarves but are highly educated – represented an ideal: a 'Turkish Dream' which implied a better future for conservative and low-income families (Interviewee 35, 2014).

As a previous study on Erdoğan underlined, 'in the eyes of ordinary people, he is a leader who speaks articulately, refrains from *haram* [wrong deeds], and takes the poor under his wing. He reflects the people's deprivation and oppression to the political arena using their body language' (E. Yıldırım et al., 2007: 13). Yıldırım et al. have also argued that 'the masses looked at how Erdoğan spoke rather than the content of what he said. His gestures, appearance, lifestyle, and tone of voice seemed more impressive than his words' (2007: 19).[16] Hence, as İnsel ironically underlined in order to illustrate Erdoğan's difference from the former generation of political leaders in Turkey, he was not simply a 'populist'; he was the 'people' (2002: 24). Therefore it was not uncommon to come across people arguing that they had cast their votes for Erdoğan instead of the JDP. However, this situation hardly indicated the charismatic-transformational effect of Erdoğan's leadership, but revealed his highly convincing 'low-populist' appeal[17] that relied on a strong sense of similarity with the electorate.

Leadership Autonomy in the JDP

According to Ansell and Fish, the most remarkable benefit of non-charismatic personalism for leaders and parties is an 'exceptional

---

[16] Throughout their study E. Yıldırım et al. (2007) argued that this situation indicated the charisma of Erdoğan. I think this was not the case. Instead, this familiarity derived from the non-charismatic situation and the highly successful 'low-populist' appeal/style of the JDP leadership discussed in detail in Chapter 3.

[17] As discussed at length in the previous chapter, I define populism as a political appeal/style and a cultural-affective bond between parties and their supporters in line with the works of Ostiguy. In particular, see Ostiguy (2009c, 2017).

degree of latitude for public maneuver in advertising their programs and their positions' and a 'tactical flexibility' (1999: 308). In the case of the relationship between Erdoğan and the JDP, a similar pattern can be observed. Nevertheless, unlike Ansell and Fish's examples of non-charismatic personalist leaderships, such as Kohl in Germany and Zhuganov in Russia, Erdoğan also benefited from a very popular public image. Hence, in the case of Erdoğan, one should talk about something beyond 'tactical flexibility', perhaps about a remarkable degree of 'leadership autonomy' constructed through robust action and the use of a 'low-populist' appeal/style.

In my fieldwork, a high-ranking interviewee from the JDP headquarters implied that Erdoğan actually did not need to have intensive consultation meetings (as will be discussed below) because he was so powerful and above the party organizations (Interviewee 37, 2014). Another interviewee also underlined the fact that nothing could happen in the JDP against the will of Erdoğan (Interviewee 9, 2014). Most JDP members would confirm the firm control and undisputable authority of Erdoğan in the party and how he was able to make decisions without any limitations stemming from within the party. Hence, from the perspective of JDP members and supporters, Erdoğan's 'robust action' seemed to be a politeness granted by him to the party rank and file. Nevertheless, as I will illustrate, from the perspective of this study, Erdoğan's leadership autonomy was constructed through these intensive meetings, endless travels and numerous speeches to the party rank and file, in other words, through 'robust action'.

Erdoğan's power depended heavily on his organizational existence and diligence, rather than his unique personal qualities and ideological inventions. Here, it can also be useful to underline the fact that, compared to leaders of personal parties (such as Berlusconi in Italy, Cem Uzan in Turkey[18] and Clive Palmer in Australia), Erdoğan, to a great extent, lacked both financial resources and media support during his rise to prominence. In the absence of economic, cultural and symbolic capital as well as of exceptional intellectual qualities, he had to rely, at least initially, on his organizational intelligence and diligence as power resources. Later on, this would certainly become a fundamental part of Erdoğan's political craftsmanship.

In the case of the JDP and Erdoğan, the impact of the subsequent consolidation of the JDP's position in power should also be underlined. The party's position in power changed the nature of personalism since

---

[18] For Uzan's Young Party, see Appendix 1 and Türk (2008).

Figure 4.2 A portrait of Erdoğan in a provincial JDP branch
Source: Photograph taken by author.

many resources, most notably public posts, were available to the JDP and its leader. Since Erdoğan had the final say on the selection of provincial chairs and candidate deputies, as well as ministers and mayors (as shown in Chapter 7), his role in the party became much more indispensable than the non-charismatic personalism in opposition. The power in the hands of Erdoğan as party leader, as well as the cabinet, provided him with an upper hand in negotiations with other power foci within the party. Hence, not only did Erdoğan emerge as an above-faction leader but he also actively prevented the formation of factions and any other minor, centrifugal power-holding groups within the JDP as demonstrated in the following chapters on the JDP's organization.

As illustrated in Table 4.1, with regard to leaders' public image and autonomy, all three forms of personalism, namely charismatic, non-charismatic and personal party personalism, tend to produce highly autonomous leaderships with strong public images. From the perspective of these features, it is highly plausible to argue that the relationship between Erdoğan and the JDP can be defined as a type of personalism. Nevertheless, these features usually led researchers to think that Erdoğan was a charismatic leader. However, as I illustrated in Table 4.1, charismatic leadership emerges under extraordinary political and social circumstances, and it usually has a decisively transformational impact on its followers and supporters. In the following sub-sections, with regard to the context of his political rise and his relation to his followers, supporters and organization, I demonstrate that Erdoğan was not a charismatic leader and that his authority was not a result of a transformational impact on his followers, but that it derived from his organizational intelligence, pragmatism and diligence.

The Context of Erdoğan's Political Ascent: Ordinary Times

As underlined by Weber and re-emphasized by Tucker, charismatic authority is usually associated with massive distress. In other words, just like charismatic personalities, charismatic situations are not ordinary occurrences. While exceptional personal qualities represent the supply side of charisma, exceptional circumstances form the demand side. Charismatic leaders usually emerge in the context of the demise of the legitimacy of existing political regimes (Rustow, 1968: 794). Hence, it is no surprise that the rise of charismatic personalities has been usually accompanied by critical, deeply destabilizing historical events such as revolution, state collapse, war, civil war, national liberation movements and decolonization.

Turkish politics has always been turbulent since the foundation of the Republic in 1923 because of military coups, social protests and political violence. Nevertheless, it has not produced a charismatic situation so far within the Turkish military and political elite after the passing of Mustafa Kemal Atatürk. The specific period that covered Erdoğan's political rise was not a particularly extraordinary one, either. After the military coup on 12 September 1980, Turkey witnessed a restoration of the political regime in line with a new conservative-nationalist identity and culture, in other words, the Turkish-Islamic Synthesis. Although Erdoğan started his political career in the youth movement of the Islamist National View tradition in the turmoil of the 1970s, his political ascent was defined by the circumstances of the 1980s: a relatively stable period compared to the polarized 1970s.[19]

Apart from the lack of a demand side of a charismatic situation, authoritative biographies of Erdoğan do not include any sign of at least a small group of early followers. Instead, Erdoğan had, for a long time, been one of the figures of a promising younger generation of the Islamist National View tradition. He was by no means an ideological shaper of this circle. He was not intellectually superior to his friends, either. On the contrary, this younger generation had preserved a brotherly solidarity among themselves until their split from the Islamist National View tradition. Erdoğan was, at most, a very active organization man (teşkilatçı),[20] but not an undisputable leader even after his mayoralty in İstanbul.[21] It was also known that, despite his disputes with the party leader Necmettin Erbakan and the Islamist National View gerontocracy, he was, at the same time, very obedient to Erbakan to the degree that he named one of his sons 'Necmettin'. He was by no means an intellectual or ideological trendsetter. He was rather a committed follower, albeit an active and highly visible one, of a loose Islamist outlook just like his peers. In short, Erdoğan had neither intellectual distinction nor did he impose a unique moral-ideological outlook of his own over his friends and supporters.

Early Life and Personality: Not a 'Prophet' But 'a Man of the People'

Biographies and studies of Erdoğan usually imply the impact of his childhood and early upbringing as the son of a low-income domestic-immigrant family in the tough neighbourhood of İstanbul, Kasımpaşa, on

---

[19] For this polarized period, see Landau (1974).
[20] See Kaplan (2007: 62–66) for Erdoğan's intense political activities as the leader and the orator of the youth branches of the Islamist National View party of the 1970s.
[21] It seems that among Bülent Arınç, Abdullah Gül and Erdoğan there was, at least, a balance of power when they were splitting from the Islamist National View tradition. See Çakır and Çalmuk (2001: 191). See also Yılmaz (2001: 204–226). Dindar also highlights the brotherly solidarity of the JDP elite until 2005 from a psychoanalytical point of view (2014). In a book-length interview, Abdüllatif Şener, one of the founders of the JDP, argued that 'at the beginning no one had envisaged this kind of charismatic leadership. Everybody was seeing each other as equals' (Toker, 2009: 308).

Erdoğan's later political career.[22] Kasımpaşa is located in the immediate periphery of the cosmopolitan Beyoğlu sub-province of İstanbul, alongside other conservative and low-income neighbourhoods, and has always been home to new provincial and poor immigrants of the city. Kasımpaşa has a peculiar location: it is neither completely isolated from the cosmopolitan city centre, like the faraway slums, nor completely identical to it. Hence, this neither central nor peripheral context of his early upbringing might have provided Erdoğan some rich experiences with different lifestyles and identities, and probably established the emotional grounds for his 'multi-faceted' political style targeting diverse audiences.

One should also keep in mind that Kasımpaşa is also known for its strict conservative, moralist and macho subculture.[23] It has always been home to certain criminal tendencies, as is the case with other similar İstanbul neighbourhoods (Çakır and Çalmuk, 2001: 11–13). According to the introduction of one of Erdoğan's biographies, Kasımpaşa has always been home to 'celebrated roughnecks [kabadayı]' in the past (Yılmaz, 2001: 31). According to Yılmaz, these roughnecks fight well, but at the same time they observe certain manners (racon), help the poor, respect the elderly and find solutions to the district's problems (2001: 31). Erdoğan argued in an interview that 'my manliness, bluntness, and principled conduct derive from my roots [in Kasımpaşa]' (Heper and Toktaş, 2003: 162). In a meeting with sports columnists, Erdoğan also implied that he knows 'every kind of world'.[24]

As a result of this early upbringing, Erdoğan was frequently called delikanlı or reis by his supporters, and kabadayı or külhanbeyi by his opponents. While delikanlı literally means 'lad' and reis means 'captain' in Turkish, referring to a moralist and macho attitude of a (young) man, the latter expressions, particularly külhanbeyi, pejoratively mean 'bully'. In both of these cases, in terms of political appeal/style, Erdoğan's personality was close to the 'low-popular' pole of the political-cultural

---

[22] See Yılmaz (2001: 30–32) and Çakır and Çalmuk (2001: 12–14).

[23] Heper and Toktaş's study highlights these features and their effects on Erdoğan: 'Erdogan is not an easygoing man, which seems to be related to the fact that he was brought up in Kasımpaşa. In Erdogan's own words, in that neighborhood "there were very close relations between families. There existed a shared conscience of the neighborhood. The people who lived there acted like the members of the same family." Kasımpaşa is well known for its bravado culture. Erdogan has pointed out its impact on him' (2003: 162).

[24] In a meeting with sports columnists in Turkey, Erdoğan was reported to have said: 'I am in a serious business now but I came from the heart of the vagabonds [kulağı kesik]. I am first of all Tayyip Erdoğan from Kasımpaşa. I know every kind of world [alem] [...] I have chosen a different path due to the manners I got from my family and due to my education. Yet I know this kind of business, too. Do not think that I am a fanatic [softa]. Most of you have not met the kind of people I know' (Güven, 2005).

axis of the high–low divide as defined by Ostiguy (2009c) with its macho and moralist features. This is why the official biography of Erdoğan put a special emphasis on Erdoğan's roots in Kasımpaşa (Besli and Özbay, 2014: 22).

It should also be kept in mind that one of the main slogans praising Erdoğan was 'Recep Tayyip Erdoğan: a man like a man! [*Adam gibi adam Recep Tayyip Erdoğan!*]' I also observed how ordinary supporters and members of the party were attaching great importance to a 'strong male leader' (Ostiguy 2009c: 9). While I was waiting for an interviewee in a sub-provincial JDP branch in Anatolia, one of the supporters of the party sitting in the waiting room told me the following as he pointed to Erdoğan's small portrait on the wall: 'Why are we here? Because this guy is a real man! [*Biz buradayız çünkü bu adam heriftir herif!*]'[25]

It is also well known that Erdoğan played football for several years and came close to becoming a professional player. However, his father did not allow him to follow a football career (Yılmaz, 2001: 49–50). After his primary school education, Erdoğan started at the Imam and Preacher School in İstanbul on the recommendation of one of his teachers. According to Erdoğan's biographies, he was not an exceptionally successful or intelligent pupil, and his records from his school years support this (Yılmaz, 2001: 40). All the evidence from his early years suggests that his personality was shaped in accordance with the 'low-populist' political appeal, and he was seen as a particularly familiar figure by low-income, peripheral sectors of Turkish society: son of a provincial low-income immigrant family, a moralistic and macho youth, and a football lover.

To a great extent, his later years bore the marks of the conditions of this upbringing. His quick temper and lack of diplomatic manners,[26] his macho and, from time to time, bullying style and harshness,[27] and his lack of interest in 'refined', intellectual debates remained constant.[28]

---

[25] Compare with Ostiguy: 'Turning from political theory to the discourse of the actors, a central element on the populist low is, as often stated in Latin America, the valuation of (strong, personalistic) leaders "with balls". "Ballsyness", however exactly defined, is a central attribute of the low in this political-cultural dimension' (2017: 82).

[26] At the Davos Economic Forum, after a harsh discussion with the Israeli prime minister, Erdoğan left the panel (CNN, 2009) and thousands of supporters were present in the airport on his return home to celebrate his attitude at Davos (*Radikal*, 2009).

[27] An opposition deputy stated that Erdoğan physically and verbally assaulted some of the deputies and ministers and also insulted them quite frequently (*Radikal*, 2013). Some newspapers also reported that Erdoğan scolded the deputies of the JDP (*Radikal*, 2004).

[28] According to a pro-JDP columnist, although Erdoğan was not very liberal or intellectual, he was the right candidate for Turkey's presidency: 'Yes, Erdoğan is not a Danish prime minister who goes to his job by bicycle. Yes, he has no titles, nor is he a good intellectual.

Nevertheless, he was extremely successful at converting these features of his personality into political assets through a conscious engagement with the 'low-populist' political appeal.

This background had a decisive influence on Erdoğan's leadership style, too, and was the dynamic behind his 'low-populist' leadership style or 'strong personalistic male leadership' (Ostiguy, 2009c: 9) in the JDP. Instead of care or attention to institutional mediation of state bureaucracy, 'procedural normalcy' (Ostiguy, 2009c: 10) and legal restrictions imposed by the judiciary,[29] Erdoğan usually preferred to rely on his personal authority and relations in conducting the day-to-day affairs of government. It should be noted that the leadership style Erdoğan embraced 'political-culturally' complemented the 'low-populist' 'socio-cultural' appeal of the JDP, as elaborated upon in the previous chapter.

It is, nevertheless, important to re-emphasize that excessive concentration of power in the hands of the leader was, mainly, an outcome achieved via non-charismatic personalistic leadership in the JDP. Non-charismatic personalism is about the mode of relationship between the leader and the party. It is characterized by the personal presence and control of the leader in organization building. Another feature of non-charismatic personalism is micro-management, by the leader, of organizational affairs that otherwise would be managed and controlled via organizational intermediaries and institutionalization. The following sections will provide evidence regarding this dynamic between the JDP and Erdoğan.

The 'Organization Man [Teşkilatçı]': Diligence and Pragmatism

Erdoğan was not an intellectual-ideological trendsetter, and he did not undertake a transformational role as a leader. Nevertheless, he was always known as a very innovative and diligent 'organization man'.[30] A biography coauthored by Hüseyin Besli, one of Erdoğan's close friends and a JDP deputy, underlines the innovations made by Erdoğan in the early years of his political career during the sub-provincial local government elections for which he was a candidate. According to this official biography, women started to actively work in the field for the first time in

He does not know any languages, either. He is not a monument of tolerance, either. But he is the right person to solve Turkey's hundred-year-old problems' (Oğur, 2014b).

[29] Erdoğan has been usually accused of disregard for judicial decisions and bureaucratic institutional restrictions by his opponents who come from very different backgrounds.

[30] See Çakır and Çalmuk (2001: 48–54) and Yılmaz (2001: 59–60).

this particular election, and Erdoğan had to struggle with the intra-party reactions of his conservative Islamist colleagues to this new method (Besli and Özbay, 2014: 44). According to the authors of the same biography, women's branches helped Erdoğan to reach the vital 'arteries' of the city and were key to his political success (Besli and Özbay, 2014: 66).

According to a balanced biography on Erdoğan, he introduced the use of women in the electoral campaigns around 1990 despite the conservative reactions that came from within the ranks of the Islamist Welfare Party. This method was dependent on house visits and vote canvassing of women members and included the distribution of a small package of Turkish coffee and a flower. This was so successful that, according to the author of the same biography, other parties started to imitate the Welfare Party's women's organization (Yılmaz, 2001: 59). Indeed, one of my interviewees underlined this aspect of the Welfare period, arguing that it was the 'discovery of the female electorate' in Turkish politics (Interviewee 19, 2014). Other interviewees also underlined the central role of Erdoğan in the active participation of women in electoral campaigns (Interviewee 29, 2014) and in the introduction of other new electoral strategies (Interviewee 14, 2014).

Public opinion surveys began to be used extensively under the direction of Erdoğan when he was a sub-provincial chair of the Beyoğlu branch (in İstanbul) of the Islamist Welfare Party. In the absence of adequate financial resources, instead of employing professionals to conduct public opinion surveys, Erdoğan started to use teams of university students (Besli and Özbay, 2014: 45). According to the same biography, the above-mentioned electoral methods –the use of women's branches and public opinion surveys – later became a model for the entire Welfare Party organization (Besli and Özbay, 2014: 61).

Authors of his official biography repeatedly underline his diligence, too. Perhaps there is a degree of exaggeration in these comments simply due to the authors' sympathy for Erdoğan. Nevertheless, anecdotal remarks about his diligence point to a very specific feature of his leadership: intensive effort put into organization building and intra-party governance. According to the authors of Erdoğan's official biography, even in his early youth he was always a participant in or the producer of the activities of youth organizations of the Islamist National View parties: 'He is always in action' (Besli and Özbay, 2014: 32).

In the same biography, one of Erdoğan's colleagues says, 'If you are working with the captain [reis], you should keep pace with him. You should always rush' (Besli and Özbay, 2014: 36). One of his political and electoral advisers also made a similar point in an interview: 'He is an extremely hard-working person. I had not witnessed this to this extent until this campaign [for the 2011 general elections]. He starts in the morning at seven or eight o'clock. Every day he has two mass rallies and five or six other programmes. Such a pace as if he is new in politics. Even until the very last moment he did not lose any determination and concentration. If I were him, after a while, I would be exhausted' (Aydıntaşbaş, 2011).

One of the focal points of Erdoğan's proactive style was organization building and dynamism, and he always expected a similar level of devotion and punctuality from other ruling cadres of the party as well (Besli and Özbay 2014: 103).

It is plausible to argue that Erdoğan's effort and vigilance in building a dynamic organization were a result of the lack of reliable financial resources for the activities of the Islamist National View parties. Hence, the most reliable resource for the electoral campaigns was an active and pervasive organization that was tightly controlled by the leadership. This was why one of Erdoğan's advisers in his local electoral victory in 1994 in İstanbul, Nabi Avcı, underlined the critical role played by a hardworking, devoted organization 'which was present even in the remotest neighbourhoods of the city' in the absence of extensive financial resources (Besli and Özbay, 2014: 121).

These components of Erdoğan's 'robust action' – his strategic inventiveness, proactive style and diligence devoted to organization building – were also supported by other personal qualities usually common to similar non-charismatic personalist leaders (Ansell and Fish, 1999: 293). Erdoğan was also known for his pragmatism, multi-faceted style, ambitions and tactical intelligence. As early as the end of the 1980s, according to Yılmaz, Erdoğan was aware of the limitations of a narrow Islamist discourse. In the elections around the turn of the decade, Erdoğan was pushing party members to reach beyond the Islamist electorate (Yılmaz, 2001: 60). Yılmaz also argued that, despite his radical speeches, Erdoğan was always telling party members that the Islamist Welfare Party should become the 'party of Turkey' (2001: 60).

Erdoğan's nomination for the mayoralty of İstanbul in 1994 made his ideological flexibility even greater. In this election, according to Yılmaz, 'Erdoğan's strategy was actually simple. He was aware of the fact that it was impossible to win the elections with the conventional votes of [the Welfare Party] and he was trying to get the support of other voters too' (2001: 80). A very similar point was made in Erdoğan's official biography, as well. In 1989, with regard to moving the Welfare Party's İstanbul provincial centre building outside Fatih, a conservative neighbourhood heavily populated by devout people, Erdoğan argued that 'the Welfare Party must go beyond Fatih. Being in Fatih isolates the party, and presents it as the specific representative of particular groups [...] If the Welfare Party is to reach broader social segments it has to get rid of this community-style [*cemaatvari*] image' (Besli and Özbay, 2014: 57). A particular incident involving Erdoğan sheds light on the transformational power of participation in electoral politics on radical political actors. According to an anecdote in two different biographies of Erdoğan (Besli and Özbay, 2014 and Çakır and Çalmuk, 2001), during their search for more votes, the Islamist political elite realized how unreliable and unsustainable it was to depend solely on the votes of devout social segments and support of religious networks. According to Besli and Özbay's biography, during a 1986 election campaign, Erdoğan could not get in touch with a member of a certain religious community. Despite of all of Erdoğan's attempts to speak to him this particular person rejected Erdoğan's proposal and said that he was a supporter of the centre-right Motherland Party. According to the biography, at that same moment, a man approached Erdoğan and his friends and invited them to his shop. His shop was a local pub, and there Erdoğan and his friends were very welcome and their speeches were listened to with enthusiasm by the customers. A witness of this event later commented that 'we have wandered in the wrong places for years, we wasted our time in the yards of mosques. This [pub] is the real wellspring [of votes]' (Besli and Özbay, 2014: 89–90).[31]

Erdoğan also literally started to reshape and deploy the party's cadres accordingly. For example, for the local election in 1989, according to his official biography, he did not find the excessively religious appearance of one of the candidates of the Welfare Party appropriate and ordered him to shave and to wear a suit (Besli and Özbay, 2014: 58–59). Another incident described in his official biography revealed his tactical intelligence and flexibility. In the local elections in 1989 he sent women without headscarves to the secularist regions of the sub-province instead of headscarf-wearing members of the party (Besli and Özbay, 2014: 44–45). This pragmatism and multi-faceted style that targeted different segments of the electorate had a deep impact on Erdoğan's personal and ideological convictions. According to Yılmaz, 'in his early years in politics [Erdoğan] did not shake the women's hands because he thought it was a "sin". But now he does' (2001: 269).

All of these experiences and his strategic learning eventually led Erdoğan in a very pragmatic direction, and this was why he rejected an

---

[31] In Çakır and Çalmuk's biography it was even argued that Erdoğan started to visit brothels for his electoral campaigns and promised the women there that he would save them from their 'dark world'. Later it was also argued that some of those women worked for Erdoğan and the Welfare Party's electoral campaigns (2001: 66–67).

'ideological party' just on the eve of the foundation of the JDP (Yılmaz, 2001: 274–275). His words 'we took off the [Islamist] National View shirt' (*Radikal*, 2003), during the foundation process of the JDP, expressed the fact that he and the JDP cadres had changed profoundly. This was the final declaration of the gradual transformation of the Islamist National View cadres on the basis of the electoral concerns outlined above. Within Erdoğan's personality we see a pragmatic and ambitious[32] politician after more votes, rather than a charismatic Islamist who exerted an ideological, intellectual and moral domination upon his followers in order to enthral and transform them. Erdoğan's personality and biography were characterized by a tactical and organizational intelligence directed towards coming to power rather than transforming his followers and the wider circumstances of the country.

The above-mentioned components of his personality, biography and the circumstances of his political rise and, more importantly, his political style after he became prime minister support the argument that Erdoğan's approach was that of non-charismatic personalism instead of charismatic leadership. The primary indicator of this was Erdoğan's 'robust action': his endless travelling to meet with party members and attend mass rallies and the excessive effort he put into intra-party governance. Through his proactive style and diligence, Erdoğan built a large and pervasive organization and tightened his direct grip on it, making himself an important cement of the diverse political, social and ethnic segments within the JDP's electoral base and within its elite coalition.

Erdoğan's 'Robust Action': Diligence in Organization Building

In contrast to the features of charismatic personalism and personal party personalism as discussed in the second section, the electoral achievements of the JDP depended on the formation of a large and pervasive membership organization personally constructed and tightly controlled by Erdoğan.[33] The members of this massive organization came from various backgrounds, and thousands of party branches that penetrated into even the smallest locales of the country were kept under the control

---

[32] An incident described by one of the deputies of the JDP, as highlighted in Dindar's book, revealed this point. In 1991, Erdoğan became a deputy, but due to a dispute over the distribution of votes within the party he lost his position. According to Mehmet Metiner, 'when Erdoğan heard that Mustafa Baş had been elected with the help of the preference votes – I know because I was beside him – he lost consciousness and fell down' (Dindar, 2014: 45). This incident was also confirmed by another essay on Erdoğan's political life (Kalyoncu, 2011).

[33] Chapter 6 focuses on the features of this organization.

of the central JDP elite, keeping Erdoğan's leadership intact throughout the organization. In order to hold this organization together and under his control, Erdoğan spent much time on intra-party governance by travelling to distinct corners of the country, by speaking to diverse audiences within the party, and by controlling minute details of candidate selection processes and the formation of provincial governing bodies. Erdoğan's robust action became visible in his central role in regular consultation activity within the JDP, his active and decisive involvement in the recruitment of the party elite, and his occupation of centre stage in meetings and mass rallies organized by party branches across the country. In addition, the party's technological surveillance on the ground provided him with superior information about the membership organization of the party as well as against other national and local power holders inside and outside the party, and consolidated his grip over the massive JDP organization.

Consultations (İstişareler) During my fieldwork, from many interviewees, I heard of the importance attached to consultation meetings by Erdoğan and the JDP elite. As a JDP deputy underlined, the JDP is a 'party of consultations' (Interviewee 29, 2014). In fact, the party leadership attached great importance to the regular consultation meetings. Intense consultation activity of the JDP started at the top of the organization. The JDP held strict weekly Central Executive Committee consultation meetings and monthly Central Decision and Administration Board consultation meetings as well as the regular weekly meetings of the cabinet (Interviewee 14, 2014). All these regular consultation meetings were held under the control and personal presence of Erdoğan (Interviewee 14, 2014). Apart from these regular consultation meetings, Erdoğan and the party elite consulted frequently with local as well as national political and economic elites. They called these meetings with the political and economic elite and opinion leaders 'private consultations [*özel istişareler*]' (Interviewee 36, 2014).

As one of my interviewees underlined, Erdoğan spent considerable time in and attached greater importance to these meetings than did leaders of other parties in Turkey (Interviewee 14, 2014). He was present in monthly regular consultation meetings with the provincial chairs and the elite of the party as well as with JDP representatives of local governments. As some of my interviewees emphasized, he was also highly accessible to even junior party members from the provinces (Interviewee 35, 2014).[34] In other

---

[34] See also Interviewee 49, 2014.

words, aside from bureaucratically arranged consultation meetings, Erdoğan also had direct control and communication with the provincial party elite and the base.

Tight Control over Elite Recruitment Erdoğan closely supervised the formation of the provincial branches as well as the candidate selection processes within the JDP. This was why one of my interviewees argued that no one can exist within the party organization against the will of Erdoğan (Interviewee 9, 2014). During my interviews, I have observed that questions regarding the candidate selection processes within the party had a straightforward answer. Headquarters, and particularly the party leader Erdoğan, had the ultimate say in the process (Interviewee 9, 2014). One of my interviewees defined the ultimate criteria in the candidate selection process within the party as 'loyalty and fidelity' to Erdoğan (Interviewee 7, 2014). It also seems that a personal relationship with Erdoğan provided great privileges for competing candidates within the JDP (Interviewee 14, 2014).[35]

Meetings Meetings and mass rallies held by Erdoğan should be seen in the context of this tireless and all-encompassing activity for intra-party governance (Interviewee 28, 2014). It should also be noted that meetings and mass rallies that Erdoğan attended should not be seen as targeting the electorate alone. The intensive meeting activity of the JDP leader also served to enforce Erdoğan's control over the provincial organizations and kept the membership of the JDP active.

Technological Surveillance Erdoğan's robust action targeting a much more coherent organization was also facilitated by other instruments. While regular public opinion surveys provided Erdoğan with superior knowledge of public tendencies *vis-à-vis* centrifugal and local forces within the party, use of technologically sophisticated central communications instruments such as AKBİS (AK Parti Bilgi Sistemi, AK Party Information System) and AKİM (AK Parti İletişim Merkezi, AK Party Communication Centre) provided Erdoğan with direct feedback from the party base and the electorate. Extremely loyal women's branches also enhanced Erdoğan's control over centrifugal tendencies within the party.

Thus, Erdoğan's proactive leadership style and his political and organizational diligence were supported by a specific organizational

---

[35] See also Interviewee 23, 2014.

mechanism outlined here and delineated in Chapter 6. As a result Erdoğan became the most vital element of the elite coalition as well as of the party's electoral coalition, which consisted of diverse social, ideological and ethnic groups. In the eyes of this diverse electoral base, Erdoğan's importance was increased by the personalistic electoral campaigns.

Discussion: Are 'Personalism' and 'Mass Membership Organization' Mutually Exclusive and Can Non-Charismatic Personalism Gradually Become Charismatic?

At first glance, personalistic leadership and mass membership organizations – like the one the JDP had in Turkey – could be seen as mutually exclusive political phenomena. After all, personalism also means the rising importance of leaders, and in the case of the JDP in Turkey we also encounter a highly popular and visible leadership. One could assume that, just like personal party of Berlusconi in Italy, Erdoğan could solely rely on his popularity, his 'low-populist' appeal and the pro-JDP media. It could even be claimed that the absence of a mass membership organization would be a better ground for personalism since there would be less constraint over the leader's will and autonomy.

This kind of approach to personalism, on the one hand, conflates personalism with personal party – a specific sub-type of the phenomenon of personalism – and, on the other hand, conflates institutionalization with the mass membership organization. 'Personalism in personal parties' should be considered a specific reflection of the phenomenon of personalistic leadership. It should be considered a very specific political response by certain leaders to very specific political circumstances underlying the rapidly rising and falling parties in Europe and some parts of Latin America. In contrast, as discussed in previous chapters, the JDP phenomenon and the rise of Erdoğan in Turkey emerged under the circumstances of deeply entrenched historical and political conflicts and it was a continuation of a much older historical divide in the country – perhaps similar to that between Peronists and anti-Peronists in Argentina (Ostiguy, 1997, 2009b).

Under these circumstances, simply relying on the popularity of the party leader, media and capital-intensive electoral strategies would be a fatal error detrimental not only to the electoral fortunes of the leader but also to the survival and interests of heterogeneous networks represented by the leader and the party. Hence, in the specific context of Turkey, the personal party would not be a feasible organizational strategy for

Erdoğan and the social segments represented by him. This was most recently confirmed by the role of the JDP organization in the failure of the coup in July 2016. If Erdoğan and the JDP elite had preferred to weaken the organization simply by relying on the media and Erdoğan's image, prospects for the coup would have been fundamentally different.[36]

Another line of reasoning which would lead to the view that personalism and mass membership organizations are mutually exclusive phenomena might stem from seeing institutionalization as identical to a highly routinized and bureaucratized mass membership organization. Indeed, mass membership organizations could be institutionalized, particularly if they survive after the disappearance of their founding leaders, if they manage to construct a stable party identity ('value fusion') and if they strictly follow written regulations they produce for themselves.[37] In this sense, it would not be easy for institutionalized organizations to coexist side by side with personalistic leadership. Nevertheless, mass membership organizations are not always and necessarily institutionalized. And it is even possible to come across highly routinized and remarkably bureaucratized organizations such as the JDP without a high degree of institutionalization. In short, 'mass membership organizations' should not be conflated with 'highly institutionalized organizations'. While logically it would be less likely to come across personalism in highly institutionalized organizations simply because of the predominance of rules and codes the organization produced in its long history for its own survival, it is much more likely to see personalism in new but highly bureaucratized and routinized organizations as long as the founding leader is present and central to the party routine and bureaucracy.

This also contains two potential routes for the 'personalistic mass party',[38] unlike with personal parties. As McDonnell (2013) and Albertazzi and McDonnell (2015) illustrate, personal parties are destined to fail if the leader disappears, decides to leave or dissolves the organization. Hence, institutionalization and organizational survival are extremely unlikely for the personal party. The predominant possibility for the organization without the leader in the personal party is dissolution since the organization is actually nothing more than the personal network

[36] I discuss the coup and the role of the JDP's organization further in Chapters 6 and 8.
[37] See Panebianco (1988: 58–59) for some of these traits of institutionalization. See also Levitsky (1998) for how he breaks down the concept and points out the importance of formal as well as informal aspects of the process.
[38] The concept of 'personalistic mass party' is delineated in Chapter 6.

of the leader, comprising friends and aidies. In contrast, in the 'personalistic mass party' (as defined in the following chapters) there are two potential trajectories. Given their highly routinized and bureaucratized intra-party structure with a permanent presence in localities and regular interactions within the party (which also creates a unique party subculture), these organizations gradually create a life of their own independent of the leader; they always have a chance to survive the disappearance of their leader, and therefore institutionalization, alongside the possibility of decline. I elaborate on these strategic and organizational points in the rest of the book.

Finally, it is necessary to evaluate Erdoğan's position in the light of recent political and geo-political crises in Turkey. As mentioned in the theoretical sections of this chapter, apart from the supply-side factors in the emergence of charismatic leadership related to personal qualities of leaders, demand-side factors or, more precisely, deeply destabilizing political circumstances, are also central to the rise of charismatic leaders. The geo-political turmoil in the south of Turkey, the waves of terror attacks this turmoil triggered within the country and, finally, the bloody coup attempt which brought Turkish society to the edge of civil war could be seen as components of a deeply destabilizing political context ripe for the rise of a charismatic leader.

While the literature on charismatic leadership, in following Weber, has usually focused on the transformation of charisma into other institutional forms of authority (Robinson, 1985), the above-mentioned circumstances in Turkey force us to put some thought into the reverse situation. Could a non-charismatic personalistic leadership gradually turn into a charismatic one? In the absence of proper supply-side factors and true charismatic leadership, it is plausible that non-charismatic leaders such as Erdoğan (who was partly responsible for the rise of the above-mentioned demand-side factors due to mismanagement such as supporting and allowing the widespread colonization of the state by a certain religious community, which was argued to have taken centre stage in the coup) can acquire charisma through the help of a supportive organization and a partisan media, both in the eyes of his followers as well as in the eyes of a broader segment of society that had been disoriented by waves of small-scale but continuous political crises.

One could even argue that the creeping replacement of secular nationalism by 'Muslim nationalism' (White, 2012) in Turkey represented the transformational impact of this leadership. In addition, after overcoming the coup in 2016 (which could be seen as a circumstance of great distress) the JDP was successful in a referendum on a constitutional amendment in 2017 which granted more power to Erdoğan and transformed Turkey from a parliamentary to a presidential system. Nevertheless, it is hard to see these social and political transformations in Turkey as the unfolding and realization of the unique intellectual vision of Erdoğan. In the first instance, the gradual rise of an assertive Muslim identity as the core of Turkish national identity can also be seen as the continuation – and logical consequence – of a long-lasting nationalist-conservative indoctrination since the 1980 coup.[39] No doubt that the JDP governments also supported a kind of slow Islamization of society, but it is hard to define whether this was a part of wider strategic plan to forge a new national identity or a simple response to the sensitivities of the party's conservative electoral base (as well as efforts to consolidate and reproduce them). And the transformation of Turkey from parliamentarism to presidentialism can well be seen as an instrument of rising competitive authoritarianism in Turkey that primarily aims to consolidate power for Erdoğan and the JDP rather than transform Turkish society according to a particular ideological-intellectual vision of the leader – as charismatic leadership had attempted in the last century. Here, the search for legal legitimacy through a referendum to support these changes in the country's political system should also be mentioned, since this does not resemble the charismatic way of changing things: 'It is written, but I say unto you.'

Thus, this kind of transformation of non-charismatic leadership should still be distinguished from genuinely charismatic leadership, which is complete with the enthralling intellectual qualities of leaders and their personal transformational impact on followers and supporters as well as on the wider circumstances of the country. Instead of calling it non-charismatic personalism turned into charismatic leadership, it is much more accurate to call this transformation the rise of 'pseudo-charisma', relying on media, populism and organized mass support.

Non-Charismatic Personalism and the Political Agency of Erdoğan's JDP

This chapter has shown that Erdoğan played a key role in the rise of the JDP. But his impact was achieved through a specific, mostly understated, way: his organizational diligence and inventiveness. Apart from his popular public image, Erdoğan was also a very diligent and pragmatic organization man (*teşkilatçı*) who was central to the construction of the massive and resilient electoral machine called the JDP. What does the role of

[39] This was demonstrated in Chapter 2.

Erdoğan tell us regarding the overall emphasis of this book on the role of agency – through populism and organization – in the rise of a competitive authoritarian regime out of a multi-party democracy under highly unfavourable circumstances?

This chapter has implied that the strategic choices and actions of leaders are extremely important. But there were also certain structural circumstances and conditions that created these leaders, who were prone to taking these particular decisions and actions. Erdoğan, as a political leader, was certainly the creation of the political hurdles and circumstances that he – and the political tradition of which he was a member – encountered in the 1980s and 1990s (as delineated in Chapter 2) and the politicized socio-cultural divides of Turkey after the transition to multi-party politics in the middle of the 1940s (as analysed in Chapter 3) as well as his particular upbringing and political biography, as examined in this chapter, stretching from the middle of the twentieth century to present. As a populist, Erdoğan was not akin to Trump or Berlusconi or Uzan. From the very beginning of his political life, he knew how important a resilient, loyal organization was for political survival. And he knew the constituencies that he represented very well from his own personal experience as the son of a low-income, domestic-immigrant family.

These structural circumstances and experiences certainly profoundly shaped the strategic choices and actions of Erdoğan, which were examined in this chapter. Erdoğan, despite his extraordinary popularity and direct appeal to the electorate, never thought of weakening or dismantling the JDP's organization simply by relying on the strength of his populist appeal. He probably never thought of transforming the JDP into a simple, empty campaign vehicle such as a 'personal party'. Hence, the particular agency of Erdoğan – which was profoundly shaped by the particular circumstances of Turkish politics and his own experience as a social and political actor in Turkey – was decisive in the formation of strategies and organizational dynamics that I will delineate in the rest of this book. These preferences defined the destiny of the JDP and, ultimately, paved the way to the rise of a unique competitive authoritarian regime in Turkey. .

Conclusion

In this chapter, I have argued that the JDP leader Erdoğan was not a charismatic leader but that his authority over the JDP was an outcome of robust action or diligence in organization building. In the theoretical part of the chapter, I argued that charismatic, non-charismatic and personal party personalism are different reflections of personalistic leadership. Although all forms usually contain a very strong public image and a highly autonomous leadership, I argued that charismatic personalism was distinguished from more common forms of non-charismatic and personal party personalism. I defined charisma as a very exceptional phenomenon that is characterized by extraordinary political and social circumstances and the transformational role of the leader on the followers stemming from a particular intellectual-ideological world-view. In cases of non-charismatic and personal party personalism, one can find neither such a transformational role nor an extraordinary political and social condition. In these forms, leaders have transactional roles among their diverse segments of supporters instead of a transformational effect that enthrals and transforms followers. However, while the non-charismatic form depends on extremely tireless political activity by the leaders that focuses on organization building, in personal party personalism one is unlikely to find this emphasis on organization building and intra-party governance.

In the sections that followed the theoretical discussion, I used this perspective to analyse the case of Erdoğan and the JDP. I examined Erdoğan's public image, the degree of his autonomy within his organization, the context of his political ascent, his personal qualities and his political style. I have demonstrated that, while Erdoğan had a very strong public image and a high degree of autonomy within the JDP, he was lacking the personal-intellectual qualities of most charismatic leaders that helped them transform their followers. However, the biographical details of his personality and political activity illustrated the fact that his 'low-populist' appeal was extremely vital for his political salience, and at the same time he was a diligent, innovative and pragmatic organization man (teşkilatçı) focusing exclusively on achieving and maintaining power. The mass membership organization that Erdoğan personally constructed and his robust action – consisting of extensive travelling to various corners of the country, numerous speeches to diverse segments inside and outside the party, and a remarkable amount of time spent on intra-party governance – was the basis of Erdoğan's authority. The wider implication of this analysis of the case of Erdoğan and the JDP is as follows: non-charismatic personalist leaders and/or the populist leaders of various personal parties are not prophets. But, the non-charismatic personalist leaders, such as Erdoğan, certainly tend to be diligent and pragmatic organization builders.

Another theoretical contention of this chapter was that personalism and highy routinized and bureaucratized organizations are not mutually exclusive political phenomena. When this analysis is placed within the general theoretical approach of the book, the picture is as follows: individual agency is certainly key for the formation of collective political actors (such as the JDP), but the individual choices and actions of the leader (Erdoğan) and his experience that shape collective agency are also the product of broader political, socio-cultural and social circumstances/structures.

5   The JDP's Strategies: Moving beyond the Basics of Turkish Party Politics

Introduction

The Justice and Development Party won numerous consecutive elections after its foundation in 2002 despite many political crises. Unlike its right-wing predecessors, such as the Democrat Party of the 1950s, the Motherland Party of the 1980s and 1990s, and the Islamist Welfare Party of the 1990s (which became the Virtue Party at the end of the 1990s),[1] the JDP showed signs neither of electoral failure nor of any considerable intra-party discontent throughout this period. What distinguished the JDP from its right-wing predecessors? What made the JDP a novel force in Turkish politics? In this chapter, I argue that the combination of a large and pervasive membership organization that was active year-round, tension-increasing electoral propaganda, and a strong and decisively pro-JDP media was vital for the electoral achievements and political resilience of the party.

The management of different and mostly diverging expectations of party members, supporters and the electoral base was central to the JDP elite's strategies. In order to understand members' and supporters' engagements with the party, I borrowed – and, to a certain extent, reinterpreted – two interrelated concepts from Panebianco (1988). These are 'collective incentives' and 'selective incentives'. Relying on Panebianco's explanations (1988: 21–32), 'collective incentives' have been identified as the extra-material ideological and emotional bonds between the party and its members and supporters. I attribute a rather broad meaning to the term to refer to every possible connection between the party and its members and supporters, other than links such as patronage and clientelism based on material benefits. These bonds can be ideological, programmatic and emotional, but they can also be a product of traditional political preferences of families as well as a strong

---

[1] For brief information on these and other parties cited throughout the chapter, see Appendices 1 and 2.

affection for party leaders. In line with Panebianco's explanations (1988: 21–32), I define 'selective incentives' mainly as individual benefits, including every kind of social, symbolic, economic and cultural capital gain expected from being a party member.

It should be also underlined that this distinction between collective and selective incentives had a very concrete reflection in party life. During my interviews, I frequently came across two different expressions used to describe party members. One of these expressions was *partili* and the other one was *partici* (Interviewee 48, 2014).[2] While the former term referred to those party members with a sincere and altruistic engagement with the party, the latter term was used by my interviewees for party members who were expecting benefits such as jobs, promotion, aid and posts, along with a wider network of potential friends and customers from the party. While *partili* represented JDP cadres driven by 'collective incentives', *partici* represented the JDP members driven by 'selective incentives', in the vocabulary of my interviewees. The balance struck between these different modes of engagement of the members and supporters with the party was central to the JDP's success.

In the second section, I briefly touch upon the potential contributions of party members coming from various different political backgrounds to the strategic inclinations of the party. In this section, I demonstrate the aspects in which the JDP was different from its right-wing predecessors in terms of organizational dynamics and electoral strategies. In the same section, I identify the JDP elite's long-term strategic aim as 'maintaining predominance', which, in the longer term, has certainly contributed to the rise of a competitive authoritarian regime in Turkey under the rule of the JDP. Despite their short-term electoral benefits, the JDP elite embraced a rather controlled approach to redistributive strategies and particularism (mainly patronage and clientelism). The party – in order to protect its autonomy and, thus, the technocratic capacity of the JDP governments – also did not compromise extensively with local power holders.

In the third section, I briefly look at what was substituted by the JDP elite for the overwhelmingly patronage- and clientelism-based strategies and agreements with local and national politically salient individuals and

---

[2] A similar differentiation was also made by Interviewee 12 (2014). One should also note that the suffix *-li* in Turkish usually indicates an organic, spontaneous, mostly ascriptive and usually emotional membership relationship. By contrast, the suffix *-ci* usually indicates somebody's trade or profession. If someone sells fabric (*kumaş* in Turkish), for example, she is called *kumaşçı*. Hence, while the *partili* implied an emotional, sincere, organic relationship with the party, *partici* implied a less emotional and, in a sense, more professional relationship depending on material expectations.

social groups. As the electoral effectiveness of 'classical patronage politics' and particularism decreased, the party elite started to invest heavily in discursive-emotional techniques in electoral propaganda in order to consolidate its electoral support. In the fourth section, I give a detailed picture of the JDP's communication instruments in which conventional, organization-based communication methods were supported by the strong pro-JDP media. I argue that, without this combination, the JDP elite's and Erdoğan's interventions in public debate would have been much less effective and the party's predominant role in Turkish politics would not have been protected.

Striking a Balance between the Islamist Past and the Centre-Right Present

The JDP and Its Right-Wing Predecessors: Moving beyond the Basics of Turkish Politics

The JDP had always been seen as a grand coalition of right-wing politicians from various diverging backgrounds under the control of a previously Islamist elite. This characteristic of the party was underlined by many students of Turkish politics as well as the party's members. Tuğal, by referring to a sub-provincial (*ilçe*) organization of the JDP, underlines the fact that even this local branch was a coalition of Islamists, the centre-right and nationalists (2009: 151). Furthermore, some prominent social democratic politicians were also involved in the foundation process and this greatly enhanced the pluralist appearance of the party organization. As Hale and Özbudun note, particularly in the 2007 general election, the JDP deliberately nominated almost 170 deputies with liberal and centre-right backgrounds, and even a politician with a social democratic background could become a minister in the JDP government after this election (2010: 43). According to a statement by Hüseyin Çelik, one of the founding figures of the party, made in 2003, this heterogeneous party structure 'is not only valid for the high echelons of the party, it is also valid for the party branches as well' (Çakır, 2003a).

It should also be mentioned that this coalitional character of the party was complemented by the diversity of its electoral base. According to the statistical analysis of the JDP's electoral base in 2002, with reference to voters' choices in the general elections in 1999, 26 per cent of the JDP's constituency voted for the first time in 2002, 22 per cent came from the Nationalist Action Party's base, 28 per cent from a Islamist National View background, 9 per cent from the Motherland Party, 7 per cent from the True Path Party and 7 per cent from the Democratic Left Party

(Erder, 2002: 129). This situation was usually evaluated as a potential problem for the party since it might have a detrimental effect on its cohesion. Yet there was also a positive contribution of this pluralism to the JDP in terms of its elite's strategic inclinations and skills. Although, the JDP located itself in the history of a longer centre-right tradition, the elite of the party were always aware of the weaknesses of the previous centre-right parties as well as of the Islamist Welfare Party thanks to their previous experiences.

It can be argued that the most crucial lesson the JDP took from the experience of its predecessors arose from the problems entailed by the heavy reliance on 'classical patronage politics' (as it is termed in this chapter).[3] During the JDP years, social expenditure by the state increased (Karagöl, 2013: 57) and this, apparently, contributed remarkably to the party's lasting electoral achievements. Nevertheless, the party was extremely successful at reducing the state budget deficit (Karagöl, 2013: 42), and during the JDP years the number of public employees did not increase significantly either (DİSK, 2014: 3–4). Limitations on the rise in the number of public employees and the balanced public budget under the rule of JDP governments suggested that the party had moved beyond 'classical centre-right patronage' in Turkey. The main indicators of classical patronage in Turkey were significant increases in the number of public employees and generous public expenditure that caused public budget deficits. Another component of classical patronage and clientelism in Turkey was the influence of powerful local and traditional actors in politics, such as tribal leaders, notable families, religious authorities and large land-owners of provincial cities, leading to the 'induced participation' of rural and urban poor to politics via these powerful intermediaries.

'Induced participation' (Özbudun, 1975) or 'vertical mobilization' (Sayarı, 1975) refers to the incorporation and mobilization of urban, and particularly rural, popular sectors of Turkish society by political parties through negotiations with local and traditional power holders. Hence, since the transition to multi-party politics in the middle of the

---

[3] By following Ayata (2010), Çarkoğlu and Aytaç (2015) and Wuthrich (2015), it is possible to distinguish between patronage and clientelism, or rural versus urban clientelism (K. Çınar, 2016), in order to understand the difference between the JDP's highly centralized clientelistic strategies and the redistributive strategies of its right-wing predecessors, which were based on local – and mostly rural – patronage networks and a large public economic sector. Yet, in the broader literature on the topic, analysts of the phenomenon do not consider patronage and clientelism separately but tend to see the former as a sub-type of the latter (see Stokes, 2007). In order to avoid the incompatibility between these different studies, I distinguish between 'classical patronage' and 'new methods of patronage'.

1940s, local patronage networks and local and traditional elites together with the resources provided by the import substitution economy created the main ground of 'classical patronage politics' in Turkey.[4] Nevertheless, since the 1980s, economic liberalization, domestic immigration and the rise of urban poverty drastically dissolved the socio-economic basis of the classical patronage.[5]

As Kopecky and Spirova (2012: 27) underline, it might be misleading to use public employment numbers and expenditure as 'proxy indicators' of party patronage. Instead they recommend the use of expert interviews to see the full extent of the phenomenon. In line with this perspective, when I argue that the JDP did not depend on classical patronage politics as much as its right-wing predecessors, I also depend heavily on my personal observations in the fieldwork.[6] However, it does not mean that the party leadership did not deploy new methods of patronage (and clientelism) (Aytaç and Öniş, 2014; Çarkoğlu and Aytaç, 2015; Marschall et al., 2016) which heavily relied on suspicious links between the private sector and public resources (Çeviker-Gürakar, 2016; Esen and Gümüşçü, 2017).[7] Highly publicized corruption probes against the JDP governments at the time of writing had something to do with these novel methods of patronage and party finance. However, from the perspective of the explanations I gave above on 'classical patronage politics' of the centre-right in Turkey, the JDP definitely represented a novel force in Turkish politics and moved beyond conventional political-electoral strategies of the right in Turkey.

---

[4] The volume edited by Akarlı and Ben-Dor is a classic explanation of classical patronage in Turkey (1975).

[5] See Kemahlıoğlu (2012) for the gradual dissolution of this classical patronage politics after the introduction of neo-liberal reforms. See also Bayraktar and Altan (2013).

[6] I illustrate details supporting this claim in Chapters 6 and 7.

[7] I briefly mention these new methods of patronage in the next chapter. It should also be noted that, particularly in peripheral and poor urban contexts, the JDP deployed redistributive strategies and created clientelistic networks. The JDP's 'low-populist' appeal delineated in Chapter 3 was central to the smooth functioning of these redistributive strategies and the transformation of clientelistic networks into votes. After all, as Auyero's excellent account (2001) of 'Peronist survival and problem-solving networks' illustrates, without the proper emotional and cultural bond between the supplier and receiver in clientelistic exchange, the clientelistic relationship cannot be sustained and cannot be transformed into electoral gains. The only difference to the JDP's redistributive strategies in localities was that, unlike Peronist personal mediation for problem solving, the JDP leadership, to a large extent, did not allow any sedimentation of brokers or patrons in localities. High degrees of rotation in JDP local governments as well as local-provincial executive branches was evidence that this rather bureaucratized and centralized clientelism depended more on 'organizational networks' than on personalized ones.

As one of my interviewees, a prominent public opinion researcher working for the JDP, emphasized, 'the JDP was aware of a Demirelist [*Demirelci*] right-wing tradition which relied heavily on limitless promises to voters' (Interviewee 38, 2014). Süleyman Demirel was always a symbolic name in Turkey, and he represented the pragmatic inclinations of the centre-right politics as well as a strategy that depended markedly on classical patronage politics, generous subsidies for agricultural products and highly unrealistic promises to the electorate. Hence, it is fair to argue that the party, unlike its centre-right predecessors, deployed a rather 'controlled'[8] approach to redistributive policies and cautiously engaged with local power holders in order to remain in power for a longer time. In this sense, it is important to take a closer look at the differences between the JDP and previous right-wing parties that deeply shaped JDP politics, namely the Islamist Welfare Party and the Motherland Party.

The Legacy of the Welfare Party: The Importance of a Large and Pervasive Membership Organization, Active Year-Round Most of my interviewees tended to see the main difference between the Islamist National View parties and the JDP on an ideological basis. It is known that the founding leader of the National View tradition, Erbakan, said many times that 'if you have faith you have opportunities [*iman var imkan var!*]' and 'I do not have supporters; I have believers', which indicated the role of ideational-emotional links between the Islamist National View tradition and its followers. Another interviewee, a knowledgeable sympathizer and bureaucrat, also underlined the same motivations of the members of the Islamist National View parties. According to him, Islamist National View members did not really observe a 'benefit–cost balance [*nimet-külfet dengesi*]' in their engagement to the party (Interviewee 19, 2014). A high-up member of the Felicity Party, the most recent party of the Islamist National View tradition, also emphasized that 'belief' was the basis of the organization in the National View tradition: 'Erbakan Hodja[9] had this expression: "if you have belief, you can squeeze milk from a billy goat [*inanç tekeden süt çıkarır*]"' (Interviewee 1, 2013). Hence, a highly motivated mass membership organization was key to the Islamist National View's strategies particularly during the 1990s.

---

[8] Öniş draws attention to this fact (2012).
[9] The term 'hodja [*hoca*]' in modern Turkish has a double meaning which refers both to men of religion and teachers in secular education institutions. In the case of Erbakan, these were inseparable since he was both an Islamist political leader and a professor of engineering.

As Delibaş (2015: 54–64) underlines, all of the Turkish political parties headed towards capital-intensive[10] and media-based electoral strategies during the 1980s and 1990s. In contrast, the Welfare Party of the Islamist National View tradition was busy from the beginning of the 1990s constructing a large membership organization that was active year-round and relied heavily on a membership profile motivated by strong collective incentives. Poor government performance, the increasing organizational decline of centre-right and centre-left parties, electoral volatility and the fragmentation of the political system (discussed at length in Chapter 2) gave an advantage to the Welfare Party's strategy of using an ideologically motivated and large membership organization, active year-round, over the clientelistic and media-oriented strategies of its electoral competitors, particularly during the mid 1990s. Beyond strategic inclinations, the Islamist Welfare Party past of the JDP made a direct contribution to the party's human resources. One of my interviewees, a sub-provincial JDP chair with a National View background, described this organizational legacy of the Islamist past of the JDP succinctly:

The organizational work and approach [teşkilatçılık] of the people coming from the [Islamist] National View past is different. There were people in the party from the Motherland Party, the True Path Party or the Republican People's Party. They cannot stand our activities. You may ask why this was the case. Our organizational activity is ballot box-based. In other words it targets ballot boxes. The main things are the ballot box representative, the neighbourhood administrations above him or her, and establishing these governing bodies in neighbourhoods. Every week there is a neighbourhood meeting. In these meetings we check whether our ballot box representatives are OK. Our work is entirely targeting the base. I still could not overcome this. There are protocol meetings and inaugurations. Believe me, I cannot attend them. Because organizational work exhausts you. Why? Every week we have different meetings in fifteen neighbourhoods. Every week, [we had] regular neighbourhood meetings, neighbourhood consultation meetings including our ballot box representatives. We put enormous effort into the organization of these meetings. People coming from other parties are not really used to this kind of party activity. They are usually used to 'high' politics. This is to say that: you go and see influential people, you talk to a single person and expect 'this many votes would come [through this person]'. They have always done this kind of politics. But this is not the case in the JDP. We try to establish one-to-one contact with every voter. You gain votes one by one, by registering [individual] members [...]

---

[10] For the distinction between labour-intensive and capital-intensive campaigning techniques, see Farrell (1996: 171). While the former depends on party workers, volunteers, canvassing, mass meetings and individual contacts with voters, the latter relies upon a network of professionals, consultants and television.

Membership enhances the link between the party and the voter [...] The people coming from other parties are not really prone to this kind of approach (Interviewee 26, 2014).

From the perspective of the distinction, I made between selective and collective incentives in the introduction, it seems that 'collective incentives' played a major role in the engagement of the members of the Islamist National View parties with the organization. The JDP elites with a National View background were aware of the benefits of collective incentives as well as of having a large and pervasive membership organization that established a direct connection between the party and the electorate, without the mediation of other channels such as influential persons. This led the JDP elite to strike a very fine balance between 'collective' and 'selective' incentives, unlike the previous centre-right parties which heavily relied on classical patronage politics and clientelistic networks. As one of my interviewees underlined, the JDP's organization 'mainly relied on the National View tradition. And the organization in the National View stemmed from the fact that the party had a strict ideology, a specific cause [dava] relying on a political movement' (Interviewee 40, 2014).

Nevertheless, the JDP could not have survived by remaining an overwhelmingly ideological-Islamist party, given the electoral and political circumstances outlined in previous chapters. The party had to sacrifice some of the benefits that might stem from strong collective incentives – in other words, the ideological, programmatic and emotional engagements of its members – in order to appeal to the median voter and come closer to a centre-right position. In this sense, the Motherland Party cadres had a quite decisive influence on the strategic inclinations of the JDP organization (Aydın and Dalmış, 2008: 201).[11] This is why it is crucial to look briefly at the difference between the organizational dynamics of the Motherland Party and the JDP.

Legacy of the Motherland Party: The Failure of Overwhelmingly Patronage-, Clientelism- and Media-Based Strategies Just after the military coup in 1980, the centre-right Motherland Party unexpectedly won the general elections in 1983 and formed a single-party majority government. The Motherland Party captured the centrist and pragmatic inclination of the Turkish electorate through a discourse around economic rationality, the free market and service delivery (Ergüder, 1991: 156–157). What characterized the Motherland Party in organizational

---

[11] For the influence of Motherland Party cadres on the JDP, see also Çakır (2003b).

terms were its solid factions. Factions in the party were kept together, to a certain extent, through the personality of the party leader Turgut Özal and, to a greater extent, by 'intra-party clientelism' (Türsan, 1995: 177) including methods such as allocating ministerships and important public posts to powerful local elites. Here, it should be noted that not only the Motherland Party, but also other centre-right parties in Turkey that preceded it – most notably the Democrat Party – had a much more tolerant intra-party political atmosphere in which the decisions of the leadership were frequently contested by intra-party factions and elites, as has been shown by Eroğul's classic account (2003: 180) and in seminal works on the Democrat Party and the Justice Party by Demirel (2004, 2011).

After Özal became president of the Republic and left the party, and after the victory of Mesut Yılmaz (the representative of the liberal faction in the 1991 convention) conservative and religious figures in the party gradually started to split away from the organization (Kalaycıoğlu, 2002: 51). As one of my interviewees, a top Motherland Party politician, argued, 'the religious, conservative masses did not enjoy the leadership of Yılmaz as much as they enjoyed the leadership of Özal, Demirel or Erdoğan' (Interviewee 22, 2014). As another of my interviewees, a former local Motherland Party executive member who would go on to become a member of the JDP, underlined, the exit of the conservative elite and thus the split of conservative figures from the party base had a corrosive effect on party activities on the ground (Interviewee 13, 2014).

The response of another top Motherland Party politician to a question regarding the superiority of the JDP over the Motherland Party accurately summarized the differences between the JDP and its centre-right predecessor:

What is different in the JDP is the fact that they are coming from the 'school of Erbakan [*Erbakan mektebi*]'. The school of Erbakan is highly disciplined and attaches great importance to technology [...] and they work for the sake of God [*Allah rızası*]. Once Yılmaz told me that we should organize like the Welfare Party. I told him that this is impossible. Because these people take part in the [Welfare] party to sacrifice not to receive benefits [...] National Salvation [the predecessor of the Islamist Welfare Party] was organized even in the apartment blocks [...] They were all spending from their own pockets [...] They were closely interested in all apartments and neighbourhoods [...] They use their own car for party activities. They fill their cars with people and take them to the meetings and to polling stations. This is amazing discipline. No other party can come close to this. Because they do this for the God's sake [...] The person who takes part in Motherland, first of all, either seeks a job for his son or he wants to be a deputy or mayor. Nevertheless, the JDP has started to change as well. Some of them say 'we were jihadists and we turned into contractors [*mücahitken mütahit olduk*]' (Interviewee 17, 2014).

Despite the decrease in the motivation of the party members, and the corrosive effects of power on collective incentives, it would not be an exaggeration to highlight the role of the Islamist National View tradition, most notably the importance attached to the 'collective incentive-driven pervasive membership organization', in the survival and electoral performance of the JDP. The most crucial lesson the JDP elite took from the Motherland Party experience must have been the problems entailed by heavy dependence on classical patronage and clientelism as well as on media- and capital-intensive strategies, which ignored the vital roles played by the party on the ground. The JDP elite were aware of this strategy's detrimental impact on the Motherland Party's electoral and political destiny.

The JDP's Long-Term Political Aim: 'Maintaining Predominance'

Considering the failures of its right-wing predecessors, it is highly plausible to argue that the JDP elite did not want simply to increase its vote share by any means at hand. Instead, the JDP struck a balance between the short-term requirements of the electoral processes (responsiveness) and the long-term requirements of being in office (responsibility).[12] One of my high-ranking interviewees from the JDP vividly described this balance: 'doing politics [for the JDP elite] is this kind of business, and I think it is the hardest part: you have to understand and appeal to the taxi driver and convince the academic at the same time' (Interviewee 36, 2014). The key instrument of this balance between the short-term requirements of elections and the long-term requirements of being in office was the highly autonomous leadership and party structure.[13]

Furthermore, as some of my interviewees mentioned, the party elite started to see the JDP as the predominant force within Turkish politics with an explicit reference to other dominant parties across the world (Interviewee 29, 2014). Hence, given the JDP's long-term aims and the party's electoral potential as revealed by previous elections, deploying full-scale vote maximization strategies such as highly redistributive policies and generous promises was not a preferable option for the JDP elite. This was why, in an answer to a question about redistributive strategies, one of my interviewees, an adviser to party leader Erdoğan and an expert

---

[12] See Mair (2013) for the dilemma between responsiveness and responsibility in Western democracies.

[13] I elaborate on this organizational architecture, which is characterized by a highly autonomous leadership and party, in the following chapters. In this chapter, I give only the general framework of this organizational-electoral strategy.

on social policies, put emphasis on the fact that, while seeking short-term solutions to poverty[14] and trying to create a welfare state, the JDP largely refrained from uncontrolled redistributive tactics. Strikingly, the same interviewee also added that 'we told ourselves at the beginning that we wouldn't surrender to the populist style of rightist politicians' (Interviewee 35, 2014).[15]

Given this interviewee's point, it is plausible that the party leadership frequently encountered demands from the provincial party elite, provincial chairs and mayors to initiate redistributive policies. However, given the state budget balance protected throughout the JDP's rule, it is possible that the leadership firmly rejected these demands in general. From the same perspective, it is also plausible that the leadership also inhibited a move towards the other extreme, protecting the party from falling into a purely technocratic, long-term political strategy that depended on drastic decreases in public spending given the volume of social policy expenditure by the party since the beginning of JDP rule. As Şentürk, a former JDP vice-chair in İstanbul, underlined, the electorate can bear unpopular measures for overcoming political and economic crises for a while, but politicians should not think that this can go on forever (2007: 186–187).

In sum, the JDP must be considered a party outside the classical patronage-based centre-right politics of Turkey explained above. Since the social and economic structure (particularly the import substitution economy) that gave rise to classical patronage politics of the centre-right had already started to decline (due to the rise of neo-liberal policies and regulations that targeted privatization and reduced the role of state in economy and accelerating urbanization during the 1980s and 1990s), the JDP was required to adopt new strategies. This peculiarity of the party was also accurately captured by Özdan (2014), a critical commentator who drew attention to the relationship between socio-economic change in Turkey (urbanization and the fall of traditional local, land-owning elites) and the rise of the JDP.

As discussed above, and as will be elaborated in the following chapters, as a part of its long-term aim of maintaining predominance, the JDP elite

---

[14] Distributing coal and food in poor neighbourhoods became a well-known practice throughout the JDP years alongside other social policy reforms and expenditures in favour of low-income social segments.

[15] It should be noted that, in the JDP discourse revealed by written material such as the party programme and speeches of its leaders and prominent figures, populism referred to highly redistributive strategies. Yet at the same time, the JDP leader Erdoğan saw 'balanced' redistributive policies that relieved the popular sectors to be, to a certain extent, necessary and legitimate.

avoided relying heavily on provincial patronage networks. The party also avoided recruiting its political cadres extensively from traditional local power holders in provincial Turkey.[16] Instead, the party tended to replace these kinds of cadres with younger, highly educated, more ambitious, career-oriented yet submissive people. As Özdan underlined, 'Prime Minister [Erdoğan]'s most important skill is to create continuous expectations and keep these expectations alive [among the party cadres]. The JDP's constant renewal of the party cadres, except the core team, creates continuous energy and enthusiasm in the party' (2014). This dynamic was also underlined by a Central Executive Committee member of the party (Interviewee 37, 2014).

Hence, the predominance of the party in power provided wider flexibility to the party elite for finding required human resources: young and ambitious people. Nevertheless, the leadership also carefully dealt with an overwhelmingly careerist inclination in the party. This was why one of the commentators close to the JDP underlined Erdoğan's talent in striking a balance between 'interests' and 'mission' (Koru, 2012). It should be also noted that this frequent rotation of executive cadres of the party, to a great extent, inhibited sedimentation of power holder intermediaries within the party and in localities. As a result of the strategic experience from the previous centre-right parties and the socio-demographic change that undermined classical patronage politics, the JDP became a genuinely novel political force in Turkish politics. The above-mentioned differences between the JDP and its right-wing predecessors are summarized in Table 5.1.[17]

Playing with Emotions with 'Controlled Tension': Erdoğan's JDP as the 'Victim-Saviour'

In the previous section, I illustrated how classical centre-right patronage declined in Turkey and how the JDP's long-term aim of becoming a predominant party ruled out highly redistributive electoral strategies. As a result, investing in discursive and emotional techniques by drawing mostly upon the party leader Erdoğan's personality and political interventions became a crucial electoral tactic for the JDP elite. Erdoğan was usually accused of 'polarizing' society and politics through his public

---

[16] I elaborate on the JDP's relationship with local political elites in Chapter 7.

[17] In this chapter, I only briefly mention the difference between the JDP's organization and intra-party governance and those of its right-wing predecessors. In the following chapters I elaborate on these dimensions of JDP politics with reference to Table 5.1.

Table 5.1 *The JDP and its right-wing predecessors*

Parties Strategies	Islamist Welfare Party	Centre-right Motherland Party	Justice and Development Party
Incentive structure	Collective	Selective	Hybrid (balance between collective and selective incentives)
Organization	Highly motivated, pervasive membership organization, active year-round	Periodically active party on the ground for ballot box safety	Pervasive membership organization, active year-round
Campaign technique	Labour-intensive (based on party members and volunteers)	Media- and capital-intensive	Hybrid (labour- and capital-intensive)
Electoral strategy	One-by-one vote canvassing	Negotiations with local and national politically salient individuals and social groups and classical patronage	Hybrid (with a special emphasis on one-by-one vote canvassing and avoiding extensive patronage and clientelism)
Degree of party autonomy*	High	Low	High
Degree of leadership autonomy*	High	Low	High
Mode of intra-party governance*	Authoritarian (no room for factions and powerful local and national figures)	Tolerant (with factions and local and national powerful figures other than the party leader)	Authoritarian (no room for factions and powerful local and national figures)
Party type*	Mass-based	Elite-based	Hybrid (personalistic mass party)

Source: Author's compilation.
Note: The distinctions marked with * are discussed at length in other chapters.

speeches.[18] Commentators in Turkey usually pointed out the potential dangers of the discriminatory tone of his speeches and complained that

[18] Although political commentators in the media tend to call this tactic 'polarization', the term in fact denotes a structural quality of party systems which is characterized by the distance of political actors on a given cleavage dimension such as left and right (Sani and Sartori, 1983). For instance, as competing political actors cumulate at the extreme poles of a left–right dimension, this means a high degree of polarization in a given party system. In the Turkish case, Erdoğan increased tensions among competing political actors, yet

Erdoğan was a highly divisive figure who separated society into camps according to people's attitudes towards conservative hegemony in Turkey. I call this electoral tactic of the JDP 'controlled tension'.[19] Controlled tension can be described as artificially increasing political tensions in pre-election periods by subtle discursive attacks on political rivals with reference to the high–low, democracy–anti-democracy and secular–religious divides. This, in turn, helped the ruling party enlarge the boundaries of its electoral base in pre-election periods by antagonizing its electoral rivals and pushing undecided voters to choose a camp. Relying on the party's 'low-populist' political appeal/style elaborated in Chapter 3, the tactic of controlled tension helped the JDP consolidate its electoral base by labelling its electoral competitors, depending on the context, as either elite, anti-democratic, anti-religious or, most recently, 'anti-native and - national [yerli ve milli]', forces against the JDP government. Yet, in every possible case, the logic remained the same: the JDP elite intentionally created simple dualities before elections and ensured the existence of a mood that elections were held mainly between the JDP and others. These interventions by the party elite, more often than not, defined the electoral drama of the country and drew the JDP's political opponents into a discursive struggle defined by the JDP.

The tactic of controlled tension always appealed to the fears of the electorate. In pre-election periods, the JDP elite convincingly created a mood that only the JDP was capable of protecting the long-lasting traditions and values of society and only it was strong enough to provide political (and, to a lesser extent, economic) stability to the country.[20] The JDP elite made great efforts to present the party as the true representative and the authentic defender of the common cultural and political values of the 'nation-people'.[21]

High voter turnout in elections as well as the declining vote share of smaller, more ideological parties in the electoral system could be considered indicators of the tactic of 'controlled tension'.[22] Through

his constant interventions in Turkish politics did not create a polarized party system. Instead it caused a 'bifurcation' (kamplaşma).

[19] The term 'controlled tension' originated with Duran (2013), and he uses it to indicate the JDP's resistance to and counter-attack on secularist actors such as the army and the bureaucracy. In this text when I use the term I imply a wider tactical inclination of the party than the one pointed out by Duran (2013).

[20] Here it should be noted that, more often than not, political crises are staged/performed by the populists even when such crises are, in reality, non-existent (see Moffitt, 2016: 113–132).

[21] It should be noted that the terms 'nation [millet]' and 'people [halk]' are used interchangeably in JDP discourse.

[22] In Turkey, voter turnout has always been very high compared to the Western democracies. Nevertheless, there has been a considerable change over time. In the 2002 general election and 2004 local elections voter turnout was below 80 per cent. After the introduction of 'tactic of controlled tension', voter turnout in elections started

increasing the fears of the low-income, conservative-religious majority of the country *vis-à-vis* the alleged threat of the elite–secularist oppression, the tactic of controlled tension consolidated the party vote[23] by transforming undecided voters into decisive supporters, decisive sympathizers into party members and party members into party activists.[24] Although it created a much more decisive opposition against the JDP, the tactic of controlled tension consolidated party cohesion as well as the party's electoral base, and at the same time increased the number of voters. For instance, in the 2014 local elections, the JDP's electoral propaganda framed the election as the 'independence struggle of the new Turkey' and depicted Erdoğan as the leader of this struggle (*Aktifhaber*, 2014). It should also be underlined that the personalization of politics also played its part in this strategy, and political divides in the country, most notably the high–low divide elaborated upon in previous chapters, also became an anti-Erdoğanism–Erdoğanism divide.

However, the party elite took great care to not be perceived in the eyes of the electorate as the aggressor driving the tension, and worked hard to protect the JDP's image as the victim. This was why Erdoğan usually used the expression 'we were not aggressive but we stand tall [*dikleşmeden dik durduk*]'. In other words, the party tried to protect an image that it had always suffered the attacks of its opponents but resisted them. One can also see great efforts of the supporters and members of the JDP in discrediting the critiques of intellectuals and political opponents of the party who argued that in order to get votes Erdoğan increased tensions. This kind of defensive position mostly justified Erdoğan's attacks on his opponents.[25]

Furthermore, the Republican People's Party's secularist critique of the JDP also provided the party elite with the upper hand in presenting the

---

to increase. In the 2011 general election, it was 83 per cent and in the local elections in 2014, 89 per cent. In the two general elections in 2015, voter turnout was 86 per cent and 87 per cent respectively.

[23] When the JDP's discourse was mainly reliant on a pro-democracy and pro-EU conservative democracy narrative, the party's vote started to decline and hit rock bottom in the local elections in 2009 with 38 per cent. Since that election, the JDP elite, and most notably the party leader Erdoğan, have tended to use tension-increasing, exclusionary language in their public speeches, particularly in pre-election periods. Since 2009, the party vote has started to increase considerably. In the 2011 election, the JDP received almost 50 per cent of the vote, and in the 2014 local elections the party got remarkably higher than the previous local election with 43 per cent of the popular vote. Although the decline and subsequent rise of the party vote over this period cannot be explained by the tension-increasing interventions of the JDP elite alone, there appears to be a strong correlation.

[24] I borrow these distinctions between supporters, members and activists from Duverger (1974: 138).

[25] For example, see Esayan (2014a).

JDP as the only party capable of protecting the conservative-religious sectors of society against the assaults of the secularist establishment and the elite (M. Çınar, 2013: 46).[26] Thus, by reframing and presenting secularist critiques as a threat to the religious, conservative sectors of society, the JDP elite reminded its electorate that its survival in power was vital for the interests and survival of Islamic identity in the cultural, intellectual and economic realms (M. Çınar, 2013: 45). This defined the character of 'survival politics' (M. Çınar, 2013: 45) as a primary component of the JDP's discursive strategy. Hence, as one of my interviewees underlined, conservative-religious (*muhafazakar-mütedeyyin*) segments of society always feared that, if the JDP were to fall from power, they would be treated unjustly (Interviewee 20, 2014). It should also be underlined that criticism of the religious appeals of JDP politicians by the Republican People's Party was usually interpreted by the JDP elite and JDP supporters as evidence of the main opposition's disdain for devout and ordinary people.

Most recently, and particularly after the corruption probes in 2013 and the failed coup attempt in 2016, the pro-JDP media and intellectuals increasingly and frequently began to depict the party and Erdoğan as being in a struggle with powerful international actors, which was, perhaps, to a certain extent compatible with reality given the increasing dislike of Erdoğan in powerful Western capitals. This also helped the JDP consolidate its position domestically by adding a new dimension to its populist script and by enriching the image that portrayed Erdoğan's JDP as the 'victim-saviour' of contemporary Turkey. As noted by Duran, after all, 'the *politics of controlled tension* [Duran's emphasis] and Erdoğan's superior performance in manipulating public debate allowed the AK Party [JDP] to effectively take advantage of these polarizations and to solidify popular support' (2013: 102).

Communication Strategy: 'Strong Organization' and the Pro-JDP Media

The JDP strategy with regard to organizational dynamics and electoral propaganda was also complemented and supported by its communication instruments. In this section, I give a detailed picture of the twofold

[26] Many of Erdoğan's speeches draw upon the theme of 'assaults by the Republican People's Party on religion'. For a news report on Erdoğan's claims with 'documents' that the Republican People's Party sold some mosques and turned some of them into storehouses during the 1930s and 1940s, see *Aktifhaber* (2012). Erdoğan also said: 'Our nation remembers well how the mosques were shut, how the call to prayer [*ezan*] was silenced, how they intervened in the way people dressed' (*Aktifhaber*, 2012).

communication strategy of the JDP. On the one hand, the JDP had the advantage of having a 'strong organization'. This is to say that, from the practical point of view of the JDP elite, the party was organized at the neighbourhood level and had large numbers of motivated and qualified members (Şentürk, 2008a: 21). On the other hand, the JDP leadership also supported the efforts of its large and pervasive membership organization with the construction of a decisively pro-JDP media. These complementary aspects of the JDP's communication activity distinguished the party from its political competitors as well as its right-wing predecessors.

'Strong Organization'

As will be illustrated in detail in the next chapter, the JDP had a highly developed organization with a large number of members organized even in the smallest corners of the country. In this section, I focus firstly on the uses of the JDP's large and pervasive membership organization as an effective communication channel.[27] As illustrated by Çaha and Guida's study of the campaigning activities of the JDP and the Republican People's Party in the 2009 local elections, the JDP had a clear superiority over other parties in preparing and motivating its organization for party activity on the ground through education (2011: 66). In my fieldwork, too, my questions about the educational activities of the JDP were usually met with an emphasis on the education of members on electoral issues (Interviewee 7, 2014). An examination of the official JDP publication, *Turkey Bulletin*, also revealed the prominence of topics on electoral affairs in the party's educational activities. In addition to members who were highly educated on electoral affairs, the JDP also had a very pervasive organization which extended to villages and neighbourhoods (Çaha and Guida, 2011: 66).

According to Çaha and Guida's observation on the eve of the 2009 local elections, other parties lacked an organization like the JDP's, which was active not only during the elections but during in other periods as well. Indeed, as one of my interviewees underlined, the JDP had a sensitivity towards keeping party organizations active even during the regular periods when there was no election approaching: 'you know the expression: "you come only around at election time" [...] We are going to every door lest people think that we only go for elections [...] This is the impression we had from the previous era' (Interviewee 10, 2014). According to Çaha and Guida, the JDP constantly kept its organizations

---

[27] In the next chapter I mainly focus on the intra-party governance and dynamics of this massive organization.

active through educational activities and the periodic and routine activities imposed on the provincial, sub-provincial, neighbourhood and village organizations of the party (2011: 67).

According to Şentürk, a former JDP executive from İstanbul, 'despite a shorter institutional history and a mass party base, the JDP members have a stronger loyalty to the party. This is because the party has a strong and active organization, and a large and active party organization enhances the loyalty of the members' (2008b: 287). Indeed, the observations of Çaha and Guida in the 2009 elections were in line with Şentürk's statement (2011: 72). One should also bring the robust and hardworking women's branches of the JDP into the picture. According to Çaha and Guida, for example, in Küçükçekmece, a sub-province of İstanbul, the JDP was able to mobilize a large army of volunteers consisting of youth and women. In line with my findings on the vitality of the women's branch of the party, Çaha and Guida argued that the JDP derived most of its dynamism from the work of young people and women (2011: 103).

Face-to-Face Interaction The first contribution of such a pervasive and effective organization to the JDP was the leverage that it provided to the party for face-to-face interaction with the electorate. The JDP elite always considered face-to-face interaction the most important method for reaching the electorate, and this situation should not be dismissed as mere rhetoric. According to Şentürk, a former JDP executive from İstanbul, the most important instrument of communication is face-to-face interaction because it is always more persuasive than other methods (2006: 119). Face-to-face interaction included house visits, workplace visits, coffee house visits and meetings organized in private halls (Şentürk, 2006: 154). Indeed, as Çaha and Guida (2011) observed in the 2009 local elections, the party took face-to-face interaction seriously in its electoral campaigns. For instance, the JDP candidate for the mayoralty in one of the central sub-provinces (Üsküdar) in İstanbul told researchers that he relied heavily on the strategy of 'warm contact [*sıcak temas*]' with the electorate (Çaha and Guida, 2011: 113).

One of the strategic assumptions of the JDP elite which led them to take face-to-face interaction seriously was the predominance of oral culture in Turkish society:

In societies where oral culture is predominant and which are characterized by a low degree of reading habits, the strength of party organizations gains a special significance. Parties with a strong and active organization are able to send their message to the electorate through one-to-one communication established by its members [...] Today the JDP runs its campaigns with its strong organizational structure [...] The JDP particularly attaches a special importance to women's branches, and hundreds of thousands homes have been visited by women and exposed to JDP propaganda (Şentürk, 2008b: 269).

Nevertheless, the JDP elite, members and strategists were also aware of the limitations of face-to-face activity. According to one of my interviewees, face-to-face interaction became less and less effective because of the change in information technologies and the rise of the social media: 'soon we might not find any people on the streets to shake their hands' (Interviewee 38, 2014). On the other hand, one of the vice-chairs of the party's İstanbul branch also told me that they saw professional campaigns and conventional face-to-face interaction as complementing each other (Interviewee 11, 2014). Therefore, the JDP had a hybrid approach to campaign techniques which blended capital- and labour-intensive strategies (also see Table 5.1).

The contribution of face-to-face interaction should not be understood only in the context of immediate electoral benefits. It seems that the importance attached to face-to-face interaction also had something to do with the desire of the JDP elite to keep party organizations active and alive with electoral work even in the periods when there was no election approaching. In addition, an active membership organization that visited the electorate and worked in the field motivated party members and supporters and provided crucial visibility to the JDP in elections as well. One should also underline the practical importance of 'strong organizations' in providing ballot box safety. As one of my experienced interviewees underlined, one of the primary roles of party organizations in Turkey was to protect the ballot boxes on election days from potential fraud (Interviewee 17, 2014).[28]

In this sense, too, the JDP had a clear advantage. In the 2014 local election in Ankara, for example, the Republican People's Party organizations were quite unsuccessful at providing ballot box records, which were necessary for appeals against disputed election results. An interview with one of the leading figures of a neutral civil organization for observing the elections highlighted this superiority of the JDP organization. According to Ayberk Yağız,

---

[28] It was really striking to see that this particular interviewee, a top Motherland Party politician with his own powerful local patronage network, had a very limited perspective on the importance of the membership organizations and considered it simply a tool for safeguarding ballot boxes in election days. This was emblematic of the perspective which caused the organizational decline of centre-right parties in Turkey during the 1990s.

the Republican People's Party organization was in such bad condition [on the election day of the 2014 local elections] that we thought that there was a conspiracy behind this. We had to collect ballot box records from the Nationalist Action Party and the Great Union Party [Büyük Birlik Partisi] independently from the Republican People's Party organizations. People did not enter results and the Republican People's Party's [online] system was down. Therefore they searched ballot box records through the internet [...] The most well-organized party was the JDP. They had at least one representative per ballot box, and there were people who were serving tea and food in the breaks. In the afternoon, other people came as replacements. While the ballot box staff of other parties were tired, the JDP brought fresh and new people. The Nationalist Action Party was quite organized too. The Republican People's Party was the worst. It had something to do with the general organization of the party (Güvenç, 2014).

Meetings Face-to-face interaction should not be seen only in the context of the work of junior party members. As one of my expert interviewees underlined, Erdoğan's meetings and mass rallies of the JDP should also be seen in this context (Interviewee 28, 2014). For example, before the 2007 general elections, it was reported that Erdoğan visited fifty-four provinces out of eighty-one, whereas his closest rival, Deniz Baykal, then the chair of the Republican People's Party, had been to only thirty-one (*Hürriyet*, 2007). Similarly, Erdoğan's performance before the 2009 elections was better, too. According to a news article published a couple of days before the elections, Erdoğan had visited fifty-seven provinces, whereas his closest rival Baykal had visited only thirty by then (*Zaman*, 2009). Erdoğan had also visited sixty-eight provinces during the 2011 election campaign (*Memurlar*, 2011). Before the 2014 local elections, Erdoğan had been to fifty-six provinces for meetings, although this time the opposition leader, the Republican People's Party's new leader Kılıçdaroğlu, had a better performance by participating in meetings in sixty provinces (*Milliyet*, 2014a).

The participation numbers were also usually remarkably higher in Erdoğan's meetings. For instance, for the 2011 general election in İstanbul, different parties had meetings in the same square, and the participation numbers varied significantly. According to police records, while 400,000 people participated in the JDP meeting in Kazlıçeşme, the Republican People's Party could attract only 82,000 people to the same square (*Milliyet*, 2011). Participation in the JDP mass rally just prior to the 2014 local elections was also another indication of its organizational capacity. Although the numbers of participants had been an issue of dispute since then, during the meeting Erdoğan claimed that there were 2 million people in the meeting space (*Radikal*, 2014a).

Mass rallies provided remarkable visibility for the JDP. It is also plausible to argue that, just like face-to-face interaction, organizing meetings might be considered a way of keeping party organizations active given the demanding work for 'filling the meeting space'. As one of my interviewees, an academic whose area of expertise is the centre-right, underlined, one of the reasons why Erdoğan organized so many meetings was to revitalize the party branches: 'When the prime minister is coming there, [for example,] the Kayseri branch of the party will start to work a week before' (Interviewee 28, 2014).

The organizational workload for the meetings also enhanced the hierarchical cohesion and solidarity of the party. Central decisions of organizing mass rallies in any part of the country started a chain reaction that went all the way down from the headquarters to the neighbourhood branches. The plans prepared by the headquarters were realized by the work of the lower rungs of the party. For example, for a meeting in İstanbul, the party headquarters in Ankara asks the provincial party branch to organize the meeting and the provincial party branch asks the sub-provincial branches to call as many people as possible from their own regions. Sub-provincial party branches also push neighbourhood representatives under their control to call as many people as possible from their neighbourhoods.

Apart from that, it also seems that Erdoğan had a special appetite for meetings, and he found refuge in mass rallies during the political crises that the JDP encountered. As one of my expert interviewees underlined, mass rallies had a therapeutic effect on Erdoğan (Interviewee 28, 2014). For instance, as a response to the summer 2013 mass protest movements in Gezi Park in İstanbul, the JDP organized two mass meetings in Ankara and İstanbul under the title of 'respect for the national will' (AA, 2013). And the response to the failed coup in 2016 mainly took the form of an 'orderly mobilization', namely the Democracy Watches (*Demokrasi Nöbetleri*), which were regular mass meetings organized by the JDP branches in the squares of every major urban centre across the country for almost a month alongside several small and big rallies that gave centre stage to Erdoğan. One should also note that Erdoğan was always present at these meetings (either personally or through his image), which were organized around his personality. It should also be underlined that Erdoğan was always a remarkable orator, and the texts of his speeches were written by talented propagandists. The JDP's use of mass rallies constructed around the presence of Erdoğan should also be seen as a dimension of the party's personalistic communication style (Interviewee 49, 2014).

Lastly, the 'strong organization' had a meaning beyond electoral purposes for the JDP elite and, as elaborated upon in previous chapters, it was also seen as a power base and/or a mobilizational resource by the (formerly Islamist) party elite against potential threats by the powerful non-party political actors in the country, such as the military, the judiciary and the bureaucracy, as well as against social discontent. Hence, besides immediate electoral benefits, the degree and nature of political conflict and divisions in the country elaborated upon in previous chapters (particularly in Chapters 2 and 3) were other factors making a year-round, large and pervasive organization indispensable for the JDP elite.

The Pro-JDP Media

Relying only on the JDP organization was felt to be insufficient by the JDP leadership, and this was why the party started to construct a strong and decisively pro-JDP media. A former chief editor of the pro-JDP daily newspaper *Star* explicitly underlined the necessity of having a media for the 50 per cent, which apparently denoted the vote share of the JDP (Karaalioğlu, 2014). Hence, it is safe to talk about a pro-JDP media consisting of at least five highly influential and strongly pro-JDP newspapers such as *Sabah*, *Türkiye*, *Star*, *Yenişafak* and *Akşam* alongside minor ones such as *Yeni Akit* and *Milat*. According to the figures of the official Press Notification Institution (Basın İlan Kurumu), the total circulation rate per day of the above-mentioned newspapers at the time of writing was close to 1 million.[29]

One should also mention the appointments of pro-JDP columnists to mainstream newspapers such as *Hürriyet* and *Habertürk* as another instrument of the JDP's grip over the media. It is also known that Erdoğan, in person, directly tried to control the news through his relationship with media bosses (*Radikal*, 2014b). There were also several pro-JDP TV channels broadcasting nationally such as *24*, *Ülke TV*, *Beyaz TV*, *TGRT*, *A Haber*, *ATV* and *Kanal 7* alongside many local newspapers and TV channels under the control of the local and provincial JDP elite. One should also add the unprecedented tight control over the official Turkish Radio Television (Türkiye Radyo Televizyonu) to the picture.

One of my expert interviewees underlined the importance of media control for the JDP through a very illustrative reference to the politics of the 1990s in Turkey. This quotation is rather important since it also underlined a couple of important features of political conflicts in Turkey, most notably the deep involvement of non-party actors in party politics:

---

[29] See the circulation rates at www.bik.gov.tr/istanbul/temmuz-2014-tiraj-raporu/ (accessed: 21 July 2014).

In the past the Motherland Party [and] the True Path Party tried to keep the mainstream media under their control through granting them priviliges in state contracts. But it was a very risky strategy. We saw this in the example of Aydın Doğan [the most influential media boss of the country] [...] The True Path Party period was a clear example of this [...] For instance, Erbakan, in the Welfare Party period, did not use a similar strategy. He thought that *Milli Gazete* alone would be sufficient. This was a huge mistake [...] At that time, during the Motherland Party period, Aydın Doğan had such an enormous influence on politics that he could push governments to change ministers [...] For instance, Aydın Doğan waged war [through his newspapers] against the minister of internal affairs of the era, Saadettin Tantan, because of his words about *Dış Bank* [...] And the Motherland Party had to change him [...] For the sake of this media power the Motherland Party sacrificed him (Interviewee 39, 2014).

Regardless of the factual validity of the incidents related by my interviewee, this kind of calculation very much reflects the strategic approach of the JDP and Erdoğan to the media. Another interviewee from the JDP also made similar observations. According to him, without the pro-JDP media created by the support of pro-government business circles, the JDP could have been crushed by powerful non-party actors such as the military and bureaucratic elite (Interviewee 7, 2014). Hence, it seems that the former media order in Turkey, and its influence on Turkish politics throughout the 1990s, led the JDP elite to construct their own media. The JDP elite strategically learned lessons from the political failures of former centre-right parties and the Islamist National View parties that had partially stemmed from the lack of a full grip over the media.

According to a news report based on leaked audio recordings of some businesspeople and government members, the JDP leadership actively collected money from businesspeople into a 'pool' in return for privileges in state bids in order to buy and run two highly influential newspapers and a TV channel as pro-JDP instruments (*Zaman*, 2014). Thus, the JDP managed to create an effective pro-JDP media, ironically, at the cost of its newspapers and TV channels being referred to by opponents of the party as the 'government bulletin [*hükümet bülteni*]', 'partisan media [*yandaş medya*]' and 'pool media [*havuz medyası*]'. Lastly, it should be mentioned that the pro-JDP media not only contributed to the JDP's visibility and electoral campaigns, but also played a vital role in the manipulation of public opinion by the interventions of party leader Erdoğan. Without the support of the pro-JDP media, the political crises that the party encountered would definitely have left much deeper wounds in the JDP organization. This necessary strategic grip over the media by the JDP has, apparently, gradually turned into one of the instruments of construction of an authoritarian regime (Yeşil, 2016).

Conclusion: The JDP and Its Right-wing Predecessors

The electoral achievements of the JDP were much more enduring than those of previous right-wing and centre-right parties in Turkey. While Democrat Party rule between 1950 and 1960 was marked by a steady decline in the party's vote share, the ruling Motherland Party of the 1980s also started to lose momentum at the beginning of the 1990s. In addition, the votes of the Islamist National View parties started to decline after reaching their peak in the mid 1990s. In contrast, the JDP increased its votes in almost every election and remained in power as the single-party majority government. The discussion in this chapter has pointed out a few distinguishing features with regard to organizational dynamics, electoral tactics and communication strategies which, together, contributed to the JDP's unprecedented electoral predominance as well as political resilience in Turkish political history which gradually turned into a hegemonic party autocracy.

First of all, previous centre-right parties in Turkey usually depended heavily on highly redistributive strategies such as classical patronage and clientelism for party cohesion as well as for vote maximization. Hence, the role of selective incentives had played a major role in those parties' survival and electoral achievements. Unlike those parties, and thanks to its Islamist National View past, the JDP leadership also attached great importance to the role of collective incentives. In order to consolidate its rank and file and its electoral base it frequently appealed to a tension-increasing discourse in which Turkish politics was depicted as a struggle between the JDP, representing the conservative downtrodden peripheral masses, and the allegedly 'elite' secularist opposition and powerful international actors.

Secondly, although previous centre-right parties had robust membership organizations, their elites usually viewed the role of the 'membership organization' from a very limited perspective: as a simple device for preventing electoral fraud. Instead of relying on their membership parties' efforts, those centre-right parties mostly depended on the support of local elites, religious communities and tribal leaders in order to protect their electoral bases. In addition, the Motherland Party in particular tended to rely on professional campaigning and gave up being interested in the membership party at the beginning of the 1990s. Hence, the membership party lost its significance for those parties and their leadership had to further compromise with particularistic interest groups outside the party. Unlike these parties, the JDP elite attached great importance to the membership party and relied on its effort in extracting votes from local constituencies through individual interactions with the electorate, in addition to the effective use of a highly developed pro-JDP media. This increased the party's autonomy *vis-à-vis* local and national power holders outside the organization.

Last but not the least, although the predecessors of the JDP were very centralized centre-right parties, historical evidence also showed that there was a much more tolerant intra-party atmosphere in those parties. Unlike the JDP, those parties' mode of centralization created space for the accumulation of power in the hands of local and national elites other than the leadership. Hence, despite the influence of the leadership in those parties, they also had to struggle with various local and national power holders. Unlike previous centre-right parties, the JDP elite embraced a much more disciplined yet consensual intra-party political conduct (delineated in the next chapter) and carefully inhibited the accumulation of power in the hands of local and national elites other than the party leadership.

All these organizational dynamics and electoral strategies depended on the autonomy of the leadership and the party and, under the circumstances of the diminishing effectiveness of classical patronage, provided better grounds for the implementation of technocratic policies. However, the JDP discursively and organizationally remained highly responsive towards its electorate. Better government performance[30] with a responsive discourse and organization, in turn, also increased the party's lasting electoral support. In the next chapter, I elaborate upon the organizational architecture on which the strategic approach of the JDP outlined in this chapter has been constructed.

---

[30] When I mention goverment performance, except for the increase in the GDP and the decrease in consumer price inflation, I am not referring to the objective and real achievements of the JDP governments. Illustrating the government's performance in those senses would require a different research agenda and method. Instead, I am referring to the *perception* of the government's performance. In line with this position, relying on statistical analysis, Gidengil and Karakoç's (2014) study on the reasons for the JDP's success illustrated that the party owed its electoral achievements to a large extent to the perception of the majority of the people that the party's government performance was successful regarding issues such as the economy and social policies.

6   The JDP Organization: A Personalistic Mass Party

Introduction

According to official records, in 2017 the Justice and Development Party had more than 9 million members[1]. These members, coming from various backgrounds, were channelled by the party to the ballot boxes along with their friends and relatives by the thousands of party branches that penetrated into even the most remote corners of the country, each of which was kept under the control of the central JDP elite. When the numerous political crises that the JDP had encountered since its foundation are taken into account, the resilience and electoral predominance of such an enormous organization seem puzzling. How was the central JDP elite able to keep this massive membership organization under its control and successfully deploy it for electoral success?

In this chapter, I propose that three practical organizational factors were central to the electoral achievements and the political resilience of the JDP. Firstly, the JDP had a very large and pervasive membership organization that was active year-round. Secondly, the JDP leadership exerted very tight control over this massive membership organization. Third, the JDP elite also paid great attention to the 'controlled participation' of the party base in order to absorb potential dissent against this firm control. These organizational factors have led me to identify the JDP as a 'personalistic mass party'.

In this chapter, before focusing on the JDP organization, I firstly take a closer look at theories on party typologies in the second section. In this literature, I paid particularly close attention to studies by Duverger (1974) and Epstein (2000), which focus on the relationships between organizational structures and changes in the electoral market. This literature led me to understand the organizational dynamics of the JDP as a specific response to the electoral market and to the broader political

---

[1] Records of the Court of Cassation (Yargıtay), www.yargitaycb.gov.tr/sayfa/faaliyette-olan-siyasi-partiler/1095 (accessed: 29 June 2017).

conflict in the country, rather than an institutional unfolding of a genetic origin, as did Panebianco in his approach (1988).[2] Hence, one of the presumptions in this chapter, and throughout the book, is that the organizational model of the JDP was directly connected to the party's electoral achievements. I consolidate the theoretical assumption expanded upon in the second section with a brief discussion on Turkish party organizations in the third section.

These rather theoretical considerations surrounding the case of the JDP also justify having a relational perspective for understanding the organizational dynamics' contributions to the party's electoral achievements and political resilience. In other words, neither a perspective exclusively focusing on the high echelons of the party – the party central office and the party in public office – nor an approach solely focusing on the grass roots would give a comprehensive understanding of the contribution of organizational dynamics to the JDP's electoral success. Instead, I prefer to focus on the relationship between these two faces of the party, both of which are central in the electoral processes: the party in central office (and more precisely the party leadership) and the party on the ground (the massive membership organization of the JDP). While the latter was an extremely important nexus for the JDP in reaching out to the electorate, the former was key to the identification of the electoral and organizational strategies of the JDP,[3] and the mode of relationship between these two faces was central to the party's lasting electoral success and political resilience which ultimately turned into authoritarian predominance.

In the fourth section, I briefly describe the legal framework relevant to the JDP organization such as the Law on Political Parties (SPK, Siyasi Partiler Kanunu) and the JDP statutes. In this section, I also give an overview of the formal organizational structure of the party: its territorial dispersion, the party's local presence and its membership structure. In the fifth and sixth sections, I illustrate the kind of instruments through which the JDP elite exerted tight control over this massive party base without causing discontent among party activists. After this empirical exposition, I evaluate the JDP organization from a broader theoretical perspective in the following section, and I argue that the JDP organization represented a hybrid party, or more precisely a 'personalistic mass

---

[2] In Panebianco's analysis (1988: 50–53), the term 'genetic origin' refers to the decisive impact on a party's future organizational development of the conditions experienced and choices made during its foundation.

[3] See Kumbaracıbaşı for the importance of the Central Decision and Administration Board of the party in the decision- and policy-making processes (2009: 133).

party', with regard to ideal typical models of the 'mass-based' and 'elite-based' parties discussed in the second section. This situation also demonstrates that, in certain respects, the mass party model has still been shaping party organizations, particularly in the developing world.[4]

Concepts and Theories of Organizational Models: A View from the Periphery

This analysis of the JDP organization mainly focuses on the complex relationships between the membership organization of the JDP and its central office.[5] The analysis, both in this chapter and throughout the book, has mostly excluded the discussion regarding the party's position in the public office vis-à-vis the party on the ground and the party in the central office. I benefited greatly from Levitsky's (2003) account in terms of my main approach to the fieldwork, which puts a special emphasis on the relationship between the various levels of a party's organization. In addition, I see parties 'as clusters of relationships rather than as unitary "black boxes"' (Massicard and Watts, 2013: 4).

In this analysis, I have used several conceptual tools derived from the literature on party organization. I use the concept of centralism to refer to the domination of the party's central office over the party's units on the ground and to the lack of any meaningful power placed in the hands of these subordinate units (Duverger, 1974: 94). The JDP's centralism and its organizational mechanics also worked in favour of 'leadership autonomy', and did not allow the formation of other strong power foci inside the party. Following the perspective of Levitsky (2003), I define 'leadership autonomy' as the party leader having a great degree of flexibility and room for manoeuvre in quick decision making without needing approval from competing individual or collective power holders within the party. A related concept here is that of 'party autonomy' and, following Panebianco (1988: 56–57), I define the term as the exclusion of

---

[4] I use the term 'developing world' to refer to a context where the liberal democratic architecture is considerably weak and where socio-economic development (of the sort we see in advanced industrial countries and which gave rise to a certain type of party organizational development in Western democracies) remained far from creating a mostly affluent society. In these contexts, political systems are usually labelled competitive authoritarianism, electoral democracy or hybrid regimes. But the term 'developing world' indicates wider circumstances that include socio-economic and socio-cultural features. For a discussion of the term and consideration of Turkey as an upper-middle-income developing country, see Calvert and Calvert (2014).

[5] For the separation of party organizations into three levels as 'party in public office', 'party on the ground' or the 'membership party', and 'the party in central office', see Katz and Mair (1993).

politically salient actors outside the party – whether national or local, collective or individual – from decision-making processes, drawing neat boundaries between the party and the wider environment surrounding it. I also draw on the literature on party typologies to develop a comprehensive view of the JDP organization. Since this research aims to explain the relationship between the electoral success of the JDP and its organizational dynamics, it has adopted an 'electoral competition approach' rather than an 'institutional' or 'sociological' approach to party typologies and organizations (Ware, 1996: 92–112). This is to say that my main understanding of party typologies is based heavily on the approaches of Duverger (1974) and Epstein (2000) and, more recently, on literature which followed the discussions developed by these scholars that understands party organizational development mainly as a response to changes in electoral markets.

Although the literature on party typologies is very rich, it is possible to define a basic distinction that is present, either implicitly or explicitly, in the majority of the works. This distinction is between 'elite-based' (cadre, catch-all, electoral-professional and cartel) and 'mass-based' (mass party) models.[6] One of the sources of this distinction, not surprisingly, is the seminal work of Duverger (1974). In this work on political parties published in the early 1950s, Duverger differentiated the 'committee' or 'caucus' organization of the 'elites' from the 'branch' organizations of the 'working classes'. Duverger associated the committee or caucus organization with cadre parties and the branch organization with mass parties (1974: 114). According to him, the difference between these two parties was related to a structural quality rather than the quantity of their members (Duverger, 1974: 106). To Duverger, mass parties were distinguished from cadre parties by the importance attached to the local presence[7] of the party and the regularity/permanence of the party's activities as well as the centrality of indoctrination and education of party members (1974: 60). Another distinguishing point of the mass party that Duverger pointed out was the importance of the financial contributions of ordinary members in this kind of organizational structure (1974: 107). In contrast, cadre parties depended on the financial means of limited interest groups as well as on technicians who know how to run campaigns (Duverger, 1974: 107). According to Duverger, electoral achievements of mass parties led many elite-based parties to adopt the organizations of mass parties and started a process of 'contagion' from the left (1974: 61–62).

---

[6] It should be noted that Ware uses a very similar distinction between 'elite-based' and 'membership-based' models (1987: 8).

[7] Szczerbiak (1999) also draws attention to this aspect of the mass party.

More than a decade after Duverger, as a result of the rise of television and the social transformations that started to dissolve the class basis of the mass parties in Western democracies, Epstein argued that the mass party was not the rule but the exception with regard to party organizational change (2000: 100). According to Epstein, the golden age of the mass parties was a very short period during the 1950s (2000: 251), which was followed by the rise of 'Americanization' or 'heavily financed mass media campaigns' (2000: 257). Epstein contended that social and technological transformations triggered counter-organizational tendencies, and therefore a process of 'contagion from the right' (2000: 260), in which active members of the parties started to be seen as liabilities rather than assets (2000: 258). Epstein even tended to see these counter-organizational trends as the future of the political party (2000: 260).

These two main analyses of the party organizational typologies gave the main lines of two ideal typical party models and two main strategic inclinations: a mass-based approach depending on tight control over a massive membership organization, and an elite-based one depending on mass communication, centralized finance, campaign technicians and professionals. Relatively recent literature has also confirmed this distinction between mass parties and more modern elite parties that rely on technological instruments instead of a massive membership organization. For instance, Panebianco differentiated the 'mass bureaucratic party' from the 'electoral-professional party' and pointed out the decline of the *classe gardée*, or the particular, insulated social segments in which parties took root as the main reason for the decline of the mass party (1988: 263). According to Panebianco, electoral-professional parties were distinguished from mass parties by the importance the former attached to campaign professionals and experts instead of the party bureaucracy (1988: 264). Electoral-professional parties targeted the 'opinion electorates' while mass parties were based on the 'electorates of belonging' (Panebianco, 1988: 264). While mass parties depended on the resources created by members, electoral-professional parties depended on financial means provided by interest groups and the state (Panebianco, 1988: 264). Panebianco also pointed out the central role of ideologies in mass parties, whereas the emphasis shifted to leaders' competence and managerial issues in electoral-professional parties (1988: 264).

Other contributions to the literature on party organizations usually followed this main distinction and elaborated on the features of the mass-based and elite-based parties in line with Duverger (1974). According to Kirchheimer, for instance, the 'mass integration party' was aimed at the 'intellectual and moral encadrement of the masses'

(1966: 184). In contrast, the catch-all party, or the elite-based parties in general, have been defined by the decline of the party's 'ideological baggage', the 'strengthening of the top leadership groups' and the 'decline of the role of individual members' (Kirchheimer, 1966: 190), which were compensated for by the closer relationship between the party and the state (Katz and Mair, 1995) and the extensive use of mass media and technology to connect the party leadership directly to the electorate (Katz and Mair, 1993: 615). Political marketing techniques, such as the frequent use of public opinion surveys, were also at the heart of catch-all strategies and elite-based parties in general (Scammell, 1999: 726–734).

As the works of Katz and Mair (1995, 2002, 2009), Mair (1992) and Blyth and Katz (2005) illustrate, more contemporary studies tended to introduce more sophisticated distinctions than the one between elite-based (cadre and catch-all) and mass-based (mass party) parties. For instance, Katz and Mair differentiated between the catch-all party and what they described as the 'cartel party' (1995). According to them, the catch-all party was a short-lived phenomenon that emerged after the historical achievements of the mass party such as the improvement of the conditions of the working classes through generous welfare regimes established under mass party rule (Katz and Mair, 1995: 12). The dissolution of the class basis of mass parties under these improved social and economic conditions led political parties in Western democracies to target a more heterogeneous electorate than before, 'an electorate made up of voters who were learning to behave more like consumers than active participants' (Katz and Mair, 1995: 7). According to Blyth and Katz, the catch-all parties were creatures of the Keynesian economies (2005: 42) and, as they increased promotion of public goods in order to appeal to a heterogeneous electorate, they reached certain fiscal limits and created apathy towards party politics (2005: 40). Hence, the catch-all model was replaced by the cartel party as parties in Western democracies moved closer to the state and started to depend increasingly on public resources (Katz and Mair, 1995).

Meanwhile, parties started to invest less and less in the party on the ground or membership parties (Mair, 1992: 4–5). According to Katz, the fall of the mass party and the rise of increasingly elite-based catch-all or cartel parties required the 'de-activation of activist members' within the parties (Katz, 2013). Katz and Mair also underline the importance of professionalized and capital-intensive campaigns for the cartel party model (2009: 755). Hence, according to Katz and Mair, for parties in Western democracies, being in government has become extremely crucial for organizational survival and, therefore, party systems dominated by cartels started to make it as hard as possible for other parties to gain prominence. This was the point at which the term 'cartel' became crucial and the label of 'cartel parties' mainly underlined the collision – or proximity – between the main parties in terms of policies and organizations in a given party system (Katz and Mair, 1995: 17). Despite the theoretical elegance of Katz and Mair's studies (particularly the one published in 1995), as Koole underlined later, the cartel party model used a systemic property to identify individual parties (1996: 508). Another criticism was that the distinction made by Katz and Mair between the state and society was far from grasping the blurred boundaries between the two (Koole, 1996: 513).

Apart from these general theoretical concerns about the concept, one of the main problems with these theoretical sophistications in the recent literature was that, from the perspective of the particular case of the JDP, and from the perspective of party politics in the developing world in general, these discussions of the nuances between various types of elite-based parties did not address the uneven socio-economic development (the weakness of the welfare regimes and the much slower development of communications and technological infrastructures) outside the Western liberal democratic contexts. Furthermore, the 'cartel party' hypothesis presumed orderly and legitimate alternation of power among parties of the cartel, but this simple condition was usually lacking in many electoral democracies or competitive authoritarian regimes in the developing world, where political developments were interrupted by coups, revolutions, insurgencies and states of emergency. The 'cartel party' hypothesis assumed that there was a basic stability in the political regime.

In the context of Western liberal democracies, the functions performed by the party organization could easily be restricted to election time, and therefore it would be plausible to assume a decline of the presence of the party on the ground and of 'warm bodies' actively working for the party (Mair, 1992: 15), the retreat of the party central office, and the rise of the party in public office since nationalized, professionalized campaigns backed by state resources would be sufficient to secure parties' remaining in power. But when party politics and electoral politics are perceived as a game played by powerful and politicized non-party actors such as armies, powerful judicial and bureaucratic elites, and allegedly mainstream but deeply partisan media groups who interfere on the grounds of uneven technological and socio-economic development, party organizations should be considered something more than a professional player in an ordinary game of electoral politics. In these kinds of circumstances, it is better to understand mobilizational functions of party organizations as 'power capabilities' available to 'power contenders'.[8]

As Roberts (2006: 137) underlined in the context of Latin America, the deeper the political conflict between a party and its opponents – whether other political parties or non-party politicized veto players – parties tend to have more solid organizations. After all, in such circumstances, 'followers not only vote; they may be called upon to mobilize for rallies and demonstrations, participate in strikes and occupations, or even take up arms to defend their leader in times of peril' (Roberts, 2006: 137). Under the conditions of uneven socio-economic development – including a weak welfare regime and lack of state capacity to fulfil some of social policy responsibilities as well as the slower development of communications and technological infrastructure – mass-based organizations not only provided superior mobilizational capacities to leaders, but they also undertook crucial roles in distributing aid in cash or in kind to the low-income segments of the electorate by providing 'warm bodies'. This canvassing and clientelistic function of party organizations made an invaluable contribution to the electoral fortunes of parties in the developing world. This is also to say that at least some of the traits of the mass party model were highly relevant for many parties outside the Western liberal democracies, and particularly in the context of electoral democracies or competitive authoritarianism. Hence, the need to 'foster a presence on the ground' for these parties was not simply due 'to the legacy of the past and to the inheritance of earlier models' (Katz and Mair, 2002: 127), but emerged as a real necessity which deeply influenced the electoral and political resilience of parties outside the Western liberal democracies.

One of the main concerns regarding the cartel party model is also the fact that the depiction of the party organizational change in Katz and Mair's approach implicitly envisaged an irreversible development towards the cartel model.[9] In other words, according to Katz and Mair, the mass party model has become obsolete, a thing of the past 'at least across Europe' (2009: 760). However, the social and technological transformations that led to the decline of mass parties and the rise of elite-based parties have not been as complete in the developing world as they have been in Western liberal democratic systems. Although the rise of television and other mass communication technologies was a global

---

[8] For the terms 'power capabilities' and 'power contenders', see Anderson (1967: 91).
[9] Koole also underlines how problematic this perception of parties, which understands organizational variance as 'stages of development' towards an up-to-date 'one best' party type, is (1996: 520).

phenomenon, in vast areas across the world the degree of technological development remained highly uneven, and therefore tightly controlled membership parties remained as highly effective linkages between parties and electorates. This is to say that, while some social segments in these kinds of political settings could be easily reached by television, mass media or the internet, to reach certain low-income segments of these societies required the presence of robust organizational leverages with strong vertical ties – more precisely, a mass-based organizational strategy. Hence, it is more plausible to expect to see in the majority of the countries outside Western liberal democratic settings a move towards the hybridization of party models instead of an irreversible trend towards the 'Americanization' or 'presidentialization' of party politics.

Even in liberal Western democracies, recent studies of party organizations and party membership underline the vital roles assumed by members and the party on the ground and the inadequacy of the exclusively elite-based strategies. According to Seyd and Whiteley, for example, the UK Labour Party's main mistake, which led the party to a series of electoral failures in the second half of the twentieth century, was the extensive use of centralized communications and campaigning (1992: 11) while ignoring an energetic grass-roots organization. Susan Scarrow's studies also demonstrate the crucial role played by the membership parties (or the party on the ground) in terms of providing legitimacy and establishing contacts with the electorate (1996, 2000, 2014). Scarrow drew attention to the fact that, even in Western democracies, parties were still organizing themselves as 'membership-based organizations' (2000: 80) and attaching importance to the benefits of an active membership body (1996: 20). Scarrow's works demonstrate the fact that, even in Western liberal democratic settings, empirical realities of party organizational change have been much more complicated than the irreversible trends envisaged by the clear-cut theoretical schemes regarding party typologies.

Instead of the demise of a certain model and the rise of another one, what we overwhelmingly witnessed could be considered to be the rise of hybrid forms (Ware, 1996: 102). Hence, despite the discussions and theoretical sophistications developed after Duverger and Epstein, a fundamental, ideal typical strategic distinction between elite-based and mass-based parties remained highly useful in understanding empirical realities of organizational change and typologies. Nevertheless, it is enormously important to underline that this distinction should not be seen as a simple, nominal dichotomy. Instead, in line with Ware (1987, 1996), I view elite-based and mass-based party models as the ideal types or extreme ends of a continuum (Ware, 1987: 6). Given the theoretical

Table 6.1 *Mass-based and elite-based organizational models as ideal types and the JDP*

Party types			
Features	Mass-based	Elite-based	JDP: a personalistic mass party
Ideology and programme	Important – rigid	Less important – vague	Less important – vague (political marketing)
Membership salience	High	Low	High
Local presence	High	Low	High
Attachment to a specific social segment	Strong (social class or denominational groups)	Weak (heterogeneous electorate)	Weak
Relationship between the party centre and local branches	Strong – hierarchical	Weak – stratarchical	Strong – hierarchical
Main campaign technique	Labour-intensive	Capital-intensive	Hybrid
Source of finance	Members	State and interest groups	Hybrid (predominantly state and elite-based)
Organizational presence and activity	Permanent – year-round	Balloons during elections	Permanent – year-round
Professionals	Not important	Important	Important
Top leadership	Less visible	Highly visible	Highly visible
Party bureaucracy	Developed	Weak	Developed

Source: Author's compilation of indicators addressed in various theoretical sources discussed in this chapter.

discussion above, I see the ideal typical elite-based and mass-based parties as related to the features mentioned so far and locate the JDP somewhere in between these two ideal types as demonstrated in Table 6.1. In the next section, I will briefly evaluate the party organizational change in Turkey from the perspective of this theoretical discussion.

Party Organizations in Turkey and the Novelty of the JDP

Turkish politics has always been overwhelmingly party-based (Özbudun, 2001: 238). However, the literature on party politics in general, and on party organizations in particular, remained unusually underdeveloped for decades until the rise of the Islamist Welfare Party[10] in the middle of the 1990s on the basis of its robust organizational structure. Until then, only a few major studies had focused on party organization in Turkey.[11] A pioneering work in this sense was Sayarı's 'Aspects of Party Organization in Turkey' (1976). One of Sayarı's assertions in this article was that, despite the rise of new social groups in Turkey, such as working-class populations in urban centres, party politics remained under the control of notable families (1976: 187). The depiction of Turkish political parties in the middle of the 1970s by Sayarı drew a picture in which parties were active only during the electoral campaigns and did not pay attention to recruiting new members (1976: 188). According to Sayarı, local party organizations in Turkey during the 1970s were weak (1976: 197) and, particularly in the provinces, politics was under the control of traditional elites (1976: 198). Hence, Sayarı argued that 'in general [...] Turkish parties have more in common with the cadre than with the mass membership model' (1976: 188). In this analysis, party politics in Turkey appeared mainly as a reflection of local patronage networks in relation to the import substitution economy and heavy dependence on patronage through state and private resources.

Later major contributions to the analysis of the main characteristics of the Turkish parties underlined similar tendencies. Özbudun, at the very beginning of his oft-cited study, argued that Turkish parties were closer to the 'cadre, catch-all or cartel' models than the 'mass party' model (2000: 74). In a different study, Özbudun (2001) also argues that some parties in Turkey could be considered cartel parties. He points out trends of professionalization, claims regarding managerial efficiency in the image-building processes of parties, the rising importance of capital-intensive methods in electoral campaigns, and parties' dependence on the state for financial resources (2001: 250).[12] He also underlines the centrality of 'personalism' and lack of issue orientation in Turkish parties

---

[10] For a brief overview of the Welfare Party and other parties mentioned in this section, see Appendices 1 and 2.

[11] Apart from Özbudun's studies cited in this section, exceptions to this lack of interest in party politics are works by Heper and Landau (1991), Rubin and Heper (2002), Sayarı and Esmer (2002), Kabasakal's *Political Party Organizations in Turkey* (1991) and Bektaş's *Leadership Oligarchy in the Process of Democratization, the Republican People's Party and the Justice Party* (1993). There are also some more up-to-date studies on party politics in Turkey approving the recent interest. See in particular Uysal and Topak (2010) and Massicard and Watts (2013).

[12] The trends mentioned by Özbudun in Turkish party politics are undeniable. Nevertheless, for the reasons discussed earlier on the wider theoretical problems of the cartel party hypothesis, and specific difficulties regarding its application to the political context of the developing world, I would refrain using the concept for identifying any Turkish party including the JDP.

(Özbudun, 2000: 86). Özbudun argues that patronage and clientelism inhibited the rise of organizations relying on common class and group interests in Turkey (2000: 82). Yet he also underlines Turkey's relatively more institutionalized parties as superior to those in many new democracies (Özbudun, 2000: 73) along with the presence of remarkably active grass-roots organizations of Turkish parties for electoral mobilization (2000: 84).

Özbudun emphasizes that the organizational capacities (and the grass-roots presence in particular) of Turkish parties disappeared after the decline of the role of the state in the economy due to the privatization and economic liberalization processes started in the 1980s (2000: 84). At the same time, during the 1980s and 1990s, Turkish parties started to rely more on 'media appeals and image building with the help of professional public relations experts' (Özbudun, 2000: 84). According to Özbudun, as a result of the convergence of these dynamics, there was a dramatic decline in the organizational capacities of the main Turkish parties (mainly centre-right parties – the Motherland Party and the True Parth Party – but also other parties on the left), particularly during the 1990s (2000: 84).[13] Hence Özbudun underlines the overall organizational decline in Turkish parties at the end of the 1990s and argues that 'Turkey seems to have made a direct leap from the cadre party to a catch-all or cartel party without having gone through a mass party phase' (2000: 99). The only exception Özbudun highlights in this sense is the Islamist Welfare Party in the 1990s: the JDP's predecessor (2000: 99). Here Özbudun considers the connection of the Islamist Welfare Party with the urban lower classes, the party's robust local presence, a grass-roots organization that is active year-round, and the importance attached by the party elite to the political indoctrination of members as indicators of being a mass party (2000: 91–92).

The literature on the party organizations in Turkey preceding the JDP demonstrates that they were elite-based entities ('cadre' and 'catch-all' are terms used in this literature) whose membership usually inflated during elections and which depended on patronage, brokerage and clientelism, and powerful traditional local elites.[14] Despite the leadership domination (liderlik sultası) taking place within these elite-based parties (Bektaş, 1993), centrifugal tendencies and traditional and powerful local elites were always central in these 'personalistic cadre parties'. Political

---

[13] See also Özbudun (2001) for a detailed exposition of organizational decline of Turkish parties.
[14] For the organizational characteristics of these parties, see Ayata (2010), Bektaş (1993), Demirel (2004, 2011), Kabasakal (1991), Sayarı (1976) and Türsan (1995).

parties in Turkey entered into a period of further 'organizational decline' after the introduction of neo-liberal reforms in the 1980s (Özbudun, 2000: 84), except in the case of the Islamist Welfare Party, the main predecessor of the JDP. It became increasingly difficult for these elite-based, centre-right parties to remain in power through previously effective means such as negotiations with traditional local elites (who possessed fewer and fewer resources), state subsidies for agricultural products, and a state of massive public employment due to rapid privatization and economic liberalization.[15]

At this critical juncture in the Turkish party system, the predecessors of the JDP embraced two different strategies. While the Motherland Party relied upon capital-intensive campaign methods, media appeals and the hiring of campaign professionals (Özbudun, 2000: 84) as well as negotiations with powerful local elites, the Islamist Welfare Party preferred (or more precisely, *were obliged*, due to lack of financial resources) to rely on a highly motivated mass membership organization compatible with urban poverty (Delibaş, 2015; White, 2002). Both strategies, however, failed to properly respond to the changing electoral, social and economic conditions of the country. While the Motherland Party lost momentum at the beginning of the 1990s, the popularity of the Welfare Party started to decrease towards the close of that decade.

In addition, these two parties and their right-wing predecessors failed to resist a series of non-party elite interventions, most notably the coups and memorandums by the Turkish Armed Forces. None of these parties was capable of resisting these interventions, either due to a lack of control over the media and hence an inability to shape public opinion (as was the case with the Welfare Party), or due to a lack of sufficient organizational capacity for rapid, effective and resilient mass mobilization (as in the case of elite-based, centre-right parties such as the Democrat Party, the Justice Party, the Motherland Party and the True Path Party). In addition, factionalism in these parties incrementally diminished their performance in government and in their campaigning activities. The organizational formation of the JDP was an innovative and formidable response (that other parties failed to formulate) to new electoral, social and economic conditions as well as to the history of wider political conflict in the country involving powerful non-party elite opponents which gave rise to the above-mentioned organizational crisis of political parties in Turkey.

---

[15] See Kemahlıoğlu (2012) for the change of patronage structures in Turkey. See also Bayraktar and Altan (2013) for the description of this dynamic through the case of local politics in Mersin.

The marked confusion in the literature about how to locate the JDP within the conventional theoretical frameworks also demonstrates this novelty of the party. Despite the marked agreement on the robust organizational presence and 'mass partyness' of the Islamist Welfare Party (Delibaş, 2015; White, 2002), the literature on the organizational characteristics of the JDP uses various labels for it. For instance, while Kumbaracıbaşı identifies the party as a 'modern party with traits of an electoral-professional party' (2009: 137), Hale and Özbudun argue that the JDP approximated a 'mass party' model (2010: 47). In fact, the JDP organization should be seen as a very innovative mixture of mass-based models (its organizational past) and elite-based methods (its organizational present). While the JDP's main predecessor, the Islamist Welfare Party, approximated the ideal typical mass party, its partial predecessor, namely the Motherland Party, was a 'personalistic cadre party' in the tradition of Turkish political parties, and supported this model with new electoral and campaign instruments. Therefore it approximated the elite-based ideal type.[16] In contrast, as can be seen in Tables 6.1 and 6.2, I describe the JDP as a hybrid organization, and more precisely as a 'personalistic mass party' that blended a pervasive, highly bureaucratized, routinized and tightly controlled membership organization that was active year-round (features of a mass-based model) with a diligent personalistic leadership relying on capital-intensive campaign methods and political marketing techniques (features of an elite-based model). In the following parts of the chapter, I present the empirical findings of my research that led me to this conclusion.

The Formal Organization: A Large and Pervasive Membership Organization, Active Year-Round

In this section, I briefly outline the legal framework in which the JDP's organizational structure was formed. I also demonstrate the territorial dispersion and the membership structure of the party. The Law on Political Parties, issued in 1983, regulates the structure of parties' central, provincial and sub-provincial units. The SPK defined the central organization of a party as a grand convention, a party chairman and other decision-making, administrative, executive and disciplinary organs

---

[16] See also Chapter 5 for the senses in which I tend to see the JDP as a novel force in Turkish politics. Besides incorporating a robust organizational network with a decisively pro-JDP media and political marketing techniques, the JDP also broke ties with 'classical centre-right patronage' and heavy dependence on local political elites, and introduced novel, more centralized forms of clientelism.

Table 6.2 *Islamist National View parties and the Motherland Party: predecessors of the JDP*

Relationship with the JDP	Direct predecessors (Islamist National View tradition)		Partial predecessor	
Parties			Motherland	
Organizational characteristics	Welfare Party (1983–1998)	Virtue Party (1998–2001)	Party (1983–2009)	JDP (2001–present)
Membership salience	High	High	Low	High
Ideology	Rigid	Vague	Vague	Vague – political marketing
Finance	Mixed (considerable membership contribution)	Mixed (considerable membership contribution)	Mixed (considerable state and elite contribution)	Mixed (considerable state and elite contribution)
Campaign technique	Labour-intensive	Labour-intensive	Capital-intensive	Hybrid (labour- and capital-intensive)
Regularity of organizational activity	Year-round	Year-round	Ballooning around elections	Year-round
Local presence	Strong	Strong	Weak	Strong
Main electoral strategy	One-by-one vote canvassing	One-by-one vote canvassing	Negotiations with local and national politically salient individuals and social groups	Hybrid with a special emphasis on one-by-one vote canvassing avoiding extensive compromise to local elites
Mode of intra-party governance	No room for factions and powerful local and national figures	Presence of factions and local and national powerful figures	Tolerant of factions and local and national powerful figures	Tight control over centrifugal tendencies and powerful local and national figures
Party type	Mass-based	Mass-based	Elite-based	Hybrid – a personalistic mass party

Source: Author's own compilation of data and comments in sources cited in the preceding section.

(SPK, 1983: 5706). The SPK also regulated the provincial (*il*) and sub-provincial (*ilçe*) organizations of parties. The main organs of provincial and sub-provincial organizations are the convention, the party chair and the administrative and disciplinary committees (SPK, 1983: 5708).

Given this highly restrictive legal framework, every political party in Turkey had a very similar hierarchical organization, both centrally and in the provinces and sub-provinces.[17] In this sense, the JDP was not an exception. However, from the mid 1990s, the Islamist National View tradition, the predecessor of the JDP, had begun developing grass-roots units such as neighbourhood representatives, ballot box committees and women's branches. Following this organizational tradition, the JDP also had neighbourhood representatives and ballot box committees as well as women's and youth branches (AK Parti, 2012a: 28). According to the JDP statutes, in line with the SPK, every level in the JDP organization consisted of the following elements: a convention, a chairman, an administration board, an executive board (in practice the highest ruling organ of party branches), a women's branch and a youth branch. Under the sub-provincial branches, special attention was paid to the neighbourhood representatives and ballot box committees (AK Parti, 2012a: 29) through which the JDP derived its main strength.

The Local Presence of the Party

In order to understand the hierarchical ties and territorial penetration of the party it would be helpful to have a closer look at a concrete example. In İstanbul, the JDP's provincial executive board consists of fourteen people while the administration board consists of fifty people at the time of writing. Thirty-nine sub-provincial branches were under the control of the provincial branch of the JDP in İstanbul. Under these sub-provincial branches one can find neighbourhood representatives (see Figure 6.1). The Bakırköy sub-provincial branch of the party in İstanbul consists of an executive board, an administration board, a women's branch and a youth branch. These units include fourteen, seventeen, thirty and twenty-eight people respectively at the time of writing. Under the Bakırköy sub-provincial branch of the party, one can find eleven neighbourhood representatives.[18] These neighbourhood representatives (*mahalle temsilcileri*) also form ballot box administration committees (*sandık yönetim kurulları*), each consisting of nine people. For instance, in Cevizlik, a

---

[17] See Kabasakal (2014) for the illustration of this formal similarity of organizations of different parties in Turkey. Works by Sayarı (1976) and Özbudun (2000) also underline this similarity. Bektaş's (1993) and Ayan Musil's (2011) studies underline the predominance of leaders and authoritarian party structures in Turkish parties in general. Ayan Musil's (2011) study also points out the variance in authoritarianism in Turkish parties.

[18] These numbers can be seen on the party branch websites of İstanbul provincial and Bakırköy sub-provincial branches of the party.

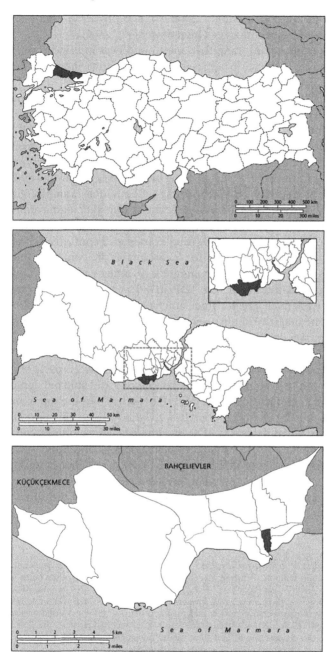

Figure 6.1: An example from İstanbul of the territorial and hierarchical relationships among branches in the provinces, sub-provinces and neighbourhoods : İstanbul, Bakırköy and Cevizlik respectively.
Source: Visual material from Wikipedia (accessed: 1 December 2015).

neighbourhood of İstanbul, Bakırköy sub-province, there are 4,450 electors and 14 ballot boxes (Interviewee 27, 2014).

Another important thing that one should bear in mind about the JDP organization in these localities is that it did not increase in the pre-election period and decrease in the rest of the year,[19] but was active year-round and constantly in touch with the electorate (Interviewee 17, 2014). Even if we consider that my interviewees from the JDP were prone to exaggerating the local presence of the JDP and the party's attention to allocating people to ballot box regions (or polling station areas), there were still other observations confirming that the JDP was very successful at the local level as well as at keeping ballot boxes under this kind of tight control, particularly on election days. Eligür, for example, gives vivid details about the robust local presence of the JDP and confirmed the superiority of the party on the ground (see in particular 2010: 259).[20] Not surprisingly, Tosun and Tosun's study also confirms the superiority of the JDP organizations in local-provincial contexts statistically. According to their study, compared to other parties in Turkey, the organizational density of the JDP in 80 per cent of the provinces in Turkey was much greater than other parties (2010: 55). This is to say that, in the majority of the provinces of Turkey, the total number of JDP members was larger than that of any other party (Tosun and Tosun, 2010: 52).

The territorial and hierarchical relationship between party branches of the JDP can be seen in Table 6.3 and Figure 6.1. Table 6.3 demonstrates the vertical, hierarchical order of JDP branches. On the top of numerous provincial, sub-provincial branches, neighbourhood representatives and ballot box committees, the JDP headquarters exerted tight control even over the smallest local party base –the ballot box committee – through the vertical ties cutting all the way down through provincial, sub-provincial branches and neighbourhood representatives. Figure 6.1, by using the example of İstanbul province, demonstrates the deep territorial penetration of the JDP organization. Turkey is officially divided into eighty-one provinces. These provinces in turn are divided into various sub-provinces,

---

[19] Most of the populist-personalistic parties, and most notably the personal parties of Berlusconi, ballooned during election periods and deflated at other times when there was no election approaching. For this, see McDonnell (2013) and Albertazzi and McDonnell (2015). For this reason, their structures are rather different from permanent membership parties, and they approximate the elite-based parties. In other words, while Berlusconi's parties are elite-based 'personal parties', the JDP in Turkey, despite the central role of Erdoğan, was a 'personalistic mass party' simply due to its massive and permanent membership organization.

[20] See also Doğan (2016) for the robust local presence of the JDP in one of the peripheral neighbourhoods of İstanbul.

Table 6.3 *The formal structure of the JDP organization, its hierarchy and the approximate number of party branches*

Numbers	Branches	
1	**JDP headquarters in Ankara**	
	Grand convention and chairman	
	Central Executive Committee and Central Decision and Administration Board	Main unit
	Executive committee and administration board	Women's branch
	Executive committee and administration board	Youth branch
81	**Provincial branches**	
	Provincial convention and chair	
	Executive committee and administration board	Main unit
	Executive committee and administration board	Women's branch
	Executive committee and administration board	Youth branch
957*	**Sub-provincial branches**	
	Sub-provincial convention and chair	
	Executive committee and administration board	Main unit
	Executive committee and administration board	Women's branch
	Executive committee and administration board	Youth branch
394*	**District branches**	
20,000*	**Neighbourhood administrations**	
170,000*	**Ballot box committees**	

Source: Author's compilation.
* Approximate numbers.

and the sub-provinces are further divided into neighbourhoods. The JDP sub-provincial branches divided these neighbourhoods into ballot box regions and attempted to allocate a committee to every single ballot box. There are approximately 170,000 ballot boxes in urban Turkey (*Hürriyet*, 2014a) and the party formed almost an equal number of ballot box committees. Each ballot box sought to include 300 voters. The JDP tried to control every ballot box through a committee of nine people: three representatives from the party's main units, three from women's branches and three from youth branches (Interviewee 4, 2013). Even at their most cautious, the JDP strove to keep each ballot box under the control of at least five members (Interviewee 13, 2014).

An interview with one of the leading figures of a neutral civil organization for observing the elections confirmed this ability of the JDP organization in 'safeguarding ballot boxes' (frequently called '*sandıkları kollamak*' or '*sandıklara sahip çıkmak*' by my interviewees). According to Ayberk Yağız, on the election day of the 2014 local elections, the 'most well-organized party was the JDP' (Güvenç, 2014). Nevertheless, even the JDP could be unsuccessful at appointing ballot box observers at times and in certain localities but this did not change the overall superiority on the ground of the JDP organization over competing parties. Considering that the JDP had 170,000 ballot box committees across Turkey, the party would have required around 850,000 active members in order to keep these ballot boxes under its firm control through ballot box committees consisting of five members. The claims of the JDP members, however, were that the party's total membership was much higher still. In the next section, I will take a closer look at the membership structure of the JDP.

The JDP's Membership Structure: 'Speed Membership' à la turca

In Kumbaracıbaşı's study it was indicated that the JDP had around 1.8 million members in 2004 (2009: 127). Hale and Özbudun's study claimed that the JDP had 3,688,761 members in 2008 (2010: 47). Tosun and Tosun's study on party membership in Turkey, however, contended that the JDP had only 1,796,799 members in 2008 (2010: 187). The difference between the numbers indicated by Hale and Özbudun's and Tosun and Tosun's studies can be explained on the ground of legal-institutional changes. According to Tosun and Tosun, during the period from 2005 to 2008, total party membership numbers in Turkey decreased more than 2.5 million due to a new electronic registration method which eliminated dual and false membership records (2010: 47). Nevertheless, a couple of years after these reforms in the official registration methods of party members, in a news report in the daily *Milliyet* it was argued that the JDP had 7,551,472 members in 2013 (*Milliyet*, 2013). In 2014, one of the founders of the JDP, Bülent Arınç, also claimed that the party had more than 9 million members (*Hürriyet*, 2014b). The records of the Chief Prosecutorship of the Supreme Court of Appeals (Yargıtay Cumhuriyet Başsavcılığı) in Turkey also confirms Arınç's claim by indicating that the JDP had 9,399,633 members by the end of 2015.[21]

These dramatic inconsistencies among various figures, and particularly these huge leaps in membership figures of the JDP from 2008 to 2013, indicate an important feature of party membership in Turkey. According to Özbudun, in Turkey, what a party member usually means is something little more than a supporter (2000: 80). If we take a party member to mean someone who has the right to vote in intra-party candidate selection processes and participate in decision-making

[21] See the membership figures at www.yargitaycb.gov.tr/sayfa/adalet-ve-kalkinma-partisi/ 1095 (accessed: 23 January 2017).

processes and who, at the same time, has the obligation of paying dues (Scarrow, 1996: 16), then most of the JDP members would not be qualified as party members in the strictest sense since most of them have no right to vote in intra-party elections and do not pay dues. However, it is plausible that these figures later indicated by the party elite and published in the national media pointed out a particular strategic inclination of the JDP leadership. What we see in these inflated membership figures is a kind of strategy, a 'speed membership'[22] à la turca, through which the JDP leadership tried to encapsulate voters by registering as many of them as possible as members. For instance, JDP activists register members during election periods in mobile registration vehicles and during spontaneous contacts with the party's supporters and sympathizers.

This tendency to register as many official party members as possible could be viewed as an inheritance of the classical strategies of the Islamist National View organizations.[23] As one of my interviewees, a subprovincial chair of the JDP in Konya, underlined, the JDP elite too paid particular attention to registering as many members as possible: 'As our prime minister said, "we are the most alive party in the world with the largest membership". Every year our member numbers increase. We always have membership forms nearby. If someone wants to become a member we immediately fill out these forms' (Interviewee 6, 2014). Registering as many members as possible might have been seen as a successful electoral strategy from the perspective of the JDP elite, similar to that of Austrian parties (Müller, 1994: 66–67). The JDP elite might have expected that a single member would bring at least one vote, if not two, in addition to his or her own and, to a great extent, previous elections demonstrated the credibility of this expectation.[24]

But what attracted enormous numbers of people to the JDP? It is not difficult to understand motivations such as the expectations for jobs and material assistance based on the JDP's position in power (Interviewee 6, 2014). However, there is a wider dynamic related to ideational motivations and collective incentives. During my fieldwork, I frequently heard

[22] In her study, Scarrow (2014) defined 'multi-speed membership' as new methods introduced by political parties in order to quickly increase membership numbers. One of the main aspects of this process has been the introduction of multiple types of membership status, each with varying degrees of rights and obligations and by using the internet for enrolment. This dynamic's emphasis on 'speed' was highly relevant for the JDP although the party did not officially have multiple forms of membership.

[23] An instruction by the Islamist Welfare Party on organization building revealed the party elite's attention to 'registering members' (Güney, 1995: 122).

[24] For example, in the local elections in 2014, the JDP received almost 18 million votes, around twice the number of its members.

from my interviewees that they attached great importance to Erdoğan himself (Interviewee 7, 2014; Interviewee 31, 2014). It is important to emphasize that the people's attachment to the party was due to Erdoğan's personality and the party's 'populist political style/appeal' (Ostiguy, 2017) in general (as elaborated in Chapter 3) as much as it was due to religiosity and nationalism. As one of my interviewees emphasized, it was Erdoğan's 'candour [*samimiyet*]' in the eyes of JDP supporters that made him such a successful politician (Interviewee 9, 2014). Therefore, the populism and personalistic leadership of the JDP, alongside religiosity, to a great extent explain how the JDP was able to construct this robust local presence and massive membership organization by recruiting members and activists from the most underprivileged sectors of Turkish society.

The massive membership organization and a robust and permanent local presence helped the JDP to establish and consolidate a strong connection with its constituency across Turkey through routine activities requiring face-to-face interaction such as regular house and workplace visits, participation in funerals and weddings, and condolence (*taziye*) visits (Doğan, 2016). As one of my interviewees told me, the electorate even value seeing party members and having a 'chat' with them from time to time (Interviewee 32, 2014). In addition, this robust and permanent local presence helped the JDP know the 'people in need [*ihtiyaç sahipleri*]' in poor local settings. The party either directly provided assistance in cash or in kind through the organization (Interviewee 32, 2014) or referred those in need to local social assistance institutions or charities (Interviewee 10, 2014).[25] Related to this clientelistic function, as Magaloni (2006: 64–68) underlines, a dense organizational network is vital for monitoring commitment problems in this kind of relationship with the electorate in an urban context. Hence, the massive and hierarchical JDP organization could also be considered a huge control mechanism over its low-income and peripheral electorate in need of the party's assistance. This organizational formation also helped the JDP

[25] The existence of a broad circle of non-governmental and charity organizations as well as an informal network of religious communities and orders strongly affiliated to the JDP should be underlined. While some of these charities and organizations were established directly by the JDP leadership, such as TÜRGEV (Charity for Youth and Service to Education), the JDP also exerted tight control over other pre-existing conservative charities and non-governmental organizations, such as İHH (Charity for Humanitarian Aid), as well as other religious communities and orders. In both cases, it was the party and Erdoğan who had the upper hand in this relationship, and it seems unlikely that these charities and religious communities forced the JDP to compromise on anything regarding the party's autonomy. For information on these charities, see Sunar (2015). For the tight control over the network of religious communities and brotherhoods, see Çakır (2014a).

gain more control over ballot boxes and polling station areas during election times and easily mobilize the party's supporters to vote. The massive, permanent and highly disciplined JDP organization helped JDP headquarters fill the public squares for Erdoğan's recurring mass rallies across distinct corners of the country.

Finally, on 15 July 2016 and in the days following, the membership organization of the JDP once again showed that it was key to the party's survival by providing rapid, effective and resilient mass mobilization in a political environment that included hostile and powerful non-party elite opponents. Despite the official narrative that people from all walks of life resisted the coup attempt, there was solid evidence that the overwhelming majority of protesters who attended the resistance against the coup and the subsequent 'Democracy Watches' (*Demokrasi Nöbetleri*) were JDP supporters and members (43 per cent and 41 per cent respectively) (Konda, 2016). This is, of course, not to say that the JDP mobilization inhibited and overcame the brute force exerted by the army. In fact, 250 people were killed and many more were wounded during the resistance. But mass mobilization certainly sent signs in the initial hours of the intervention that there was massive popular discontent and that the coup was going to fail (Waldman and Çalışkan, 2017: 43). It is plausible that this signal inhibited further high-ranking soldiers to jump on the bandwagon of the pro-coup segments, and incrementally dissolved the coup coalition within the army.

The importance the JDP elite attached to forming a large and pervasive membership party that was active year-round was a legacy of the Islamist National View politics of the 1990s and a response to the weakening and eventual demise of centre-right parties in Turkey during the same period as a consequence of their heavy dependence on media-based and capital-intensive organizational strategies as well as their underestimation of the critical functions played by the party on the ground (Delibaş, 2015: 54–64).[26] Hence, the JDP developed a mass-based face – a massive membership organization firmly controlled by the centre – to counterbalance the insufficiencies of elite-based models in the Turkish context. The JDP elite also developed appropriate organizational solutions that kept this massive membership organization under firm central leadership control without alienating the party base. Hence, the massive membership of the party was, in a sense, monitored and contacted by a large,

---

[26] Tanıyıcı also emphasizes how the Islamist Welfare Party 'avoided the organizational decline' of the Turkish political parties throughout the 1990s (2003: 469).

tightly controlled activist organization.[27] In the following section, I will have a closer look at these mechanisms.

Leadership Control

It has already been emphasized that the JDP exerted very tight control over the party base (Kumbaracıbaşı, 2009: 78), yet little effort has been made to illustrate the instruments and methods of this control. In this section, I illustrate the crucial instruments of control for the JDP over party activities on the ground. Firstly, I look at the role of centrally conducted public opinion surveys. I then draw attention to the role of technologically sophisticated communication channels. I also underline the importance of centrally appointed party co-ordinators, the rotation of ministers and deputies by the party leadership, and party funding by the elite in the tight central control of the provincial and local party life of the JDP.

Public Opinion Surveys or 'Questionnaires [Anketler]': The JDP and Political Marketing

One of the most important instruments for the JDP leadership in maintaining control of the party base was public opinion surveys. These surveys were demanded by the headquarters and provincial branches of the JDP and conducted by professional research companies close to the party. Surveys were conducted nationally or among the electorate of a certain region in order to understand the electoral inclinations as well as the attitude of the people with regard to certain, mostly unpopular, policies of the party.

It was frequently mentioned both in the media and by popular commentators that the JDP relied heavily on public opinion surveys for its decisions (Dalay, 2014; Soyoğul, 2013). Indeed, most of my interviewees underlined the importance attached to public opinion surveys or 'questionnaires [anketler]', as they were called by my interviewees, in the decision-making processes of the party (Interviewee 5, 2014).[28] Besides regular monthly public opinion surveys on the general inclinations of the electorate, the party also used many specified opinion surveys on its important national as well as minor and regional decisions (Interviewee

---

[27] It would be misleading to argue that the JDP organization worked equally well in various corners of the country. There were decisive dysfunctionalities in certain localities (Ocaklı, 2015). Overall, however, the JDP organization was a well-functioning machine.
[28] See also Interviewee 35, 2014.

38, 2014). Several of my interviewees noted that the party did not rely on a single research company but used a few different companies in order to get reliable results.[29]

In discussions of the opinion polling activity of the party, a remarkable difference occurred between the narratives of high-ranking party members and the narratives of junior members, failed candidates and former party members. While the former tended to underline the importance of public opinion surveys for overcoming the blindness caused by 'local-provincial organizational solidarity [teşkilat taassubu]' (Interviewee 18, 2014), the latter – in other words, failed candidates, junior party members and former party members – underlined the problems of opinion surveys.[30] This difference could be seen as evidence of the role of public opinion surveys as a central control mechanism.

An interview with the owner of one of the research companies working for the JDP provided some solid information on the uses of public opinion surveys by the party. My interviewee emphasized that 'question-naires' were a decision support mechanism and that the party regularly conducted research once a month. He underlined that when there were specific agendas the JDP tended to conduct surveys much more frequently. According to my interviewee, it was the public opinion surveys that illustrated to the party leadership that they should get rid some of the ideological-programmatic principles of the Islamist National View tradition right on the eve of the foundation of the JDP. He argued that the research conducted by his company prior to the foundation of the JDP revealed that the anti-EU and anti-globalization discourse as well as the redistributive 'Just Order [Adil Düzen]' promise of the Islamist Welfare Party were not embraced by the majority of the population. He argued that, through these surveys, the party leadership could see the 'pro-market' orientation of the electorate.

Hence, the rise of the JDP could also be seen as the decisive victory of political marketing techniques over redistributive, contentious and somehow more idealistic Islamist politics in Turkey. The rise of the JDP in a sense was an outcome of 'tailor[ing] the product according to consumer taste' (Scammell, 1995: 8). As my interviewee bluntly put it: 'There is this concept of "political marketing" [said in English]. The JDP uses this with fidelity. In other words, the party conducts careful market analysis before the decision-making process' (Interviewee 38, 2014).

Relying on the data gathered via public opinion surveys, the party also began to change its strategy towards local power holders in some

---

[29] See Interviewee 23, 2014; Interviewee 29, 2014; Interviewee 35, 2014.
[30] See Interviewee 8, 2014; Interviewee 10, 2014; Interviewee 15, 2014.

provinces (Interviewee 38, 2014). My interviews with failed candidates just before the local elections in 2014 strengthened this impression. For example, one of those failed candidates – most probably a local boss located in the middle of a small local patronage network – complained that, after the failure of his candidacy within the party, he did not know what to do with his hundreds of supporters in the sub-province (Interviewee 15, 2014). It seems that the party did not trust the claims of the local elite. Instead, the party centre conducted surveys in these regions and measured the real support for local bosses. Even if the claims of local bosses were proven true by the surveys, the JDP leadership tended to choose more competent and obedient people if it was possible to win elections with such candidates.

Nevertheless, one of my interviewees, a chair of a provincial party branch, also highlighted the fact that the party handled the local power holders and networks carefully, too (Interviewee 43, 2014). Although the party did not rely on specific persons or families, it could get votes from tribal families and religious communities as well in that particular province. This was to say that although the party leadership, to a great extent, did not compromise with local, regional power holders, they did not alienate them, either. It is plausible that extensive and frequent use of public opinion surveys provided the party leadership with superior knowledge regarding the inclinations of the electorate and enhanced leadership control over provincial and local branches of the party and local elites.

Use of Technology for Surveillance of Party Activity on the Ground: Unmediated Connections Between the Electorate, Activists and Leadership

The knowledge generated by the public opinion surveys was also supported by the knowledge gathered by the party headquarters about local and provincial party life. Regarding the control of party activities, one of my interviewees mentioned the highly sophisticated monitoring of the activities of the local-provincial organizations. According to the numbers she provided, 1.2 million households in İstanbul were continuously contacted by teams of three party members (each team consisting of a woman and two men). These visits were recorded and monitored with a barcode system (Interviewee 11, 2014).

In 2003, the party also launched a centralized communications centre. According to official party documents, every year tens of thousands of applications were received by AKİM via phone or email or in person, and the majority of demands and problems expressed in these applications were responded to by the party's professional staff (AK Parti, 2004). According to Eligür, in these communication centres – both in head-quarters and in the provinces – all citizens were allowed to express their complaints and demands and discuss them with party members (2010: 245). She also underlines the fact that all of the problems expressed in these communication centres were transmitted to the relevant state authorities by AKİM workers and followed up by party staff until they were responded to (Eligür, 2010: 245).

AKBİS, an intra-party online system for the surveillance of the party activities of provincial branches, should also be included in the picture (Interviewee 13, 2014). In an interview, the İzmir party chair described how AKBİS worked:

Headquarters can see the deputy's performance by pressing a key [...] Our sub-provincial chairs and the vice-chairs of municipal assembly groups are asked, 'Who are the ones who participate in the meetings for the municipality assembly, who are the ones who attend the party's activities? Who are the ones who pay their dues?' This is party identification. 'Does this member do the work she's been assigned by the party? Does she visit villages, does she visit the citizens, does she participate in party activities?' The provincial vice-chair responsible for the local government there provided us with records for all members of the municipal assembly. Who participated and how many times did they participate in the group meeting about the metropolitan municipality? We even know how long they stayed in the meeting. Sometimes, they just show up, sign the sheet and leave. But we have records. Sooner or later you definitely face these records (Soyoğul, 2013).

The party directly evaluated and controlled local-provincial party activity via AKBİS. As one member of headquarters told the system's users in local-provincial party branches, 'the headquarters can watch provincial and sub-provincial party activity by pressing a single key' (AK Parti, 2011). The party heavily relied on technology to surveil local-provincial organizational activity (Interviewee 28, 2014). Thus, while the party leadership established a direct connection with the electorate via AKİM, the party headquarters used AKBİS and its information about the minute details of party activity on the ground to enhance its position against provincial and local party branches, bypassing the organizational medium between the party leadership and the electorate on the one hand, and party activists on the ground and the party headquarters on the other.

Party Co-ordinators: The Bureaucratic Face of the JDP

The party co-ordinators also tightened the control of JDP headquarters over the provincial and sub-provincial branches through their personal presence. The JDP headquarters divided Turkey into several regions, and each region was supervised by a regional co-ordinator from either the Central Executive Committee or the parliamentary group of the party. These regions were further divided into sub-regions according to the provincial borders, with each sub-region supervised by the deputy of another city. Kumbaracıbaşı gives a detailed picture of these regions created by the JDP headquarters (2009: 133). He indicates that the JDP divided Turkey into two main domains: east and west. While the east comprised seven regions, the west comprised six. And these regions constituted several cities and were kept under the control of JDP deputies (Kumbaracıbaşı, 2009: 133).

As Kumbaracıbaşı indicates, these deputies were not locals of these regions and cities, and this was why they could take an objective stance in local politics and give detailed accounts to JDP headquarters about the local political situation (2009: 133). Thus, provincial politics were kept under control by centrally appointed party co-ordinators who were not a part of local politics. For example, a deputy from an inner Anatolian city could be the co-ordinator of the Eastern Black Sea region (*Haberler.com*, 2013). The role of city and regional co-ordinators was to provide constant and neutral feedback to the party leadership from the provincial branches. Particularly during the candidate selection processes, reports from the regional and city co-ordinators might provide neutral information to the party leadership that was oriented to the general party interest.

The same model was applied to the provincial level as well. Sub-regions created by the provincial party branch of a city were supervised and kept under control by co-ordinators appointed by the provincial party branch.[31] Thus, the control exercised over provincial party branches by headquarters was complemented by the control exercised over sub-provincial party branches by the provincial party organizations (Interviewee 6, 2014). Regions comprising only a few neighbourhoods were also supervised by co-ordinators appointed by the sub-provincial party branch.[32] The party exerted intense central control even over the most minor segments of party organization. To this end, the party leadership carefully appointed outsiders to these settings in order to

---

[31] In a news article, it was indicated that İzmir had been divided into six sub-regions by the provincial party branch, and each of these regions, consisting of five or six sub-regions, was allocated a co-ordinator by the provincial branch (*Milliyet*, 2014b).

[32] On the website of one of the provincial branches of the JDP it was reported that a certain neighbourhood of the Kepez sub-province was visited by the co-ordinator appointed by the sub-provincial branch (Akpartikepez, 2013).

protect their neutral, central stance against local politics. These control mechanisms alone created a considerable bureaucracy in the JDP.

Control by Ministers and Deputies: Elected Elites as Agents of the JDP Central Office

The rotation of JDP ministers and deputies also played a crucial role in the central control of party activities in provinces and local settings. One of my interviewees drew attention to the fact that the formation of the JDP cabinets revealed a certain pattern in the distribution of minister-ships (Interviewee 29, 2014). For example, a look at the JDP cabinets formed after the 2011 general elections revealed that the party leadership allocated and distributed ministerships to as many different influential cities as possible. Not only İstanbul and Ankara, but also other major provincial power centres of Turkey such as Bursa, Konya, Kayseri, İzmir, Diyarbakır, Trabzon, Gaziantep, Mersin, Kocaeli, Samsun and Rize were represented by ministers in the cabinet. These ministers were not necessarily locals of these provinces, and some of them were deliberately nominated by the party headquarters for these cities. The result was the headquarters' tighter control over these cities through the intervention of ministers in some of the important decision-making processes at the provincial level, such as candidate selection and the identification of governing bodies of the party. These ministers, under the control of the party leadership, also responded to the particularistic demands of the electorate in these cities without entirely surrendering to local politics. Hence, allocating ministerships to different cities enhanced party centralism[33] and, at the same time, absorbed the reactions of local party bases through the centrally supervised direction of selective resources.

A very similar dynamic was followed in the use of deputies. For example, a member of the JDP elite from İstanbul, based on her family origins in a provincial city in Anatolia, could be nominated to represent this city by the demand of the party headquarters. This, in turn, provided the party leadership with stronger leverage over both the deputy and local politics because in the general elections, as most of my interviewees underlined, the electorate usually voted for the personality of Erdoğan and the party rather than for the individual candidates. As a conse-quence, most, if not all, JDP deputies were more likely to defend head-quarters' opinion against local dynamics. As one of my interviewees from a provincial city said, 'here, deputies are like civil servants [of the party

---

[33] Bayraktar and Altan (2013) also illustrate a very similar dynamic.

headquarters]' (Interviewee 44, 2014). Although Turkish politics has always been prone to the predominance of party leaders in candidate selection processes in localities, the presence of many colourful and powerful figures (mostly relying on extensive local patronage networks) has always been one of the characteristics of the Grand National Assembly of Turkey. As discussed in the next chapter, the JDP central elite had a surprisingly deep suspicion towards local elite and local politics, and this was one of the reasons behind the JDP elites' strategy of effectively inhibiting the presence of powerful local personalities in the parliament. In this context, the rotation of ministers and deputies and the detachment of individual JDP politicians from their local settings gave the central party leadership an upper hand over both provincial and local settings as well as over the ministers and deputies themselves.

Party Finance by the JDP Elite

The essential component of the highly centralized JDP organization was party finance by the elite. Central party finance has always been a consolidating element of party centralism in Turkey (Gençkaya, 2002: 44–45). Within the framework of existing laws regarding political parties, state subsidies to the parties were allocated centrally, and the party headquarters had the power to decide how to distribute these resources. At the same time, parties could collect only scant membership dues, and most of the party branches relied on the central funding of activities and on resources generated by local party elite (Uysal and Topak, 2010: 209). This picture of party finance in Turkey was, to a great extent, applicable to the JDP as well. As the ruling party and winner of several elections, the JDP received a considerable amount from the state for party activities,[34] and the party also used public facilities for its electoral campaigns.[35]

Two of my interviewees told me of some typical incidents revealing the dynamics of party finance in the JDP. One of my interviewees, regarding a question about party finance in the sub-provinces, underlined the resources generated by the local elite (Interviewee 7, 2014). Another interviewee drew attention to the role of the party's central finance in its foundation and pointed out that this was one of the origins of leadership domination within the JDP. It seems that, alongside the role of state

[34] According to the JDP website, 96.9 per cent of the party's income comes from state subsidies. See www.akparti.org.tr/site/akparti/gelir-gider (accessed: 25 February 2015).
[35] Ferries and buses of the Municipality of İstanbul took thousands of people to the meeting space in Yenikapı for the JDP meeting in the summer of 2013 (Ntvmsnbc.com, 2013).

aid, party leaders' financial autonomy in the foundation of parties is a crucial element for the future domination of party life by the leader:

Finance is important because of this: he who financially supports a party actually owns the party [...] [When the JDP was founded] Mr Tayyip[36] rented a headquarters building at the monthly cost of 36 billion liras. We had seventy-three founders and not one among them put their hand in their pocket. This is very important. The whole rent was a serious amount by then [...] Mr Tayyip paid the rent alone. When saying this – of course perhaps he had collected money from various sources – I am trying to underline that he did not receive any money from the founders. And at that moment, Mr Tayyip actually owned the party. Like an asset, like owning a flat. The property of the party belongs to Mr Tayyip (Interviewee 21, 2014).

Apparently, the party relied heavily on the resources generated by its central and provincial elite for its activities. JDP predominance in local government should also be kept in mind since municipal resources provided a considerable financial resource to the local JDP elite. However, the autonomous financial resources provided by the JDP municipalities for the local JDP elite should not be considered something that enhanced the local elites since the central JDP elite always had a close eye even on the minor centrifugal dynamics within local politics (as elaborated upon in the next chapter). Close relationships with business circles were also vital for central party finance, particularly for the building of a strong pro-JDP media.[37]

Controlled Participation

In this section, I focus on three key mechanisms of the JDP organization that provided a very strong sense of participation to the party base and diminished the potential corrosive effects of tight central control over the

---

[36] The particular interviewee, who knew Erdoğan personally and had interacted with him for a long time, called him Mr Tayyip (Tayyip Bey) in this interview because of their acquaintance. It is common to hear ordinary supporters of the party using this form of reference too. This is another indicator of the solid populist rapport between Erdoğan and his supporters. It should also be noted that it is common to see some opponents of the JDP call Erdoğan simply Tayyip (without the honorific Bey); in this latter situation, the aim is, apparently, to deprecate him.

[37] As an initial evaluation, these relationships between businesspeople and the JDP elite could also be considered 'new patronage relationships' of the JDP years which replaced the old-style, centre-right patronage in Turkey (explained in the previous chapter), which mainly relied on heavy state subsidies and massive public employment. The examination of this aspect of JDP politics would be very interesting, yet it is beyond the scope and extent of this research. For a very detailed account of the patronage triangle among the JDP elite, pro-JDP businesses and JDP voters, see the study by Esen and Gümüşçü (2017). See also Çeviker-Gürakar (2016).

massive membership organization of the party. These are 'regular consultations', 'non-binding elections among selected party members' and the 'extensive use of women's branches for party activity'.

Regular Consultations (İstişareler): Listening to Activists and Keeping Them Busy

The most pronounced instrument revealed through my interviews for controlling the participation of the party base in the decision-making processes of the JDP was that of 'consultations'.[38] The intense consultation activity of the JDP started at the top of the organization. The JDP held weekly Central Executive Committee consultation meetings and monthly Central Decision and Administration Board consultation meetings as well as regular weekly meetings of the cabinet (Interviewee 14, 2014). All of these regular consultation meetings were held in the personal presence of Erdoğan. One of my interviewees, a former JDP member and a critical observer of the party, very neatly described this attention of Erdoğan with a humorous exaggeration: 'I do not think that there has ever been a single meeting in the history of the JDP without the attendance of Erdoğan' (Interviewee 21, 2014).

Erdoğan was also always present in the regular monthly consultation meetings with the eighty-one provincial chairs, provincial mayors and sub-provincial mayors of the party (Interviewee 14, 2014). One of my interviewees, a provincial chair, described the function of regular consultation meetings and pointed out the reasons for the great importance attached to these meetings by the party leader Erdoğan:

At the moment the prime minister [Erdoğan] is in his twelfth year as the party chair. Is he not? If he does not gather provincial party chairs for the [monthly] consultation meeting for three or five months no one would say why this party does not conduct the [monthly] consultation. But he gathers these people for the monthly consultation meeting. We also do consultation meetings here [in the province]. In other words we always come together through these consultation meetings and people sometimes criticize this. Other parties do not bother themselves with such meetings. In the sub-provinces, too, [you have] weekly sub-provincial meetings and extended consultation meetings [genişletilmiş danışma meclisi toplantısı], weekly provincial meetings as well as weekly meetings of the executive committee of the provincial party branch. In addition you have the meetings of provincial mayors and the meetings of members of the provincial municipality assembly. Sometimes even we criticize this: 'we should do these meetings in three months' time, monthly meetings are too frequent'. But even the constant movement for these meetings increases the motivation. This

---

[38]   See Interviewee 14, 2014; Interviewee 29, 2014; Interviewee 34, 2014.

was one of the reasons why the JDP was so dynamic and alive. The prime minister knew this. We learned this by experience. [When you do these meetings] people [party members] do not speak [about the problems of the party] in coffee houses or in other irrelevant places. They come to the meeting and criticize the provincial chair in the party and you get something from him/her. You say, 'There is a problem in one of our sub-provinces. I shall go there.' But if you want to know about these problems you have to conduct these frequent meetings. You also transmit to them what you have received in Ankara. He/she [the provincial party activist] does not know every detail. You cannot learn everything from the TV and from newspapers. You [as the provincial chair] go to Ankara and come back and transmit these details to them [. . .] And you also discuss what works [need] to be completed. You control [the sub-provincial organizations]: 'Are your ballot box observers OK? Have you conducted your consultation meetings?' (Interviewee 4, 2013).

It is apparent that regular consultations enhanced the intra-party connections of the hierarchical units of the JDP, and frequent meetings also kept the JDP activists busy permanently. One could also presume that these regular meetings had also contributed to the emergence of a party sub-culture. The JDP headquarters also carefully controlled whether the local-provincial branches held their own weekly consultation meetings for party administration and monthly consultation meetings with the sub-provincial chairs (Interviewee 6, 2014). The provincial governing bodies of the party also ensured that the same meetings were held at the sub-provincial and neighbourhood levels (Interviewee 7, 2014). One of my senior interviewees argued that the intensity and frequency of these consultation meetings were unique to the JDP, and that other political parties in Turkey hardly ever attributed such importance to consultations (Interviewee 14, 2014).

For example, one of my interviewees, a sub-provincial mayor who had previously had political experience in the centre-right Motherland Party, and later in the JDP, related an incident where he missed a consultation meeting at the JDP headquarters in Ankara due to his work in his sub-province. Unlike in the Motherland Party period, he told me that he was immediately called by a vice-chair from the headquarters and was asked the reason for his absence (Interviewee 30, 2014). As one of my interviewees pointed out, these meetings not only provided feedback to the party headquarters from local-provincial branches, but also motivated the local-provincial activists of the party: '[when you do these meetings] you also provide motivation. These people say that "they [the headquarters] are taking me seriously"' (Interviewee 39, 2014).

It should also be noted that the term *istişare* has a religious connotation as well and implies the political superiors' obligation to consult subordinates before making decisions in accordance with verdicts of the Quran.

Nevertheless, one of my interviewees, a highly critical member, provided vivid details about the nature of central consultation meetings of the party in which high-ranking members of the party had so little time to express their opinions (Interviewee 21, 2014). Yet, most of my interviewees who had high-ranking positions in the party implied that, despite the authoritarian appearance of Erdoğan from the outside, he was tolerant towards intra-party negotiations, and he allowed space for lively discussions (Interviewee 35, 2014). Yet, it would be really misleading to consider the results of these meetings binding for the leadership (Interviewee 34, 2014). Instead, it was considered a method deployed by the JDP leadership to replace intra-party democracy (Interviewee 37, 2014).[39]

A Central Executive Committee member of the JDP explained to me why the consultation meetings were not binding through a distinction he made between 'mass-oriented [kitle temelli]' and 'principle-based [ilke temmelli]' tendencies (Interviewee 34, 2014). According to him, it was not always healthy to follow the tendencies of the majority, or mass-oriented inclinations, in consultation meetings since the majority might be prone to observing short-term interests and solutions. Hence, for him, there was no problem at all about the fact that consultation meetings were not binding in the JDP. His narrative implied an identification of elite choices with long-term, general interests and principles. One should also note that, as one of my interviewees highlighted, consultation meetings were much more binding for the provincial administrators than the party chair and the national party elite (Interviewee 40, 2014). This also entailed less autonomy for provincial chairs over provincial activists and kept them weaker as compared both to the provincial party base and to the party headquarters. This situation should also be considered a side effect of consultation meetings, which increased the party leadership's autonomy vis-à-vis provincial party bosses and local power holders.

At first glance, these consultation meetings appeared to be an opportunity for junior party members and the party base to express their ideas and demands. However, these meetings were not only a means of getting feedback from the party base, but were also an instrument through which the party leadership could persuade less senior and junior party

---

[39] According to one of my interviewees, a JDP Central Executive Committee member, consultations 'are extremely important in the Islamic world [...] The consultation tradition is a more developed form of democracy. The JDP is the only and most important party using the consultation tradition and never concedes on this point' (Interviewee 37, 2014).

administrators and the party base to accept headquarters' decisions.[40] One should therefore note the double role of these regular consultation meetings: feedback and control/persuasion. As one of my interviewees implied, in cases where the leadership made unpopular decisions, they also made great efforts to convince the provincial and local party branches to accept them (Interviewee 36, 2014). However, it is plausible to argue that regular consultations provided a strong sense of participation for the party base and provincial organizations. Hence, the party base tended to embrace even the most unpopular decisions made by the party leadership, and consultations increased the legitimacy of the JDP leadership in the eyes of the party on the ground.

Non-Binding Elections among Selected Party Members (Teşkilat Temayül Yoklamaları): Giving a Voice to Party Members

Another important instrument used to control the participation of the party base in the party's decision-making processes, as outlined by my interviewees, was that of non-binding elections among selected members of the party. According to JDP statutes, the party could conduct 'elections for defining organizational tendencies [teşkilat temayül yoklaması]' in order to choose its candidates (AK Parti, 2012a: 74). But just like the consultation meetings, these elections did not produce binding results for the party leadership. Instead, the results of these elections, which were conducted among the party elite, high-ranking party members and members of the administration boards in a given province, were considered only a component of a wider decision-making mechanism. The results of these elections were not usually publicized and were made available only to the party leadership. Since, the party base had no information on the results of these non-binding elections, the party leadership did not take the risk of facing bottom-up dissent and, since the results were not publicized, the party leadership could also use these elections to explain the failure of certain candidates who were not approved by headquarters.[41]

As one of my interviewees underlined, there were many examples in which the results of non-binding elections did not match the desires of the party leadership (Interviewee 4, 2013). In these cases, the decisions of the party leadership were usually accepted by the provincial and local

---

[40] Numerous videos of consultation meetings of the JDP in which the provincial and local party leaders explain JDP policies to party members can be found on YouTube. For example, see www.youtube.com/watch?v=t3c9DUIm6_k (accessed: 27 May 2016).

[41] I elaborate on candidate selection processes in the next chapter.

organizations since there was widespread trust in the personality and political experience of Erdoğan. Non-binding elections provided feedback to the party leadership about organizational inclinations by officially asking the opinion of the party base via a simple vote-casting procedure. More importantly, non-binding elections fulfilled the party base's desire to participate in the decision-making process. This is why one of the elites of the JDP and the Islamist National View organizations, in his guide to aspiring politicians, argued that non-binding elections were held to appease the party base (Şentürk, 2006: 99).

During the interviews, a certain pattern appeared when high-ranking party members tried to explain why the results of intra-party elections for defining organizational inclinations (*teşkilat yoklamaları*) in the JDP were not considered binding by the party leadership. Senior party members frequently argued that provincial organizations and local politics were prone to particularistic tendencies and driven by local interests. Some of my interviewees called this tendency 'organizational conservatism [*teşkilat taassubu*)]' or 'organizational nationalism [*teşkilat milliyetçiliği*]', which denotes a local organizational solidarity that is not considerate of the general interest of the party and the country.[42] It was, therefore, not surprising that party leader Erdoğan, in a party consultation meeting prior to the 2014 local elections, emphasized that non-binding elections would not be the only decision-making instrument in the candidate selection processes: 'Our aim is not to provide posts to some people. Our aim is to produce service for our cities. We know, in too many places, there is serious institutional nationalism [*kurumsal milliyetçilik*]. Non-binding election [*teşkilat yoklaması*] results would not be decisive. We know how, sometimes, these elections are held' (*Hürriyet*, 2013). This shows that Erdoğan himself thought that local politics and local organizational solidarity could produce inappropriate candidates for elections. Non-binding elections were therefore another instrument for controlling the participation of the party base while helping the leadership avoid 'organizational conservatism' in the provincial and local branches.

Women's Branches as the Main Tool of Party Activity:
Reaching Out to Low-Income, Conservative Households

Another channel that fulfilled the JDP base's desire to participate in politics and which significantly helped the party get in touch with the

---

[42] See Interviewee 15, 2014; Interviewee 18, 2014; Interviewee 35, 2014.

electorate was the activity of women's branches. Most of my interviewees underlined the extraordinary role played by women's branches in party activity,[43] and even neutral observers confirmed their vital role (Interviewee 39, 2014). As one of my interviewees described it, the Welfare Party phase of the Islamist National View tradition was the 'discovery of the female electorate' (Interviewee 19, 2014). And, it seems that one of the most crucial organizational inheritances of the JDP from the National View tradition was women's branches and the importance attached to the female electorate (Interviewee 1, 2013). In fact, Erdoğan attached great importance to women throughout the JDP years, too. Hence, there was a remarkable women and youth quota in the JDP, albeit an unofficial one.[44]

According to my interviewees, the primary benefit of strong women's branches was the opportunities that the presence of women provided to access conservative and low-income households in Turkey.[45] According to my interviewees involved with women's branches of the JDP, the women in the household could change the men's decision (Interviewee 10, 2014). At the least, the activity of women's branches helped persuade women to vote differently from their husbands (Interviewee 49, 2014). Hence, the women's branches had also a particular importance as the primary medium of one of the important communication methods of the party underlined in the previous chapter: 'face-to-face interaction with the electorate' (Mercan, 2003: 12). Women's branches also played a vital role in distributing aid in cash or in kind in low-income neighbourhoods (Interviewee 10, 2014). Hence, active women's branches also weakened the connection between local power holders and selective resources distributed to the low-income electorate, therefore inhibiting the development of local political machines.

The work of JDP women's branches also established an emotional link with the electorate (Interviewee 32, 2014). During my interviews, I observed that members of the women's branches tended to be motivated more by collective incentives than the selective incentives that party life provided as a result of the charity-like nature of the party activity conducted by the women's branches. It is plausible that most of the members of the women's branches enjoyed the spiritual satisfaction of helping the poor and viewed the party activity from this perspective. The

---

[43] See Interviewee 4, 2013; Interviewee 29, 2014; Interviewee 35, 2014.
[44] There used to be an official quota implemented by the party but this was later removed. Nevertheless, according to research regarding women's branches of the party, there was an unofficial quota which anticipated 30 per cent female participation (Tür and Çıtak, 2010: 620). See also Interviewee 49, 2014.
[45] See Interviewee 10, 2014; Interviewee 28, 2014; Interviewee 49, 2014.

women's branches of the JDP also showed striking loyalty to Erdoğan. One of the substantial reasons behind women's participation in the JDP was their affection for Erdoğan and their belief in his 'rightness, sincerity, manners, diligence, charisma, leadership and the importance he attached to women' (Tür and Çıtak, 2010: 622).

In accordance with the vital duties of the party's women's branches, as one of my interviewees underlined, the party leadership systematically privileged women: 'sometimes [...] the party nominates women from some provincial cities; and local politicians of these cities just argue that "this region cannot tolerate women". In these cases the party leadership strongly supports the women' (Interviewee 49, 2014). This statement was confirmed by another study as well, where participants from the women's branches of the party argued that Erdoğan himself attached great importance to the representation of women in the party life and in elected positions (Tür and Çıtak, 2010: 620). As one of my interviewees argued, the JDP strongly encouraged the participation of women and youth in politics (Interviewee 29, 2014).

The importance attached to women's branches, as well as to the youth ones, also had a centralizing effect. Since women and young people tended to be more loyal to the leadership and less competitive over selective incentives as a consequence of the charity-like nature of their engagement with the electorate, relying on these secondary branches for party activity could be considered a deliberate strategy of party centralization. After all, as one of my interviewees from a sub-provincial women's branch pointed out, 'actually women are not into politics; they are mainly concerned about the spiritual [manevi ve vicdani] aspect of the activity' (Interviewee 32, 2014).[46] However, the main reason behind the intensive use of women's branches was to easily get in touch with the low-income and conservative households of Turkey. Greater autonomy of the party leadership vis-à-vis the local-provincial party bosses and the elite was an unintended consequence of the extensive use of women's branches.

In this section, I have illustrated that the potential dissent towards the tight central control of party activity on the ground was carefully managed by the JDP elite. To this end, the party elite attached great

---

[46] Here it should be carefully noted that the participation of women in politics through the JDP remained within the boundaries of a mainly patriarchical division of labour that allocated charity-like activities to women and reserved 'serious politics' mainly for the men. For instance, the women ministers from the ranks of the JDP have been usually responsible for issues regarding family, woman and education. However, there is also reason to think that this division of labour was compatible with the populist appeal of the JDP and that it resonated with expectations of the party's electorate.

importance to regular consultations, held non-binding elections among selected JDP members in the provincial and local branches, and intensively employed its women's branches. These methods together provided the party base with a strong sense of participation and remarkably increased the legitimacy of the party leadership. As a result, authoritarian intra-party governance of the JDP was tolerated remarkably by the JDP activists since they had a strong sense of participation in the decision-making processes and activities of the party.[47]

Conclusion: The Personalistic Mass Party in Perspective

The organizational dynamics of the JDP, as elaborated above, paint a remarkably different picture from that of party organizational change in Western democracies. As discussed above in the section on concepts and theory, many students of party organizations have contended that the mass party lost its significance with the rise of elite-based 'catch-all' or 'cartel parties'. The literature usually argued that massive membership organizations lost their importance in most Western democracies.[48] In contrast, the JDP elite carefully protected and improved the party's membership organization, increased the number of JDP members and made great efforts to build party branches in even the remotest and smallest corners of the country. This situation was also a divergent strategic choice compared to those made by most of the JDP's predecessors in the 1990s and its current competitors in the Turkish party system.

The JDP elite, primarily through central interventions, created a highly centralized, hierarchical, bureaucratized, large and pervasive membership organization that was active year-round, and as a result the JDP approximated to a mass-based party. Nevertheless, the JDP also attached importance to public opinion surveys, direct communication channels with the electorate and a communications strategy that placed Erdoğan at its centre. The party leadership created a strong, pro-JDP media and used political marketing techniques in general under the control of a highly personalistic leadership (elaborated upon in Chapters 4 and 5). Hence, the JDP also had the face of an elite-based party. Figure 6.2

---

[47] 'Controlled participation' should also be seen as central to the 'clandestine authoritarianism' in Turkish parties as identified by Ayan Musil (2011). According to Ayan Musil, in this sort of intra-party authoritarianism, ideational interests play a central role (2011: 164). It seems that vigorous intra-party participation mechanisms could also play an important role in absorbing dissent against firm central control.

[48] For a critical discussion on the party decline literature, see Ignazi (1996). According to Ignazi the literature on 'the crisis of party' misled researchers into thinking that there was a general decline in party politics.

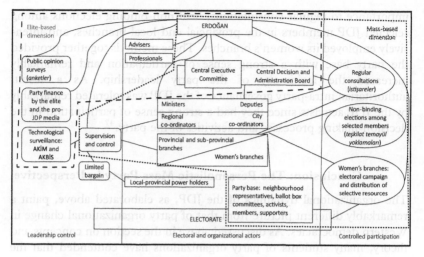

Figure 6.2: The JDP as a personalistic mass party: elite-based and
mass-based dimensions
Source: Author's compilation.

illustrates these two faces of the party and provides a general diagram of
the JDP's organizational mechanics. (See also Table 6.1, Table 6.2 and
Table 5.1 for various organizational and strategic characteristics of the
JDP that made the party a hybrid electoral machine and distinguished it
from its right-wing predecessors in Turkish politics, namely the Islamist
Welfare Party and Virtue Party and the centre-right Motherland Party as
well as from a series of centre-right parties preceding the Motherland
Party which can be called 'personalistic cadre parties'.) The hatched lines
indicate the components of the elite-based dimension of the party, and
the dotted lines cover the elements in which the JDP resembled a mass-
based model. Thus, the JDP can be identified as a hybrid electoral
machine: an organization that blended the mass-based and elite-based
party models and which targeted electoral predominance through robust
organizational leverage supported by political marketing techniques.
Given the centrality of the party leader Erdoğan in this massive membership organization, it could be called a 'personalistic mass party'.

In this innovative mixture of various traits of the mass-based and
elite-based party models, the JDP elite were also able to overcome the
potential problems entailed by both models.[49] Bureaucratic and

---

[49] For these problems, see Ignazi (1996).

ideological rigidity and lack of flexibility (a problem of the mass party model) were ruled out by the creation of an autonomous party leadership through the use of public opinion surveys, technological surveillance techniques and central party finance. The party also overcame its members' lack of motivation (a problem of elite-based models). Through regular consultations, non-binding elections among selected members and active women's branches, the JDP elite were able to provide a strong sense of participation, and thus motivation, throughout this massive membership organization. As a result of the simultaneous use of these instruments, the JDP was able to form a highly autonomous leadership, as well as a highly autonomous party, and overcome the problems entailed by the purely mass-based and elite-based parties while benefiting from the electoral advantages of both models.

It should also be added that the routinization and bureaucratization of the party, in combination with its populist appeal (delineated in Chapter 3) and personalistic conduct (analysed in Chapter 4), to a certain extent, solved problems regarding the establishment of trust among various party hierarchies and among the JDP elite. While routinization, bureaucratization and the regular rotation of elites provided a sense of stability and foreseeable career paths among the JDP elite, the strong sense of similarity with the party leader Erdoğan, which was felt by the lower echelons of the organization (stemming from the populism and personalism of the JDP organization as delineated in Chapters 3 and 4), helped the party elite to sustain trust in the leadership. In other words, rotation of elites (elaborated in Chapter 7), and the bonds between the party leader and the unprivileged party base constructed through populism, personalism and the organizational dynamics outlined so far, helped the JDP elite solve a fundamental dilemma regarding the principal–agent model.[50]

The principal–agent model implies that authority stems from the unprivileged majorities and that it is delegated to the chosen elites on behalf of the masses. The principal–agent model, as generated from the politics of Western democracies, also presumes a basic distrust between the principal (the constituency of the party and the party base) and the agent (which includes local and national party leaders, as well as party members in both central and public office) due to the superior access to information and the self-interest of the latter. Yet, as Ayan Musil demonstrates, it is much more useful to understand the principal–agent relationship in the reverse order in the context of Turkish party politics

---

[50] For a very useful illustration of the principal–agent model and its implications for the Turkish party politics, see Ayan Musil (2011: particularly 58–65).

(2011: 63). This is to say that politicians at the top of power hierarchies of authoritarian parties in Turkey usually play the role of principals and delegate authority to the local political activists. The principals in Turkey, in practice, were not the party base or constituencies but the national party leaders (either at the top of the party in the central office or holding influential positions in the party in public office).

In this reverse functioning of the principal–agent model, one would expect a much deeper problem of distrust between party hierarchies since the sectors of the party who were nominally 'principals' had so little power to shape the decision- and policy-making processes of the party. However, the subordinate segments of the JDP organization and the party's constituency always had a very strong sense that they were delegating authority from the bottom and that their agents were fulfilling what they desired. Alongside material benefits to the masses, I contend that the innovative combination of populism, personalism and the model of mass membership organization created by the JDP elite (the personalistic mass party) helped the party overcome this exacerbated dilemma regarding the principal–agent model in the context of Turkish party politics. This was crucial in sustaining popular support for and legitimacy of the JDP for a remarkably long time, which ultimately gave rise to competitive authoritarianism in Turkey.[51]

As briefly discussed in the section on theories on the party typologies, this mixture achieved by the JDP was a response to the political context (analysed in Chapter 2 in detail) and the electoral market (analysed in Chapter 5) which gave rise to the JDP. Under these circumstances, the JDP could not risk exclusively relying on elite-based models given the resistance triggered among powerful non-party political actors by the rise of the JDP and due to the party's strictly Islamist past. Apart from this, the JDP elite also took lessons from the previous centre-right parties' organizational decline in the 1990s and the electoral costs entailed by this organizational decay. Hence, the JDP adopted techniques from modern elite-based parties but carefully combined them with a mass-based model. This not only provided an upper hand to the party in elections, but also consolidated its resistance against hostile non-party political opponents. The case of the JDP illustrates that, in the context of developing countries where social and technological change did not match the pace of that of liberal Western democracies, some aspects of the mass party model have still been shaping party organizations. Here, the broader theoretical implication is this: a non-critical engagement with

---

[51] I focus on the transformation of the political regime in Turkey from an electoral democracy to competitive authoritarianism in Chapter 8.

party models predominantly based on theories of the cases of Western liberal democratic settings might be misleading in explaining the party organizational development in the developing world.

In the context of the general approach and argument of the book, this chapter also puts a strong emphasis on the organizational agency of the party (alongside parts of Chapters 3–5). But, like previous chapters, this chapter has also evaluated the party's agency in a dynamic interaction with the political environment; it has considered the 'personalistic mass party' a strategic response to the constraints and opportunities within the political and electoral context of a developing country. More precisely, this chapter has highlighted the role of the agency of the JDP elite in creating the agency of the JDP as a collective actor. Hence, while viewing the JDP as a coherent collective actor and agent, this particular chapter has refrained from taking this fact as a given. In fact, this chapter (in combination with Chapters 4 and 5) has put a strong emphasis on the fact that the JDP emerged as a coherent, strategic and ultimately politically successful[52] actor mainly as a result of the labour-intensive, successful management by its leadership and, most prominently, as a result of the agency of Erdoğan himself (as delineated in Chapter 4).

With respect to the authoritarian turn of the JDP as well as the rise of competitive authoritarianism in Turkey, this chapter has some important implications. In the absence of reliable economic and symbolic resources, a successful organizational arrangement that could effectively absorb potential dissent, keep centrifugal tendencies within the party organization in check and control clientelistic practices (which rely on limited economic resources) had a central role in the construction of a hegemonic party autocracy. In other words, theories about hegemonic party autocracies or authoritarian dominant party systems should also seriously take into account the organizational characteristic of hegemonic-dominant parties alongside 'structural-economic factors' (Magaloni, 2006) and 'the strategic and organizational formation of rival political parties in a given dominant party system' (Greene, 2007). This point will be discussed further in the conclusion, where I address the theoretical implications of the case of the JDP within the context of the literature on Islamism, populism and authoritarianism.

---

[52] As I indicated in the introduction, I use this term in its Machiavellian sense of meaning the ability to stay in power for a prolonged period of time under profoundly hostile circumstances. The issue of the managerial and long-term success of Erdoğan and the party with regard to the development of Turkey, not only in economic terms but also in terms of the quality of its human resources and welfare, is an entirely different, and debatable, issue.

From the perspective of this chapter, a couple of future trends can also be identified with regard to the evolution of the JDP's organizational dynamics. It is plausible that, while the JDP remains in power, as the party elite start to feel themselves more secure against the non-party political opposition, and as the party's supporters take advantage of the party's position in power for upward socio-economic mobilization, the party might move closer to elite-based models. It can also be expected that, as the party remains in power, its incorporation with the state apparatuses might also enhance this trend towards the adaptation of more elite-based models. The wider socio-economic transformation of Turkey throughout the JDP years might also have a deep impact on the JDP's long-term evolution. As income levels of voters increase, internet use becomes widespread, and the rise of consumerism in Turkey gains a new momentum and provides social activities to the conservative JDP supporters that are more interesting than party activism, the party elite might increasingly need to adapt elite-based models. And the *de jure* presidentialization of Turkish political system (which is elaborated upon in Chapter 8) might also require the JDP to move incrementally in an elite-based direction. Hence, the depiction of the JDP's organization in this chapter, and in the book in general, should be considered as a picture taken at a certain point in time rather than a comprehensive story of the party's organizational evolution.

7 Elite Recruitment in the JDP: 'You Do Not Want These Kinds of People in the Parliament'

Introduction

Since its foundation, the JDP's ruling cadres have been considered highly competent by the majority of the electorate, and this perception contributed significantly to electoral support for the party, as previous research (Gidengil and Karakoç, 2014) has illustrated. This was why the JDP's political appeal (as outlined in Chapter 3) always contained the claim that 'service delivery [*hizmet*]' by the 'hard-working', 'competent' cadres was essential to the party's mission. Hence, it is crucial to understand the dynamics of the JDP's elite recruitment processes in order to understand its claim of managerial competence and the party's electoral support that partly relies on this claim. The dynamics of elite recruitment processes within the party were also important for providing the JDP with the coherence that was required for the rise of a competitive authoritarian regime in Turkey in the absence of vast economic and symbolic resources. In this sense, this chapter can be seen as a natural extension of the previous chapter (with a particular focus on the intra-party and elite-level political dynamics of the JDP), which examined the overall organizational dynamics and structure of the party.

How did the JDP choose its candidates for crucial posts like local and national government and provincial governing bodies of the party? In this chapter, I argue that the party leadership[1] was able to select and support competent (in other words, highly educated and experienced) and

---

[1] The term 'leadership' with regard to JDP intra-party politics specifically refers to party chair Erdoğan. It also covers some other high-ranking, but not very visible, JDP members and advisers around Erdoğan who had strong leverage in the party's decision-making processes. Although it is hard to single out names of these people, one of my interviewees, for example, underlined the influence of a powerful group around Erdoğan, three or four people who ultimately chose the candidates of the party (Interviewee 9, 2014). Regarding other fields of decision making in the party, 'the leadership' can refer to a wider group such as the Central Executive Committee. However, it would not be unfair to argue that Erdoğan had an overwhelming dominance over these secondary segments of the leadership whose positions were usually granted personally by him.

obedient candidates instead of popular local bosses by inhibiting factionalism through robust interventions into local and provincial party life. The JDP leadership carefully designed the formation of provincial governing bodies of the party, and this in turn provided it with almost indisputable authority over the party candidate selection processes, inhibited centrifugal tendencies and opened up room for the JDP elite to elevate competent candidates.

As noted in Chapter 6, in this book, party organizations are seen 'as clusters of relationships rather than as unitary "black boxes"' (Massicard and Watts, 2013: 4). Hence, it is vital to elaborate upon the recruitment processes since this is one of the most important activities in intra-party politics, where researchers are able to see these 'clusters of relationships' among party hierarchies. As Hazan and Rahat underline, candidate selection processes are 'the best points at which to observe the distribution of power within the party' (2010: 8). Candidate selection dynamics illustrate vital features of party organization (Hazan and Rahat, 2010: 10). In line with Hazan and Rahat, I understand the various methods of candidate selection processes to fall mainly on a scale between the 'most exclusive' and 'most inclusive' extremes, where the former represents the selection by one person (the party leader) and the latter represents selection by all voters (2010: 35).

In the second section, I briefly describe the rise of leadership domination in the JDP and the formation of provincial governing bodies since these were key to inhibiting factionalism within the party and, therefore, central to bringing the candidate selection processes under the control of the party leadership. In the third section, I elaborate on candidate selection processes. I pay special attention to the different perceptions of candidate selection processes by people at different hierarchical levels of the party. I demonstrate that the party leadership had the ultimate say in the candidate selection processes and, despite the 'official story' (Katz and Mair, 1994) described in the party statutes, the JDP elite embraced a highly exclusive selection method. Nevertheless, the party leadership mostly took the results of public opinion surveys into account and made great efforts to make the party base feel that they had influence over the candidate selection processes through the use of non-binding elections among selected party members.

Inhibiting Factionalism: Leadership Domination and Local-Provincial JDP Branches

In this section, I firstly demonstrate the legal basis for the rise of central leadership domination in the JDP over both the central and provincial party elite, and the consolidation of party centralism in general. Afterwards, I illustrate briefly the extent and functioning of this central control over the provincial and local branches of the party through the example of the contentious JDP provincial branch convention in İstanbul in 2009. In the last part of the section, I draw attention to the general lines of the JDP elite's outlook towards local-provincial politics.

The Rise of Leadership Domination in a Young Organization: 'This Is His Shop'

Most of my interviewees agreed that the party leadership had tight control over provincial organizations. Some of my interviewees argued strongly that no one could remain within the organization, in central or provincial branches, against the will of Erdoğan (Interviewee 9, 2014).[2] As one of my interviewees told me, there was a well-known expression used by party members which indicated the tight grip of Erdoğan even over the smallest localities of the organization: 'this is his shop [dükkan onun]' (Interviewee 9, 2014). According to JDP statutes, the party leadership had the right to remove and change party chairs on the grounds of loosely defined reasons which weakened the legal protection of subordinate segments of the party vis-à-vis the central leadership (AK Parti, 2012b: 36; articles 58 and 58.1). Apart from this, the party leadership also had the right to appoint party chairs and the governing bodies of the party (AK Parti, 2012b: 36; article 57).

According to one of my interviewees, a former JDP deputy, the first party statute of the JDP was written by a commission chaired by Hayati Yazıcı, a figure close to party chair Erdoğan (Interviewee 23, 2014). The same interviewee also argued that the first statute of the party was 'unrealistically' democratic and that it gave too much power to ordinary party members and too little authority to the executive positions within the governing bodies of the party. Therefore, the same interviewee asked the commission to rewrite the statute before it was too late and to place more power in the hands of provincial and sub-provincial chairs as well as the chairman of the party. As he mentioned, this statute of the party changed repeatedly even before the first general convention of the party.

The amendments to the first party statute in 2001, where provincial party administrations and delegates were selected according to the 'blanket list [çarşaf liste]' method, should be particularly highlighted. The 'blanket list' method in the identification of party governing bodies was

---

[2] See also Interviewee 10, 2014.

much more democratic since the delegates had a chance to identify individual members among a larger set of names for governing bodies of party branches instead of voting using an already prepared committee list for a given candidate for the chairmanship, as is the case with the 'bloc listing [blok liste]' method. With the amendments to article 30.7 and 46.7 of the JDP statute in 2003, these positions started to be filled by the demands of the provincial party chairs. In addition, later amendments also granted the provincial and sub-provincial party chairs the right to define the composition of the local party executive committees.[3] These amendments to the first party statute pushed the JDP in a much more hierarchical and centralized direction.

This picture was also complemented by the consolidation of the party leader's power vis-à-vis the Central Decision and Administration Board of the party in 2003. This tight control by the leadership, and by Erdoğan in particular, was gradually constructed within the JDP through the collaboration between Erdoğan and the founders' committee of the party and sustained through regular interventions by the party headquarters. This was mainly done through the consolidation of the party leader's say in the appointment of national and provincial party executive committees and by truncating every potential accumulation of power at the local level through careful candidate selection processes. One of my interviewees, who was one of the founders of the party in a province, described the development of leadership domination in the JDP right at the beginning of the party's political life in a detailed way. It should also be underlined that, in the beginning, the JDP had some really high standards, ideals and goals about intra-party democracy:[4]

We held the general election in 2002. Two months before the general election they [most probably Erdoğan and his close colleagues] called upon the founders' committee to make a statute change. In that meeting Mr Tayyip said, 'we are approaching the general election'. When we were approaching the general elections we were [around] 120 people: 73 founders and 51 deputies. He [Erdoğan] said, 'We are approaching the general elections. Dear founder friends, I do not want to put you in a bad position before provincial and sub-provincial chairs. If we go to the election with these articles [granting too much power to the party base and ordinary members in the identification of candidates], in order to become candidate deputies you might be a toy to provincial and sub-provincial chairs and members. And probably most of you

---

[3] See articles 33 and 38 of the JDP statutes (AK Parti, 2012b: 25–26).
[4] The first JDP promotional video, from 2001, can be seen on YouTube. In this video, one of the repeated themes is the importance attached to intra-party democracy within the JDP. See the video entitled *AK Parti'nin İlk Tanıtım Filmi* (*The JDP's First Promotion Video*) at www.youtube.com/watch?v=YZrGqyKnIPY (accessed: 27 May 2016).

would not be able to be nominated. This is why we have to change these articles.' At the end, the committee voted through the changes [proposed by Erdoğan]. The result was this: 117 people voted yes for the changes and 3 people voted no. And people gave the chairman a five-minute standing ovation (Interviewee 21, 2014).[5]

The centralization within the party and the accumulation of power in the hands of the party leader continued after the above-mentioned changes. In 2003, the party leadership abolished the articles on the election of the Central Decision and Administration Board of the party via a 'blanket list' and instead adopted the 'bloc listing method', so a single list prepared by the candidate for the chairmanship was voted on in the party's grand convention. In addition to this, articles in the party's first 2001 statute regarding the formation of the Central Executive Committee with an election among the Central Decision and Administration Board members of the party was amended in 2003 as well (Interviewee 21, 2014). The new regulation reduced the strength of the Central Decision and Administration Board vis-à-vis the party leader (Interviewee 21, 2014).[6]

Figure 7.1 illustrates how the first JDP statute envisaged a more or less even distribution of power within the party and how quickly this idea was abandoned by amendments to the first party statute. At the beginning, ordinary party members had a greater say in the formation of governing bodies in the localities and the party elite (the Central Decision and Administration Board) also had some sort of control over the formation of the Central Executive Committee – and, therefore, over the party leader. After the amendments, the party leader acquired the right to select all members of the Central Executive Committee, and the headquarters gained the right to define minute details of the provincial governing bodies through the abolition of the blanket list method. As a result, the party leader's power vis-à-vis the party elite and the party base increased enormously in formal terms, and the JDP organization became very hierarchical and centralized.

---

[5] In this particular example the complicity between Erdoğan and the founding elite of the party must be highlighted. At a very early stage, the central, ruling elite of the party started to concentrate power in their hands at the expense of local-provincial branches and ordinary members, which ultimately created the indisputable position of Erdoğan within the party. This of course once again confirms one of the contentions of Michels (1966) that authority tends to gather in the hands of a very few people in organizations. One of the reasons for this situation is apparently the common interests of elites against the masses, as this particular example makes clear.

[6] See article 79 of the JDP statute (AK Parti, 2012b: 47).

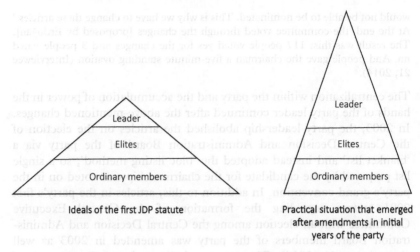

Ideals of the first JDP statute	Practical situation that emerged after amendments in initial years of the party

Figure 7.1: Approximate graphic representation of the change in the distribution of power, degree of centralization and hierarchy within the JDP after amendments to the 2001 party statute
Source: Author's compilation.

The party leadership not only exerted tight control over the formation of party governing bodies in provinces but also took great care to create an image of a highly unified and cohesive party organization in the eyes of the electorate. The party headquarters encouraged provincial branches to decide who would be party chair by an internal discussion within local organizations before local-provincial conventions. That is to say, most of the JDP provincial conventions were only held to vote on a single candidate and an administration list (Çarkçı, 2006: 9). Needless to say, it was much easier for the party leadership to shape local-provincial intra-party politics behind closed doors than in open competition between different lists in party conventions.

An Example of the Central Intervention in Provincial Organizations: The JDP İstanbul Branch Convention in 2009

There were several exceptions to this imposition of the party leadership over the provincial branches in previous years. A particularly important exception was the 2009 party branch convention in İstanbul, where two candidates – and, therefore, two different lists – were presented to the provincial party delegates. The convention resulted in the victory of the then İstanbul chair, who was supported personally by Erdoğan and the party headquarters.[7] In this convention, despite his support among the party base, the failed candidate was not able to overcome the support of the party leadership for the existing party chair of İstanbul. According to an observer of the convention process, one of the reasons behind the support of the party leadership for the existing chair was the failed candidate Metin Külünk's influence on the party base (Çetiner, 2009).

Here, one should also note that Külünk's political background was very similar to Erdoğan's. He came from the party base and had worked at almost every level of the Islamist National View parties. He was also a remarkable orator and was, just like Erdoğan, known as a talented 'organization man [teşkilatçı]' (Interviewee 16, 2014). Hence, it is highly credible to think that Erdoğan did not want a potential competitor at the top of the İstanbul organization. However, one should also add that, during this period, Külünk carefully refrained from open confrontation with Erdoğan and publicly praised him (*Aktifhaber*, 2009). Eventually, Külünk was nominated as a candidate in the 2011 general elections and became a deputy in the Grand National Assembly of Turkey. Although the new title sounds like a promotion, it was not exactly a better and more influential position than being the İstanbul chair of the ruling party.[8]

This convention indicated that the party leadership carefully designed and supervised provincial organizations and inhibited the rise of powerful local bosses. Yet, one should also note cautiously that, given its importance, İstanbul was too big a party branch for the party leadership to lose its grip over the local organization. However, throughout this book, I have illustrated that the party leadership wanted to tighten its grip even over much less significant local-provincial segments of the party. This was why, as one of my interviewees underlined, the party headquarters always encouraged provincial party organizations to have a single

---

[7] According to a news article, the party convention was held in a tense atmosphere where there was competition between Metin Külünk, who was supported by the party base, and Aziz Babuşcu, who was supported by the party headquarters (*Milliyet*, 2009).

[8] It is possible to consider Külünk's candidacy for the İstanbul chairmanship a deliberate tactic to make himself more visible and acquire a position within the party. In this way, he managed to gain the party's nomination for the Grand National Assembly of Turkey. This tactic of aspiring politicians 'gaining position by candidacy' has been underlined by various sources. According to Şentürk's guide to aspiring politicians, 'if you think that there is a chance to benefit in future you should become a candidate within the party, even when you are sure that the party will not choose you as its candidate for general or local elections this time. As a result, party administrators may later nominate you for another post [albeit a smaller one]' (Şentürk, 2006: 72). This can be considered a well-established pattern, a 'tactic' (de Certeau, 2002) of the weak within the ruling parties.

candidate and, thus, a single party administration list in provincial party conventions (Interviewee 16, 2014). As I have already mentioned, it was much easier for the party leadership to influence discussions behind closed doors than to guarantee success in the transparent competition of different candidates and lists in conventions. Nevertheless, if the party leadership encountered such open competition, they did not refrain from explicitly supporting one of the candidates (Çetiner, 2009).

Legitimizing Rationales Behind the Central Interventions: Central Suspicion of Local Politics

It is safe to argue that the party leadership attached great importance to the formation of provincial governing bodies of the party. According to one of my interviewees, a hard-working provincial chair always made a huge difference, and supervision by the headquarters of the provincial organizations was necessary for inhibiting the development of 'particularistic relations', in other words, the growth in the local branches of centrifugal, provincial power-holding groups/coalitions and local political machines (Interviewee 49, 2014). The same interviewee also told me that the party paid great attention to the formation of party governing bodies in order to eliminate the presence of, for example, two members with a business partnership or familial relationship. The party leadership usually did not allow the existence of strong particularistic coalitions at provincial or sub-provincial levels.

Another interviewee, an executive committee member of a provincial party organization, argued that, unlike previous parties in south-east Turkey, the JDP was always careful not to be seen as strongly identified with a specific social group in the city (Interviewee 46, 2014). Hence, according to my interviewees' narratives, the party tried to reflect the plurality of the electorate in party governing bodies. And this situation was often used as the justification for regular interventions by the party headquarters in local politics. The party leadership usually pointed out the potential damage to the general interests of the party that might arise from the nature of local politics and its particularistic tendencies, and used this reasoning as the basis for central interventions. Hence, the party leadership had a firm belief in the necessity of close supervision by headquarters and weak trust in the spontaneity of local politics.

This picture should also be complemented by the frequent rotation in party governing bodies due to interventions by the party leadership. As one of my senior interviewees underlined, the benefit of this rotation was the revitalization of the party governing bodies by new, enthusiastic, aspiring people (Interviewee 37, 2014). But it seems that another benefit of the frequent rotation of provincial governing bodies as well as parliamentary deputies was the inhibition of any potential consolidation of factions or particularistic interest circles other than the leadership within the party. Another indicator of this strategy was the discussions within the JDP over the 'three-term rule' in the party statute. According to these articles, the party leader, deputies, mayors and provincial, sub-provincial and town chairs from the JDP could not run as candidates for a fourth subsequent term.[9] Although at the time of writing this regulation would affect seventy-three existing deputies of the party, including several ministers and executive committee members, it was not changed (*Sabah*, 2014).

Elevating Competent Candidates

In this section, I take a closer look at the JDP's candidate selection processes. I firstly illustrate the formal regulations of the party and draw attention to the difference of the processes in practice from those in written regulations – or the 'official story', as Katz and Mair (1994) have termed it. Next, I demonstrate two competing views on the candidate selection processes, those of the party elite and the party rank and file. These different points of view specifically illustrated the highly 'exclusive' approach to candidate selection in the JDP. In the last part of this section, I illustrate the strategy of the central JDP elite towards local and provincial power holders in the party's candidate selection processes.

Formal Regulations and Practical Realities

According to the written party regulations, three methods were used in the identification of the candidates for local and general elections, and the party had the right to use different methods in different instances of candidate selection: 'primary elections [*önseçim*]', 'non-binding elections among selected party members [*teşkilat temayül yoklaması*]' (or 'organizational roll calls' as they were termed in the English translation of the JDP statute) and the 'central roll call [*merkez yoklaması*]' (AK Parti, 2012b: 69). According to the JDP statute, 'an organizational roll call is an event which is held for the purpose of [the] identification and ranking of candidates of the party by [. . .] members of the party, who are considered voters for the organizational roll call, using the method of

---

[9] See articles 24, 31, 36, 75 and 132 of the JDP statute (AK Parti, 2012b).

secret ballot and open counting under judicial supervision and audit in accordance with the principles and methods laid down in the Law on Political Parties' (AK Parti, 2012b: 70). By contrast, the 'central roll call', according to the JDP statute, 'is an event which is held for the purpose of [the] identification and ranking of candidates of the party directly by the central decision and administrative committee' (AK Parti, 2012b: 70).

What distinguished the organizational roll calls from primary elections was the specific definition of the people eligible to vote in these elections, most of whom came from the executive positions of the party organizations. More importantly, unlike primary elections, organizational roll calls did not produce binding results for the party headquarters and were seen only as a decision support mechanism, a single component of a wider set of data received by the party headquarters. One should also add that 'organizational roll calls', or 'non-binding elections among selected party members' as I will henceforth refer to them in this book, were used to examine the inclinations of party branches. This is why it was called *teşkilat* or *temayül yoklaması* in Turkish, which literally translates as 'organizational inclination examination' in English. Although the party statute indicated that the counting of the votes for these elections would be open and in public view, there was also evidence that the results were usually not declared to the party base by headquarters (Çarkçı, 2006: 6). According to the JDP statute, the individuals eligible to vote in the 'non-binding elections among selected members' were mostly active and former members of the party with high-ranking, executive positions (AK Parti, 2012b: 70).

However, most of my interviewees underlined three methods in their narratives on candidate selection processes, and it seems that the practical realities of these processes were quite different from those set out in the written regulations of the party. The methods indicated by my interviewees were the above-mentioned 'non-binding elections among selected members [*teşkilat temayül yoklaması*]', 'public opinion surveys conducted by the party headquarters' (popularly known as 'questionnaires', or *anketler*, among the party members) and 'consultations of the party headquarters' (popularly known as *istişareler* among the party members). According to the views of a high-ranking member in the official publication of the party, the *Turkey Bulletin*, the candidate selection process appeared to be an evaluation of the data in the party headquarters received through questionnaires, consultations and non-binding elections (Çetinkaya, 2003: 51). Apparently, the last word in the candidate selection process belonged to the party headquarters as it did with the formation of provincial governing bodies. Apart from these mechanisms, the role of the deputies and ministers from the region was influential in the process (Interviewee 8, 2014).[10]

Thus, the tight control over provincial organizations and local politics by the party leadership described above was complemented by close supervision of the candidate selection processes. Nevertheless, candidate selection processes reflected the main problems of tight leadership control over provincial branches: tension between provincial organizations, the party base and the party leadership, or tension between 'inclusive' and 'exclusive' methods in candidate selection processes. Such tension paved the way for two different narratives of candidate selection processes: the narrative of the party elite vs the narrative of the 'true democrats', junior members and failed candidates. Here, I argue that these two narratives were two sides of the same coin and the JDP leadership was usually successful at striking a fine balance between these segments' diverging expectations within the organization. The autonomy of the JDP leadership, which was reliant upon tight leadership control, on the one hand, and the controlled participation of the party base, on the other hand, as illustrated in the previous chapter, was key to this capacity of the JDP leadership.

Two Narratives: The Party Elite vs 'True Democrats'

There was a particular advantage in my interviewing party members from different hierarchical levels of the organization and with different positions within the party. These different points of view illustrated the uneven distribution of power within the organization and demonstrated how the lack of any meaningful power in the hands of the party base was justified and explained by more senior members of the party. These narratives of the members of different levels of the party also illustrated the fragile balance between the leadership and the grass-roots organization. They revealed how important it was for a party to protect the balance between 'responsiveness and responsibility' and between 'popularity and merit'. In other words, as discussed in previous chapters, striking a fine balance between the 'short-term requirements of electoral processes' and the 'long-term requirements of being in office' was one of the main achievements of the JDP leadership. Overcoming the potential discontent of the party base stemming from the central interventions

---

[10] See also Interviewee 5, 2014; Interviewee 9, 2014; see Soyoğul (2013) for an interview with the JDP İzmir chair. In this interview the JDP chair described an incident in which a deputy asked him to add a particular person to the JDP's candidate lists for the municipality assembly in a sub-province of the city.

through constant negotiations and diligence in intra-party governance was key to this achievement.

During my interviews, I observed that questions regarding candidate selection processes within the party received a straightforward answer. The headquarters, and particularly the party leader Erdoğan, had the ultimate say in the process (Interviewee 9, 2014). Most of my interviewees told me that public opinion surveys (questionnaires) were the main instrument used in the decision-making processes of the party headquarters.[11] Nevertheless, one of the interviewees also told me that non-binding elections among selected members made a difference if there were two good candidates from the same branch of the party (Interviewee 18, 2014).

Apart from this, my interviewees often told me that even very limited personal contact with Erdoğan provided a huge advantage in party candidate selection processes. One of my high-ranking interviewees, who occupied a senior ministerial post, told me that he had just been physically present with Erdoğan in the same place a couple of times and Erdoğan did not forget this (Interviewee 14, 2014). Another interviewee, who was a former deputy, also underlined the importance of personal contact with Erdoğan. The crucial part of this example was that it showed how a personal reference from Erdoğan bypassed the local dynamics by implanting half of the deputies in this particular interviewee's native city from among non-locals (Interviewee 23, 2014).

According to my interviewees, Erdoğan's main criteria in this selection were loyalty and obedience to the leadership (Interviewee 7, 2014). This dynamic in the candidate selection processes should also be considered one of the very fundamental aspects of personalism in the JDP, elaborated upon in depth in Chapter 4. Thus, in his book, written in an ironic style, Şentürk (a former member of the Islamist National View parties and a current member of the JDP) illustrated the leadership's domination over the candidate selection processes in Turkey's political parties with the following joke:

> a deputy who had been elected to the parliament for a couple of consecutive terms was asked about the reasons for his achievement. He neatly replied, 'I do whatever my electorate says.' Then he was asked, 'How is it possible to do whatever you are told by thousands of people?' He replied, 'I do not have thousands of voters. I have only a single electorate. He is my chairman. I do whatever he asks' (Şentürk, 2006: 43).

---

[11] See the section on 'public opinion surveys' in the previous chapter.

In the following sub-sections, I demonstrate how this overwhelming domination of the party centre and this highly exclusive method of candidate selection was rationalized and legitimized by the party elite and to what extent these justifications were accepted by the party rank and file.

Party Elites Assessing the Candidate Selection Processes: 'You Do Not Want These Kinds of People in the Parliament'

During my interviews, I observed that there were some regular patterns of justification used by the party headquarters against local branches. For example, one of my interviewees told me that when the party needed some people with particular expertise for bureaucratic positions, it became natural – and, most of the time, inevitable – to ignore the choices of local party branches (Interviewee 12, 2014). The need for experts within the parliament, local government and local assemblies was underlined repeatedly by my interviewees as one of the reasons for central intervention into local-provincial politics.

It should be noted that the higher the position of the party member, the more likely it was that s/he highlighted the necessity of having experts and well-educated people within the party ranks. High-ranking party members were also more likely to say that 'tricks' and 'ruses' were used by the people in the lower party hierarchies in candidate selection processes. One of my interviewees told me that non-binding elections among selected party members cannot be considered a reliable method without reservation. He explained this opinion with a fictional example: 'if the only criterion in candidate selection process was the success of the candidate in the non-binding election [*teşkilat yoklaması*], a local mafia boss could have easily provided the support of some of the members of the local branch through money. You do not want these kinds of people in the parliament' (Interviewee 14, 2014).

Another high-ranking interviewee highlighted a similar explanation for the necessity of mechanisms other than non-binding elections in candidate selection processes. According to this interviewee there was a tendency called 'organizational conservatism [*teşkilat taassubu*]'. This tendency simply referred to the local party branches' tendency to support candidates from within the local organization. He argued that:

Local party branches might tend to support their own people even if they are incompetent. This is why there are questionnaires [public opinion surveys] and reliable people who provide references for candidates. Take a candidate with a graduate degree from abroad and who is really competent and has the required skills and expertise as an example. The local organization and electorate of the region do not know this candidate (Interviewee 18, 2014).

Indeed, it seems that the party elite usually did not rely on the view of the local-provincial party branches and the base, and thought that relying on them might be misleading, as Şentürk, one of the JDP elites, implied in an interview: 'Sometimes, the selectorate attaches too much importance to themselves and tends to choose candidates among themselves. However, the party has to provide a vision to society' (Çarkçı, 2006: 6).

Hence, the party elite thought that 'it would be misleading only to rely on views stemming from the party branches' (Çarkçı, 2006: 11). Thus, it seems that in order to resolve the contradiction between organizational belonging and merit, and between responsiveness and responsibility, the party elite saw the headquarters' intervention as inevitable. In other words, in order to provide competent enough cadres, the JDP elite sometimes had to intervene into local politics and implant candidates preferred by the party headquarters in place of candidates proposed by local JDP organizations. However, these interventions were made in such a way – through the use of non-binding elections and consultations – that the party base did not feel that they lacked any say in the process. To a certain extent, ignoring local-provincial choices was, in fact, necessary to elevate competent candidates within the party for a massive organization like the JDP.[12] Yet these explanations could also be considered justifications for central leadership domination within the JDP.

Reflections of Disappointed Candidates, the Rank and File and 'True Democrats'

Not surprisingly, lower-ranking members or members with looser links with the party due to their failure in intra-party competition tended to be more critical of the candidate selection processes. The party rank and file complained about the interventions and resistance of high-ranking members to the wishes of local JDP branches. Nevertheless, the party rank and file usually had no problem with the final say of the party leader Erdoğan, but they tended to complain about the 'manipulative interventions' of deputies, ministers or influential people in the decisions of the leader (Interviewee 8, 2014). As the party became more and more centralized, as illustrated in the previous section, public opinion surveys conducted by the party headquarters became much more

---

[12] This, however, does not necessarily mean that candidates supported by local organizations or local elites were, by definition, incompetent. Local figures and local power holders might well be highly competent, well-educated candidates. But when this was not the case the JDP headquarters did not refrain from intervening despite the popularity of these kinds of candidates.

effective than non-binding elections among selected party members in the identification of candidates. It also seems that candidates close to decision makers in the headquarters were always in a better position than other candidates with weaker ties to the centre (Interviewee 10, 2014).

Nevertheless, particularly in the identification of candidates for local elections, local party branches had some leverage in the process, especially through non-binding elections among selected party members. For example, in local elections, according to one of my interviewees, it was almost impossible to nominate a candidate for the mayoralty if the entire local branch of the party was against her/him (Interviewee 9, 2014). This was why, in his guide to aspiring politicians, Şentürk, a former JDP vice-chair in İstanbul, underlined the necessity of being supported by the local party organization and the base since 'the [high-ranking party members] need to include the candidate who is liked by the party branches in the middle of the list though not at the top' (Şentürk, 2006: 71). Hence, it seems that, especially in local elections, local party branches might not have been successful at identifying a candidate supported by the local branch but they could stop the nomination of a candidate who was disliked by the entire branch. Thus, local party branches had a kind of negative force in the candidate selection processes within the party, particularly in local elections.

There were also other factors and instruments influential in the party candidate selection process. According to one of my interviewees, a deputy from one province was sent to another province as a neutral observer of the local candidate identification process (Interviewee 7, 2014). Another interviewee, a neighbourhood representative, also told me that regions with deputies and ministers were less successful in the local elections due to the influence of these people from the higher levels of the party in the local candidate identification process. He also expressed his doubts about the public opinion surveys used by the party headquarters in the identification of candidates (Interviewee 8, 2014). Indeed, as Şentürk, a JDP executive from İstanbul indicated, it seems that public opinion surveys could also be manipulated (Çarkçı, 2006: 7).

Another interviewee also described the candidate selection process within the party in line with the above accounts. According to her, people close to the headquarters always had the upper hand in the candidate identification processes (Interviewee 10, 2014). Therefore, particularly in the identification of candidates for the parliament, local party organizations were not really influential. According to one of my interviewees, the effect of local party branches was, at most, 10 per cent. For instance, non-binding elections (teşkilat temayül yoklamaları), according to him, had almost no effect in the identification of candidates for parliamentary elections (Interviewee 9, 2014). This statement was confirmed by Şentürk in his interview on intra-party democracy. According to Şentürk:

Usually particular people had already been designated by the party headquarters. They ask the organization in order to legitimize this decision. They do not declare the results either. In other words there is a secret ballot, and secret counting. Votes are secret but counting should be transparent. But in those years no single result of non-binding elections was declared to the organizations. Because they usually did not observe the results. If they thought it was appropriate they just told people that 'brother, you wanted this' but usually they remained silent (Çarkçı, 2006: 6).

Instead, according to one of my interviewees, candidates for the parliamentary group were chosen by (then) Prime Minister Erdoğan and his three or four close colleagues (Interviewee 9, 2014). As underlined above, a question regarding the criteria used by decision makers in the candidate selection process also revealed the hierarchical, centralized and personalistic characteristics of the JDP organization. Not surprisingly, one of my interviewees defined the ultimate criteria in the candidate selection process within the party as 'loyalty and fidelity' to Erdoğan (Interviewee 7, 2014).

Despite the tight grip of the leadership over provincial organizations, during my interview process I also noticed that there was also a particular gap between provincial and sub-provincial party branches in big cities such as İstanbul, Ankara and Konya. One of my interviewees told me that local dynamics played a major role in the sub-provincial branches of the party. According to him, sub-provincial party chairs were directly exposed to the local demands. He argued that sub-provincial and neighbourhood levels were the main levels where you 'do politics' (Interviewee 12, 2014). As a result, despite the tight control of the party leadership over provincial organizations, it seems that a particular gap started to appear between sub-provincial party organizations and the provincial and national leadership.

This gap could even be observed between the two different narratives of the party members on the dynamics of the organization. While the party elite tended to underline the necessity of leadership interventions due to the technocratic requirements of the governmental processes, the party base tended to complain about the weakness of the leverage of ordinary members in the formation of governing bodies and identification of candidates. While the former legitimized its intervention through pretending to be the defenders of the general interests of the party and the country, the latter complained about the party's disregard of local dynamics. Yet the latter did not show massive dissent against the central interventions at the level of local-provincial politics due to their trust in Erdoğan and the controlled participation channels illustrated in the previous chapter.

Coping with Local Bosses and Centrifugal Tendencies

As illustrated in the previous section, the formation of provincial party branches was closely supervised by the headquarters, and the party leadership constantly impeded the development of centrifugal tendencies as well as the accumulation of power in the hands of local elites. In order to do this, the party mainly relied upon specific candidate and local chair profiles in provinces and localities. These people in the key executive positions of the party in the provinces revealed a particular socio-economic similarity. For instance, none of my interviewees from the executive circles of the party in the provinces came from rich, influential local families, and they did not have any power base of their own. Most of them were rather submissive, civil-servant-type administrators with white-collar jobs and a fairly good education instead of rich, local bosses with influence in city politics. Indeed, more than half of the party provincial chairs had white-collar jobs at the time of writing of this book.[13] Only thirteen of these provincial chairs were businesspeople or owners of small businesses (*esnaf*). The rest of the provincial chairs were lawyers, engineers, financial advisers and pharmacists; in other words they had white-collar occupations and highly educated backgrounds compared to the average Turkish citizen. The professional distribution of JDP provincial chairs can be seen in Table 7.1.

This pattern is also compatible with the importance attached to the candidates' educational level by the party leadership. Despite the 'low-populist' political appeal of the party illustrated in Chapter 3, there was a strong tendency in the preferences of the party leadership towards competency and education over popularity in the recruitment of its national and local elites.[14] It seems that, to a great extent, the same pattern was valid for deputies of the party and candidate profiles in general in provincial cities. The party leadership preferred relatively more obedient but well-educated candidates for general elections. Hence, this pattern is concrete evidence of the fact that the party leadership had a remarkably 'high' attitude towards intra-party politics.

All of these methods, in the context of the above-mentioned identification of the local and provincial party governing bodies and deputies,

---

[13] For the backgrounds of JDP executives I mainly relied on the short biographies of the provincial JDP chairs on the websites of the party's provincial branches.
[14] See Interviewee 12, 2014; Interviewee 36, 2014; and Interviewee 49, 2014.

Table 7.1 *Professions of JDP provincial chairs in 2014*

Professions	Numbers
Lawyer	28
Businessperson, small business owner	13
Engineer	8
Financial adviser	3
Pharmacist	2
Civil servant, bureaucrat	2
Dentist	1
Unidentified	24
Total	81

Source: Author's compilation of the information in short biographies of JDP provincial executives on JDP provincial branch websites.

provided strong leverage to the party leadership *vis-à-vis* local and provincial power holders. In interviews, party members tended to emphasize that ordinary people were able to gain strength against local elites through the support of party headquarters (Interviewee 49, 2014). To a great extent this was, indeed, the strategy of the JDP leadership. One indication of this strategic tendency was, as mentioned in the previous chapter, the women and youth quotas that the party implemented. Nevertheless, it seems that the party leadership also did not hesitate to nominate local bosses as long as they remained loyal to the leadership. This was why one of my interviewees, the chair of one of the south-eastern provinces, underlined the success of the party in his region, where traditional-local elite such as elders of tribal families and religious figures had a remarkable influence over politics (Interviewee 43, 2014).

However, compared to its right-wing predecessors (as elaborated upon in Chapter 5), the JDP leadership tended to establish less compromising links with those groups that had the potential to cast bloc votes consisting of thousands. In other words, instead of accepting all the demands raised by powerful groups and individuals in localities and negotiating with the representatives of these communities for votes, as the former centre-right parties did, the JDP elite usually preferred reaching voters individually through its robust membership organization and through bypassing powerful intermediaries whenever possible. After all, as one of my interviewees explained in great detail, relying on powerful intermediaries also entailed specific problems that the JDP wished to avoid:

When you put a tribe's [*aşiret*] candidate [on the candidate list for the office] and when he is elected by a slim margin by the support of his tribe you usually lose the votes of other electors in the region. What the JDP underwent in 2009 was this [...] When you ignore all these options and nominate ordinary candidates from among the people you get 63 per cent [...] These guys [candidates of tribes] come to interviews for the candidacy and argue, 'I have this many guaranteed – bloc votes [*paket oy*]. Therefore nominate me and win the election. If you do not nominate me you won't win.' There is this arrogance [*küstahlık*] too. Until now, every right-wing party believed this and was afraid of challenging this force [of local power holders]. It is pragmatic too: 'Why shall I fight with these people. Put the guy on the list, after all he has bloc votes.' This [strategy] even has short-term [negative] consequences. Because when you put tribal candidates you make them happy but you upset the rest of the electorate [...] When you do not develop alliances with the tribes the only option remains for protecting your power is collaborating with masses in the region. This is what the JDP does (Interviewee 38, 2014).

In order to target voters individually the JDP, as mentioned in the previous chapter, developed elaborate ballot box committees.[15] As one of my interviewees from the south-eastern region of the country underlined,

through a ballot box-based approach, the JDP tries to activate all individual members of the party [...] A ballot box-based approach is this: there are approximately 350 members in each ballot box [region] [...] and in these ballot box [regions] the party has approximately twenty to thirty members. The party chooses an administration board from among these members of the ballot box [region]: the ballot box committee. This committee organizes a meeting with all party members in this ballot box [region]. We call this a ballot box consultation meeting. And, in these meetings, [the party] tries to activate the members and tries to reach all the voters in this ballot box [region] through its members. This is to say that party members are constantly in touch with voters on behalf of the party (Interviewee 46, 2014).

As another interviewee pointed out, 'the aim here is to reduce the election campaign to the level of the ballot box. Man-to-man marking [*Bire bir markaj!*]. This is a much more effective method than speaking to an audience in a coffee house, in a meeting with the microphone in your hand' (Interviewee 7, 2014).

A strong indication of this strategic tendency was the JDP's approach to the powerful İzol tribe in Urfa in the 2011 general election. In this election, the JDP headquarters did not nominate the candidate of the İzol tribe. Apart from him, it seems that the party leadership avoided

---

[15] The importance of these nerve endings of the JDP organization was examined in the previous chapter.

nominating any tribal leader in the city.[16] Indeed, as I illustrated in the previous chapter, the JDP headquarters used public opinion surveys in order to examine the validity of the claims of the local-provincial power holders. As one of my interviewees underlined, party research conducted prior to the 2011 general elections in Urfa revealed that the existing local political elite in the city at that time had not really been embraced by the electorate of the province (Interviewee 38, 2014). Thus, the party leadership was able to reject the demands of local power holders.

It seems that not only in Urfa but also in Diyarbakır the JDP leadership was able to nominate people other than local power holders (Gürses, 2011). This situation illustrates the role of public opinion surveys in the concentration of power in the hands of the central JDP leadership. As some of my interviewees underlined, there was already a weakening of the local political elites' power base in the region due to the PKK's assaults on tribal leaders and the accelerating urbanization and improvements of mass communication channels (Interviewee 38, 2014).[17] Hence, tribal vote blocs had already started to dissolve. As one of my interviewees underlined, even if a tribal leader decisively supported a non-JDP candidate, a considerable number of people from that tribe, because of their sympathy towards Erdoğan, would vote for the JDP (Interviewee 44, 2014).

It seems that public opinion surveys provided the party with a much more solid idea about inclinations in local politics, and thus encouraged the party leadership to deploy a centralized strategy in the region for candidate selection processes. Indeed, particularly in Urfa in the 2011 general elections, the JDP was very successful using the abovementioned strategy, winning ten seats out of twelve. As underlined by a local journalist, JDP candidates, as a result of coming from a different background than tribal families, were more prone to co-operation in that particular election, and this convinced the electorate that the JDP as a team would be beneficial to the city. He also argued that 'the election in Urfa revealed the following truth: the predominace of tribes' influence on politics in Urfa is over. From now on, tribal candidates should not argue that 'I have this many votes' [...] Now in every tribe every individual has dared to cast his/her vote according to his/her own logic' (Kapaklı, 2011). Thus, while indicating the gradual decline of feudal ties in the city, the local election results in Urfa also confirmed the JDP leadership's firm

---

[16] According to a news article, with one exception, the JDP did not nominate any tribal leader for the twelve chairs allocated to Urfa in the Grand National Assembly of Turkey in the 2011 general elections (Takvim, 2011).
[17] See also Interviewee 44, 2014.

grip on provincial organizations and local politics. This was even the case in a city like Urfa where informal-primordial networks had such a remarkable influence on party politics.[18] Thus, it would be plausible to argue that the JDP leadership established unprecedented control over provincial, local politics across Turkey.

Conclusion

In this chapter, I have illustrated how the central JDP leadership constantly intervened in the formation of local-provincial governing bodies of the party across Turkey and how they elevated competent yet obedient candidates within the party. The party leadership decisively tried to inhibit the formation of strong local particularistic coalitions through constant interventions and frequently changed governing bodies in local branches. The JDP elite legitimized central interventions in local politics through highlighting the potential dangers to the party's general policies that could stem from the popular but incompetent candidates chosen by local party branches. Therefore, the JDP candidate selection processes were 'highly exclusive'. Total control by the JDP leader Erdoğan over the identification of candidates for local and national governments inhibited the rise of local political elites with strong support bases. Instead, the JDP leadership preferred highly obedient but well-educated and competent candidates. These candidates selected by party leader Erdoğan, in turn, remained loyal to the general party policies and to Erdoğan, and could not develop strong particularistic interests or local political machines.

Potential dissent against the highly exclusive candidate selection processes was also absorbed by the party leadership. On the one hand, on the basis of their trust in Erdoğan's personality and political experience, the party base tended to approve the interventions of the centre in local politics. Intensive consultation meetings (*istişareler*) and non-binding elections among selected party members (*teşkilat temayül yoklamaları*) also provided a strong sense of participation by the party base in candidate selection processes. On the other hand, the direct appeal of Erdoğan to the electorate and public opinion surveys conducted by the headquarters left the local-provincial power holders in a weaker position *vis-à-vis* the central JDP leadership and made resistance to the central elite interference in local politics a highly risky strategy. Despite its 'low-populist' political appeal, the JDP elite had a strikingly 'high' attitude with regard to the party's recruitment processes. This highly exclusive

---

[18] For the influence of tribes on the local politics of Urfa, see Çelik and Uluç (2009).

candidate selection strategy, without the alienation of the party base and local elites, gave rise to more competent yet obedient candidates within the party and enhanced the local and national government performance of the party in the eyes of the electorate. The image of the party's managerial competence, in turn, consolidated the JDP's electoral achievements.

More importantly, as a natural extension of the intra-party arrangements within the JDP that were analysed in the previous section, the particular elite recruitment dynamics of the JDP demonstrated in this section allowed the party to construct a level of coherence and autonomy that distinguished it from its right-wing predecessors. Without this coherence and autonomy the JDP would have been remarkably vulnerable in the face of the political crises it has encountered since its foundation. Here again, the agency of the party elite, and its careful management of elite recruitment processes within the party, were key in providing electoral and political resilience to the party – ultimately paving the way for the rise of a competitive authoritarian regime in Turkey under the personalistic rule of Erdoğan. In the conclusion, I will elaborate on the theoretical implications of the case of Erdoğan's JDP with regard to the literature on Islamist parties, populism and authoritarianism. But before that, I will put the case of the JDP into historical perspective and illustrate the course of political developments that led to the rise of a competitive authoritarian political regime in Turkey.

8   'The New Regime': The Role of Agency in the Rise of Competitive Authoritarianism in Turkey

Introduction

On 15 July 2017 the Turkish people witnessed the first anniversary commemorating the tragic events of the failed coup the previous year. Contemplating these events, it was hard to miss the implicit implication embedded in the way the events were organized: the JDP had already established a 'new regime',[1] a rather more authoritarian one that was reliant on the support of popular sectors of Turkish society. The organization of the anniversary was telling in a specific respect: it was in full contradistinction with early Republican authoritarianism and the contemporary Kemalist public imagination in the sense that it gave centre stage to the masses, Erdoğan and the JDP.[2]

The failed coup on 15 July 2016 and its anniversary one year later were two major events emblematic of the transformation of Turkey's political system since the rise of Erdoğan's JDP. The coup and the following events, reactions and regulations helped Erdoğan to *de facto* terminate Turkey's powerful elite contenders and remove all doubts regarding the new authoritarian turn. The second event signified the rise of a new regime in Turkey (a hegemonic party autocracy under the personalistic rule of Erdoğan) by ritualizing the resistance to the coup on 15 July 2016, this moment of violence and Erdoğanism's victory.

In this chapter, I use three interrelated concepts to explain the overall transformation of Turkish politics throughout the JDP's rule: electoral democracy, competitive authoritarianism and political regime. By following Duverger's definition in his work on 'political regimes'

---

[1] In this respect, I am not claiming that the new authoritarian regime has already been consolidated and institutionalized. The JDP and the party's new allies are still struggling to leave the current transition phase behind. Yet, there is no doubt that after the coup in 2016 Turkey has entered into a profound qualitative transformation which complemented the more incremental change since the JDP's rise.

[2] See Plaggenborg (2015) for the distance of the Kemalist regime from the masses, not only in terms of its world-view, but also in the construction and organization of its public image and activity.

(1994), I define the term 'regime' as the mode of the relationship between rulers and the ruled on a scale between liberal and authoritarian methods regarding the restrictions on the rulers' authority. If the political regime restricts the authority of the ruler in favour of the ruled, it approximates the liberal democratic pole of the scale, and if it is the opposite it approximates the authoritarian pole (Duverger, 1994: 10). In this view, a regime change is understood as a movement along this scale that qualitatively transforms the mode of the relationship between the rulers and the ruled.

I will also use two concepts borrowed from the literature on authoritarianism in order to define the qualitative transformation that the democratically deficient Turkish regime has undergone throughout the JDP years. These are 'electoral democracy' and 'competitive authoritarianism'. Although it is usually hard to distinguish the two regime types, by the former term, in line with Schedler, I understand an ultimately democratic framework in which opposition parties can win elections despite the deficiencies of the regime regarding the institutionalization of 'the rule of law, political accountability, bureaucratic integrity, and public deliberation' (Schedler, 2002: 37). In contrast, a competitive authoritarian regime (or 'electoral authoritarianism', as Schedler terms it)[3] is an ultimately authoritarian regime in which the opposition has little possibility of winning elections due to decisive and effective restrictions on their activity, on the judiciary and on the media (Levitsky and Way, 2002: 53). Hence, I understand electoral democracy and competitive authoritarianism as two qualitatively different regime types located in the middle of Duverger's regime scale, which stretches between full-scale democracy and full-scale authoritarianism.[4] An illustration of this scale combined with Mudde and Kaltwasser's demonstration (2017: 87) can be seen in Figure 8.1.

In order to understand the dynamics of these changes, I will also use two other concepts borrowed from the literature on democratization. These are *reforma* and *ruptura*. But, diverging from their use in the literature for describing processes leading to pluralist democracies,[5] I use these concepts to define the dynamics of the processes leading to the rotation of power-holding elite groups and the regime change this entails in deficient democracies. These changes could well produce further democratization but, as the case of Turkey demonstrated, they can also lead to the deterioration of an already deficient democracy.

[3] O'Donnell (1994) terms the same phenomenon 'delegative democracy'.
[4] For a very similar distinction, see also Özbudun (2011: 39–43).
[5] For an example of this literature, see Linz and Stepan (2011).

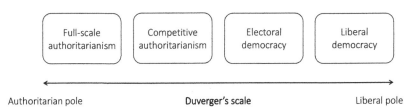

| Full-scale authoritarianism | Competitive authoritarianism | Electoral democracy | Liberal democracy |

Authoritarian pole   **Duverger's scale**   Liberal pole

Figure 8.1 Regime types on the authoritarianism–liberal democracy scale
Source: Author's compilation of Mudde and Kaltwasser (2017) and Duverger (1994).

Hence, I am using the terms *reforma* and *ruptura* independent of the normative load they bear in democratization studies. I use the term *reforma* to refer to a long process including conflicts, negotiations and compromises as well as co-operation between old and new elite groups in the struggle for power. I use the term *ruptura* to imply a sudden *de facto* and *de jure* change in the course of political developments after a direct – and symbolically or physically violent – confrontational moment between contending elite groups.

In this chapter, I will put the agency of Erdoğan's JDP into historical perspective[6] and illustrate how a post-Islamist reaction to the authoritarian legacy of Turkish politics (that is, the democratically deficient context of Turkey, or the electoral democracy under military-bureaucratic tutelage) has gradually turned into a competitive authoritarian regime under the rule of a hegemonic party with popular sector support. In the first part of the chapter, I will briefly reiterate the democratically deficient context of Turkey. But unlike the emphasis put on the broader political-electoral context in Chapter 2, in this chapter I will emphasize the impact of this authoritarian legacy on the Islamist political actors of Turkey, most notably the Gülen Community and the National View parties, the predecessors of Erdoğan's JDP. In the third section, I look at the relationship between the Gülen Community and the JDP along with the demise of this powerful post-Islamist alliance around 2012. I will also analyse the manoeuvres of Erdoğan in the realm of political elites. In Section 4, I will focus on the aftermath of the coup, which *de facto* and *de jure* marked the transition to a hegemonic party autocracy in Turkey. Finally I will discuss and summarize the role of the party's agency which

---

[6] For a detailed and up-to-date account of Turkish politics stressing the the majoritarian political system of the country and the change of the role of the army since the rise of the JDP, see Waldman and Çalışkan (2017).

gradually led Turkey from democratically deficient parliamentarism (electoral democracy) to competitive authoritarian presidentialism.

The Authoritarian Legacy of Turkish Politics: A Brutal 'State of Nature' for Collective Actors?

Turkey has never been a full, liberal, pluralist democracy at any time in its history of multi-party politics. Since its transition to multi-party politics in the middle of the 1940s, the public political space of Turkey has developed under strict regulations imposed by the founding state elite. With regard to party politics, for example, the ban on ideological parties (combined with the historical sociological dynamics of the development of the party system in Turkey, as outlined in Chapter 3) has resulted in the absence of parties representing certain ideologies (such as socialism or Islamism) or social segments (such as ethnic groups or classes). As a result, Turkish parties, in ideological terms, have always presented themselves as representative of the 'whole nation' (Wuthrich, 2015). It was not surprising that parties on the right or the left of the political spectrum were forced to use centrist appeals in favour of national integration, and when they moved away from this centrist appeal they have always been harshly penalized by powerful elite groups located in the heart of this semi-democratic status quo. Socialist, pro-Kurdish, Islamic-leaning parties have been banned in Turkey on numerous occasions since the transition to multi-party politics. The counterpart of these restrictions regarding party politics in the sphere of civil society was strict control over religious brotherhoods and communities as well as secular associations, which were considered dangerous for national integration.

However, except for the transitory military regimes after successful coups in 1960 and 1980, Turkey was an 'electoral democracy' in which incumbents have changed frequently through free and fair elections since the 1950s, albeit under the tutelage of the military-bureaucratic and judicial state elite. Nevertheless, this democracy was characterized by many authoritarian tendencies of its own (as delineated in Chapter 2). Political actors in Turkey, therefore, should always be evaluated against the background of this authoritarian legacy which relied on the strategy of selective pluralism (again delineated in Chapter 2). In this particular section, I am not going to elaborate on actors other than the Islamists, yet it is necessary to underline the fact that the political actors in civil society and party politics have either embraced the rules imposed by this authoritarian logic of Turkish politics or faced measures driving them either to political decline or to underground political activism and violence. Hence, this particular legacy of Turkish politics can also be seen as a peculiar kind of 'state of nature' in Turkey among the influential collective political actors with high levels of intra-group solidarity *(asabiyet)* and low levels of trust towards their rivals in the political game.

This was certainly the case for Islamist political actors in Turkey, including the predecessors of the JDP (the National View parties) and other powerful religious communities and groups. In previous chapters of this book, I elaborated on how the particular political circumstances of Turkey have shaped the JDP (and its predecessors) strategically and organizationally. In order to contend with the concentrated leverages of powerful elite groups in Turkey, the Islamist elites developed very resilient organizations that relied on the power of numbers. At the same time, they usually downplayed their Islamist discourse (see Interviewee 1, 2013).

While this was the case for the representatives of Islamic identity in party politics, in the sphere of civil society, in order to protect themselves from the interventions of secularist state actors, religious communities in Turkey embraced very tight and opaque organizational strategies. One of the most notable examples of this was the Gülen Community,[7] which created a network of semi-clandestine elite organizations based on, the colonization of the state through negotiations with centre-right parties in power (including the JDP), and highly educated cadres from the private schools and colleges of the community.

In short, the authoritarian legacy of Turkey not only shaped the mainstream and destroyed the genuinely left-wing movements in Turkey, but it also drove the influential actors representing Islamic identity in Turkey to construct a powerful mass membership organization on the one hand (the personalistic mass party of Erdoğan) and a semi-clandestine elite organization on the other (the Gülen Community) (Baykan, 2015a). Despite the hostility between them, these two powerful political entities, which played a power game in Turkey according to their unique rationale (by downplaying their Islamic credentials and overstating their commitment to democratization while embracing a Machiavellian strategic approach to politics), nevertheless formed an alliance of convenience against Turkey's secularist establishment elite during the initial years of the JDP's rule. In the next section, I will focus on the operational logic of this alliance and its gradual demise, which gave way to the further concentration of power in Erdoğan's hands.

---

[7] I elaborate on the Gülen Community in the following sections.

Eroding the Power of the Old Establishment through *Reforma*: The JDP's Political Manoeuvres

In this part of the chapter, I will firstly focus on the alliance between the Gülen Community and the JDP, which gradually undermined the power of the old establishment in Turkey. I will also briefly discuss Erdoğan's manoeuvres in elite-level interactions in party politics. Then, in the main part of this section, I will analyse the demise of the post-Islamist alliance between the Gülen Community and the JDP and the worsening of the state of democracy in Turkey after a series of critical developments.

The Tactical Post-Islamist Alliance and Its Demise: The Gülen Community and the JDP against the Kemalist Elite

The Gülen Community,[8] an influential religious group, has become one of the main components of the elite-level power structures in Turkey during JDP rule, alongside the populist JDP elite and Erdoğan, nationalist secularist (*ulusalcı*) intelligentsia and pro-Western secularists, far-right Turkish political elites, left-leaning liberal intellectuals in academia and journalism, and pro-Kurdish political elites. Yet the Gülen Community has never become an important electoral player. The Gülen Community has strategically always depended on the highly educated cadres implanted in state apparatuses and has embraced a highly elitist, bookish interpretation of Islam, disseminated by the leader of the Community, which targets the upbringing of an elite 'golden generation [*altın nesil*]' in Turkey. This organizational/strategic inclination and this highly elitist world-view made the Gülen Community in Turkey a strong example of elitist Islamism.

When the JDP and the Gülen Community were allies, prosecutors allegedly affiliated with the Gülen Community carried out high-profile cases against the systemic elite opposition in Turkey. There was evidence that the legal struggle against the secularist elite was embraced by the JDP elite, too. In his book about the 'democratic struggle methods against coups and memorandums', Hulusi Şentürk, a JDP elite who has been cited numerous times in this book, has repeatedly underlined the importance of legal struggles against coups and coup attempts (2007: 199). He has also underlined the importance of a strong press (2007: 178–180) and a strong police (2007: 195–198). The JDP also undermined the legal bases of the power of secularist elites. Institutions such as

---

[8] For some balanced views on the subject in English and Turkish, see works by Çobanoğlu (2012), Kozanoğlu (1997) and Tittensor (2014).

the National Security Council were abolished (Şentürk, 2007: 117–120), and the JDP governments empowered the civilian authorities *vis-à-vis* the military. In response to rising numbers of attacks by secularist actors during 2007 and 2008 (such as the e-memorandum and the legal interventions for banning the JDP, as illustrated in Chapter 2), the JDP elite used Gülenist cadres in the judiciary to initiate sensational (and widely disputed) legal cases called *Ergenekon* and *Sledgehammer* (*Balyoz*) against so-called coup attempts and terror organizations. The JDP–Gülen Community alliance also discredited the systemic elite opposition by placing their names alongside the well-known names of Turkey's underground mafia and gangs in these trials.[9] There were strong indications that some of the evidence used in these cases was manufactured by the so-called Gülenist prosecutors (Rodrik, 2011). This became evident just after the conflict between the Gülen Community and the JDP government became public. For example, Erdoğan's chief political adviser, Yalçın Akdoğan, blamed the Gülen Community for 'hatching a plot against the national army of the country' (2013).

Yet the alliance between the Gülen Community and the JDP had lasted long enough for them to arrange and win a referendum for constitutional amendments. In 2010, amendments to several articles of the constitution of 1982 were passed. The JDP and the Gülen Community achieved the results they desired. Both acquired more power and influence over the judicial institutions at the expense of the secularist Kemalist elite. Another important gain for Erdoğan with a previous referendum in 2007 during this period was the amendment regarding the election of the president of the Republic. The new regulations in the constitution allowed the election of the president by popular vote.

Later the amendment in 2010, and the newly acquired power of the Gülen Community within the judicial apparatuses, would be used against the JDP. Thus, the decreasing leverage of the military in Turkish politics was achieved through the misuse of legal instruments, through the increasing colonization of state apparatuses by members of the Gülen Community, and via Machiavellian methods in general. As a result, these developments, which seemed positive at first glance, neither contributed to the further democratization of Turkey nor improved the rule of law. The result has been the reproduction of the authoritarian logic of the Turkish party system, outlined in the previous section, under the control of a new conservative elite alliance, and then solely by the populist JDP elite.

---

[9] See Jenkins (2009 and 2011).

Incorporation and Destruction on the Right

Meanwhile, the JDP also actively intervened in the developments of centre-right political circles in Turkey. The JDP accurately defined the rise of potential electoral competitors within the wider right/centre-right electoral market. In some cases, Erdoğan and the JDP elite incorporated or absorbed the elites of other right-wing parties who had considerable electoral-leadership potential. In other cases, the JDP elite actively inhibited the development of right-wing parties that might have decreased the JDP's share of the vote.

Incorporation of Promising Figures on the Right: Kurtulmuş and Soylu One of these right-wing elites whom the JDP preferred to incorporate was Numan Kurtulmuş. Kurtulmuş, a young member of the National View tradition, became the leader of the National View Felicity Party in 2008. After the leadership of Kurtulmuş, the Felicity Party of the National View tradition increased its votes from 2.5 per cent in the 2007 general elections to 5 per cent in local elections in 2009. Neverthe-less, due to pressure from the old guard of the party and from the family of Erbakan (the perennial leader and the founder of the Islamist National View movement), Kurtulmuş and his friends split from the National View tradition and founded a new party, the People's Voice Party (Halkın Sesi Partisi), along the same lines as the JDP but with a special emphasis on social justice.[10] The party was not successful in general elections in 2011 and was seen as a niche party that combined the reformist and democratic appetite of the JDP with an agenda of left Islamism and social justice (Çakır, 2012). Afterwards, Kurtulmuş and his supporters in the party decided to merge with the JDP at Erdoğan's suggestion in 2012 (*Sabah*, 2012b). In fact, this was hardly a merger but rather, as Çakır underlined, the People's Voice Party was swallowed by the JDP (2012). Later, Kurtulmus would become one of the vice-chairs of the JDP and assume high-ranking positions in JDP cabinets.

Another promising stirring in the centre-right political field was that of the leadership of Süleyman Soylu in the Democrat Party (before 2007 this party was named the True Path Party) (*Yenişafak*, 2008). Soylu's leader-ship was seen as an attempt to revitalize the centre-right in Turkey (*Aksiyon*, 2008). He was a fierce critic of the JDP (*Gazetevatan*, 2012), and he was not discredited like other centre-right elites such as Erkan Mumcu and Mehmet Ağar after they supported the political

---

[10] See the aims of party in the party statute at www.yargitaycb.gov.tr/Partiler/kimlik/hsp.pdf (accessed: 21 July 2014).

interventions of the military and high judiciary during the crises of 2007 and 2008 (elaborated in Chapter 2). On the contrary, Soylu criticized the intervention of the high judiciary (*Yeniasya*, 2009) and military (*Taraf*, 2009) in Turkish politics. In 2009, Soylu lost the struggle for the chairmanship in the party convention to the old guard centre-right elite of the Democrat Party, and in 2012 he joined the JDP after he was excluded from the leadership circle of the party. The incorporation of Soylu, alongside Kurtulmuş and his People's Voice Party, not only enhanced the centre-right identity of the JDP but also inhibited the development of potential electoral competitors in the JDP's electoral market.

The Method of Destruction: Uzan's Fall However, the JDP leadership was not always polite and conciliatory to electoral competitors whom they suspected of searching for votes in the JDP's electoral market. In the 2002 general elections, it was not only the JDP but another new party, the Young Party (Genç Parti) of Cem Uzan, who were in competition for the votes of a disillusioned electorate. Uzan was a Turkish business tycoon, and his party was mainly a personalistic entity without any significant organizational structure and programmatic commitment (Türk, 2008: 178–197). The party was founded a couple of months before the election, and it mainly relied on the personality of its leader, professional advertising and the newspapers and TV channels Uzan owned, as well as a catchy neo-fascist and redistributive discourse that included reducing the cost of diesel fuel to one Turkish lira per litre (Türk, 2008: 197–238). In the 2002 elections the Young Party gained 7 per cent of the popular vote. Although the JDP ultimately benefited from the existence of the Young Party in these elections since its share of votes pushed some right-wing parties below the 10 per cent electoral threshold (Tezcür, 2012: 121), at the same time the Young Party was probably viewed by the JDP leadership as an electoral threat.[11] In the following years, rumours of corruption in Uzan's companies led to financial investigations and resulted in the confiscation of some of his wealth (Türk, 2008: 88–99). Later, the Young Party lost its momentum, and Uzan had to flee the country; he took up residence in France.[12] Hence, it is safe to argue that the JDP has cunningly protected its

---

[11] In 2003, in a meeting with provincial chairs Erdoğan said that the JDP's only rival is the Young Party since it was the only party after the 2002 elections which had been increasing its vote (Sabah, 2003).

[12] According to Uzan, in 2009 a Gülenist prosecutor, Zekeriya Öz, threatened him and asked him to withdraw his legal cases against Turkey for his confiscated property (T24, 2013).

electoral market from other political entrepreneurs in order to sustain its political power and resilience.

The Demise of the Post-Islamist Alliance

As the JDP eliminated its elite competitors, increased its power and secured its position in office with the help of the Gülen Community, the tension between these two powerful actors started to grow. The alliance between the Gülen Community and the JDP started to break down, initially on the grounds of struggle for further power (Çakır, 2014b). The first move came from the Gülen Community when (allegedly Gülenist) prosecutors wanted to take Erdoğan's intelligence chief, Hakan Fidan, into custody for negotiations with the PKK in order to resolve the armed conflict between the state and the armed pro-Kurdish organization. In response, the JDP wanted to ban all private education institutions under the control of the Gülen Community. This was an extremely important move because the Gülen Community, as mentioned above, had always relied upon these institutions in terms of human resources and finance. Afterwards, the struggle between the Gülen Community and the JDP passed a point of no return, leading to catastrophic consequences in subsequent years, which are analysed later in this chapter.

Another serious non-electoral challenge to the JDP stemmed from snowballing environmentalist protests in İstanbul. The protests against the demolition of Gezi Park in Taksim, İstanbul, were crushed harshly by police forces at the beginning of June 2013. This disproportionate police intervention rapidly triggered an unprecedented wave of social protest across Turkey that lasted for weeks. In the end, the JDP was able to suppress the protests at the cost of the lives of eight young protesters due to the inordinate use of force by the police. During the protests, the pro-JDP media presented the riots as an attempted coup against the JDP government staged by foreign powers (*Yenişafak*, 2013). The JDP deputies explicitly called the protests a coup attempt (*Ahaber*, 2013).

In the following months, the Gülen Community initiated its counter-attack against Erdoğan and the JDP. On 17 December 2013, just a couple of months before the local election in 2014 (allegedly Gülenist), prosecutors initiated corruption probes against four ministers of the JDP government. The JDP responded with the dismissal and relocation of tens of allegedly Gülenist prosecutors and hundreds of allegedly Gülenist police officers. The pro-JDP media presented the corruption probes as a 'civilian coup' against the JDP government. The pro-JDP media called the Gülenists in bureaucracy 'a parallel state' and started to argue that they were being manipulated by international powers. Erdoğan's chief adviser not only blamed the community for being a tool of foreign powers but also argued that they had inherited the spirit of the bureaucratic and military tutelage (Akdoğan, 2014). In short, thanks to the pro-JDP media, the JDP elite effectively presented the corruption probes as an attempted coup against the elected government, and this strategy was ultimately successful. In the local elections on 30 March 2014 the JDP received 45 per cent of the popular vote.

The Road to the Failed Coup: The Demise of the Kurdish Opening and the First Electoral Failure of the JDP

A couple of months after the local elections in 2014, the Turkish people voted in the first popular election for the president of the Republic. In this election, there were three candidates: besides Erdoğan, Ekmeleddin İhsanoğlu and Selahattin Demirtaş competed for the presidency. The joint candidate of the Republican People's Party and the Nationalist Action Party, Ekmeleddin İhsanoğlu, received slightly less than 40 per cent of the popular vote. The outcome was another victory for Erdoğan and the JDP, with 52 per cent of the total vote, and Erdoğan became the first president of the Turkish Republic to be elected by popular vote.

One of the surprising outcomes of Turkey's first presidential election was the success of Selahattin Demirtaş, the co-chair of the pro-Kurdish Peoples' Democratic Party. Demirtaş, with the support of Kurds and socialist, left-leaning segments of the electorate, obtained 10 per cent of the total vote. This certainly paved the way for the future decision of the pro-Kurdish elite to take part in the general elections as a party.[13] In becoming the president of the Republic, due to constitutional requirements, Erdoğan had to step down from the chairmanship of the JDP and left his place to Ahmet Davutoğlu, the former minister for foreign affairs.

Decline of the Kurdish Opening Meanwhile, the ongoing efforts to solve the Kurdish problem (which was termed the Kurdish Opening (*Kürt Açılımı*) by the government) came to a conclusion at the beginning of 2015. The representatives of the JDP government and the pro-Kurdish Peoples' Democratic Party declared an agreement consisting

---

[13] Because of the 10 per cent threshold, the pro-Kurdish elite usually participate in elections as independent candidates and, in the Grand National Assembly of Turkey, they reunite under the banner of their party. For how this success in the presidential elections changed the minds of the pro-Kurdish elite regarding this strategy, see Bora (2015).

of ten articles regarding a peaceful solution to the Kurdish issue on 28 February 2015 in Dolmabahçe Palace. This agreement included the regulation of the return of PKK fighters to civilian politics, the devolution of power to local governments and the right to education in one's mother tongue (*Hürriyet*, 2015). However, within a couple of weeks, Erdoğan declared that he did not ultimately approve this meeting and the agreement that had been declared, which had begun to be known as the 'Dolmabahçe Agreement [*Dolmabahçe Mutabakatı*]' (*Gazetevatan*, 2015).

Various explanations were offered regarding this sudden change in Erdoğan's attitude towards the negotiations to solve the 'Kurdish issue'. But Erdoğan's concerns related to the upcoming general elections in the summer of the same year seem to have played a decisive role. One interpretation was that Erdoğan did not get what he expected from the peace negotiations in electoral terms and decided to renounce the entire process before it was too late, in other words, before the general elections on 7 June 2015 (*Cumhuriyet*, 2015; *Yarın*, 2016).

General Elections on 7 June 2015: A Return to Pluralism? The general elections on 7 June 2015 indeed validated Erdoğan's observations that the negotiations aimed at resolving the Kurdish issue did not favour the JDP in electoral terms.[14] The results were shocking for the JDP, which lost the majority needed to form a single-party government, despite gaining more than 40 per cent of the total votes. Both the Peoples' Democratic Party and the Nationalist Action Party – two parties located at the extreme opposite ends of the ethnic axis of Turkish politics – comfortably passed the 10 per cent electoral threshold and got almost 30 per cent of all votes in total. The Republican People's Party got 25 per cent of all votes. This formed a problematic composition for an anti-JDP coalition, since the two parties located on the opposing ends of the ethnic axis of Turkish politics did not want to take part in the same coalition in the parliament. The following months were therefore characterized by unproductive negotiations among these parties to form a coalition, most notably the tedious and time-consuming negotiations between the Republican People's Party and the JDP.

Meanwhile, the conflict between the PKK and state security forces had a resurgence in the summer months with the assassination of two police officers. Later, sporadic conflicts between the two sides grew into urban warfare in various Kurdish cities of south-eastern Turkey. Due to the trenches dug by PKK members, these urban conflicts, which lasted the

---

[14] For an analysis of the election, see Baykan (2015c).

entirety of a long and bloody summer, became known as the 'Trench Wars [*Hendek Savaşları*]'. The human and economic cost of these catastrophic months was enormous. Hundreds of security personnel and PKK militants, as well as non-combatant civilians, were killed, residential areas home to thousands were destroyed, and many people had to leave their homes during the conflicts. The consequences of the war extended beyond the region. Academics who criticized the heavy-handed state intervention in these cities in a petition (which was later known as the Peace Petition) were exposed to heavy pressure from government circles, including Erdoğan. In the following days and months, many of them were tried for supporting a terrorist organization and expelled from their posts.

Riding the Nationalist Wave: The Snap Election of 1 November 2015
The negotiations for a coalition government after the 7 June 2015 elections ended in deadlock, thanks in part to the interventions of Erdoğan. This resulted in a decision to call a snap election. Meanwhile, the urban warfare between the PKK and the security forces gradually came to an end, and mainly resulted in the victory of the latter. With the support of Erdoğan's nationalist-hawkish attitude towards the PKK, the JDP successfully attracted the vote of the nationalist segments of the electorate. In the snap elections on 1 November 2015 Erdoğan's JDP regained the parliamentary majority required for a single-party government.

Among these developments, Erdoğan started to reconsider the position of Davutoğlu, the trustee (*emanetçi*) he left in his place at the top of the JDP when he became president. There were rumours that Erdoğan thought the reason behind the electoral failure of the party in the first general election of 2015 was Davutoğlu's poor performance. At the same time, it is plausible that Erdoğan was not impressed with the independent behaviour of Davutoğlu, who was an ambitious intellectual with a degree of organizational intelligence. Erdoğan was, presumably, not very happy with Davutoğlu's reluctance to back a constitutional amendment which would grant more power to Erdoğan himself as the president, either. In an extraordinary convention Binali Yıldırım, an Erdoğan loyalist, replaced Davutoğlu as the chair of the JDP and became the new prime minister of Turkey.

The Failed Coup on 15 July 2016: On 15 July 2016 these circumstances culminated in a bloody coup in an attempt to topple Erdoğan and the JDP. From the perspective of this book's approach, it is possible to see the coup as an anti-populist reaction to the populist predominance of

Erdoğan's JDP.[15] As the elite, other than the populist JDP leadership, had been sidelined through the tactics and instruments I have explained in this chapter (and in this book in general) so far, hostilities among elite-level power contenders in Turkey grew intolerably strong. It is also plausible that these elite-level power players in Turkey had begun to think that it was almost impossible to replace the JDP via elections due to the party's overwhelming organizational penetration into Turkish society and its ability to generate massive popular support. The man-oeuvres of the JDP after its first electoral failure in June 2015 must have been another clear indicator for the anti-populist elite that Erdoğan and the JDP would not hand over power easily. There is convincing evidence to suggest that infiltrated members of the Gülen Community in the Turkish Armed Forces also played a central role in the putsch alongside other elite groups hostile to Erdoğan and the populist JDP.

The coup hastily triggered a popular resistance led and organized by JDP branches across Turkey. Around 250 people, mostly from the lower strata of Turkish society, were killed by pro-coup soldiers. Many more were wounded during the clashes on 15–16 July 2016. The robust JDP organization certainly played a central role in the rapid, effective and resilient mass mobilization against the coup[16] alongside the unorganized masses that poured into the streets at Erdoğan's urging.[17] It is plausible that the mass mobilization in the initial hours of the coup, the signs that success would be achieved only at an extremely high human cost, per-haps even in a civil war-like situation where the army and the police remained divided, helped to stop more anti-Erdoğanist soldiers from jumping onto the pro-coup bandwagon. There was also evidence that the intra-army coalition behind the coup consisted of ideologically diverse segments (Gürcan, 2016). The resistance and mass mobilization against the coup, therefore, had a decisive impact in dissolving the coup coalition within the army. In the next section of this chapter, I will focus on the aftermath of the failed coup and the tightening of the JDP's control over Turkish politics and society.

[15] For a detailed analysis of the coup, see Baykan (2017c).
[16] The research conducted just after the coup by Konda (2016) illustrates that the overwhelming majority of protesters who took part in the resistance were JDP members or supporters.
[17] In a live broadcast on CNNTurk a couple of hours after the putsch began, Erdoğan invited his supporters to the streets: 'I invite our nation to the squares of our cities, our airports. Let's gather in the squares, in the airports. Let this minority group come with their tanks and arms; let's see what they can do. I have not known any other power above the power of the people. And this won't change.' See www.youtube.com/watch?v= 7LEfGo0uN-o (accessed: 26 December 2017).

The *Ruptura*: Crystallization of the Hegemonic Party Autocracy

In this section, I will focus on the *de facto* and *de jure* transition to a hegemonic party autocracy in Turkey that had been in the making at least since the Gezi protests. Here, I will focus on the measures that followed the state of emergency and some crucial political interventions by the JDP leadership that allowed them to shape the political space and would guarantee the predominance of the JDP in the coming elections.

Declaration of a 'State of Emergency'

A couple of days after the coup was repelled by the JDP's mass mobilization, the government declared a state of emergency that granted President Erdoğan the power to use decree laws and bypass the parliament in order to deal with the delicate situation that developed after the coup. In the initial days, it was argued that the state of emergency would be effective only for a couple of months. Nevertheless it became clear as the months passed that the state of emergency would not be lifted quickly.

The following months brought several consecutive decree laws from Erdoğan that were not directly related to the consequences of the failed coup. The optimism during the immediate aftermath of the coup that the JDP would seek consensus and return to the path of democratization gradually disappeared. The decree laws were not used only to expel alleged members of the Gülen Community from their public posts. They were also used to penalize opponents of the JDP government, such as the academics who signed the Peace Petition in the summer of 2015. The number of people expelled from their positions in the state institutions grew enormously in the months that followed the coup, and many associations, institutions and media outlets were shut down (*Duvar*, 2017a). Meanwhile, the collaboration between the JDP and the Nationalist Action Party that had emerged after the snap elections in November 2015 grew even deeper after the coup. The Nationalist Action Party and its leader strongly supported the harsh measures implemented by the JDP to shape Turkish politics and started to become the 'loyal opposition' of the new regime.

The JDP's control over the judiciary also helped them to shape the party's opponents on the left, too. Just a couple of months after the coup, the leadership circles of the legal pro-Kurdish opposition were taken into custody on the accusation that they were affiliated with a terrorist organization, namely the PKK.[18] Selahattin Demirtaş, Figen Yüksekdağ and Ahmet Türk were among the most high-profile targets in this purge. The months following the coup attempt were also characterized by the imprisonment of many left-leaning critical journalists, including people such as Kadri Gürsel and Ahmet Şık. Another journalist, who was a Republican People's Party deputy, was also imprisoned on the allegation that he was affiliated with the Gülen Community, or to the 'Fethullahist Terror Organization' (FETÖ), as it was called in the official narrative of the JDP.

The decline of the rule of law in Turkey was accelerated as the state of emergency was repeatedly extended. A decree law made it possible for the government to remove popularly elected mayors and appoint government trustees (kayyumlar) instead. During the state of emergency and after the removal of many judges affiliated with the Gülen Community, these seats have begun to be filled by JDP loyalists such as former local chairs and executives of the party (Cumhuriyet, 2017b). And more recently, with another, ambiguously formulated decree law, the government sparked heated debates as to whether it was preparing the grounds of impunity for violent assaults on opponents. This decree law, declared on 24 December 2017, stated that civilians who took part in the suppression of the coup and the following 'terror' events would not be subject to penal responsibility (Karar, 2017). Not surprisingly, this regulation has been widely evaluated as a loosely defined one that could provide immunity to the violence against the government's opponents in the current conditions in Turkey.

The Constitutional Referendum of 16 April 2017: The De Jure Move from an Electoral Parliamentary Democracy to a Competitive Presidential Authoritarianism

Under these circumstances of progressive decline of the state of law in Turkey, Erdoğan pushed for a referendum on a constitutional amendment that would transform Turkey into a presidential system in which

---

[18] In contrast to the expectation that these high-profile arrests would cause massive discontent, particularly among the country's Kurdish population, the arrests did not trigger any notable protest at all. The state of emergency and the repressive measures in effect, as well as the disappointment among the Kurdish population because of the PKK's decision to engage in conflicts in urban settings, certainly played a role in this silence. It is, however, plausible that by using public opinion research the JDP might have measured the potential reaction against this kind of heavy-handed intervention beforehand. Hence, the potential role of political marketing techniques in the growth of a competitive authoritarian regime should be taken seriously into account.

Erdoğan could accumulate extraordinary powers. Not surprisingly, the content of the constitutional amendment triggered heated debates and drew substantial criticism from opponents.[19] The proposal to shift the political system in Turkey to presidentialism included many changes that reduced the control of the legislative branch of the government over the executive branch (i.e., the president) and enlarged the authority of the latter to an unprecedented extent in Turkish political history. The amendment also granted the president the power to rule by decree in his executive duties. This was certainly a major intrusion into the legislative branch by the executive. The proposal also granted almost complete penal immunity to the president.

Besides changes to the relationship between the executive and legislative branches of the government, the proposal also contained many changes to the relationship between the executive and the judicial branch. Not surprisingly, the proposal included amendments granting extraordinary powers to the president in the formation of the high governing bodies of the judiciary. Hence, the proposal also included the subordination of the judicial branch to the president. As one of the prominent legal scholars of Turkey, Kemal Gözler, argued, this 'abusive constitutional change' was designed to accumulate all of the powers in the hands of the president (2017: 7).

During the process leading to election day, independent observers pointed out the negative impact of the state of emergency on free and fair campaigning for the opposition. Immediately after the referendum on 16 April 2017, many rumours regarding irregularities in the conduct of elections emerged. For a couple of days, opponents of the JDP protested the results in major urban centres of the country (DW, 2017), but the protests gradually came to an end. Nevertheless, the final report of the independent observation body, the Office for Democratic Institutions and Human Rights, indicated that the deeply unfair competition was certainly an outcome of the state of emergency (OSCE/ODIHR, 2017: 1). In the following section, I will focus on a few crucial intra-party developments within the JDP since Erdoğan became the president in 2014. These developments represent an inseparable side story related to the rise of a hegemonic party autocracy in Turkey under the control of the personalistic rule of Erdoğan.

---

[19] For a detailed legal evaluation of each amendment, see the report by the Turkish Bar Association, http://anayasadegisikligi.barobirlik.org.tr/Anayasa_Degisikligi.aspx (accessed: 27 December 2017).

The JDP Organization after the Presidential Elections in 2014 and the Referendum in 2017

After Erdoğan became the president of the Republic in 2014, under the constitutional constraints effective at that time, he had to step down as chairman of the JDP. For this position, Erdoğan selected Davutoğlu, the JDP's minister for foreign affairs and an academic in the social sciences. Although Davutoğlu was not an experienced organization man like Erdoğan (as delineated in Chapter 4), there were many indications of sympathy towards him in JDP organizations across Turkey.[20] There were also signs that, after Davutoğlu became the prime minister and the chair of the JDP, he attempted to reshape the JDP party organizations across Turkey according to his views and needs (*Cumhuriyet*, 2016; *Sözcü*, 2016). Later on, in a Central Decision and Administration Board meeting, the powers of the party chair regarding appointments and removals within the JDP organizations across Turkey were reduced at the request of Erdoğan (*Cumhuriyet*, 2016).

An aggressive social media campaign followed these developments. A blog post, later called the 'Pelican Brief', was published at the beginning of May 2016 that accused Davutoğlu of being 'vain', of betraying Erdoğan in several issues including not backing the presidential cause adequately, and of creating his own media and power base within the party by relying on 'well-educated' advisers.[21] A couple of days later, Davutoğlu declared that he had resigned from his post. This was followed by an extraordinary JDP convention at the end of May 2016 in which an Erdoğan loyalist and former minister for transport, Binali Yıldırım, became chairman of the party and prime minister. Under Yıldırım's leadership, the JDP campaigned for the constitutional amendment on 16 April 2017 and, ironically, Yıldırım's success deprived him of his power. He fulfilled his role flawlessly as a 'trustee'.

The return of Erdoğan as president and chair of the JDP after the constitutional amendment in 2017 quickly triggered changes in the

[20] During my fieldwork, I heard from many interviewees that, after Erdoğan, Davutoğlu was the most liked national personality within the JDP organization. For example, see Interviewee 9 (2014).

[21] For how populism has played a role in this intra-party struggle it is remarkable to see the following expressions regarding Davutoğlu and his advisers/supporters in this highly debated blog post called the Pelican Brief: 'These are all "well-educated" kids. They are very well educated. You have not seen such a thing. They are all graces of God. The Hodja [Professor Davutoğlu has been called "Hodja" in reference to his academic title] is "well-educated" too. The Reis [Erdoğan] is from Kasımpaşa. Is it possible. No? Is it going well? It is not going well! Therefore they need to rule [instead of Erdoğan].' For the blog post, see https://pelikandosyasi.wordpress.com/ (accessed: 28 December 2017).

organization. In a parliamentary group meeting of the JDP, Erdoğan stated that there was 'metal fatigue' within the JDP organizations (*Evrensel*, 2017). The following weeks and months were characterized by the removal of and changes in many provincial governing bodies of the party. Erdoğan continued to attend the provincial consultation meetings and conventions, and many provincial organizations were reshuffled in line with his preferences (*AA*, 2017; *Duvar*, 2017b).

One of Erdoğan's main targets in his interventions in the party organizations across Turkey after the constitutional amendment was to change some of the powerful provincial mayors of his party (Selvi, 2017). In a series of negotiations with these powerful local patrons within his party, Erdoğan requested them to step down. Several mayors, including the mayors of İstanbul and Ankara, resigned from their positions (*Habertürk*, 2017; *Hürriyet*, 2017). The removals of Kadir Topbaş and Melih Gökçek were particularly remarkable since they had been ruling the municipalities of İstanbul and Ankara for years. Topbaş remained the JDP mayor of İstanbul for more than a decade, and Gökçek had been the mayor of Ankara for more than two decades – initially as a member of the Islamist National View parties and then the JDP.[22]

It is plausible that they (and particularly Gökçek) would have developed powerful patronage networks to support them. Their removal, however, once again illustrated the relevance of the main argument of this book regarding the JDP: Erdoğan and the JDP centre actively inhibited the rise of powerful patrons within the JDP organization and kept provincial mayors of the party under tight control. So, it seems that the local power base of prominent provincial figures of the party have always remained below a certain threshold that kept them weaker *vis-à-vis* the party centre. Even after spending decades at the top of two of Turkey's largest cities as mayors, none of these people was powerful enough to challenge Erdoğan and claim popular legitimacy and backing.

The concentration of power in the hands of Erdoğan continued after he became president in 2014. The personalization of power within the JDP took a further step through the changes made in 2015 to the central ruling cadres of the party. Erdoğan first implanted his son-in-law, Berat Albayrak, a 37-year-old businessman with no previous experience in party politics, into the Central Decision and Administration Board of

---

[22] Another comment on the removal of these two important mayors draws attention to the public opinion research conducted on the orders of Erdoğan. According to Yalçın (2017), this public opinion research on local governments demonstrated to Erdoğan that these mayors were performing poorly and that this was decreasing support for the JDP.

the party alongside other loyalists during the crisis with Davutoğlu. In the months following the removal of Davutoğlu, Albayrak became the minister for energy and natural resources (*Ahaber*, 2017).

This was symbolically a crucial move. Although personalism has always been a fundamental aspect of Turkish party politics, the rise of such a close relative of the prime minister or president to such a high-ranking official position was unprecedented in Turkish politics. There were many times, of course, where relatives of top politicians had socially or economically benefited from the positions of their powerful patrons, or informally influenced political decisions. However, while it was very common in many Middle Eastern dictatorships, in Turkey the existence of this kind of close relationship between the head of the executive branch and those occupying high-ranking political office had always been seen as something that should be avoided. Therefore, the rise of Albayrak was another indicator of the exceptional degree of personalization of power in the case of the JDP in Turkey and the party's unique position in the history of Turkish politics. This picture was also complemented by the rising public visibility of Erdoğan's wife, son and daughter, and perhaps of the rising influence of family members and relatives over his political decisions in general.[23]

From a Slow and Tumultuous *Reforma* to an Unexpected *Ruptura*: Numbers against Instruments

In the second section, I drew attention to the authoritarian dynamics of Turkish politics since the transition to a multi-party system and how these dynamics have ignited distrust and opportunism among Turkey's powerful collective actors. For instance, while the JDP elite had been in a seemingly natural alliance with the Gülen Community in the initial years of its rule in order to curb the power of the secularist Kemalist establishment elite, as their relationship grew increasingly tense the JDP could develop alliances with secular and conservative nationalist forces in Turkey. But the authoritarian nature of Turkish politics has remained intact, and the alliances and conflicts among the powerful collective actors in Turkish politics could not bring democratization since the distrust between them never disappeared.

---

[23] One of my interviewees underlined this dynamic as a general trend in Turkish politics. According to this particular interviewee, top Turkish politicians have always turned towards their families for advice and consultation for political decisions as they get older. He also implied that this is a factor that contributes to their fall because it is impossible to change one's family members, like other advisers, when they fail to provide good advice (Interviewee 21, 2014).

As I have illustrated so far, the rise of the JDP emerged in a state-of-nature-like context for collective political actors, and the decades preceding the rise of the JDP saw the creation of various elite groups with different power resources and strategies. In order to curb the power of the elites of the former status quo in Turkey the JDP engaged in a process of *reforma* by observing the rules of the virtual consensus with the secularist political actors through avoiding violence and other non-electoral political methods. When these strategies were not enough, the JDP formed an alliance with another powerful conservative collective actor, the Gülen Community. By deploying the community's infiltrated cadres within the security and judicial apparatuses of the state, the JDP elite successfully curbed the power of the secularist elite and consolidated its position within Turkey's democratically deficient system through passive, legalist methods while avoiding any overt confrontation with these forces.

This process of long and tumultuous *reforma* targeting the replacement of secularist elites with a new generation of conservative elites through non-violent but hardly legitimate means turned into a dangerous conflict when the main drivers of the process, the JDP and the Gülen Community, parted ways. The gradual but progressive demise of Turkey's electoral democracy accelerated after the end of this post-Islamist alliance. The failed coup, and the developments of its aftermath analysed in this chapter, has shown that the process of *reforma* turned into an unexpected *ruptura* with the coup. The following months brought the further decline of democracy in Turkey and the *de facto* and *de jure* rise of a competitive authoritarian regime and an all-powerful presidential system characterized by the concentration of powers in the hands of the populist Erdoğan. Meanwhile, and through the resistance to the failed coup, Erdoğan acquired new symbolic importance and new symbolic resources that could form the basis of a new authoritarian regime. It should be noted here that the authoritarian legacy of Turkish politics and the distrust and opportunism it inflicted upon the organizational and strategic behaviour of Turkey's powerful collective actors were decisive in the rise of a competitive authoritarian regime.

Yet the particular (and perhaps contingent) outcome of these processes – in other words, a competitive authoritarian regime under the populist predominance of the JDP – needs to be explained. The role of the party's agency was certainly key in this case, too. As stated above, powerful collective political actors responded with different organizational and political strategies to the authoritarian legacy of Turkish politics. For example, while secular, ethnically Turkish sectors of Turkey mostly relied on powerful state institutions to defend their interests and identity, left-leaning secular Kurds were predominantly led by an armed opposition which, time and again, embraced terror and violence as an instrument for achieving their political aims. On the other hand, one of the influential organized actors from the religious sectors, namely the Gülen Community, chose the strategy of semi-clandestine elite infiltration of state institutions and usually refrained from mass mobilization techniques. This gradually led to the rise of an authoritarian and elitist Islamism which unfolded in the form of a bloody coup on 15 July 2016.

The only winning political strategy in the 'state of nature' of Turkish politics belonged to Erdoğan's JDP. The combination of populism and the personalistic mass party was the most reliable strategy in a moment of unexpected *ruptura* after a long process of *reforma* that profoundly transformed state apparatuses and deprived the secularist elite sectors of their age-old leverages. But it was also superior to the strategy of the Gülen Community and the armed Kurdish opposition since it allowed the encapsulation of broad social sectors through the organizational, discursive, stylistic and clientelistic links demonstrated throughout this book. When everything collapsed on 15 July 2016, only Erdoğan's JDP was powerful and organized enough to seize the moment because only the strategy of populism and the personalistic mass party relied on 'numbers'. Under the unique political circumstances of Turkey, political strategies relying on powerful 'instruments' (state apparatuses, semi-clandestine elite organizations, armed struggle) failed decisively.[24] Only a strategy that relied on encapsulating and mobilizing large numbers of people and a skilful pragmatism at the elite level which could engage in a series of fluid coalitions could be victorious. The authoritarian outcome was certainly normatively not desirable, but the mastery of political craftsmanship is undeniable.

Conclusion

In this chapter, I have placed the agency of Erdoğan's JDP in historical perspective. I have drawn attention to the authoritarian legacy of Turkish politics and its impact on powerful collective political and social actors in Turkey. In the third section, I focused on the long and tumultuous process of *reforma* in Turkey that resulted in the replacement of the secularist elite of the country with a new conservative elite alliance. In the next section, I drew attention to the *ruptura*, or the sudden *de facto*

---

[24] See Arendt (1969). It is striking that it was only the most majoritarian force to ever occur in Turkish politics that was aware of the simple fact that political power relies on numbers, not instruments.

and *de jure* rise of a competitive authoritarian regime in Turkey after rifts and tensions appeared within this conservative bloc and the demise of this post-Islamist alliance gave rise to a bloody coup in the summer of 2016. In the final section of the chapter, I argued that the impact of the unique dynamics of the democratically deficient context of Turkish politics (its peculiar electoral democracy) and its effect on powerful collective actors in Turkey have paved the way for the victory of Erdoğan's JDP in a moment of *ruptura*. Populism and the personalistic mass party helped Erdoğan and the JDP elite to successfully resist the bloody coup and take advantage of the institutional crises that followed this catastrophic moment to build a competitive authoritarian regime. Without encapsulating and mobilizing people in the way analysed in this book, the consequences of the coup and the political prospects for Erdoğan and the JDP elite would have been remarkably different.

9   Conclusions: Findings, Implications, Future Research

The Puzzle, Main Arguments and Empirical Findings of the Research

This book has focused on the reasons for the electoral success and political resilience of the Justice and Development Party (JDP, Adalet ve Kalkınma Partisi) in Turkey. At the time of writing, despite many social, political and economic crises, which would have destroyed many governments in liberal democratic settings, the subject matter of this research was still very much alive and perhaps stronger than ever. How has this new party, coming from a strictly Islamist political tradition, begun to dominate Turkish politics and ultimately pave the way for the rise of competitive authoritarianism in the presence of powerful (secularist and other) elite contenders, even in the absence of facilitating economic and symbolic resources for authoritarian rule? In this book, I have proposed answers to the puzzle of the JDP's electoral and political predominance from a party agency perspective. Proximity to the people through diligent organizational activity as well as through a 'low-populist' political appeal/style was always central to the JDP's electoral and political resilience. In other words, party agency – organization, strategies and political appeals – was the key to the JDP's electoral and political resilience.

In empirical terms, I have argued that the combination of a 'low-populist' political appeal/style and a large and pervasive membership organization, active year-round, tightly controlled by a diligent leadership and supported by political marketing techniques and extensive media control (a personalistic mass party), was central to the electoral achievements and political resilience of the JDP for more than fifteen years, and this gradually paved the way for the rise of a competitive authoritarian regime in Turkey. Hence, the primary contribution of this book is the detailed empirical illustration of the functioning of the JDP's organization and the demonstration of the party's 'low-populist' political appeal to the economically disadvantaged majority of the country who were also usually looked down on socio-culturally. Thus, from a broader, theoretical point of view, this research has highlighted the importance of party agency alongside external-structural economic, social and political reasons when it comes to explaining electoral and political success.

In the Introduction to the book, I focused on existing explanations for the JDP's electoral and political achievements. I have pointed out how the majority of these explanations highlighted external-structural economic and social reasons as the basis for the rise and electoral predominance of the JDP. Although these structural factors were vital for the rise of the party in Turkey, this rise and the electoral achievements of the JDP as a post-Islamist party, and then its transformation into a hegemonic party, were made possible by a specific 'party agency' that capitalized on these suitable social, political and economic circumstances. Hence, I highlighted the importance of focusing on party agency, and more precisely on the organizational agency of the party, for a better understanding of the JDP's electoral and political predominance.

In Chapter 2, I analysed the historical, political and social background of the transformation of Islamism and the rise of the JDP in Turkey. Here, in contrast to many studies relying on the secular–religious dichotomy, I began with underlining the 'virtual consensus' between the Islamist elite and the so-called secularist establishment elite of Turkey, which became particularly visible after the September 1980 military coup. This virtual consensus granted a remarkable tolerance for the Islamic activism in the country that other political forces, which had the potential to channel lower-class support, could not enjoy. Hence, I argued that the destruction of the leftist organizational networks after the coup in 1980, the introduction of the new conservative and nationalist official indoctrination programme of Turkish-Islamic Synthesis, and new legal and constitutional regulations implemented in line with the strategy of 'selective pluralism' opened up unexpected room for manoeuvre for the Islamist elite in post-coup Turkish politics.

Not surprisingly, the JDP elite did almost nothing to change this restrictive political framework, including the unusually high 10 per cent electoral threshold and many other legal and constitutional impediments for new political entrepreneurs and other elite groups. Other empirical evidence in this chapter showed that not only external systemic pressure but, first and foremost, the internal debates of the Islamist elite and their revising of strategies as a consequence of electoral failures were the main causes for the transformation of Islamism and the rise of post-Islamist JDP. The most important feature of the political struggles illustrated in this chapter was that they included not only political parties competing for power, but also other significant non-party power contenders such as the army and the high judiciary. This particular nature of political conflicts in the country deeply shaped the organizational formation of the Islamist parties and, later, the JDP as discussed at length in Chapter 6.

In Chapter 3, after a theoretical discussion on concepts of cleavage, divide and populism and a brief illustration of the relevance of the high-low divide in Turkey (see also Appendices 1 and 2), I elaborated on the JDP's political appeal and demonstrated how the party elite and the pro-JDP media located the party and its leader within Turkish politics. I argued that, more than the left–right or secular–religious divides, the high–low divide as the 'manifestation in politics of social and cultural inequalities' (Ostiguy, 2009c: 2) was the main framework of the JDP's political appeal. Although emphases on religious sentiments and right-ist-conservative motives were also central to the JDP's political appeal, all these motives were turned into political assets through a 'low-populist' political appeal/style in which the JDP leadership and the pro-JDP media decisively depicted JDP cadres as the authentic representative of the despised, belittled, socially and culturally excluded, and downtrodden segments of the society. Here it should also be noted that, particularly for Erdoğan, the 'low-populist' political appeal/style was not simply the product of an artificial image-making activity but was embedded naturally in Erdoğan's biographical background, political experience and style (this was a point I delved into further in Chapter 4 on the JDP leadership). The 'low-populist' appeal not only provided the party with a great degree of flexibility in terms of its programme and ideology, but also helped the JDP elite to protect a strong emotional link with low-income, conservative and peripheral segments, and thereby provided collective incentives for the masses comprising very diverse social, ethnic and political groups.

In Chapter 4, I gave a detailed picture of the JDP leadership. In this chapter, in contrast to the loose uses of the concept of charisma in studies of Turkish politics, and by relying on the original exposition of the concept by Weber (1974), I proposed to take charismatic personalism as a genuinely rare phenomenon characterized by a strong transformational impact of the leader on his followers, supporters and organization. Drawing on an analysis of secondary sources such as biographies of Erdoğan as well as my interviews, I described the case of Erdoğan's leadership as an example of 'non-charismatic personalism' following the conceptual proposition of Ansell and Fish (1999). In this sense, while charismatic leaders are akin to architects in terms of introducing novel narratives – which could be integrative as well as divisive, plausible as well as irrational – to their followers, non-charismatic personalist leaders such as Erdoğan resemble engineers focusing on achieving concrete-functional and pragmatic goals. From a broader theoretical point of view, in this chapter I also drew attention to the compatibility between personalism and the mass membership organization despite the seeming contradiction between two. In order to do this, I pointed out the distinction between institutionalization and routinization-bureaucratization. I argued that the JDP was a highly routinized and bureaucratized massive membership organization under the control of a highly personalistic leadership, but it was by no means a highly institutionalized one at the same time.

In Chapter 5, I argued that the JDP had a highly cautious approach to classical redistributive strategies used by its centre-right predecessors in Turkey. I underlined how the JDP's politics diverged from 'classical centre-right patronage' in which generous state subsidies for agricultural products, massive public employment and 'induced participation' of poor rural and provincial masses through traditional-local elites had been central pillars of party politics for a very long time. In this chapter, I also demonstrated that, with regard to organizational and electoral strategies, the JDP diverged remarkably from its right-wing predecessors and targeted electoral and political predominance; they strategically aimed for long-lasting rule from the very beginning of the JDP's term of office. In order to maintain predominance, the JDP departed significantly from the Islamist National View tradition in terms of its communications strategy and put heavy emphasis on having a tight grip over a decisively strong pro-JDP media and political marketing techniques in general. In addition, the party also diverged from its centre-right predecessor, the Motherland Party, in terms of its attention to protect the tightly controlled, large and pervasive membership organization that was active year-round for one-to-one vote canvassing activities. The main benefit for the party elite of this autonomous party structure and leadership, supported by a pro-JDP media, was the ability to strike a balance between the short-term requirements of elections (responsiveness) and the long-term requirements of being in office (responsibility), and between the collective and selective incentives, between the mission and material expectations, and, last but not least, between the idealist and pragmatist cadres of the party.

Yet, inheriting the organizational culture of the Islamist National View tradition (Delibaş, 2015), the JDP also relied upon year-round activity and a massive membership organization consisting of 8–9 million members (or supporters encapsulated as members) that penetrated into even the smallest corners of the country such as sub-provincial neighbourhoods. In Chapter 6, I highlighted that this massive membership organization was kept under the tight control of the central JDP elite through public opinion surveys (*anketler*, as popularly known in Turkish), through technological surveillance instruments such as AKİM (the JDP Communications Centre) and AKBİS (the JDP Information Centre) and through party co-ordinators, deputies and ministers in person. Yet this firm control was also balanced through 'controlled participation' channels within the JDP such as regular consultations (*istişareler*), non-binding elections among selected members (*teşkilat temayül yoklamaları*) and an active women's branch which, together, created a very strong sense of participation in decision-making processes and party activities among the activists of this tightly controlled, massive membership organization.

From a broader theoretical perspective, and through a critical evaluation of the recent literature on party organizational change and party decline, I argued that, given the importance attached by the party elite to a tightly controlled massive membership organization and political marketing instruments such as public opinion surveys as well as a decisively pro-JDP media, the JDP organization should be identified as a 'personalistic mass party'. In Chapter 6, I described the JDP as a hybrid electoral machine which blended the mass-based party model (a tightly controlled, hierarchical, massive membership organization that is active year-round and has a robust and permanent local presence) and elite-based party model (a party with a less ideological orientation and highly visible leadership groups supported by professionals, political marketing techniques and extensive use of media). In the specific case of Turkey, where the party organizations represented something more than an instrument of electoral mobilization for political entrepreneurs (instead representing a wider power capability against non-party political challengers as well as an instrument of redistributive tactics in poor urban contexts), various traits of the mass-based party model were still indispensable for electoral success.

In Chapter 7, I elaborated further on the JDP's intra-party governance through focusing on the increasing leadership domination just after the party's foundation and the formation of provincial governing bodies and candidate selection processes within the party. I have demonstrated that, immediately after its foundation, the JDP's remarkably democratic first statute was changed through the collaboration of the party leader Erdoğan and the founding committee. A series of amendments to the first statute granted extensive rights to party chair Erdoğan and created leadership domination at a very early stage of this organization's life. I also argued that the party centre designed the minute details of the local-provincial branches of the JDP through careful interventions and this, in turn, enhanced the say of the party leadership in the candidate selection process. I showed that candidate selection was highly 'exclusive' (Hazan and Rahat, 2010: 35) within the JDP: party leader Erdoğan was almost the only selector of the party's candidates, even for those coming from relatively insignificant local settings.

Considering the separate accounts of senior party members, junior members, critical former party members and 'true democrats' regarding the candidate selection process within the party, I have also shown how these frequent interventions in local politics were legitimized by the JDP leadership, pointing out the 'organizational conservatism [teşkilat taassubu]', which refers to the local party branches' tendency to bear in mind the day-to-day interests of local politics but not to consider the general interest of the party and the country – and, therefore, their inclination to support so-called incompetent candidates coming from among the ranks of the local branch. Another consequence of this deep suspicion towards local politics by the JDP elite was the party's cautious approach to the local political elite and power holders inside and outside the party.

In Chapter 8, I framed the JDP's agency, and particularly its manoeuvres at the elite level, against a historical backdrop. I have argued that the strategic and organizational orientation of the JDP leadership were the product of the authoritarian legacy of Turkish politics, which had already inflicted a deep distrust among powerful collective political actors of Turkey. This authoritarian legacy (or the electoral democracy of Turkey since the transition to multi-party politics), which made Turkish politics a 'state of nature' for collective political actors, prepared the ground for the unprecedented pragmatism and opportunism that characterized the JDP leadership. Riding on various fluid and, to a certain extent, mutually exclusive elite alliances from the beginning of the 2000s, the JDP got rid of other collective – and individual – power contenders within the Turkish political system at the expense of an intolerable increase in tensions among elite groups.

Accompanying these manoeuvres, the JDP has driven the already authoritarian system of Turkey – its electoral democracy – in a rather more authoritarian direction, in other words into competitive authoritarianism. When the bloody coup in 2016 failed as a result of the party's mass mobilization, the JDP was the only political actor that was capable of taking advantage of this unexpected political and institutional crisis in terms of its strategic and organizational orientation. After the coup, the process of the long, initially post-Islamist, and then populist, *reforma* in Turkey that gradually replaced secularist elites with a bloc of conservative elites, turned into a *ruptura* through the declaration of a state of emergency just after the coup in 2016. The *de facto* rise of a competitive authoritarian regime in Turkey was complemented by the *de jure* change of Turkey's political system to presidentialism, where the populist Erdoğan accumulated unprecedented powers through the constitutional referendum in 2017.

Some Methodological and Theoretical Implications

These findings of my research primarily enlarged our empirical knowledge of the JDP's organization and Turkish party politics in general, but they also have the potential to contribute to the larger literature on party organizations, in particular those on party typologies, intra-party governance, party leadership, candidate selection processes and the relationship between these organizational traits and authoritarian predominance.

What Is Party Agency? A Critical Approach to Loosely Used Concepts

Focusing on the role of agency in the electoral success and political resilience of the JDP also required very careful handling of a couple of interrelated concepts regarding the analysis of Turkish politics. These are populism, personalism and charisma. Various loose uses of these concepts lead many researchers either to simply underline the role of Erdoğan's image and his direct appeal to the electorate or to highlight the redistributive methods used by the party as the basis of the JDP's popular durability. When, on the one hand, populism was understood as referring to redistributive mechanisms or discourse and, on the other hand, charisma and personalism were understood as signifying a popular image of a national leader, a very narrow understanding of party agency automatically prevailed in the literature.

One of the main contentions in this book when arguing that 'agency matters' is that the electoral success of the JDP was not simply an outcome of the image of a popular leader and redistributive mechanisms, as many studies on the party using concepts of populism, personalism and charisma implied. Behind the electoral success and political resilience of the JDP there was a much more complicated, agency-based dynamic: not simply the image of the party leader and redistributive mechanisms, but a specific mode of interaction between the leader and various diverse elements of a broader organization as well as organizational links between the party and electorate.

In addition to the fieldwork, careful theoretical considerations on concepts of populism, personalism and charisma were essential for understanding this specific mode of agency. Hence, in this book, in line with Ostiguy (2017) I avoided seeing populism as a set of redistributive tactics, as a (thin) ideology/discourse (as mere words), or as an (organizational) strategy, and I proposed instead to understand it as a political appeal/style emotionally connecting the JDP with the popular sectors (the low-income, conservative, peripheral and provincial majority) of Turkish society. In the case of charisma, too, by remaining loyal to Weber's original usage, I proposed to embrace a very cautious approach to the concept, which particularly focuses on the transformational impact of the leadership. In the usage of the concept of personalism, I again tried to define a specific dynamic with the concept that surpasses the centrality of the leader's image and focuses on his/her organizational role. The discussions of these concepts might be helpful in the future, too, in the analyses of actors in Turkish politics other than the JDP.

Moving Beyond the Secular–Religious Polarization Perspective

This cautious approach to commonly used concepts in the literature on Turkish politics in this book was also complemented by a similarly cautious evaluation of the paradigmatic centre–periphery approach to Turkish politics. Thus, another implication of the research was that the centre–periphery or the secular–religious divide, which formulates the struggle between Islamists and so-called secularist establishment elites as an antagonism, could be misleading for the analysis of the political opportunity structures available to the Islamists and post-Islamists across the Muslim world. After all, the rise of Islamism – and then post-Islamism – in Turkey benefited greatly from the conservative and nationalistic views of the so-called secularist establishment elite of the country.

A secular–religious divide does not help a full understanding of political appeals in Turkey, either. In this book, it has been made clear that the JDP's political appeal had something to do with the 'populist emphasis' (Worsley, 1969) of Turkish politics, and the secular–religious divide was only a single element of this wider 'populist script' (Ostiguy, 2017) deployed by the JDP. Hence, the findings in this book might have also implications regarding the study of politics of other Muslim countries. Approaching these contexts either primarily or solely through the 'secular–religious polarization perspective', as Turam (2012) terms it, could lead scholars to ignore vital elements of political divisions such as the manifestation of socio-cultural inequalities.

Another problem with the centre–periphery narrative was that it also led many analysts to outdated perceptions of Turkish politics in which the 'induced participation' of the 'peripheral' and conservative majority of the country through powerful local and traditional elites was central. The examination of the case of the JDP (particularly in Chapter 5) presented some evidence about the fact that, at least since the 1980s, the central role of local-provincial power holders and 'classical patronage networks' deteriorated as a result of socio-economic changes in Turkey. This classical patronage politics (and rural poverty as the basis of it) was replaced, to a large extent, by new, more centralized forms of clientelism (with urban poverty in the background), which gave rise to the unprecedented electoral success of the JDP. Understanding these new circumstances requires researchers to think outside the box of the 'basics of Turkish party politics' and move beyond the centre–periphery narrative.

A Critical Engagement with the Literature on Party Typologies

In this book I also critically reinterpreted some of the concepts derived from the party politics literature. In contrast to the party decline literature, which argued that the mass party died out many years ago, this research has revealed the fact that various features of the mass-based party models, such as hierarchical, permanent and massive membership organizations, are still alive and can produce electoral success in combination with other contemporary electoral techniques. In other words, instead of pushing the empirical reality to fit into already existing ideal types and theoretically rigid categories, it is much more fruitful to focus on the interaction within organizations and hybrid forms in the analyses of party organizations outside Western liberal democracies.

The Importance of Focusing on Intra-Party Organizational Dynamics

In this book, I have primarily pointed out the importance of looking at the internal organizational dynamics of parties in power in order to understand the contribution of their organization to their electoral resilience as well as to the larger hegemonic impact of a political movement on society in general. The literature on the JDP's hegemony (its cross-class political and electoral coalition) usually assumed the JDP to be an already unified political actor and a simple reflection of the social forces behind it, such as the Islamic bourgeoisie or the low-income and conservative segments of society.

One of the theoretical implications of this research in line with a recent study (Massicard and Watts, 2013) is that political parties should not be seen as unified actors exerting hegemony over society or as unified mediums used by dominant sectors for producing consent. On the contrary, various chapters in this book have shown that consent was produced primarily within the organization by incorporating subordinated and dominant segments through organizational techniques. The production of consent, in other words, requires a great amount of party organizational effort on the part of the elites or dominant sectors.

From a methodological point of view, understanding party organizations as complex power relationships also indicates the necessity of looking at intra-party political dynamics and informal interactions among various components of parties beyond formal organizational features. Apart from the nexus between the party and the electorate, researchers should also take formal, informal and practical intra-party organizational dynamics into consideration if they want to properly understand the contribution of organizations to the electoral success and political resilience of parties.

This point also has implications for studies on competitive authoritarian regimes. In the absence of exceptional symbolic and economic resources at the disposal of authoritarian regimes, and without the construction of a more or less coherent, well-functioning party machinery, it is very difficult to create and sustain a competitive authoritarian regime. Hence, studies on authoritarianism should also go beyond the analysis of (clientelistic) linkages between hegemonic parties and their electorates (Magaloni, 2006) and the relationships between dominant parties and their contenders (Greene, 2007), and instead delve more deeply into the intra-party operations of ruling hegemonic parties – particularly the relationships between elite and grass-roots levels within these parties (Somer and Baykan, 2018). In other words, apart from economic and repressive tactics, hegemonic parties that rise within contexts similar to the one that characterized the JDP's rise certainly need a skilful, labour-intensive agency in order to construct the necessary organizational leverage and keep these organizations unified and well-functioning.

Synthesizing the Lessons from the Case of Erdoğan's JDP: Islamist Parties, Populism and Authoritarianism

From Islamism to Populism

From a much broader theoretical perspective, this book has highlighted the importance of taking party agency seriously (political appeal, leadership, party strategy, intra-party organizational dynamics – such as control over the party grass roots – and elite recruitment processes as well as strategic manoeuvres at the elite level) in explaining electorally successful 'normalization' of Islamist parties and, therefore, the rise of the post-Islamist party and one of the routes that this post-Islamist transformation can lead to.

The rise of Islamist parties, and later post-Islamist parties, emerges in relatively permissive political contexts. These contexts could be 'electoral democracies' or 'competitive authoritarianisms', but even in full-scale authoritarian regimes establishment elites have allowed (or turned a blind eye to) the formation and grass-roots organization of various Islamist actors.[1] One of the main characteristics of political conflict in these contexts is the presence of powerful non-party political actors, such as armies, monarchies, excessively strong presidents, self-proclaimed dynasties and restrictive state institutions including high judicial and bureaucratic authorities. Furthermore, due to uneven socio-economic development in these contexts, large sectors of society cannot enjoy some of the basic comforts of voters in Western liberal democracies such as generous welfare regimes and access to mass communications channels, most notably the internet. Therefore, the peripheral, considerably poor and politically extremely salient rural and urban popular sectors are a decisive social force in these countries. Islamist parties need to respond organizationally and strategically to the above-mentioned external circumstances in order to achieve electorally successful normalization and to pave the way for the creation of post-Islamist parties.

In addition, the major organizational and strategic (or agency-based) problems encountered in the process of Islamist party normalization are pluralization within the party organization (both in the central leadership groups and in local-provincial branches) and the problem of a 'dual constituency' (Mecham and Hwang, 2014b): in other words, the fragmentation of the formerly homogeneous leadership, membership structure and electoral base of the Islamist party due to its enlargement after normalization. In the socio-economic context in which Islamist parties emerged, this problem was exacerbated by another one: the socio-economic diversity of the post-Islamist party's electorate, which includes low-income and peripheral segments of society with relatively better-off middle-class median voters at the same time. If the post-Islamist party is going to remain unified and reach these diverging

---

[1] For this dynamic, see various country studies in the volume by Bayat (2013b). In this volume, it is made clear by various authors that many authoritarian and hybrid regimes permitted the formation and grass-roots work of various Islamist groups, either in order to increase the regime's legitimacy or in order to keep dissident Islamists under surveillance through legal incorporation. See also the studies on 'upgraded authoritarianisms' in the Middle East by Heydemann (2007) and 'liberalized autocracies' by Brumberg (2002) for repertoires of various authoritarian regimes for absorbing dissent.

segments of its electorate, its leadership should strike a balance between elite-based and mass-based party models, selective and collective incentives, careerist and idealistic party cadres, and capital-intensive and labour-intensive campaign techniques. At this point, the post-Islamist leadership encounter a specific problem regarding the rights- and liberties-based post-Islamist discourse and identity, which would appeal only to the reformist Islamist intelligentsia and upper- and middle-class median voters. This would be a very restrictive discursive framework for the post-Islamist party elite in striking a balance between components of the party elite and the membership, between the two segments of its dual constituency, and between elite-based and mass-based approaches.

The case of the JDP revealed that one way to overcome these problems is 'the personalistic mass party', or more precisely an organizational-strategic model combining highly autonomous leadership with a tightly controlled, large membership organization, active year-round, supported by a strong partisan media and political marketing techniques. In the case of the JDP, this organization also adopted a 'low-populist' appeal which could articulate diverging segments of the dual constituency of the party and which could, most notably, incorporate popular sectors.[2] If the post-Islamist party returns to an Islamist discourse in order to consolidate support among radical-leaning grass roots and fails to appeal median voters, it will cost the party the strong electoral support that could provide it with electoral legitimacy against pressure from the establishment elite. And, if the post-Islamist party insists on the rights- and liberties-based discourse of post-Islamism and fails to appeal to the popular sectors, this would cost the post-Islamist party the electoral support of popular sectors and organizational capacity to resist the inter-ventions of powerful non-party actors through non-violent mobilizational techniques. To appeal to these diverging segments within the post-Islamist party and its electoral base at the same time requires a very specific organizational and discursive strategy elaborated upon in detail in this book: the combination of a 'low-populist appeal' with the 'personalistic mass party'.

The main contradiction in this process, however, is this: in order to remain in power as a unified political actor and survive, the normaliza-tion of the Islamist party should become deeper – it should increasingly

[2] See also Schwedler (2006: 195–196) for how, in terms of 'moderation', the better-organized Islamist Action Front (the party of the Muslim Brotherhood) in Jordan was much more successful than the loosely organized Islah Party in Yemen, which relied on a fragmented coalition of various Islamist and tribal groups.

adapt itself to the 'rules' of contexts that are already democratically deficient, and it should abandon the rights- and liberties-based post-Islamist discourse together with a decisively Islamist one. As a result, the rights- and liberties-based post-Islamist identity declines and the majoritarian kernel of Islamism fully unfolds in the form of a 'low-populist' appeal and personalism with conservative, nativistic and nationalistic repercussions.[3] The growth of this populist core, to a great extent, destroys the Islamist and post-Islamist shells or reduces them to residual, sporadic and peripheral elements of the discourse and appeal of the successfully normalized Islamist party.

As the case of the JDP reveals, a successfully normalized post-Islamist party starts to exploit the political, legal and institutional framework created by the strategy of selective pluralism and eventually ceases to be post-Islamist. In other words, as a populist and personalistic mass party, the successful post-Islamist party starts to take advantage of the already existing restrictive political, institutional framework – or the weakness of the liberal democratic architecture in the political context in which they emerged – and becomes highly averse to further democratization, either of the environment in which it sits or of its own structures. In addition, the robust organizational leverages inherited by the successful post-Islamist party from its Islamist past, together with the advantages of being in power, create a fundamentally asymmetric electoral competition for its opponents and increase frustrations and hostilities in the political system. Hence, successful normalization of an Islamist party in a democratically deficient context, to say the least, does not create highly propitious conditions for further democratization.

In fact, the instruments and strategies (in the case of the JDP, the personalistic mass party and populism) for successful normalization in a democratically deficient context (in Turkey's case, an electoral democracy) pave the way for a deep power asymmetry between the predominant (initially post-Islamist) populist party and the opposition. This creates convenient conditions for the further deterioration of the already democratically deficient context. The specific combination of populism, personalism and the mass membership organization was the basis for this asymmetry in Turkey.

---

[3] Here it is tempting to argue that if the Freedom and Justice Party (the party of the Muslim Brotherhood) in Egypt had embraced a pro-democracy populist appeal and sustained the support of secular sectors alongside its core Islamist constituency, the prospects for Abdel Fattah el-Sisi's coup would have been remarkably different. For information on the Freedom and Justice Party and the Muslim Brotherhood, see Hamid (2014).

Towards a 'Hegemonic Party': Populism, Personalism, Organization

The transformation of Islamism in Turkey, first to post-Islamism, and then to populism combined with a 'personalistic mass party', also has implications for the literature on populism. One of the main theoretical implications of the case of the JDP, therefore, is the fact that populism can be found with or without solid organizational structures. In other words, in contrast to the emphasis of Weyland (2001: 14), the JDP illustrates that populism can coexist with a strong organization unless the concept of populism is reduced to rapidly rising and declining, maverick, personalistic leaderships that depend on the extensive use of media and patronage. The case of the JDP illustrates that populism can even coexist with very hierarchical and routinized organizations. Unlike some of the Latin American populisms, particularly that of Peronism (Levitsky, 2003) and Chavismo (Hawkins, 2010), which had a massive grass roots but which lacked strong, routinized, hierarchical connections with those grass roots, populism was shown to be able to coexist with highly hierarchical and routinized organizations, including a massive grass roots. Hence, the case of the JDP supports a recent clarification in the literature on populism that organizational traits should not be included in the definition of populism (Ostiguy, 2017; Albertazzi and McDonnell, 2015). If researchers take populism to be a style or political appeal in line with the framework proposed by Ostiguy, it would be much easier to detach the phenomenon from organizational characteristics.

The populist aspect of the JDP also illustrates the fact that without any systematic appeal to populism as an ideology in the party programme and policies, such as anti-immigration and anti-minority regulations, a party could still be decisively populist in style. For this reason, it would be quite hard to capture this dimension of JDP politics through the use of the conceptual approaches offered by Mudde (2004), Hawkins (2010) and Albertazzi and McDonnell (2015), which take populism as a 'thin ideology' or 'world-view' reflected in party programmes, speeches and the party discourse and policies in general.

The case of the JDP also demonstrates the fact that populism does not necessarily need to include patronage or clientelism. This point has been already underlined by a series of works on 'neo-liberal populism' which emphasized the surprising coexistence of neo-liberal policies with populist leaderships in Latin America and Turkey (Bozkurt 2013; Roberts, 1995; Weyland, 1999, 2001, 2003). The JDP's controlled approach to redistributive policies since the very beginning of the party's rule has proved the validity of the previous statements regarding the relationship between populism and patronage. Thus, it is not surprising to come across cases of populism in which parties have a very cautious approach to full-scale redistributive strategies (or 'classical patronage', as it is termed in this book).

This situation also points to the fact that populist parties can pursue prudent technocratic policies when in power. In line with the findings of the recent study by Albertazzi and McDonnell (2015), populists in power can be quite responsive while also being responsible in government. The case of the JDP is just another example of this situation, which defies the intuitive arguments that populists in power are destined to fail. Here again, understanding populism as a style/appeal and detaching it from organizational and ideological traits help researchers avoid seeing populism as identical to administrative irresponsibility. Hence, the expectation that negative incumbency effects would have deeper impacts in cases of populism should be questioned since populists in power can rule quite responsibly, or, at least, they can be quite successful at creating the image in the eyes of the electorate that they can rule responsibly and effectively. For this reason the contention that populism is an 'episodic' (Taggart, 2000: 1) phenomenon should be interrogated, too.

This point also sheds considerable light on another relevant puzzle. Why do some contemporary populist parties try to build solid organizational networks with massive grass roots when their leader has such an enormous impact on their policies and electoral achievements? One of the main answers to this question is that, apart from providing legitimacy to the leader, a solid organizational network reduces the potential negative impacts of incumbency and also equips populists with a robust mobilizational resource to defend against powerful elite contenders within the party system (particularly if this system is democratically deficient). A tightly controlled, solid, routinized and hierarchical mass membership organization that deploys political marketing techniques is vital for populists in power to persuade the party's low-income supporters of the necessity of technocratic measures and to absorb potential dissent against any political prudence required by the government. In addition to bringing very concrete electoral advantages, a solid organization is a *sine qua non* if the populist party wants to remain in power for a long time.

Yet, one should also consider the puzzle the other way around. Why would political entrepreneurs need a populist political appeal/style when they also have a massive grass roots that is encapsulated with a highly routinized and hierarchical organizational structure? At least from the perspective of the JDP, the answer is obvious: without the 'low-populist' political appeal/style it would have been extremely difficult to construct this massive organization and penetrate into the low-income, peripheral and provincial, conservative households of Turkey. Hence, a 'low-populist' appeal is much more compatible with a personalistic mass party like the JDP. Without the populist appeal, even controlled redistributive strategies would fail, for when political actors take the emotional advantages of a populist political appeal/style and avoid being seen as 'patrons', then patronage and/or distributing food or coal in exchange for votes become a very effective electoral strategy.

The case of the JDP also sheds some light on the relationship between the concepts of populism and personalism. The importance of the leader in the majority of the populist parties has also made most of these parties personalistic organizations in which the party leader has great authority within the organization and becomes the symbol of the populist party. In the case of Erdoğan, in other words, in the case of non-charismatic personalism, there is a very heavy emphasis on a robust organizational network, and the personalist leader's political existence was deeply embedded in the organization and his contact with various hierarchies of it. In these cases, the party leader appears, first and foremost, as a diligent and cunning organization man (*teşkilatçı*). In the case of the personal party, however, the leader has no concern in building a massive organization, and in fact he or she avoids this kind of grass-roots organization in order to protect the leadership's autonomy (McDonnell, 2013: 224).

In contrast, in the case of the JDP, I have revealed an obsessive attention to constructing a hybrid organization which blended the mass party with some of the traits of elite-based party models such as the use of media and of political marketing techniques. Hence, it was not at all surprising that the JDP leader Erdoğan has always been a talented organization man on the one hand and a very telegenic politician on the other. However, following Ostiguy (2017), I see personalism as a fundamental aspect of populism since populist audiences are, by definition, inclined to respond well to the personal embodiment of power. On the other hand, this does not mean that personalism is always populist, and there could be forms and instances of personalistic leadership lacking a populist appeal/style.

Populism and Competitive Authoritarianism

As I have illustrated throughout this book, the phenomenon of populism and the linkage structures between populist parties and masses are much more complicated, and most of the time are a combination of selective and collective incentives, clientelistic exchanges and proximity to people, patronage, and a robust organizational presence of the populist party.

The works that focus only on the redistributive strategies of the party or repressive measures give us only a partial story regarding the rise of competitive authoritarianism in Turkey under the rule of a populist party. In fact, the case of the JDP has illustrated that the generation of consent through discursive, stylistic and organizational techniques was key in compensating for the lack of symbolic and economic resources that other ruling parties in authoritarian or semi-authoritarian systems enjoyed. Hence, the literature focusing on the 'coercive' – either direct, physical coercion or economic coercion[4] – aspect of the JDP would, for instance, fall short of providing a means of understanding why people sacrificed themselves for the government on 15 July 2016.

Despite this, it is hardly possible to ignore the relevance of some of the 'high' critiques regarding the JDP's predominance in Turkey. As elaborated upon in Chapter 8, the past several years of JDP rule have witnessed a concrete erosion of the rule of law, the independence of the judiciary,[5] and basic rights and liberties in Turkey.[6] Not only has domestic pro-democracy criticism against the party by the opposition started to be labelled treason against the country, but also the international critiques regarding the negative situation of rights and liberties have been usually rejected by the JDP elite as part of an international conspiracy against the expression of the popular national will in Turkey.

Therefore, apart from the contradictions regarding the normalization outlined above, the other major contradiction revealed by the case of JDP

[4] For example, the 'punishment regimes' underlined by Magaloni (2006).
[5] One of the JDP members admitted that in Turkey there is no such thing as judicial independence. See T24 (2015).
[6] According to a Freedom House report in 2015, Turkey has been considered partly free (Freedom House, 2015: 3). In a Human Rights Watch report in 2015, it was indicated that Turkey had many problems regarding judicial independence and freedom of expression (HRW, 2015). According to the World Press Freedom Index in 2015, Turkey is ranked 149th of 180 countries, doing slightly better than the Russian Federation. See https://rsf.org/en/ranking/2015 (accessed: 13 November 2015). According to the Economist Intelligence Unit, Turkey was ranked 98th in the world, and the country has been considered a 'hybrid regime' rather than a 'flawed democracy' (Economist Intelligence Unit, 2015: 32), as stated by the previous version of the report regarding the state of democracy in Turkey. According to the Corruption Perceptions Index of Transparency International (2015), Turkey's situation is not bright, either. According to UN Development Programme's Human Development Report 2014, Turkey was ranked behind Venezuela and Costa Rica and just above Kazakhstan (UNDP, 2014: 161). According to OECD data, too, Turkey's mediocre performance does not change. OECD data on Turkish students' performance in mathematics in 2012 shows that the country is better than only a few OECD countries such as Indonesia, Brazil, Mexico and Chile, and is behind most OECD countries. See https://data.oecd.org/turkey.htm (accessed: 28 November 2015). The critics pointing out Turkey's mediocre performance in these international indexes has been usually ignored by the JDP elite and the pro-JDP media as simply a distortion of Turkey's image by international forces.

pertains to the relationship between populism and democracy. Although populism is not necessarily an anti-democratic force, the personalistic element of the phenomenon or, from a broader perspective, its 'immediacy' and 'anti-institutional' nature that is hostile to liberal checks and balances is in full contradistinction to party predominance in liberal democratic settings. The predominance of the populist party is achieved at the cost of the corrosion of liberal democratic institutional architecture. The case of the JDP (and perhaps the case of Venezuela, too) has illustrated that populist predominance is destined to be achieved at the cost of denying the minimum conditions of an electoral democracy – alternation in power – by creating deeply unfair conditions for opposition parties in elections through the use of government power and extensive and unfair control over the media. Hence, it is highly likely that populist predominance comes at the cost of gradual growth of authoritarianism. As repeatedly argued throughout this book, the robust organizational leverage constructed and controlled by the JDP organization had a central role in this 'political success'.

In the democratically deficient context of Turkey – a context characterized by the influence of selective pluralism and the weakness of liberal democratic institutions – promises of post-Islamism were forgotten quickly and easily and, unlike liberal democratic Western settings (Mudde and Kaltwasser, 2012), populism had no corrective influence over the deficiencies of democracy. On the contrary, populist political actors can start to damage the already fragile institutional balance of electoral democracy through the mobilization asymmetry[7] that stems from the robust organizational leverages and political stylistic skills of populists in mobilizing and organizing numbers for electoral victory. Hence, although it seems straightforward to remedy this by recommending the consolidation of democratic institutions to overcome democratic reversals in those countries under the influence of populist predominance, at the same time it is unrealistic to expect that the very same populist actors – who have become in Turkey a hegemonic party – would strengthen liberal democratic institutions, the weakness of which worked to their benefit.

A much more realistic remedy for creating checks and balances over the populist predominance in the short term, and for inhibiting further democratic reversals in those countries, includes a much stronger and unified opposition, various coalitions of pro-democracy forces, collaboration at the grass-roots level among opposition parties, and, most

---

[7] For the concept of 'mobilization symmetry', see Angrist (2004) and Mufti (2015).

importantly, a political stylistic strategy that aims to break the monopoly of the populist predominance at the low end of the high–low divide in the country.[8] While populist predominance and its authoritarian implications pave the way to frustration and dissent among large sectors of society, this proposition should be seen as a remedy for channelling the political energy of anti-populist sectors from non-democratic strategies (such as favouring non-electoral and institutional interventions by anti-populist elite groups in the form of coups,[9] memorandums, politicized legal cases and supporting forms of political activism with violence) towards electoral politics. For this reason a strong and unified opposition in electoral politics is not only necessary for reconsolidating democracy (or an authoritarian reversal) under the conditions of populist predominance, but it is also the most logical route to follow for the ruling populist party too since, without democratic pressure, the populist party is strongly inclined to fall into the trap of authoritarian-majoritarian politics, which is corrosive to long-term political and economic stability. It is only this stalemate in strength between populists and the opposition that can create opportunities for a negotiation of the construction of genuinely liberal democratic institutions.

Hypotheses for Future Research

Theoretical implications of the case of the JDP regarding the party's populism have shown the necessity of looking at populists as perennial political actors. In a recent study, this potential of populism has already been demonstrated by Albertazzi and McDonnell (2015), according to whom populism is not necessarily an 'episodic' phenomenon and populist parties are not destined to fail in government (2015: 3). The case of the JDP discussed throughout this book has consolidated this recent statement on populists. Yet this particular case, at the moment of writing, represents something more than a mere case of populism that was not episodic and that did not fail in government.

---

[8] One of the obvious difficulties for the opposition parties in Turkey in pursuing this kind of strategy is the political violence that still poisons the country. Armed conflict between PKK militants and security forces has, for years, destroyed coalition potential against conservative and nationalist populist hegemony in Turkey and caused a mobilization asymmetry. As armed conflict has continued in Turkey, many Turkish people have remained indifferent towards the democratic demands of Kurdish people and distanced themselves from secular-left movements led by Kurds.

[9] One of the most frequently adopted strategies against predominant populist actors across the world is a military coup backed by the middle and upper classes.

The case of the JDP, in fact, is a case of 'populist predominance' that has driven Turkey from an electoral parliamentary democracy to competitive presidential authoritarianism.[10] This case, therefore, can be considered a pioneering example that illustrated the dynamics of populist predominance and some of its costs and consequences. This book, then, has in a sense focused on the dynamics of the rise and electoral consolidation of a 'populist hegemonic party'. Some initial hypotheses of this book for future research on other cases of 'populist predominance' could be as follows: the deeper the democratic deficiency of a country, the stronger the organization of populists will be. The stronger the grassroots organization and the tighter the control over this organization, the more resilient the populist party will be. The tighter the grip over the media, in combination with this tightly controlled grass-roots organization, the more likely populist predominance will be. It is highly likely that, despite the initial democratizing impact, the extended rule of populists will drive electoral democracies to competitive authoritarianism. These hypotheses must be tested properly and systematically with other cases of populist predominance or long-term populist rule as well as similar hegemonic parties in other parts of the world. Peronism in Argentina and Chavismo in Venezuela, as well as the Party of Institutional Revolution in Mexico, could be considered to be potential comparative cases in this regard.

Not wholly independent from the first potential research agenda, the case of the JDP and the contribution of its specific organizational model to the party's electoral success and political resilience could be framed from a comparative perspective that focuses on the relationships between populism, personalism and mass membership organizations. It seems very promising to evaluate the case of the JDP from the perspective of a systematic comparison that focuses on rapidly rising and falling personal and populist parties in Europe and Latin America, such as the parties of Berlusconi and Fujimori, as well as organizationally more rigorous and historically more resilient entities such as the Peronist Justicialist Party (Partido Justicialista) in Argentina and Maduro's United Socialist Party of Venezuela (Partido Socialista Unido de Venezuela).

---

[10] In this regard, I am inclined to differentiate populist predominance from predominant parties in liberal democratic settings such as those in Canada, Sweden and Japan. While the electoral predominance of these parties in liberal democratic settings was reliant on producing consent, even among the opponents of the party, and on remaining bound to the liberal democratic institutions, populist predominance, as the case of the JDP illustrates, has relied on dividing society into hostile camps and on the denial of the institutional framework of the liberal democratic setting, except for 'free elections'.

This kind of comparative research could shed light on the dynamics of the relationship between party institutionalization and personalistic leadership. Under which kind of political and social circumstances do personalistic leaderships prefer more rigorous and stable organizational leverages that could be potentially institutionalized? What kind of social, economic and political conditions are conducive to creating, on the one hand, erratic personal parties and, on the other hand, much more entrenched organizational structures such as the JDP that lead their political systems to competitive authoritarianism? Future comparative research that focuses on these kinds of questions can contribute remarkably to improving our understanding of the relationship between populism, personalism, party organizations and democratization.

Appendix 1 Political Parties in Turkey

Republican People's Party (1923–present)

The Republican People's Party was established by the founder of the Turkish Republic, Mustafa Kemal Atatürk, and his supporters just after the victory in the National Independence War. The party ruled in a one-party state between 1923 and 1945 and it was, to a large extent, incorporated into state institutions. The party has always been seen as the representative of the secularist establishment elite of the country. Among its various principles, secularism later became the party's hallmark in its struggles against a series of conservative and populist parties ranging from the Democrat Party of the 1950s to the JDP of present-day Turkey. Except for a brief period during the 1970s, the party's continuous attempts to become a genuinely left-wing populist party failed. Organizationally, the Republican People's Party was not different from other Turkish parties in terms of its leadership's domination over provincial politics. But its grass-roots organizations have been usually much weaker and less active than those of the JDP (and its right-wing predecessors), the size of its membership has been much smaller and its intra-party communications were irregular. For further information, see Ayata (2002), Karpat (1991) and Turan (2006).

Democrat Party (1946–1961)

The Democrat Party was founded by a small group of dissident Republican People's Party members. Initially the Democrat Party attempted to take a more liberal political and economic position than the Republican People's Party. However, immediately after its foundation, the party started to represent the victims of the secular nation-building process initiated by the Kemalist Republican People's Party and became the first in a series of populist and conservative centre-right parties including its followers, the Justice Party of Demirel, the Motherland Party of Özal, the True Path Party of Demirel and, finally, the JDP of Erdoğan. When the party was at the peak of its strength, its majoritarian inclinations started to make Kemalist segments of society, and most notably the army, deeply uncomfortable. Overlapping this creeping authoritarianization was a deteriorating economy, which paved the way to a military coup and, hence, to the end of the Democrat Party. The Democrat Party was organizationally a remarkable force that could develop party branches even in the remotest provincial corners of the country. However, the influence of local bosses over the local-provincial branches of the party and local patronage was always central. For further information, see Demirel (2011), Eroğul (2003) and Sarıbay (1991).

Justice Party (1961–1981)

The Justice Party was founded just after the military coup in 1960 as the continuation of the Democrat Party. After its initial years the party chose Süleyman Demirel as its leader. Unlike the leadership of its predecessor Democrat Party, Demirel neither came from a provincial notable family nor from the traditionally predominant educational institutions of the Republic such as Mülkiye and Harbiye. The Justice Party was often in government throughout the period between two military coups in 1960 and 1980. The military junta after the 1980 coup closed down the parties, including the Justice Party, and banned their leaders. This ban on leaders was lifted with a referendum in 1987. The Justice Party also inherited the organizational effectiveness of the Democrat Party, and it was always more successful in poor, urban contexts of Turkey than the left-wing parties, with its robust grass-roots presence and through better incorporation of local elites. For further information, see Demirel (2004), Levi (1991) and Sherwood (1967).

Labour Party of Turkey (1961–1980)

The Labour Party of Turkey was founded by leftist intellectuals and representatives of trade unions under the conditions of the relatively pluralist political and legal environment of the post-coup period during the 1960s. The party was the first influential socialist organization of the country represented in the Grand National Assembly of Turkey. The chair of the party, Mehmet Ali Aybar, was a lawyer, and came from a notable İstanbul family. He advocated a more liberal form of socialism, which drew much criticism from hard-liners in his party and from the wider left-wing circles in the country. Despite its socialist discourse, the party's touch with low-income and provincial social segments of the country was remarkably weak. The party, organizationally, always suffered from factionalism on an ideological basis, and its grass-roots presence, despite its efforts in shantytowns of big cities, was not impressive. The party was banned twice, in 1971 and 1980. For further information, see Lipovsky (1991) and Ünsal (2002).

National Order Party (1970–1971) (Islamist National View tradition I)

The National Order Party was founded by Erbakan as the first representative of the Islamist National View tradition in Turkey. The party was supported by more religious, conservative and provincial small- and medium-sized business-owners of the country as a reaction to the uncomfortable situation created by the Justice Party's encouragement of foreign capital and trade. The party did not survive long and in 1972 faced the first in a series of interventions by the establishment elite that the Islamist National View parties would face throughout their long political journey. For further information, see Eligür (2010).

National Salvation Party (1972–1981) (Islamist National View tradition II)

The National Salvation Party was the second party of the Islamist National View tradition. The National Salvation Party managed to survive until the military coup in 1980. Under the rule of Erbakan, it achieved an influential position in the Grand National Assembly of Turkey as a king-maker and was part of various coalition governments throughout the 1970s. The party's founders came from notable provincial families, and it was supported by provincial small- and medium-sized business-owners in Turkey. The party was banned in 1980 by the military junta alongside other Turkish parties. Organizationally, until the rise of the Welfare Party in the mid 1990s, the National View parties were not effective entities. They mainly relied on isolated, religious, informal networks and lacked a vigorous grass-roots presence, particularly in low-income regions of urban centres. For further information, see Eligür (2010).

Nationalist Action Party (1969–present)

The Nationalist Action Party was founded by former colonel Alpaslan Türkeş towards the end of the 1970s. The party's political stance during the 1970s was one of authoritarian Turkish nationalism. The party found the opportunity to take part in a couple of conservative-nationalist coalition governments during the 1970s alongside the Justice Party and the National Salvation Party. Another mark the party left on Turkish politics was its engagement in political violence against leftist groups in the country. The party, despite the background of its leader in the Turkish military, received much sympathy from lower- and lower-middle-class urban and rural social sectors. The party was banned by the military junta after the coup in 1980 but reappeared several years later. After the death of its founding leader and under the new leadership of Devlet Bahçeli, the party carefully avoided street violence and embraced a softer nationalistic stance during the 1990s and 2000s. The leader has always been extremely powerful in the party as a result of the authoritarian nationalist ideology, and the party always had a remarkable grass-roots presence that relied mainly on its youth branch, the Grey Wolves (Ülkü Ocakları). For further information, see Landau (1982), A. Çınar and Arıkan (2002) and Bora and Can (2004).

Motherland Party (1983–present)

The Motherland Party was founded by Turgut Özal, a former bureaucrat, just after the military coup in 1980. The Motherland's electoral victory in this election against parties supported by the military regime was the least desired outcome by the military junta. The Motherland Party embraced a radical liberal economic programme including drastic international trade liberalization and privatization, and politically it claimed to contain four different tendencies: nationalism, conservatism, liberalism and social democracy. The party was supported by urban and upwardly mobile middle classes as well as low-income conservative social segments, at least during its initial years. It was seen as an attractive option for conservative and religious people since Özal was also a spontaneously religious man. The party started to lose momentum in the 1990s after a leadership change, and in the 2002 election it was *de facto* erased from Turkish political life. Organizationally, the party always suffered from intra-party factionalism. The grass-roots presence in localities for the party was not a priority and was considered merely a tool for preventing fraud on election days. For further information, see Ergüder (1991) and Kalaycıoğlu (2002).

Nationalist Democracy Party (1983–1986)

The Nationalist Democracy Party was one of the two parties that emerged after the coup in 1980 with the open encouragement of the military junta. The chair of the party was a retired general and ambassador, and it was expected to be the centre-right party submissive to the military regime. In the first election after the coup, the party received many fewer votes than expected and two years later dissolved itself. Some of its deputies joined the Motherland Party group, while some founded the True Path Party in the parliament. See Turan (1988).

Populist Party (1983–1985)

The Populist Party was the other party the military junta allowed to participate in the first 'free' elections in 1983 after the coup. At first, the party received a degree of support from former Republican People's Party supporters (the Republican People's Party was banned by the junta after the coup in 1980) and secured more votes than the Nationalist Democracy Party, which was explicitly supported by the junta and became the main opposition. Nevertheless, with the emergence of the Social Democracy Party as the true heir of the Republican People's Party, the Populist Party lost much of its support and merged with this party in 1985. See Turan (1988).

Social Democratic Populist Party (1985–1995)

The merger between the Populist Party and the Social Democracy Party, which was established by Erdal İnönü, created the Social Democratic Populist Party in 1985. The Social Democracy Populist Party attempted to locate itself in a modern social democratic position, and the party also took part in coalition governments in the first half of the 1990s. After the removal of the ban on the parties of the pre-coup period, the Republican People' s Party re-emerged, and some of the deputies of the Social Democratic Populist Party joined the Republican People's Party. These very similar parties coexisted in the parliament for a short period and merged in 1995. For further information, see Mango (1991).

True Path Party (1983–present)

After the removal of the ban on politicians of the pre-coup period, Demirel could participate in elections with the True Path Party that he founded in 1983. The True Path Party, under the leadership of Demirel, was seen as the direct heir to the Democrat Party and the Justice Party. The only difference this time was that the True Path Party had to share the votes of this political tradition with Özal's Motherland Party. The difference between these two centre-right parties was also related to the personal hostility between their second-generation leaders, Tansu Çiller of the True Path Party and Mesut Yılmaz from the Motherland Party. The True Path Party *de facto* disappeared from Turkish politics after its leader Süleyman Soylu joined the JDP in 2012. A vigorous local presence in provincial Turkey side by side with local patronage was a main organizational trait of the party. For further information, see Acar (1991) and Cizre (2002).

Democratic Left Party (1985–present)

The Democratic Left Party was founded in 1985 by the wife of Bülent Ecevit, the prominent leader of the Republican People's Party before the 1980 military coup. The party was slightly more nationalist than other left-wing parties of the era. The party's most successful period occurred in 1999 when it secured the biggest share of seats in the Grand National Assembly of Turkey and took part in a coalition government with the Nationalist Action Party and the Motherland Party. This coalition government was under pressure after its inability to cope with the devastating consequences of the İstanbul earthquake in 1999 and had to call for a snap election in 2002 after the economic crises in 2000 and 2001. The party *de facto* disappeared from Turkish political life after its vote share plummeted from 22 per cent in 1999 to 1 per cent in 2002. In organizational terms, the party was not more impressive than other left-wing parties, and the leadership was extremely cautious about expanding the party's membership organization. For further information, see Kınıklıoğlu (2002).

Welfare Party (1985–1998) (Islamist National View tradition III)

The Welfare Party, established in 1985, was the third and the most influential party of the Islamist National View tradition. After the removal on the ban on the political leaders in 1987, the founder of the National View tradition, Erbakan, returned to politics, and the Welfare Party, for the first time after the coup, reappeared in the parliament through an electoral coalition with the Nationalist Working Party (which would later become the Nationalist Action Party). The Welfare Party, through its redistributive promises that appealed to the urban and rural poor and through its robust organization, started to gain momentum in the middle of the 1990s and became the top vote-winner in the 1995 election. The coalition government formed by the Welfare Party and the

True Path Party came to an end when the military openly declared its reaction to the sensational public activities of the Welfare Party including pro-sharia speeches by prominent members. The party was closed down by the Constitutional Court in 1998 on the grounds of anti-secular activities. The party, with its attention to vigorous local presence in low-income settings, a membership organization that was active year-round, and Islamist indoctrination of these members, was the closest organization to the classical mass party model in the history of Turkish party politics. For further information, see White (2002), Eligür (2010) and Delibaş (2015).

Virtue Party (1998–2001) (Islamist National View tradition IV)

The Virtue Party was founded just before the ban on the Welfare Party and was used by former Welfare Party members. Although the Virtue Party was the direct continuation of the Islamist Welfare Party, the normalization of the Islamist movement in Turkey started with the Virtue Party. On issues such as the European Union, relations with the West, free market economics and secularism, the Virtue Party was noticeably more liberal than its predecessor. Nevertheless, this liberalization did not stop the Constitutional Court – and therefore the establishment elite of the country – and the party was closed down in 2001. The Virtue Party period of the Islamist National View tradition also witnessed intra-party factionalism between the 'traditionalist [gelenekçi] old guard and the younger 'reformist [yenilikçi]' wing, resulting in the foundation of two parties after the ban on the Virtue Party. One of these parties was Erdoğan's JDP and the other was the Felicity Party of the old guard under the influence of Erbakan. For further information, see Yeşilada (2002) and Eligür (2010).

Felicity Party (2001–present) (Islamist National View tradition V)

The Felicity Party was founded just before the JDP and it represented a return to mainstream Islamist politics by the old guard National View elite after the Virtue Party period. The party remained loyal to the Islamist National View tradition's founder Erbakan and his teachings and ideas. It did not gain any seats in the parliament after the 2002 elections. See S. Şen (2004).

Pro-Kurdish parties (1994–present)

Since the beginning of the 1990s, parties defending Kurdish rights appeared in the parliament through various methods (such as running as independents and being nominated from other parties' lists) despite the unusually high 10 per cent national threshold. These parties are the Peoples' Democracy Party, Democratic People's Party, Democratic Society Party, Peace and Democracy Party and, more recently, the Peoples' Democratic Party. All of these parties represented an ideology that was a blend of socialism and Kurdish nationalism. Pro-Kurdish parties in Turkey have been predominantly supported by the Kurds living in poor urban and rural Turkey and by certain segments of left-wing Turkish voters. However, the relationship between pro-Kurdish parties and the armed Kurdistan Workers' Party has been extremely problematic for the former since the armed Kurdistan Workers' Party has usually been the predominant part of this close relationship. Recently, the last chain of the tradition, the Peoples' Democratic Party, created an optimism among left-liberal circles of the country with its radical democracy programme and its strategy of becoming the party of Turkey (*Türkiyelileşme*), but this normalization was blocked after the Kurdistan Workers' Party engaged in armed struggle with the security forces following a two-year ceasefire. Organizationally, pro-Kurdish parties have always had an almost unchallenged vigorous local presence in south-east Turkey, and this has been complemented by its presence in low-income Kurdish-majority neighbourhoods of big cities such as İstanbul and Ankara. Pro-Kurdish parties also have always been highly capable of mobilizing their supporters for elections as well as for protest marches and mass rallies. Given the centrality of nationalist-socialist ideology for its members and supporters, and its overwhelming reliance on Kurdish ethnicity, pro-Kurdish parties have approximated the mass- based party model. For further information, see Watts (2010).

Young Party (2002–present although inactive)

The Young Party was founded by a business tycoon, Cem Uzan, just a couple of months prior to the 2002 election. As a genuinely personal party without any permanent membership organization, the Young Party solely relied on its leader's higly telegenic image, oratorical skills and the television channels and financial resources owned by him. The Young

Party unexpectedly received 7 per cent of the vote in the 2002 election simply by relying on its leader's image and several redistributive promises. The party disappeared from Turkish politics after corruption investigations targeting Uzan's companies and Uzan's flight to France. For further information, see Türk (2008).

	Far left (Kurdish nationalist since the 1980s)	Left	Centre-left	Centre-right	Right-Islamist	Far right (Turkish nationalist)
High 4			Republican People's Party I (1923–1945)			
High 3			Republican People's Party II (1945–1960)			
High 2		Labour Party of Turkey	**Republican People's Party IV** (1987–present)			
High 1			Democratic Left Party			
Low 1		Social Democratic Populist Party Republican People's Party III (1960–1980)		Democrat Party, Motherland Party, True Path Party, Justice Party	National Order Party, National Salvation Party, Felicity Party (Islamist National View I, II and V respectively)	**Nationalist Action Party II** (1983–present)
Low 2	Pro-Kurdish (I) parties of the 1990s and 2000s	**Pro-Kurdish (II) Peoples' Democratic Party**			Virtue Party (Islamist National View IV)	Nationalist Action Party I (1969–1980)
Low 3				**Justice and Development Party – Erdoğanism**	Welfare Party (Islamist National View III)	Young Party
Low 4						

Note: Currently active and major parties are indicated with bold characters. In this study I embrace a particular definition of populism that allows researchers to locate parties on a scale stretching from extremely anti-populist (or 'high') to extremely populist ('low'), a scale similar to that between the far left and the far right. In this table, 'High 4' indicates an extremely anti-populist stance and 'Low 4' an extremely populist one.

Bibliography

Interviews

Interviewee 1 (2013, 2 September). Personal interview with Felicity Party Central Executive Committee member.

Interviewee 2 (2013, 4 September). Personal interview with expert academic working on JDP.

Interviewee 3 (2013, 5 September). Personal interview with former JDP provincial chair.

Interviewee 4 (2013, 6 September). Personal interview with former JDP provincial chair.

Interviewee 5 (2014, 14 January). Personal interview with former JDP sub-provincial mayor in Konya.

Interviewee 6 (2014, 14 January). Personal interview with JDP sub-provincial chair in Konya.

Interviewee 7 (2014, 15 January). Personal interview with JDP sub-provincial vice-chair in Konya.

Interviewee 8 (2014, 15 January). Personal interview with JDP sub-provincial neighbourhood representative in Konya.

Interviewee 9 (2014, 17 January). Personal interview with JDP sub-provincial chair in Konya.

Interviewee 10 (2014, 18 January). Personal interview with JDP sub-provincial women's branch chair in Konya.

Interviewee 11 (2014, 22 January). Personal interview with JDP provincial vice-chair in İstanbul.

Interviewee 12 (2014, 6 February). Personal interview with former JDP provincial youth's branch chair and candidate deputy in İstanbul.

Interviewee 13 (2014, 7 February). Personal interview with former JDP sub-provincial vice-chair and candidate for mayoralty in İstanbul.

Interviewee 14 (2014, 10 February). Personal interview with JDP vice-minister and former JDP provincial chair and deputy.

Interviewee 15 (2014, 19 February). Personal interview with former JDP sub-provincial vice-chair and candidate for mayoralty in İstanbul.

Interviewee 16 (2014, 20 February). Personal interview with former JDP sub-provincial vice-chair and candidate for mayoralty in İstanbul.

Interviewee 17 (2014, 25 February). Personal Interview with former Motherland Party minister.

Interviewee 18 (2014, 26 February). Personal interview with JDP founder and former JDP provincial chair.
Interviewee 19 (2014, 26 February). Personal interview with bureaucrat and close observer of Islamist politics.
Interviewee 20 (2014, 26 February). Personal interview with bureaucrat and close observer of Islamist politics.
Interviewee 21 (2014, 28 February–4 March). Personal interviews with JDP founder and former JDP deputy.
Interviewee 22 (2014, 5 March). Personal interview with former Motherland Party minister.
Interviewee 23 (2014, 7 March). Personal interview with JDP founder and former JDP deputy.
Interviewee 24 (2014, 18 March). Personal interview with former JDP provincial chair.
Interviewee 25 (2014, 21 March). Personal interview with former JDP provincial chair.
Interviewee 26 (2014, 4 April). Personal interview with JDP sub-provincial chair in İstanbul.
Interviewee 27 (2014, 5 April). Personal interview with JDP sub-provincial neighbourhood representative in İstanbul.
Interviewee 28 (2014, 10 April). Personal interview with expert academic on centre-right in Turkey.
Interviewee 29 (2014, 16 April). Personal interview with JDP deputy.
Interviewee 30 (2014, 19 April). Personal Interview with JDP sub-provincial mayor in Trabzon.
Interviewee 31 (2014, 20 April). Personal interview with JDP sub-provincial youth's branch chair in Trabzon.
Interviewee 32 (2014, 20 April). Personal interview with JDP sub-provincial women's branch chair in Trabzon.
Interviewee 33 (2014, 21 April). Personal interview with JDP provincial vice-chair in İstanbul.
Interviewee 34 (2014, 22 April). Personal interview with JDP Central Executive Committee member.
Interviewee 35 (2014, 22 April). Personal interview with adviser to Party Chair Erdoğan.
Interviewee 36 (2014, 24 April). Personal interview with JDP Central Decision and Administration Board member.
Interviewee 37 (2014, 24 April). Personal interview with JDP Central Executive Committee member.
Interviewee 38 (2014, 25 April). Personal interview with research company director.
Interviewee 39 (2014, 2 May). Personal interview with expert journalist on JDP.
Interviewee 40 (2014, 2 May). Personal interview with JDP sub-provincial chair in Ankara.
Interviewee 41 (2014, 3 May). Personal interview with former JDP provincial vice-chair in Mardin.

Interviewee 42 (2014, 3 May). Personal interview with former vice-chair of JDP provincial youth branch in Mardin.

Interviewee 43 (2014, 3 May). Personal interview with JDP provincial chair.

Interviewee 44 (2014, 4 May). Personal interview with JDP provincial vice-chair in Batman.

Interviewee 45 (2014, 5 May). Personal interview with JDP provincial vice-chair in Mardin.

Interviewee 46 (2014, 6 May). Personal interview with JDP provincial vice-chair in Mardin.

Interviewee 47 (2014, 6 May). Personal interview with JDP sub-provincial chair in Mardin.

Interviewee 48 (2014, 6 May). Personal interview with JDP provincial vice-chair in Urfa.

Interviewee 49 (2014, 8 May). Personal interview with member of JDP women's branch at headquarters.

Primary and Secondary Sources

AA (2013). '"Milli İradeye Saygı" mitingleri başlıyor', 11 June 2013, www.aa.com .tr/tr/rss/192005–quot-milli-iradeye-saygi-quot-mitingleri-basliyor, accessed: 27 May 2016.

—— (2017). 'AK Parti'de 'metal yorgunluğu' bayrak değişimiyle aşılacak', 13 August 2017, http://aa.com.tr/tr/gunun-basliklari/ak-partide-metal-yor gunlugu-bayrak-degisimiyle-asilacak/883364, accessed: 28 December 2017.

Acar, F. (1991). 'The True Path Party: 1983–1989', in M. Heper and J. M. Landau (eds.), *Political Parties and Democracy in Turkey*, London: I. B. Tauris, pp. 188–201.

Açıkel, F. (2006). 'Entegratif toplum ve muarızları: 'merkez-çevre' paradigması üzerine eleştirel notlar'. *Toplum ve Bilim*, 105, 30–69.

Ahaber (2013). 'Şamil Tayyar: Gezi 5. Darbe provası', 13 June 2013, www.ahaber.com.tr/Gundem/2013/06/13/samil-tayyar-gezi-5-darbe-provasi, accessed: 20 July 2014.

—— (2017). 'Berat Albayrak Enerji ve Tabii Kaynaklar bakanı oldu', 24 November 2015, www.ahaber.com.tr/gundem/2015/11/24/berat-albayrak-enerji-ve-tabii-kaynaklar-bakani-oldu, accessed: 28 December 2017.

Ahıska, M. (2006). 'Hayal edilemeyen toplum: Türkiye'de "çevresiz merkez" ve garbiyatçılık'. *Toplum ve Bilim*, 105, 11–29.

Ahmad, F. (2003a). *The Making of Modern Turkey*. London: Routledge.

—— (2003b). *Turkey: Quest for Identity*. Oxford: One World Publications.

AK Parti (2004). 'Vatandaşın bilgi kapısı'. *Türkiye Bülteni*, 19: 55.

—— (2007). *22 Temmuz 2007 genel seçimleri milletvekili adayları seçim kılavuzu*. No Place.

—— (2011). 'AKBİS bilgilendirme toplantısı yapıldı', www.akpartiankara.org/ akbis-bilgilendirme-toplantisi-yapildi/, accessed: 16 June 2014.

—— (2012a). *AK Parti tüzüğü*. No place.

(2012b). 'By-law of the Justice and Development Party with Amendments Affected in 2012', www.akparti.org.tr/english/akparti/parti-tuzugu, accessed: 27 May 2016.

Akarlı, E. and G. Ben-Dor (eds.) (1975). *Political Participation in Turkey.* İstanbul: Boğaziçi University Publications.

Akdoğan, Y. (2004). *Ak Parti ve Muhafazakar Demokrasi.* İstanbul: Alfa.

(2013). 'Ellerinde nur mu var, topuz mu?', 24 December 2013, http://haber .stargazete.com/yazar/ellerinde-nur-mu-var-topuz-mu/yazi-820061, accessed: 20 July 2014.

(2014). 'Hesap günü', 4 February 2014, http://haber.stargazete.com/yazar/ hesap-gunu/yazi-838486, accessed: 20 July 2014.

(2017). *Lider: Siyasi Liderlik ve Erdoğan.* İstanbul: Turkuvaz Kitap.

Akgün, B. (2000). Türkiye'de siyasal güven: nedenleri ve sonuçları. *Ankara Üniversitesi SBF Dergisi,* 56 (4), 1–23.

(2007). *Türkiye'de Seçmen Davranışı, Partiler Sistemi ve Siyasal Güven.* Ankara: Nobel Yayın.

Akpartikepez (2013). '3 mahalle ziyaret edildi', www.akpartikepez.org.tr/index_ tr.asp?mn=7&in=589, accessed: 22 August 2015.

Aksiyon (2008). 'Dededen demokrat Soylu'nun bilinmeyen hikayesi', 14 January 2008, www.aksiyon.com.tr/aksiyon/newsDetail_openPrintPage.action? newsId=16314, accessed: 21 July 2014.

Aktifhaber (2009). 'Külünk AKP İstanbul İl Başkanı Adayı', 11 June 2009, www.aktifhaber.com/kulunk-akp-istanbul-il-baskani-adayi-226976h.htm, accessed: 27 May 2016.

(2012). 'İşte CHP'nin sattığı camiler!', 24 April 2012, www.aktifhaber.com/ iste-chpnin-sattigi-camiler-592280h.htm, accessed: 27 May 2016.

(2014). 'AKP'den başbakan'a yeni slogan', 28 January 2014, www .aktifhaber.com/akpden-basbakana-yeni-slogan-925624h.htm, accessed: 27 May 2016.

Albertazzi, D. and D. McDonnell (2015). *Populists in Power.* London: Routledge.

Almond, G. A. and S. J. Genco (1977). 'Clouds, Clocks, and the Study of Politics'. *World Politics,* 29 (4), 489–522.

And, M. (1977). *Dünyada ve Bizde Gölge Oyunu.* Ankara: İş Bankası Kültür Yayınları.

(2001). 'Karagöz', in B. Topaloğlu et al. (eds.), *İslam ansiklopedisi, cilt XXIV,* İstanbul: İsam, pp. 401–403.

Anderson, C. W. (1967). *Politics and Economic Change in Latin America.* Princeton: D. Van Nostrand Co.

Angrist, M. P. (2004). 'Party systems and regime formation in the modern Middle East: explaining Turkish exceptionalism'. *Comparative Politics,* 36 (2), 229–249.

Ansell, C. K. and M. S. Fish (1999). 'The Art of Being Indispensable: Non-Charismatic Personalism in Contemporary Political Parties'. *Comparative Political Studies,* 32 (3), 283–312.

Arditi, B. (2005). 'Populism as an Internal Periphery of Democratic Politics', in F. Panizza (ed.), *The Mirror of Democracy,* London and New York: Verso, pp. 72–98.

Arendt, H. (1969). *On Violence*. New York: HBJ.

Atacan, F. (2005). 'Explaining Religious Politics at the Crossroad: AKP–SP'. *Turkish Studies*, 6 (2), 187–199.

Atasoy, Y. (2009). *Islam's Marriage with Neo-Liberalism*. New York: Palgrave Macmillan.

Auyero, J. (2001). *Poor People's Politics*. Durham, NC, and London: Duke University Press.

Ayan Musil, P. (2011). *Authoritarian Party Structures and Democratic Political Setting in Turkey*. New York: Palgrave Macmillan.

—— (2015). 'Emergence of a Dominant Party System after Multipartyism: Theoretical Implications from the Case of the AKP in Turkey'. *South European Society and Politics*, 20 (1), 71–92.

Ayata, A. G. (2002). 'The Republican People's Party', in B. Rubin and M. Heper (eds.), *Political Parties in Turkey*, London: Frank Cass, pp. 102–121.

—— (2010). *CHP: örgüt ve ideoloji*. İstanbul: Gündoğan Yayınları.

Aydemir, Ş. S. (1981). *Tek Adam, Vols. I, II, III*. İstanbul: Remzi Kitabevi.

Aydın, E. and I. Dalmış (2008). 'The Social Bases of the Justice and Development Party', in U. Cizre (ed.), *Secular and Islamic Politics in Turkey: The Making of the Justice and Development Party*, London: Routledge, pp. 201–222.

Aydıntaşbaş, A. (2011). 'İşte %50'yi getiren 7 strateji' (interview with Ertan Aydın, chief adviser to Erdoğan), *Milliyet*, online interview, 14 June 2011, www.milliyet.com.tr/iste-50-yi-getiren-7   strateji/siyaset/siyasetyazardetay/14.06.2011/1402165/default.htm, accessed: 27 May 2016.

Aymes, M., B. Gourisse and E. Massicard (eds.) (2015). *Order and Compromise*. Leiden: Brill.

Aytaç, S. E. and Z. Öniş (2014). 'Varieties of Populism in a Changing Global Context: The Divergent Paths of Erdoğan and Kirchnerismo'. *Comparative Politics*, 47 (1), 41–59.

Bakırezer, G. and Y. Demirer (2009). 'AK Parti'nin sosyal siyaseti', in İ. Uzgel and B. Duru (eds.), *AKP Kitabı: Bir Dönüşümün Bilançosu*, Ankara: Phoenix Yayınevi, pp. 153–178.

Balmas, M., G. Rahat, T. Sheafer and S. R. Shenhav (2014). 'Two Routes to Personalized Politics: Centralized and Decentralized Personalization'. *Party Politics*, 20 (1), 37–51.

Baran, Z. (2000). 'Corruption: The Turkish Challenge'. *Journal of International Affairs*, 54 (1), 127–146.

Bartolini, S. (2000). *The Political Mobilization of the European Left, 1860–1980*. Cambridge: Cambridge University Press.

Bartolini, S. and P. Mair (1990). *Identity, Competition, and Electoral Availability: The Stability of European Electorates, 1885–1985*. Cambridge: Cambridge University Press.

Başlevent, C. (2013). 'Socio-Demographic Determinants of the Support for Turkey's Justice and Development Party'. *Economics Bulletin*, 33 (2), 1215–1228.

Başlevent, C., H. Kirmanoğlu and B. Şenatalar (2005). 'Empirical Investigation of Party Preferences and Economic Voting in Turkey'. *European Journal of Political Research*, 44 (4), 547–562.

Bayat, A. (1996). 'The Coming of a Post-Islamist Society'. *Critique: Critical Middle Eastern Studies*, 5 (9), 43–52.

(2007). *Making Islam Democratic: Social Movements and the Post-Islamist Turn.* Stanford: Stanford University Press.

(2013a). 'Post-Islamism at Large', in A. Bayat (ed.), *Post-Islamism: The Changing Faces of Political Islam*, Oxford: Oxford University Press, pp. 3–32.

Bayat, A. (ed.) (2013b). *Post-Islamism: The Changing Faces of Political Islam.* Oxford: Oxford University Press.

Baykan, T. S. (2014). 'Halkçılık and Popülizm: "Official-Rational" versus "Popular" in the context of "Turkish Exceptionalism"'. Sussex European Institute Working Paper No 137.

(2015a). 'Contradictions of Post-Islamism: Evidence from Turkey', LSE Middle East Centre Blog, http://blogs.lse.ac.uk/mec/2015/07/30/contradictions-of-post-islamism-evidence-from-turkey/, accessed: 24 December 2017.

(2015b). 'Türkiye siyasetinde iki anlayış: idare-i maslahatçılık ve otoriter iradecilik'. *Birikim*, 313, 76–93.

(2015c). 'The 2015 Turkish General Election: Mobilisational Symmetry and Another Major Victory for Democracy', EPERN Blog, https://epern.wordpress.com/2015/06/30/the-2015-turkish-general-election-mobilisational-symmetry-and-another-major-victory-for-democracy/, accessed: 25 December 2017.

(2017a) Review of Akdoğan's *Lider: Siyasi Liderlik ve Erdoğan (The Leader: Political Leadership and Erdoğan)*, *Turkish Studies*, 18 (4), 754–758

(2017b). 'Halkçılık ve popülizm: Türkiye vakası ve bir kavramın kullanımları'. *Mülkiye Dergisi*, 41(1), 157–194.

(2017c). '"May God protect us from the evil of the well-educated": The Failed Coup, Populism and the JDP Organization in Turkey'. Paper presented at the ECPR meeting in Oslo.

Bayraktar, U. and C. Altan (2013). 'Explaining Turkish Party Centralism', in E. Massicard, E. and N. F. Watts (eds.), *Negotiating Political Power in Turkey: Breaking Up the Party*. London: Routledge, pp. 17–36.

Bektaş, A. (1993). *Demokratikleşme Sürecinde Liderler Oligarşisi: CHP ve AP (1961–1980)*. İstanbul: Bağlam.

Belge, M. (2008). 'Türkiye'de sosyalizm tarihinin ana çizgileri', in M. Gültekingil (ed.), *Modern Türkiye'de Siyasi Düşünce, Cilt VIII, Sol*, İstanbul: İletişim, pp. 19–48.

Besli, H. and Ö. Özbay (2014). *Bir Liderin Doğuşu: Recep Tayyip Erdoğan.* İstanbul: Yeni Türkiye Yayınları.

Bianet (2008). 'AKP'ye kapatma iddianamesinin tam metni', 17 March 2008, www.bianet.org/bianet/siyaset/105636-akp-ye-kapatma-iddianamesinin-tam-metni, accessed: 27 May 2016.

Blondel, J., et al. (2010). *Political Leadership, Parties and Citizens.* London: Routledge.

Blyth, M. and R. Katz (2005). 'From Catch-All Politics to Cartelisation: The Political Economy of the Cartel Party'. *West European Politics*, 28 (1), 33–60.

Bobbio, N. (2005). *Left and Right: The Significance of a Political Distinction.* Cambridge: Polity Press.

Böhürler, A. (2013). 'Ey aday adayı kardeşlerim!', 26 October 2013, http://
yenisafak.com.tr/yazarlar/AyseBohurler/ey-aday-adayi-kardeslerim/40238,
accessed: 27 May 2016.

Bora, T. (2015). 'HDP eş genel başkanı Selahattin Demirtaş'la söyleşi: "İddiamız
seçime parti olarak girmeyi gerektiriyor"' (interview with Selahattin Demirtaş, co-chair of Peoples' Democratic Party), Birikim, online interview,
9 January 2015, www.birikimdergisi.com/guncel-yazilar/1145/hdp-es-genel-
baskani-selahattin-demirtas-la-soylesi-iddiamiz-secime-parti-olarak-girmeyi-
gerektiriyor#.WkEB2uNuJdj, accessed: 25 December 2017.

Bora, T. and K. Can (2004). Devlet ve Kuzgun: 1990'lardan 2000'lere MHP.
İstanbul: İletişim.

Boratav, K. (2005). Türkiye İktisat Tarihi 1908–2002. Ankara: İmge.

(2009). 'AKP'li yıllarda Türkiye ekonomisi', in İ. Uzgel and B. Duru (eds.),
AKP Kitabı: Bir Dönüşümün Bilançosu, Ankara: Phoenix Yayınevi,
pp. 463–472.

Bourdieu, P. (1984). Distinction (Trans. Richard Nice). Cambridge, MA: Har-
vard University Press.

Bozarslan, H. (2008). 'Türkiye'de Kürt sol hareketi', in M. Gültekingil (ed.),
Modern Türkiye'de Siyasi Düşünce, Cilt VIII, Sol, İstanbul: İletişim,
pp. 1169–1207.

Bozkurt, U. (2013). 'Neoliberalism with a Human Face: Making Sense of the
Justice and Development Party's Neoliberal Populism in Turkey'. Science
and Society, 77 (3), 372–396.

Brumberg, D. (2002). 'The trap of liberalized autocracy'. Journal of Democracy,
13 (4), 56–68.

Buğra, A. (1997). Devlet ve İşadamları. İstanbul: İletişim.

(1998). 'Class, Culture, and State: An Analysis of Interest Representation by
Two Turkish Business Associations'. International Journal of Middle East
Studies, 30 (4), 521–539.

Buğra, A. and Ç. Keyder (2006). 'The Turkish Welfare Regime in Transformation'. Journal of European Social Policy, 16 (3), 211–228.

Bugün (2012). 'Erdoğan'ın konuşmasının tam metni', 30 September 2012, http://
politika.bugun.com.tr/erdoganin-konusmasinin-tam-metni-haberi/207046,
accessed: 20 July 2014.

Burns, J. M. (2010). Leadership. New York: Harper Collins.

Çağaptay, S. (2017). The New Sultan. London: I. B. Tauris.

Çaha, Ö. and M. Guida (2011). Türkiye'de Seçim Kampanyaları. Ankara: Orion
Kitabevi.

Çakır, R. (2003a). 'Tayyip Bey'in gözleriyle sözleri uyuşuyor' (interview with
Hüseyin Çelik, a JDP founder). Vatan, 2 Oct., 15.

(2003b). 'Milli Görüş değil ANAP geleneği' (interview with Ahmet Çiğdem,
academic). Vatan, 2 Oct., 15.

(2012). 'Bir HAS Parti vardı', 20 September 2012, www.gazetevatan
.com/rusen-cakir-481994-yazar-yazisi-bir-has-parti-vardi/, accessed: 21 July
2014.

(2014a). 'İslami cemaatleri AKP ve Erdoğan'dan koparmak mümkün mü?',
Rusencakir.com online essay, 1 March 2014, www.rusencakir.com/

Islami-cemaatleri-AKP-ve-Erdogandan-koparmak-mumkun-mu/2518, accessed: 23 January 2017.

(2014b). *100 Soruda: Erdoğan x Gülen Savaşı*. İstanbul: Metis.

Çakır, R. and F. Çalmuk (2001). *Recep Tayyip Erdoğan: Bir Dönüşüm Öyküsü*. İstanbul: Metis.

Calise, M. (2005). 'Presidentialization, Italian Style', in T. Poguntke and P. Webb (eds.), *The Presidentialization of Politics*, Oxford: Oxford University Press, pp. 88–106.

Calvert, P. and S. Calvert (2014). *Politics and Society in the Developing World*. London: Routledge.

Canovan, M. (1999). 'Trust the People! Populism and the Two Faces of Democracy. *Political Studies*, 47 (1), 2–16.

Çarkçı, A. (2006). 'AK Parti İstanbul İl Başkan Yardımcısı Hulusi Şentürk ile "Parti İçi Demokrasi" ve siyasetin pratik gerçeklerini' konuştuk' (interview with Hulusi Şentürk, a high-ranking JDP member). *Yerel Siyaset*, 9, 4–12.

Çarkoğlu, A. (2000). 'Summary', in A. Çarkoğlu (ed.), *Siyasi Partilerde Reform*, İstanbul: Türkiye Ekonomik ve Sosyal Etüdler Vakfı, pp. 21–27.

(2007). 'A New Electoral Victory for the "Pro-Islamists" or the "New Centre-Right"? The Justice and Development Party Phenomenon in the July 2007 Parliamentary Elections in Turkey'. *South European Society and Politics*, 12 (4), 501–519.

Çarkoğlu, A. and S. E. Aytaç (2015). 'Who Gets Targeted for Vote-Buying? Evidence from an Augmented List Experiment in Turkey'. *European Political Science Review*, 7(4), 547–566.

Çarkoğlu, A. and E. Kalaycıoğlu (2009). *The Rising Tide of Conservatism in Turkey*. New York: Palgrave Macmillan.

Çavdar, T. (2008). *Türkiye'nin Demokrasi Tarihi 1950'den Günümüze*. Ankara: İmge.

Çelik, A. and A. V. Uluç (2009). 'Yerel siyasette temsil üzerine bir çalışma: Şanlıurfa örneği'. *İ. Ü. Siyasal Bilgiler Fakültesi Dergisi*, 41, 215–231.

Çetiner, H. (2009). 'AK Parti İstanbul Kongresinde Külünk Babuşçu çarpışmasına az kaldı', Istanbultimes.com.tr online essay, 15 June 2009, www .istanbultimes.com.tr/yazarlarimiz/huseyin-cetiner/ak-parti-istanbul-il-kon gresinde-kulunk-ve-babuscu-carpismasina-az-kaldi-h1672.html, accessed: 27 May 2016.

Çetinkaya, N. (2003). 'Genel seçimlerdeki başarımızı yerel seçimlerle taçlandıracağız' (interview). *Türkiye Bülteni*, 7, 50–52.

Çeviker-Gürakar, E. (2016). *Politics of Favoritism in Public Procurement in Turkey*. New York: Palgrave Macmillan.

Çınar, A. and B. Arıkan (2002). 'The Nationalist Action Party: Representing the State, the Nation or the Nationalists?', in B. Rubin and M. Heper (eds.), *Political Parties in Turkey*, London: Frank Cass, pp. 25–40.

Çınar, K. (2016). 'A Comparative Analysis of Clientelism in Greece, Spain, and Turkey: The Rural–Urban Divide. *Contemporary Politics*, 22 (1), 77–94.

Çınar, M. (2006a). 'Turkey's Transformation under the AKP Rule'. *The Muslim World*, 96 (3), 469–486.

(2006b). 'Kültürel yabancılaşma tezi üzerine'. *Toplum ve Bilim*, 105, 153–165.

(2013). 'Explaining the Popular Appeal and Durability of the Justice and Development Party in Turkey', in Elise Massicard and Nicole F. Watts (eds.), *Negotiating Political Power in Turkey: Breaking Up the Party*, London: Routledge, pp. 37–54.

Cizre, Ü. (1998). *Muktedirlerin Siyaseti: Merkez Sağ–Ordu–İslamcılık* (Trans. Cahide Ekiz). İstanbul: İletişim.

(2002). 'From Ruler to Pariah: The Life and Times of the True Path Party', in B. Rubin and M. Heper (eds.), *Political Parties in Turkey*, London: Frank Cass, pp. 82–101.

(2008a). 'Introduction. The Justice and Development Party: Making Choices, Revisions and Reversals Interactively', in Ü. Cizre (ed.), *Secular and Islamic Politics in Turkey: The Making of the Justice and Development Party*, London: Routledge, pp. 1–14.

Cizre, Ü. (ed.) (2008b). *Secular and Islamic Politics in Turkey: The Making of the Justice and Development Party*. London: Routledge.

CNN (2009). 'Peres, Erdogan in "amicable talks" after Davos spat', 30 January 2009, http://edition.cnn.com/2009/WORLD/europe/01/30/davos.erdogan.peres/index.html?iref=newssearch, accessed: 27 May 2016.

Çobanoğlu, Y. (2012). *'Altın Nesil' in Peşinde*. İstanbul: İletişim.

Copeaux, E. (2006). *Türk Tarih Tezi'nden Türk-İslam Sentezi'ne*. İstanbul: İletişim.

Cornell, S. E. (1999). 'Turkey: Return to Stability?' *Middle Eastern Studies*, 35 (4), 209–234.

Coşkun, B. (2007). 'Göbeğini kaşıyan adam…', 2 May 2007, www.hurriyet.com.tr/yazarlar/6449176.asp?yazarid=2, accessed: 27 May 2016.

Cumhuriyet (2015). 'Erdoğan masayı neden devirdi?', 18 September 2015, www.cumhuriyet.com.tr/haber/siyaset/371753/Erdogan_masayi_neden_devirdi_.html#, accessed: 25 December 2017.

(2016). 'Davutoğlu kontrolü kaybetti', 30 April 2016, www.cumhuriyet.com.tr/haber/siyaset/525193/Davutoglu_kontrolu_kaybetti.html#, accessed: 28 December 2017.

(2017a). 'Kendine "Kasabanın Şerifi" diyen AKP'li başkan kendini böyle tarif etti: Bazı kabiliyetlerim var; biraz fırıldak, biraz üçkağıtçıyım', 31 July 2017, www.cumhuriyet.com.tr/haber/siyaset/793288/Kendine__Kasabanin_Serifi__diyen_AKP_li_baskan_kendini_boyle_tarif_etti__Bazi_kabiliyetlerim_var__biraz_firildak__biraz_uckagitciyim.html, accessed: 18 December 2017.

(2017b). 'CHP'li vekilden çarpıcı iddia: AKP'li 800 avukat hakim yapıldı', 26 April 2017, www.cumhuriyet.com.tr/haber/siyaset/728580/CHP_li_vekil den_carpici_iddia__AKP_li_800_avukat_hakim_yapildi.html#, accessed: 26 December 2017.

Dağı, İ. (2008). 'Turkey's AKP in Power'. *Journal of Democracy*, 19 (3), 25–30.

Dalay, G. (2014) 'AK Parti'de liderlik ve kadro', www.aljazeera.com.tr/gorus/ak-partide-liderlik-ve-kadro, accessed 27 May 2016.

de Certeau, M. (2002). *The Practice of Everyday Life* (Trans. S. Rendall). Berkeley: University of California Press.

de la Torre, C. (1992). 'The Ambiguous Meanings of Latin American Populisms'. *Social Research*, 59 (2), 385–414.

(2000). *Populist Seduction in Latin America*. Athens, OH: Ohio University Press.

Deegan-Krause, K. (2007). 'New Dimensions of Political Cleavage', in R. J. Dalton and H. Klingemann (eds.), *Oxford Handbook of Political Behavior*, Oxford: Oxford University Press, pp. 538–556.

Delibaş, K. (2015). *The Rise of Political Islam in Turkey: Urban Poverty, Grassroots Activism and Islamic Fundamentalism*. London: I. B. Tauris.

Demirdöğen, İ. (2007a). 'Sezer'li 7 Yıl (1)', 22 April 2007, www.radikal.com.tr/ haber.php?haberno=219108, accessed: 27 May 2016.

(2007b). 'Sezer'li 7 Yıl (4)', 25 April 2007, www.radikal.com.tr/haber.php? haberno=219414, accessed: 27 May 2016.

(2007c). 'Sezer'li 7 Yıl (5)', 26 April 2007, www.radikal.com.tr/haber.php? haberno=219434, accessed: 27 May 2016.

(2007d). 'Sezer'li 7 Yıl (7)', 28 April 2007, www.radikal.com.tr/haber.php? haberno=219694, accessed: 27 May 2016.

Demirel, T. (2004). *Adalet Partisi: İdeoloji ve Politika*. İstanbul: İletişim.

(2009). '1946–1980 döneminde "sol" ve "sağ"', in T. Bora and M. Gültekin (eds.), *Türkiye'de Siyasi Düşünce, Cilt IX, Dönemler ve Zihniyetler*, İstanbul: İletişim, pp. 413–450.

(2011). *Türkiye'nin Uzun On Yılı Demokrat Parti İktidarı ve 27 Mayıs Darbesi*. İstanbul: Bilgi.

Dexter, L. A. (1970). *Elite and Specialized Interviewing*. Evanston: Northwestern University Press.

Dinçşahin, Ş. (2012). 'A Symptomatic Analysis of the Justice and Development Party's Populism in Turkey, 2007–2010'. *Government and Opposition*, 47 (4), 618–640.

Dindar, C. (2014). *Bi'at ve Öfke: Recep Tayyip Erdoğan'ın Psikobiyografisi*. İstanbul: Telos.

DİSK (2014). *DİSK genel iş sendikası kamu istihdam bülteni*. Ankara: DİSK.

Doğan, S. (2016). *Mahalledeki AKP*. İstanbul: İletişim.

Duran, B. (2008). 'The Justice and Development Party's "New Politics": Steering Toward Conservative Democracy, a Revised Islamic Agenda or Management of New Crises?', in Ü. Cizre (ed.), *Secular and Islamic Politics in Turkey: The Making of the Justice and Development Party*, London: Routledge, pp. 80–106.

(2013). 'Understanding the AK Party's Identity Politics: A Civilizational Discourse and Its Limitations'. *Insight Turkey*, 15 (1), 91–109.

Duvar (2017a). '1 yıla damga vuran 26 KHK', 20 July 2017, www.gazeteduvar.com.tr/gundem/2017/07/20/1-yila-damga-vuran-26-khk/, accessed: 26 December 2017.

(2017b). 'AK Parti'de değişim: bir taşla üç kuş!', 25 August 2017, www.gazeteduvar.com.tr/gundem/2017/08/25/ak-partide-degisim-bir-tasla-uc-kus/, accessed: 28 December 2017.

Duverger, M. (1974). *Siyasi Partiler* (Trans. Ergun Özbudun). Ankara: Bilgi Yayınevi.

(1994). *Siyasal Rejimler* (Trans. Teoman Tunçdoğan). İstanbul: İletişim.

DW (2017). 'Referandum protestoları sürüyor', 18 April 2017, www.dw.com/tr/ referandum-protestolar%C4%B1-s%C3%BCr%C3%BCyor/a-38458761, accessed: 27 December 2017.

Economist Intelligence Unit (2015). 'Democracy Index 2014 – Democracy and Its Discontents', www.eiu.com/public/topical_report.aspx?campaignid= Democracy0115.

ECtHR (European Court of Human Rights) (2003). 'Case of Refah Partisi (The Welfare Party) and others v. Turkey', ECtHR decision, 13 February 2003, http://hudoc.echr.coe.int/sites/eng/pages/search.aspx?i=001-60936# {"itemid":["001-60936"]}, accessed: 27 May 2016.

Ekzen, N. (2009). 'AKP iktisat politikaları 2002–2007', in İ. Uzgel and B. Duru (eds.), AKP Kitabı: Bir Dönüşümün Bilançosu, Ankara: Phoenix Yayınevi, pp. 473–491.

Eligür, B. (2010). The Mobilization of Political Islam in Turkey. Cambridge: Cambridge University Press.

Ensonhaber (2009). 'Bazı monşerler İsrail'e restimizi anlamaz', 30 January 2009, www.ensonhaber.com/Politika/183114/bazi-monserler-israile-resti mizi-anlamaz.html, accessed: 27 May 2016.

Epstein, L. D. (2000). Political Parties in Western Democracies. New Brunswick, NJ, London: Transaction Publishers.

Erder, N. (2002). Türkiye'de Siyasi Partilerin Yandaş Seçmen Profilleri. İstanbul: TÜSES Vakfı.

Erdoğan, N. (1998). 'Demokratik soldan devrimci yol'a: 1970'lerde sol popülizm üzerine notlar'. Toplum ve Bilim, 78, 22–37.

(2000). 'Devleti idare etmek: maduniyet ve düzenbazlık'. Toplum ve Bilim, 83, 8–31.

Ergin, S. (1997). 'Tarikat iftarı bardağı taşırdı', 23 August 1997, http://hurarsiv .hurriyet.com.tr/goster/haber.aspx?id=-260952, accessed: 27 May 2016.

Ergüder, U. (1991). 'The Motherland Party. 1983–1989', in M. Heper and J. M. Landau (eds.), Political Parties and Democracy in Turkey, London: I.B. Tauris, pp. 152–169.

Ergün, N. (2015). Adım Adım Siyaset. İstanbul: Alfa.

Eroğul, C. (2003). Demokrat Parti. Ankara: İmge.

(2007). 'Cumhurbaşkanlığı seçimi bunalımından çıkarılabilecek dersler'. Ankara Üniversitesi SBF Dergisi, 62 (3), 167–181.

Esayan, M. (2014a). 'Kutuplaşmanın 200 yıllık hikayesi', 27 March 2014, http:// yenisafak.com.tr/yazarlar/MarkarEsayan/kutuplasmanin-200-yillik-hikayesi/ 51004, accessed:27 May 2016.

(2014b). 'Beyaz Türklerin halk ile entegrasyonu', 2 June 2014, http://yenisafak .com.tr/yazarlar/MarkarEsayan/beyaz-turklerin-halk-ile-entegrasyonu/54133, accessed: 27 May 2016.

Esen, B. and S. Gümüşçü (2016). 'Rising Competitive Authoritarianism in Turkey'. Third World Quarterly, 37 (9), 1581–1606.

(2017). 'Building a Competitive Authoritarian Regime: State–Business Relations in the AKP's Turkey'. Journal of Balkan and Near Eastern Studies, 20 (4), 1–24, https://doi.org/10.1080/19448953.2018.1385924, accessed: 24 January 2018.

ESI (European Stability Initiative) (2005). 'Islamic Calvinists Change and Conservatism in Central Anatolia', 19 September 2005, www.esiweb.org/index .php?lang=tr&id=156&document_ID=69, accessed: 27 May 2016.

Evrensel (2017). 'Erdoğan: metal yorgunluğu var, teşkilatları yenileyeceği', 30 May 2017, www.evrensel.net/haber/321629/erdogan-metal-yorgunlugu-var-teskilatlari-yenileyecegiz, accessed: 28 December 2017.

Farrell, D. (1996). 'Campaign Strategies and Tactics', in L. LeDuc, R. G. Niemi and P. Norris (eds.), *Comparing Democracies*, London: Sage, pp. 160–183.

Freedom House (2015). *Freedom in the World 2015: Highlights from Freedom House's Annual Report on Political Rights and Civil Liberties*. Washington, DC, and New York.

Gazetevatan (2009). '3 Karaman koyunu ver güdemez kaybederler', 20 April 2009, www.gazetevatan.com/3-karaman-koyunu-ver-gudemez-kaybederler-229055-siyaset/, accessed: 27 May 2016.

——— (2012). 'AKP'yi bu sözlerle eleştirmişti!', 16 August 2012, www.gazetevatan.com/akp-yi-bu-sozlerle-elestirmisti–474572-siyaset/, accessed: 21 July 2014.

——— (2015). 'Erdoğan, Dolmabahçe'ye de sert çıktı', 22 March 2015, www.gazetevatan.com/erdogan-dolmabahce-ye-de-sert-cikti–752383-gundem/, accessed: 25 December 2017.

Geertz, C. 1993. *Interpretation of Cultures*. London: Fontana Press.

Gençkaya, Ö. F. (2002). *Devletleşen Partiler*. Ankara: Anadolu Stratejik Araştırmalar Vakfı.

Gidengil, E. and E. Karakoç (2014). 'Which Matters More in the Electoral Success of Islamist (Successor) Parties – Religion or Performance? The Turkish Case'. *Party Politics*, 22 (3), 325–338.

Gönenç, L. (2006). '2000'li yıllarda merkez–çevre ilişkilerini yeniden düşünmek'. *Toplum ve Bilim*, 105, 129–152.

Gözler, K. (2017). '16 Nisan'da Oylayacağımız Anayasa Değişikliği Bir "Suistimalci Anayasa Değişikliği" midir?', legal commentary, 1 March 2017, www.anayasa.gen.tr/suistimalci.pdf, accessed: 27 December 2017.

Greene, K. F. (2007). *Why Dominant Parties Lose: Mexico's Democratization in Comparative Perspective*. Cambridge: Cambridge University Press.

Gümüşçü, Ş. and D. Sert (2009). 'The Power of the Devout Bourgeoisie: The Case of the Justice and Development Party in Turkey'. *Middle Eastern Studies*, 45 (6), 953–968.

Güney, A. (1995). *Refah Partisi Samsun Merkez İlçe Teşkilatı Çalışma Modeli*. Samsun: Refah Partisi.

Gürcan, M. (2016). 'Why Turkey's Coup Did Not Stand a Chance', 17 July 2016, www.al-monitor.com/pulse/originals/2016/07/turkey-kamikaze-coup-attempt-fails.html, accessed: 15 October 2016.

Gürgür, N. (2009). '27 Mayıs'tan günümüz Türkiye'si için çıkarılacak dersler'. *Türk Yurdu*, 262, 2–3.

Gürses, E. (2011). 'Tarihi revizyonun perde arkası', 12 April 2011, www.ntvmsnbc.com/id/25202176, accessed: 27 May 2016.

Güven, E. (2005). 'Her alemi bilirim', 31 August 2005, www.milliyet.com.tr/2005/08/31/spor/axspo05.html, accessed: 27 May 2016.

Güvenç, D. (2014). 'Sandık gönüllüleri "Suçüstü yakaladık"' (interview with Ayberk Yağız, founder of the NGO Oy ve Ötesi), *POSTA212*, online interview, 21 April 2014, http://posta212.com/guncel/sandik-gonulluleri-sucustu-yakaladik, accessed: 21 July 2014.

Haberler.com (2013). 'AK Parti il koordinatörleri toplandı', www.haberler.com/ak-parti-il-koordinatorleri-toplandi-4237401-haberi/, accessed: 27 May 2016.

(2014a). 'Başbakan Erdoğan'ın cumhurbaşkanlığı adaylığı konuşması', www.haberler.com/basbakan-erdogan-cumhurbaskanligi-adayi-konusmasi-6213688-haberi/, accessed: 20 July 2014.

(2014b). 'Cumhurbaşkanı nikah şahitliği yaptı, yeni çiftten 4 çocuk istedi', 14 September 2014, www.haberler.com/cumhurbaskani-erdogan-dort-olur-bereket-olur-6482173-haberi/, accessed: 27 May 2016.

Habertürk (2017). 'Melih Gökçek istifa etti', 28 October 2017, http://www.haberturk.com/son-dakika-melih-gokcek-istifa-etti-1690878, accessed: 12 January 2018.

Hale, W. and E. Özbudun (2010). *Islamism, Democracy and Liberalism in Turkey: The Case of the AKP*. London: Routledge.

Hamdan, Z. A. (2009). 'The Government Policies and Military Methods against the PKK in the 1990s'. Unpublished MSc Disertation. Ankara: Middle East Technical University.

Hamid, S. (2014). *Temptations of Power*. Oxford: Oxford University Press.

Hanioğlu, M. Ş. (1997). 'Garbcılar: Their Attitudes Toward Religion and Their Impact on the Official Ideology of the Turkish Republic'. *Studia Islamica*, 86, 133–158.

(2011). *Ataturk: An Intellectual Biography*. Princeton: Princeton University Press.

Hawkins, K. A. (2010). *Venezuela's Chavismo and Populism in Comparative Perspective*. Cambridge: Cambridge University Press.

Hay, C. (2002). *Political Analysis*. New York: Palgrave.

Hazan, R. Y. and G. Rahat (2010). *Democracy Within Parties Candidate Selection Methods and Their Political Consequences*. Oxford: Oxford University Press.

Heper, M. and J. M. Landau (eds.) (1991). *Political Parties and Democracy in Turkey*. London: I. B. Tauris.

Heper, M. and Ş. Toktaş (2003). 'Islam, Modernity, and Democracy in Contemporary Turkey: The Case of Recep Tayyip Erdoğan'. *The Muslim World*, 93, 157–185.

Heydemann, S. (2007). *Upgrading Authoritarianism in the Arab World*. Saban Center for Middle East Policy at the Brookings Institution.

Hoşgör, E. (2011). 'Islamic Capital/Anatolian Tigers: Past and Present'. *Middle Eastern Studies*, 47 (2), 343–360.

HRW (Human Rights Watch) (2015). *World Report 2015: Events of 2014*. No place.

Hürriyet (2007). 'Miting rekoru Erdoğan'ın', 20 July 2007, www.hurriyet.com.tr/gundem/6928772.asp, accessed: 27 May 2016.

(2008). '1997'deki Refah Partisi kapatma davası iddianamesi', 14 March 2008, www.hurriyet.com.tr/dunya/8460645.asp, accessed: 27 May 2016.

(2013). 'Başbakan: temayül yoklamaları tek belirleyici olmayacak', 2 November 2013, www.hurriyet.com.tr/gundem/25030834.asp, accessed: 27 May 2016.

(2014a). 'YSK seçmen sayısını açıkladı', 24 February 2015, www.hurriyet.com.tr/gundem/25873952.asp, accessed: 27 May 2016.

(2014b). 'Arınç: bazılarının dili varmıyor ama …', 3 May 2014, www.hurriyet.com.tr/gundem/26345490.asp, accessed: 27 May 2016.

(2015). '10 Madde Diyor ki', 2 March 2015, www.hurriyet.com.tr/10-madde-diyor-ki-28334292, accessed: 25 December 2017.

(2017). 'Kadir Topbaş istifa etti', 23 September 2017, www.hurriyet.com.tr/kadir-topbas-istifa-etti-40587764, accessed: 12 January 2018.

Ignazi, P. (1996). 'The Crisis of Parties and the Rise of New Political Parties'. *Party Politics*, 2 (4): 549–566.

İnsel, A. (2002). 'Olağanlaşan demokrasi ve modern muhafazakarlık'. *Birikim*, 163–164, 21–28.

(2003). 'The AKP and Normalizing Democracy in Turkey'. *South Atlantic Quarterly*, 102 (2/3), 293–308.

Jalali, R. (2002). 'Civil Society and the State: Turkey after the Earthquake'. *Disasters*, 26 (2), 120–139.

Jang, J. H. (2005). 'Taming Political Islamists by Islamic Capital: The Passions and the Interests in Turkish Islamic Society'. Unpublished PhD dissertation, University of Texas at Austin.

Jenkins, G. (2003). 'Muslim Democrats in Turkey?' *Survival*, 45 (1), 45–66.

(2009). 'Between Fact and Fantasy: Turkey's Ergenekon Investigation'. Central Asia – Caucasus Institute: Silk Road Paper, August 2009.

(2011). 'Ergenekon, Sledgehammer, and the Politics of Turkish Justice: Conspiracies and Coincidences'. *MERIA Journal*, 15 (2), www.gloria-center.org/2011/08/ergenekon-sledgehammer-and-the-politics-of-turkish-justice-consp iracies-and-coincidences/, accessed: 21 July 2014.

Kabasakal, M. (1991). *Türkiye'de Siyasal Parti Örgütlenmesi 1908–1960*. İstanbul: Tekin.

(2014). 'Factors Influencing Intra-Party Democracy and Membership Rights: The case of Turkey'. *Party Politics*, 20 (5), 700–711.

Kalaycıoğlu, E. (2002). 'The Motherland Party: The Challenge of Institutionalization in a Charismatic Leader Party'. *Turkish Studies*, 3 (1), 41–61.

(2010). 'Justice and Development Party at the Helm: Resurgence of Islam or Restitution of the Right-of-Center Predominant Party?' *Turkish Studies*, 11 (1), 29–44.

Kalyoncu, C. A. (2011). 'Yusuf'u kuyudan çıkaran, bir gün mührü size de verir', 13 June 2011, www.aksiyon.com.tr/aksiyon/haber-29663-37-%E2%80%9Cyusufu-kuyudan-cikaran-bir-gun-muhru-size-de-verir%E2%80%9D.html, accessed: 12 August 2014.

Kapaklı, Ö. (2011). 'AK Parti ve BDP'nin Başarısı', 13 June 2011, www.guneydogutv.com/ak-parti-ve-bdpnin-basarisi-yazisi-837.html, accessed: 27 May 2016.

Kaplan, H. (2014). 'Erdoğan'ın hikayesi', 4 July 2014, yenisafak.com.tr/yazarlar/HilalKaplan/erdoganin-hik%C3%A2yesi/54649, accessed: 27 May 2016.

Kaplan, Sam (2006). *Pedagogical State*. Stanford: Stanford University Press.

Kaplan, Sefa (2007). *Recep Tayyip Erdoğan*. İstanbul: Doğan Kitap.

Karaalioğlu, M. (2014). 'Ergenekoncuların, laikçilerin, cemaatin, marjinal solun medyası olsun ama yüzde 50'nin olmasın, öyle mi?', 10 February 2014, http://haber.stargazete.com/yazar/ergenekonun-laikcilerin-cemaatin-marj inal-solun-medyasi-olsun-ama-yuzde-50nin-olmasin-oyle-mi/yazi-840890, accessed: 27 May 2016.

Karagöl, E. T. (2013). *AK Parti Dönemi Türkiye Ekonomisi*. Ankara: SETA.

Karaömerlioglu, M. A. (1998). 'The Village Institutes Experience in Turkey'. *British Journal of Middle Eastern Studies*, 25 (1), 47–73.

Karaömerlioğlu, M. A. (2006). *Orada Bir Köy Var Uzakta: Erken Cumhuriyet Döneminde Köycü Söylem*. İstanbul: İletişim.

Karar (2017). 'Tartışalan 696 sayılı KHK maddesi ne? 121. madde neyi düzenliyor?', 26 December 2017, www.karar.com/guncel-haberler/tartisalan-696-sayili-khk-maddesi-ne-121-madde-neyi-duzenliyor-15-temmuz-haberleri-702135, accessed: 26 December 2017.

Karpat, K. (1991). 'The Republican People's Party, 1923–1945', in M. Heper and J. M. Landau (eds.), *Political Parties and Democracy in Turkey*, London: I. B. Tauris, pp. 42–64.

Katz, Richard (2013). 'Political Parties and Democracy'. Lecture presented at European Consortium for Political Research Summer School on Political Parties and Democracy, Leuphana University of Lüneburg, Germany.

Katz, R. S. and P. Mair (1993). 'The Evolution of Party Organizations in Europe: the Three Faces of Party Organization'. *American Review of Politics*, 14 (4), 593–617.

(1994). 'Preface and Acknowledgements', in Richard Katz and Peter Mair (eds.), *How Parties Organize*, London: Sage, pp. vi–vii.

(1995). 'Changing Models of Party Organization and Party Democracy: The Emergence of the Cartel Party'. *Party Politics*, 1 (1), 5–28.

(2002). 'The Ascendancy of the Party in Public Office: Party Organizational Change in Twentieth-Century Democracies', in R. Gunther, J. R. Montero and J. Linz (eds.), *Political Parties: Old Concepts and New Challenges*, Oxford: Oxford University Press, pp. 113–135.

(2009). 'The Cartel Party Thesis: A Restatement'. *Perspectives on Politics*, 7 (4), 753–766.

Kemahlıoğlu, Ö. (2012). *Agents or Bosses? Patronage and Intra-Party Politics in Argentina and Turkey*. Colchester: ECPR.

Keyder, Ç. (2003). *Türkiye'de Devlet ve Sınıflar*. İstanbul: İletişim.

Kınıklıoğlu, S. (2000). 'Bülent Ecevit: The Transformation of a Politician'. *Turkish Studies*, 1 (2), 1–20.

(2002). 'The Democratic Left Party: Kapıkulu Politics Par Excellence', in B. Rubin and M. Heper (eds.), *Political Parties in Turkey*, London: Frank Cass, pp. 4–24.

Kirchheimer, O. (1966). 'The Transformation of the Western European Party Systems', in J. L. Palombara and M. Weiner (eds.), *Political Parties and Political Development*. Princeton: Princeton University Press, pp. 177–200.

Kıvılcımlı, H. (1974). *Türkiye'de Sınıflar ve Politika*. İstanbul: Tarih ve Devrim Yayınevi.

Knight, A. (1998). 'Populism and Neo-Populism in Latin America, Especially Mexico'. *Journal of Latin American Studies*, 30 (2), 223–248.

Konda (2016). *Demokrasi Nöbeti Araştırması - Meydanların Profili*, İstanbul, http://konda.com.tr/demokrasinobeti/, accessed: 17 October 2016.

Koole, R. (1996). 'Cadre, Catch-All or Cartel? A Comment on the Notion of the Cartel Party'. *Party Politics*, 2 (4), 507–523.

Kopecky, P. and M. Spirova (2012). 'Measuring Party Patronage through Structured Expert Interviews', in P. Kopecky et al. (eds.), *Party Patronage and Party Government in European Democracies*, Oxford: Oxford University Press, pp. 17–28.

Koru, F. (2012). 'Tayyip Erdoğan'ı anlamak …', 14 June 2012, http://haber.stargazete.com/yazar/Tayyip_Erdogani_anlamak/yazi-609459, accessed: 27 May 2016.

Kozanoğlu, C. (1997). *İnternet, Dolunay, Cemaat*. İstanbul: İletişim.

Kriesi, H. (1998). 'The Transformation of Cleavage Politics: The 1997 Stein Rokkan Lecture'. *European Journal of Political Research*, 33 (2), 165–185.

Küçükömer, İ. (1994). *Düzenin Yabancılaşması: Batılaşma*. İstanbul: Bağlam.

Kumbaracıbaşı, A. C. (2009). *Turkish Politics and the Rise of the AKP: Dilemmas of Institutionalization and Leadership Strategy*. London: Routledge.

Laclau, E. (2005). *On Populist Reason*. London and New York: Verso.

Landau, J. M. (1974). *Radical Politics in Modern Turkey*. Leiden: E. J. Brill.

(1982). 'The Nationalist Action Party in Turkey'. *Journal of Contemporary History*, 17 (4), 587–606.

Laponce, J. A. (1981). *Left and Right: The Topography of Political Perceptions*. Toronto: University of Toronto Press.

Levi, A. (1991). 'The Justice Party, 1961–1980', in M. Heper and J. M. Landau (eds.), *Political Parties and Democracy in Turkey*, London: I. B. Tauris, pp. 134–151.

Levitsky, S. (1998). 'Institutionalization and Peronism: The Concept, the Case and the Case for Unpacking the Concept'. *Party Politics*, 4 (1), 77–92.

(2003). *Transforming Labor-Based Parties in Latin America: Argentine Peronism in Comparative Perspective*. Cambridge: Cambridge University Press.

Levitsky, S. and L. Way (2002). 'The Rise of Competitive Authoritarianism'. *Journal of Democracy*, 13(2), 51–65.

Linz, J. J. and A. Stepan (2011). *Problems of Democratic Transition and Consolidation: Southern Europe, South America, and Post-Communist Europe*. Baltimore: Johns Hopkins University Press.

Lipovsky, I. (1991). 'The Legal Socialist Parties of Turkey, 1960–1980'. *Middle Eastern Studies*, 27 (1), 94–111.

Lipset, S. M. and S. Rokkan (1967). 'Cleavage Structures, Party Systems, and Voter Alignments: An Introduction', in S. M. Lipset and S. Rokkan (eds.), *Party Systems and Voter Alignments: Cross-National Perspectives*, New York: Free Press, pp. 1–64.

Magaloni, B. (2006). *Voting for Autocracy: Hegemonic Party Survival and Its Demise in Mexico*. Cambridge: Cambridge University Press.

Mair, P. (1992). 'Party Organizations: From Civil Society to State', in R. S. Katz and P. Mair (eds.), *How Parties Organize*. London: Sage, pp. 1–22.

(2013). *Ruling the Void: The Hollowing of Western Democracy.* New York: Verso Books.

Mango, A. (1991). 'The Social Democratic Populist Party', in M. Heper and J. M. Landau (eds.), *Political Parties and Democracy in Turkey*, London: I. B. Tauris, pp. 170–187.

Marcus, A. (2007). *Blood and Belief.* New York: New York University Press.

Mardin, Ş. (1973). 'Centre–Periphery Relations: A Key to Turkish Politics?' *Daedalus*, 102 (1), 169–190.

Marschall, M., A. Aydogan and A. Bulut (2016). 'Does Housing Create Votes? Explaining the Electoral Success of the AKP in Turkey'. *Electoral Studies*, 42, 201–212.

Massicard, E. and N. F. Watts (2013). 'Introduction: Reconsidering Parties, Power and Social Forces', in Elise Massicard and Nicole F. Watts (eds.), *Negotiating Political Power in Turkey: Breaking Up the Party*, London: Routledge, pp. 1–16.

Mazzoleni, G. (2000). 'A Return to Civic and Political Engagement Prompted by Personalized Political Leadership?' *Political Communication*, 17 (4), 325–328.

Mazzoleni, G. and W. Schulz (1999). '"Mediatization" of Politics: A Challenge for Democracy?' *Political Communication*, 16 (3), 247–261.

McAllister, I. (2007). 'The Personalization of Politics', in R. J. Dalton and H. Klingeman (eds.), *The Oxford Handbook of Political Behavior*, Oxford: Oxford University Press, pp. 571–588.

McDonnell, D. (2013). 'Silvio Berlusconi's Personal Parties: From Forza Italia to the Popolo Della Liberta'. *Political Studies*, 61 (S1), 217–233.

Mecham, R. Q. (2004). 'From the Ashes of Virtue, a Promise of Light: The Transformation of Political Islam in Turkey'. *Third World Quarterly*, 25 (2), 339–358.

Mecham, Q. and J. Chernov Hwang (2014a). 'Introduction: The Emergence and Development of Islamist Political Parties', in Q. Mecham and J. Chernov Hwang (eds.), *Islamist Parties and Political Normalization in the Muslim World*, Philadelphia: University of Pennsylvania Press, pp. 1–16.

Mecham, Q. and J. Chernov Hwang (eds.) (2014b). *Islamist Parties and Political Normalization in the Muslim World.* Philadelphia: University of Pennsylvania Press.

Meeker, M. (2001). *A Nation of Empire: The Ottoman Legacy of Turkish Modernity.* Berkeley: University of California Press.

Memurlar (2011). '3 liderin karnesi', 11 June 2011, www.memurlar.net/haber/197925/2.sayfa, accessed: 27 May 2016.

Mercan, M. (2003). 'AK Parti'nin toplumla iletişimi'. *Türkiye Bülteni*, 5, 12–15.

Metinsoy, M. (2011). 'Fragile Hegemony, Flexible Authoritarianism, and Governing from Below: Politicians' Reports in Early Republican Turkey'. *International Journal of Middle East Studies*, 43(4), 699–719.

Michels, R. (1966). *Political Parties: A Sociological Study of the Oligarchical Tendencies of Modern Democracy* (Trans. Eden Paul and Cedar Paul). New York: Free Press.

Milliyet (2008). '"AK Parti kapatılmasın" kararı çıktı', 30 July 2008, www.milliyet.com.tr/karar–font-color-red-bugun-mu—font-aciklanacak-/

siyaset/siyasetdetay/30.07.2008/972729/default.htm, accessed: 27 May 2016.

(2009). 'İki Adaylı Kongre Sıkıntısı', www.milliyet.com.tr/Siyaset/ HaberDetay.aspx?aType=HaberDetayArsiv&ArticleID=1111565&Kategor iID=4, accessed: 27 May 2016.

(2011). 'Liderlerin 1.5 aylık maratonu böyle geçti', 9 June 2011, www .milliyet.com.tr/Siyaset/SonDakika.aspx?aType=SonDakika&ArticleID=14 00456&Date=27.06.2011&Kategori=siyaset&b=Liderlerin%201.5%20ayli k%20maratonu%20boyle%20gecti, accessed: 27 May 2016.

(2013). 'AK Parti'nin kıskandıran rekoru', 13 February 2013, http://www .milliyet.com.tr/ak-parti-nin-kiskandiran-rekoru/siyaset/siyasetdetay/13.02.2013/ 1668351/default.htm, accessed: 27 May 2016.

(2014a). 'Liderlerin miting karneleri', 29 March 2014, www.milliyet.com.tr/ liderlerin-miting-karneleri/gundem/detay/1858751/default.htm, accessed: 27 May 2016.

(2014b). 'AK Parti İzmir'de altı bölge başkanı ve sekiz ilçe koordinatörü', 27 April 2014, www.milliyet.com.tr/ak-parti-izmir-de-6-bolge-baskani-ve-izmir-yerelhaber-167501/, accessed: 27 May 2016.

Moffitt, B. (2016). *The Global Rise of Populism*. Stanford: Stanford University Press.

Mudde, C. (2004). 'The Populist Zeitgeist'. *Government and Opposition*, 39 (4), 542–563.

Mudde, C. and C. R. Kaltwasser (eds.) (2012). *Populism in Europe and the Americas: Threat or Corrective for Democracy?* Cambridge: Cambridge University Press.

Mudde, C. and C. R. Kaltwasser (2017). *Populism*. Oxford: Oxford University Press.

Mufti, M. (2015). 'Democratizing Potential of the "Arab Spring": Some Early Observations'. *Government and Opposition*, 50 (Special Issue 3), pp 394–419.

Müller, W. (1994). 'The Development of Austrian Party Organizations in the Post-War Period', in R. S. Katz and P. Mair (eds.), *How Parties Organize*. London: Sage, pp. 51–79.

Ntvmsnbc.com (2013). 'Otobüs ve vapurlar kiralandı', 19 June 2013, www.ntvmsnbc.com/id/25449811/#storyContinued, accessed: 27 May 2016.

Ocaklı, F. (2012). 'Electing the Pious: Islamist Politics and Local Party Strategies in Turkey'. PhD dissertation, Brown University, Providence, RI.

(2015). 'Notable Networks, Elite Recruitment, Organizational Cohesiveness, and Islamist Electoral Success in Turkey'. *Politics and Society*, 43 (3), 385–413.

O'Donnell, G. A. (1994). 'Delegative Democracy'. *Journal of Democracy*, 5(1), 55–69.

Oğur, Y. (2014a). 'Muhalefetin çatı adayı aslında kimdir?', 20 June 2014, www.turkiyegazetesi.com.tr/yildiray-ogur/581078.aspx, accessed: 27 May 2016.

(2014b). 'Filmin katarsis anı ...', 2 July 2014, www.turkiyegazetesi.com.tr/ yazarlar/yildiray-ogur/581244.aspx, accessed: 27 May 2016.

Öniş, Z. (2001). 'Political Islam at the Crossroads: From Hegemony to Co-existence'. *Contemporary Politics*, 7 (4), 281–298.

(2003). 'Domestic Politics Versus Global Dynamics: Towards a Political Economy of the 2000 and 2001 Financial Crises in Turkey'. *Turkish Studies*, 4 (2), 1–30.

(2012). 'The Triumph of Conservative Globalism: The Political Economy of the AKP Era'. *Turkish Studies*, 13 (2), 135–152.

OSCE/ODIHR (Office for Democratic Institutions and Human Rights) (2017). 'Republic of Turkey Constitutional Referendum 16 April 2017', 22 June 2017, www.osce.org/odihr/elections/turkey/324816?download=true, accessed: 27 December 2017.

Ostiguy, P. (1997). 'Peronism and Anti-Peronism: Social-Cultural Bases of Political Identity in Argentina'. Paper presented at the Latin American Studies Association meeting in Mexico.

(2009a). 'The High and the Low in Politics: A Two-Dimensional Political Space for Comparative Analysis and Electoral Studies'. Kellogg Institute Working Paper No. 360.

(2009b). 'Argentina's Double Political Spectrum: Party System, Political Identities, and Strategies, 1944–2007' (No. 361). Kellogg Institute Working Paper No. 361.

(2009c). 'The High–Low Political Divide Rethinking Populism and Anti-Populism'. Committee on Concepts and Methods Working Paper No. 35.

(2013). 'The Way to Do It: The Appeals of High and Low in Politics'. Paper prepared for the workshop "The Concept of Populism", Sussex University, Brighton.

(2017). 'Populism: A Socio-Cultural Approach', in C. R. Kaltwasser et al. (eds.), *The Oxford Handbook of Populism*, Oxford: Oxford University Press, pp. 73–97.

Owen, R. (2002). *State Power and Politics in the Making of the Modern Middle East*. London: Routledge.

Özbek, M. (1991). *Popüler Kültür ve Orhan Gencebay Arabeski*. İstanbul: İletişim.

Özbudun, E. (1975). 'Political Participation in Rural Turkey', in E. Akarlı and G. Ben-Dor (eds.), *Political Participation in Turkey*, İstanbul: Boğaziçi University Publications, pp. 33–60.

(2000). *Contemporary Turkish Politics*. Boulder: Lynne Rienner Publishers.

(2001). 'The Institutional Decline of Parties in Turkey', in L. Diamond and R. Gunther (eds.), *Political Parties and Democracy*, Baltimore: Johns Hopkins University Press, pp. 238–265.

(2006). 'From Political Islam to Conservative Democracy: The Case of the Justice and Development Party in Turkey'. *South European Society and Politics*, 11 (3–4), 543–557.

(2011). *Otoriter Rejimler, Seçimsel Demokrasiler ve Türkiye*. İstanbul: Bilgi.

(2013). *Party Politics and Social Cleavages in Turkey*. Boulder: Lynne Rienner Publishers.

(2014). 'AKP at the Crossroads: Erdoğan's Majoritarian Drift'. *South European Society and Politics*, 19 (2), 155–167.

(2015). 'Turkey's Judiciary and the Drift Toward Competitive Authoritarianism'. *International Spectator*, 50 (2), 42–55.

Özdan, V. (2014). 'AKP'nin sandık başarısının sırrı', 14 April 2014, http://t24.com.tr/yazarlar/vedat-ozdan/akpnin-sandik-basarisinin-sirri-ne,9020, accessed: 27 May 2016.

Özdil, Y. (2007). 'Bidon kafa …', 13 August 2007, www.hurriyet.com.tr/yazar lar/7074842.asp, accessed: 27 May 2016.

Özkök, E. (2006). 'Beyaz Türklerin tasfiyesi mi', 21 April 2006, I http://hurarsiv .hurriyet.com.tr/goster/haber.aspx?id=4289630&tarih=2006-04-21, accessed: 13 January 2015.

Öztop, T. (2014). 'AKP mitinginde bir çapulcu', 24 March 2014, sarapvepeynir.blogspot.co.uk/2014/03/akp-mitinginde-bir-capulcu.html, accessed: 27 May 2016.

Padgett, J. F. and C. K. Ansell (1993). 'Robust Action and the Rise of the Medici, 1400–1434'. *American Journal of Sociology*, 98 (6), 1259–1319.

Pamuk, O. (2012). *İstanbul*. İstanbul: İletişim.

(2015). *Kafamda Bir Tuhaflık*. İstanbul: YKY; published in English as *A Strangeness in My Mind* (Trans. Ekin Oklap). London: Faber & Faber 2015.

Panebianco, A. (1988). *Political Parties: Organization and Power* (Trans. M. Silver). Cambridge: Cambridge University Press.

Pınarcıoğlu, M. and O. Işık, (2001). *Nöbetleşe Yoksulluk*. İstanbul: İletişim.

(2008). 'Not Only Helpless But Also Hopeless: Changing Dynamics of Urban Poverty in Turkey, the Case of Sultanbeyli, Istanbul'. *European Planning Studies*, 16 (10), 1353–1370.

Plaggenborg, S. (2015). *Tarihe Emretmek: Kemalist Türkiye, Faşist İtalya, Sosyalist Rusya* (Trans. H. Demirel). İstanbul: İletişim.

Radikal (1998). 'Muhtar bile olamayacak', 24 September 1998.

(2003). 'AKP'nin yeni zarfı', 26 December 2003, www.radikal.com.tr/haber .php?haberno=100157, accessed: 27 May 2016.

(2004). 'Erdoğan'dan vekillere azar', 3 November 2004, www.radikal.com.tr/ haber.php?haberno=133156, accessed: 27 May 2016.

(2009). '"Dünya basını Davos şokunu böyle duyurdu', 30 January 2009, www.radikal.com.tr/dunya/dunya_basini_davos_sokunu_boyle_duyurdu-919321, accessed: 27 May 2016.

(2010). 'Başbakan: Twitter boş tezek kokusu gerçek', 26 November 2010, www.radikal.com.tr/politika/basbakan_twitter_bos_tezek_kokusu_gercek-10 30303, accessed: 27 May 2016.

(2013). 'BDP'li Tan: Başbakan Erdoğan en az üç bakanı tekme tokat dövdü', 12 November 2013, www.radikal.com.tr/politika/bdpli_tan_basbakan_erdo gan_en_az_uc_bakani_tekme_tokat_dovdu-1160434, accessed: 27 May 2016.

(2014a). 'AK Parti Yenikapı mitingi: Erdoğan konuşurken alan boşaldı', 23 March 2014, www.radikal.com.tr/politika/ak_parti_yenikapi_mitingi_ erdogan_konusurken_alan_bosaldi-1182817, accessed: 27 May 2016.

(2014b). '"Alo Fatih" Habertürk gazetesinin künyesinden çıktı', 4 March 2014, www.radikal.com.tr/turkiye/alo_fatih_haberturk_gazetesinin_kunye sinden_cikti-1179441, accessed: 27 May 2016.

Rahat, G. and T. Sheafer (2007). 'The Personalization(s) of Politics: Israel, 1949–2003'. *Political Communication*, 24 (1), 65–80.

Roberts, K. M. (1995). 'Neoliberalism and the Transformation of Populism in Latin America: The Peruvian Case'. *World Politics*, 48 (1), 82–116.

(2006). 'Populism, Political Conflict, and Grass-Roots Organization in Latin America'. *Comparative Politics*, 38 (2), 127–148.

Robinson, J. C. (1985). 'Institutionalizing Charisma: Leadership, Faith and Rationality in Three Societies'. *Polity*, 18 (2), 181–203.

Rodrik, D. (2011). 'Ergenekon and Sledgehammer: Building or Undermining the Rule of Law?' *Turkish Policy Quarterly*, 10 (1), 99–109.

Romano, D. (2006). *The Kurdish Nationalist Movement*. Cambridge: Cambridge University Press.

Rose, R. and T. Mackie (1983). 'Incumbency in Government: Asset or Liability?', in Hans Daalder and Peter Mair (eds.), *Western European Party Systems: Continuity and Change*. London: Sage, pp. 115–137.

Rubin, B. and M. Heper (eds.) (2002). *Political Parties in Turkey*. London: Frank Cass.

Rustow, D. A. (1968). 'Atatürk as Founder of a State'. *Daedalus*, 97 (3), 793–828.

Sabah (1997). 'Erbakan'ın özel iftarına tepki', 11 January 1997, http://arsiv .sabah.com.tr/1997/01/11/f10.html, accessed: 27 May 2016.

(2003). 'Rakibimiz Uzan', 4 June 2003, http://arsiv.sabah.com.tr/2003/06/04/ p01.html, accessed: 21 July 2014.

(2012a). 'Bürokratik oligarşi var', 18 December 2012, www.sabah.com.tr/Eko nomi/2012/12/18/burokratik-oligarsi-var, accessed: 27 May 2016.

(2012b). 'HAS Parti kapandı rota AK Parti', 20 September 2012, www.sabah.com.tr/Gundem/2012/09/20/has-parti-kapandi-simdi-rota-ak-parti, accessed: 21 July 2014.

(2014). 'AK Parti'de üç dönem kuralı devam edecek', 3 May 2014, www.sabah.com.tr/Gundem/2014/05/03/ak-partide-3-donem-kurali-devam-edecek, accessed: 27 May 2016.

Sambur, B. (2009). 'The Great Transformation of Political Islam in Turkey: The Case of Justice and Development Party and Erdogan'. *European Journal of Economic and Political Studies*, 2 (2), 117–127.

Sani, G. and G. Sartori. (1983). 'Polarization, Fragmentation and Competition in Western Democracies', in H. Daalder and P. Mair (eds.), *Western European Party Systems Continuity and Change*, London: Sage, pp. 307–340.

Sarıbay, A. Y. (1991). 'The Democratic Party: 1946–1960', in M. Heper and J. M. Landau (eds.), *Political Parties and Democracy in Turkey*, London: I. B. Tauris, pp. 119–133.

Sayarı, S. (1975). 'Some Notes on the Beginnings of Mass Political Participation', in E. Akarlı and G. Ben-Dor (eds.), *Political Participation in Turkey*, İstanbul: Boğaziçi University Publications, pp. 121–133.

(1976). 'Aspects of Party Organization in Turkey'. *Middle East Journal*, 30 (2), 187–199.

(2007). 'Towards a New Turkish Party System?' *Turkish Studies*, 8 (2), 197–210.

Sayarı, S. and Y. Esmer (eds.) (2002). *Politics, Parties and Elections in Turkey*. Boulder: Lynne Rienner Publishers.

Scammell, M. (1995). *Designer Politics: How Elections Are Won*. New York: St. Martin's Press.

(1999). 'Political Marketing: Lessons for Political Science'. *Political Studies*, 47 (4), 718–739.

Scarrow, S. (1996). *Parties and Their Members: Organizing for Victory in Britain and Germany*. Oxford: Oxford University Press.

(2000). 'Parties Without Members? Party Organization in a Changing Electoral Environment', in R. J. Dalton and M. P. Wattenberg (eds.), *Parties Without Partisans: Political Change in Advanced Industrial Democracies*, Oxford: Oxford University Press, pp. 79–101.

(2014). *Beyond Party Members: Changing Approaches to Partisan Mobilization*. Oxford: Oxford University Press.

Schedler, A. (2002). 'The Menu of Manipulation'. *Journal of Democracy*, 13 (2), 36–50.

Schwedler, J. (2006). *Faith in Moderation: Islamist Parties in Jordan and Yemen*. Cambridge: Cambridge University Press.

Scott, J. C. (1990). *Domination and the Arts of Resistance*. New Haven and London: Yale University Press.

Selçuk, O. (2016). 'Strong Presidents and Weak Institutions: Populism in Turkey, Venezuela and Ecuador'. *Southeast European and Black Sea Studies*, 16 (4), 571–589.

Selim, Y. (2002). *Yol Ayrımı*. Ankara: Hiler Yayınları.

Selvi, A. (2014). 'Ekmeleddin İhsanoğlu neyin projesi', 18 June 2014, yenisafak.com.tr/yazarlar/AbdulkadirSelvi/ekmeleddin-ihsanoglu-neyin-pro jesi/54386, accessed: 27 May 2016.

(2017). 'Erdoğan'dan yeni kriterler ve seçim takvimi', 16 August 2017, www.hurriyet.com.tr/yazarlar/abdulkadir-selvi/erdogandan-yeni-kriterler-ve-secim-takvimi-40551398, accessed: 28 December 2017.

Şen, M. (2010). 'Transformation of Turkish Islamism and the Rise of the Justice and Development Party'. *Turkish Studies*, 11 (1), 59–84.

Şen, S. (2004). *AKP Milli Görüşçü mü?*. İstanbul: Nokta.

Şener, N. (2001). *Tepeden Tırnağa Yolsuzluk*. İstanbul: İmge.

Şentürk, H. (2006). *Siyasetçinin Yol Haritası: Parti İçi ve Partiler Arası Mücadele Taktikleri*. İstanbul: Okutan Yayınları.

(2007). *Darbelere ve Muhtıralara Karşı Demokratik Mücadele Yöntemleri*. İstanbul: Okutan Yayınları.

(2008a). *Adaylar İçin Kampanya Yönetimi*. İstanbul: Okutan Yayınları.

(2008b). *Seçmenin DNAsı Seçmen Tercihlerini Etkileyen Faktörler*. İstanbul: Okutan Yayınları.

(2008c). *Merkezden Yerele Siyaset*. İstanbul: Plato Yayınları.

(2011). *İslamcılık*. Ankara: Çıra Yayınları.

Sewell, W. H. Jnr (1992). 'A Theory of Structure: Duality, Agency, and Transformation'. *American Journal of Sociology*, 98 (1), 1–29.

Seyd, P. and P. Whiteley (1992). *Labour's Grass Roots: The Politics of Party Membership*. Oxford: Oxford University Press.

Sherwood, W. B. (1967). 'The Rise of the Justice Party in Turkey'. *World Politics*, 20 (1), 54–65.

Sikk, A. (2009). 'Parties and Populism'. Centre for European Politics, Security and Integration Working Paper.

Şimşek, S. (2004). 'New Social Movements in Turkey Since 1980'. *Turkish Studies*, 5 (2), 111–139.

——— (2005). '"People's Houses" as a Nationwide Project for Ideological Mobilization in Early Republican Turkey'. *Turkish Studies*, 6 (1), 71–91.

Somer, M. (2007). 'Moderate Islam and Secularist Opposition in Turkey: Implications for the World, Muslims and Secular Democracy'. *Third World Quarterly*, 28 (7), 1271–1289.

——— (2016). 'Understanding Turkey's Democratic Breakdown: Old vs. New and Indigenous vs. Global Authoritarianism'. *Southeast European and Black Sea Studies*, 16 (4), 481–503.

Somer, M. and T. S. Baykan (2018). 'Hybrid Party Dilemmas and the Rise of Turkey's AKP as a Dominant Party'. Koç University Draft Paper.

Soyoğul, G. (2013). 'Aziz Bey Gökçek Taktiği Güdüyor' (interview with Ömer Cihat Akay, the JDP İzmir chair), *Ege'de son söz*, online interview, 16 September 2013, www.egedesonsoz.com/roportaj/Aziz-Bey-Gokcek-taktigi-guduyor/320, accessed: 27 May 2016.

Sözcü (2016). 'Erdoğan'ın Davutoğlu pişmanlığı!', 10 February 2016, www.sozcu.com.tr/2016/gundem/erdoganin-davutoglu-pismani-1083592/, accessed: 28 December 2017.

SPK (1983). '2820 Sayılı Siyasi Partiler Kanunu', *Resmi Gazete*, no: 18027, pp. 5703–5741.

Stokes, M. (1992). *The Arabesk Debate: Music and Musicians in Modern Turkey*. Oxford: Oxford University Press.

Stokes, S. C. (2007). 'Political Clientelism', in C. Boix and S. C. Stokes (eds.), *The Oxford Handbook of Comparative Politics*. Oxford: Oxford University Press, pp. 649–673.

Sunar, L. (2015). 'Civil Islamic Actors Versus the State in Turkey: The Structural Transformation of Islamic Non-Governmental Organisations'. Paper presented at BRISMES Annual Conference at LSE, UK, 26 June.

Szczerbiak, A. (1999). 'Testing Party Models in East-Central Europe'. *Party Politics*, 5 (4), 525–537.

T. C. Resmi Gazete (1998). 'Anayasa Mahkemesi Kararları', Constitutional Court Decision on pp. 19–349, 22 February 1998, www.resmigazete.gov.tr/arsiv/23266.pdf, accessed: 27 May 2016.

T24 (2013). 'Cem Uzan: Yılmaz Özdil ve Fatih Çekirge'nin başında olduğu Star'da Hurşit Tolon'un talimatıyla manşet atıldığını bilmiyordum', 7 August 2013, http://t24.com.tr/haber/cem-uzan-darbeci-gazeteciler-icin-ifade-veririm,241354, accessed: 25 December 2017.

——— (2014). 'AKP'nin 6 bin kişilik iftarına ünlüler akın etti', 19 July 2014, http://t24.com.tr/haber/akpnin-6-bin-kisilik-iftarina-unluler-akin-etti,264856, accessed: 27 May 2016.

——— (2015). 'Cemil Çiçek: Mahkemelerin Bağımsızlığı Ölmüştür', 3 January 2015, http://t24.com.tr/haber/cemil-cicek-mahkemelerin-bagimsizligi-olmustur,247527, accessed: 13 November 2015.

Taggart, P. (2000). *Populism*. Buckingham: Open University Press.

Takvim (2011). 'AK Parti Şanlıurfa'da Rekor Peşinde', 4 June 2011, www.takvim.com.tr/Siyaset/2011/04/15/ak-parti-sanliurfada-rekor-pesinde, accessed: 27 May 2016.

Tanıyıcı, S. (2003). 'Transformation of Political Islam in Turkey: Islamist Welfare Party's Pro-EU Turn'. *Party Politics*, 9 (4), 463–483.

Taraf (2009). 'Demokrat Parti'de eski kafa kazandı', 17 May 2014, www.taraf.com.tr/haber-yazdir-33874.html, accessed: 20 July 2014.

Taşkın, Y. (2008). 'AKP's Move to "Conquer" the Center-Right: Its Prospects and Possible Impacts on the Democratization Process'. *Turkish Studies*, 9 (1), 53–72.

TBMM (No date). 'Constitution of the Republic of Turkey', https://global .tbmm.gov.tr/docs/constitution_en.pdf, accessed: 27 May 2016.

Tezcür, G. M. (2010). *Muslim Reformers in Iran and Turkey: The Paradox of Moderation*. Austin: University of Texas Press.

(2012). 'Trends and Characteristics of the Turkish Party System in Light of the 2011 Elections'. *Turkish Studies*, 13 (2), 117–134.

Thelen, K. (1999). 'Historical Institutionalism in Comparative Politics'. *Annual Review of Political Science*, 2 (1), 369–404.

Tittensor, D. (2014). *The House of Service: The Gulen Movement and Islam's Third Way*. Oxford: Oxford University Press.

Toker, Ç. (2009). *Abdüllatif Şener: 'Adım da Benimle Beraber Büyüdü'*. İstanbul: Doğan Kitap.

Toprak, B. (2005). 'Islam and Democracy in Turkey'. *Turkish Studies*, 6 (2), 167–186.

Tosun, T. and G. E. Tosun (2010). *Türkiye'de Siyasal Parti Üyeliği ve Katılım*. İstanbul: Kalkedon.

Transparency International (2015). Corruption Perceptions Index. Berlin.

Trthaber (2014). 'İstanbul'un refah seviyesi en yüksek ilçesi', 1 February 2014, www.trthaber.com/haber/turkiye/istanbulun-refah-seviyesi-en-yuksek-ilcesi-117016.html, accessed: 27 May 2016.

Tucker, R. C. (1968). 'The Theory of Charismatic Leadership'. *Daedalus*, 97 (3), 731–756.

Tuğal, C. (2009). *Passive Revolution: Absorbing the Islamic Challenge to Capitalism*. Stanford: Stanford University Press.

Tür, Ö. and Z. Çıtak (2010). 'AKP ve kadın teşkilatlanması, muhafazarlık ve kadın', in İ. Uzgel and B. Duru (eds.), *AKP kitabı: bir dönüşümün bilançosu*. Ankara: Phoenix Yayınevi, pp. 614–629.

Turam, B. (ed.) (2012). *Secular State and Religious Society*. New York: Palgrave Macmillan.

Turan, İ. (1988). 'Political Parties and the Party System in Post-1983 Turkey', in M. Heper and A. Evin (eds.), *State, Democracy and the Military in the 1980s*. Berlin: Walter de Gruyter.

(2006). 'Old Soldiers Never Die: The Republican People's Party of Turkey'. *South European Society and Politics*, 11(3–4), 559–578.

Türk, H. B. (2008). *Şirket ve Parti*. İstanbul: İletişim.

Turkish Statistical Institute (2012). *Milletvekili genel seçimleri 1923–2011*. Ankara: Turkish Statistical Institute.

(2013). *Seçilmiş Göstergelerle İstanbul 2013.* Ankara: Turkish Statistical Institute.

Türsan, H. (1995). 'Pernicious Party Factionalism as a Constant of Transitions to Democracy in Turkey'. *Democratization,* 2 (1): 168–184.

Uluengin, H. (2006). 'Ayakkabı kokusu', 22 June 2006, www.hurriyet.com.tr/ yazarlar/4295236_p.asp, accessed: 27 May 2016.

UNDP (United Nations Development Programme) (2014). *Human Development Report 2014. Sustaining Human Progress: Reducing Vulnerabilities and Building Resilience.* New York.

Ünsal, A. (2002). *Umuttan Yalnızlığa: Türkiye İşçi Partisi, 1961–1971.* İstanbul: Tarih Vakfı.

Uygur, E. (2001). *Krizden Krize Türkiye: 2000 ve 2001 Kasım ve Şubat Krizleri.* Ankara: Türkiye Ekonomi Kurumu.

Uysal, A. and Topak, O. (2010). *Particiler Türkiye'de Partiler ve Sosyal Ağların İnşası.* İstanbul: İletişim.

Waldman, S. A. and E. Çalışkan (2017). *The New Turkey and Its Discontents.* Oxford: Oxford University Press.

Ware, A. (1987). 'Introduction: Parties under Electoral Competition', in A. Ware (ed.), *Political Parties Electoral Change and Structural Response,* Oxford: Basil Blackwell, pp. 1–23.

——— (1996). *Political Parties and Party Systems.* Oxford: Oxford University Press.

Watts, N. F. (2010). *Activists in Office: Kurdish Politics and Protest in Turkey.* Seattle: University of Washington Press.

Weber, M. (1946). *From Max Weber: Essays in Sociology* (Trans. H. H. Gerth and G. Wright Mills). New York: Oxford University Press.

——— (1974). *On Charisma and Institution Building* (Trans. S. N. Eisenstadt). Chicago and London: The University of Chicago Press.

Weyland, K. (1999). 'Neoliberal Populism in Latin America and Eastern Europe'. *Comparative Politics,* 31 (4), 379–401.

——— (2001). 'Clarifying a Contested Concept: Populism in the Study of Latin American Politics'. *Comparative Politics,* 34 (1), 1–22.

——— (2003). 'Neopopulism and Neoliberalism in Latin America: How Much Affinity?' *Third World Quarterly,* 24 (6), 1095–1115.

White, J. B. (2002). *Islamist Mobilization in Turkey: A Study in Vernacular Politics.* Seattle: University of Washington Press.

——— (2008). 'Islam and Politics in Contemporary Turkey', in R. Kasaba (ed.), *The Cambridge History of Turkey, Volume IV, Turkey in the Modern World,* Cambridge: Cambridge University Press, pp. 357–380.

——— (2012). *Muslim Nationalism and the New Turks.* Princeton: Princeton University Press.

Worsley, P. (1969). 'The Concept of Populism', in G. Ionescu and E. Gellner (eds.), *Populism: Its Meaning and National Characteristics,* London: Weidenfeld & Nicolson, pp. 212–250.

Wuthrich, F. M. (2015). *National Elections in Turkey.* Syracuse: Syracuse University Press.

Yabancı, B. (2016). 'Populism as the Problem Child of Democracy: The AKP's Enduring Appeal and the Use of Meso-Level Actors. *Southeast European and Black Sea Studies,* 16 (4), 591–617.

Yalçın, S. (2017). 'Topbaş-Gökçek vd. götüren araştırmacı', 19 October 2017, www.sozcu.com.tr/2017/yazarlar/soner-yalcin/topbas-gokcek-vd-goturen-arastirmaci-2054757/, accessed: 12 January 2018.

Yalman, G. (2012). 'Politics and Discourse under the AKP's Rule: The Marginalisation of Class-Based Politics, Erdoğanisation, and Post-Secularism', in S. Coşar and G. Yücesan-Özdemir (eds.), *Silent Violence: Neo-Liberalism, Islamist Politics and the AKP Years in Turkey*, Ottawa: Red-Quill Books, pp. 21–42.

Yarın (2016). 'Demirtaş: Erdoğan, HDP'nin barajı aşacağını görünce, "Kandırıldım" deyip masayı devirdi', 28 February 2016, www.yarinhaber.net/gun cel/35658/demirtas-erdogan-hdpnin-baraji-asacagini-gorunce-kandirildim-deyip-masayi-devirdi, accessed: 25 December 2017.

Yavuz, H. (2006). 'The Role of the New Bourgeoisie in the Transformation of the Turkish Islamic Movement', in M. H. Yavuz (ed.), *The Emergence of a New Turkey*, Salt Lake City: University of Utah Press, pp. 1–19.

——— (2009). *Secularism and Muslim Democracy in Turkey*. Cambridge: Cambridge University Press.

Yeniasya (2009). '367 krizi 28 şubat işi', 4 February 2009, www.yeniasya.com.tr/ 2009/02/04/haber/h1.htm, accessed: 21 July 2014.

Yenişafak (2008). 'DP'de başkan Süleyman Soylu', 6 January 2008, http:// yenisafak.com.tr/politika-haber/dpde-baskan-suleyman-soylu-06.01.2008-91754, accessed: 20 July 2014.

——— (2013). 'Gezi'de darbe girişimi deşifre oldu', 15 June 2013, http://yenisafak .com.tr/gundem-haber/gezide-darbe-girisimi-desifre-oldu-15.06.2013-533006, accessed: 20 July 2014.

Yeşil, B. (2016). *Media in New Turkey: The Origins of an Authoritarian Neoliberal State*. Urbana: University of Illinois Press.

Yeşilada, B. (2002). 'The Virtue Party', in B. Rubin and M. Heper (eds.), *Political Parties in Turkey*, London: Frank Cass, pp. 62–81.

Yetkin, M. (2007). 'E-muhtıra Erken Seçimi Gündeme Taşıdı', 29 April 2007, www.radikal.com.tr/haber.php?haberno=219781, accessed: 27 May 2016.

Yıldırım, D. (2009). 'AKP ve Neo-liberal Popülizm', in İ. Uzgel and B. Duru (eds.), *AKP Kitabı: Bir Dönüşümün Bilançosu*, Ankara: Phoenix Yayınevi, pp. 66–107.

Yıldırım, E. (2013). 'Erdoğan'ın ontolojisine kaygılılar', 3 June 2013, http:// yenisafak.com.tr:999/yazarlar/ErgunYildirim/erdoganin-ontolojisine-kaygili lar/38381, accessed: 12 August 2014.

Yıldırım, E., H. İnaç and H. Özler (2007). 'A Sociological Representation of the Justice and Development Party: Is It a Political Design or a Political Becoming?' *Turkish Studies*, 8 (1), 5–24.

Yıldız, A. (2008). 'Problematizing the Intellectual and Political Vestiges from "Welfare" to "Justice and Development"', in U. Cizre (ed.), *Secular and Islamic Politics in Turkey: The Making of the Justice and Development Party*, London: Routledge, pp. 41–61.

Yılmaz, T. (2001). *Tayyip Kasımpaşa'dan Siyasetin Ön Saflarına*. Ankara: Ümit Yayıncılık.

Yücesan-Özdemir, G. (2012). 'The Social Policy Regime in the AKP Years: the Emperor's New Clothes', in S. Coşar and G. Yücesan-Özdemir (eds.), *Silent Violence: Neo-Liberalism, Islamist Politics and the AKP Years in Turkey*, Ottawa: Red-Quill Books, pp. 125–152.

Zaman (2009). 'Erdoğan, miting sayısında muhalefete fark attı', 23 March 2009, www.zaman.com.tr/politika_erdogan-miting-sayisinda-muhalefete-fark-atti_829129.html, accessed: 21 July 2014.

—— (2011). 'Başbakan Erdoğan'ın konuşmasının tam metni', 15 October 2011, www.zaman.com.tr/politika_basbakan-erdoganin-konusmasinin-tam-metni_1190950.html, accessed: 20 July 2014.

—— (2014). 'Sabah ve Atv için iş adamlarından ihale karşılığı para toplanmış', 1 February 2014, www.zaman.com.tr/politika_sabah-ve-atv-icin-isadamlarin dan-ihale-karsiligi-para-toplanmis_2196892.html, accessed: 16 June 2014.

Zürcher, E. J. (2004). *Turkey: A Modern History*. London: I. B. Tauris.

Index

315